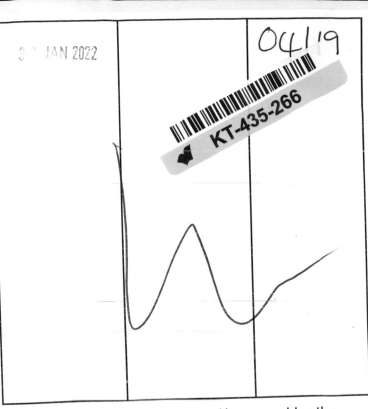

DK EYEWITNESS

GREEK ISLANDS

CONTENTS

DISCOVER 6

Welcome to the Greek Islands 8

Reasons to Love the
Greek Islands.................................. 10

Explore the Greek Islands 14

Getting to Know the Greek Islands...16

Greek Islands Your Way 20

A Year in the Greek Islands 44

A Brief History 46

EXPERIENCE 52

The Ionian Islands 54

The Argo-Saronic Islands 88

The Sporádes and Évvia 102

The Northeast
Aegean Islands 120

The Dodecanese 152

The Cyclades 200

Crete 244

Athens 282

NEED TO KNOW 296

Before You Go 298

Getting Around 300

Practical Information 304

Index 306

Phrasebook 314

Acknowledgments 319

Left: A bright blue door on a yellow house in Kefaloniá
Previous page: Shipwreck Bay on Zákynthos

DISCOVER

The colourful Assos village, Kefaloniá

Welcome to the Greek Islands 8

Reasons to Love the Greek Islands...10

Explore the Greek Islands.......................14

Getting to Know the Greek Islands....16

Greek Islands Your Way...........................20

A Year in the Greek Islands....................44

A Brief History..46

WELCOME TO THE GREEK ISLANDS

From the breathtaking beaches to the pretty ports, the Greek Islands are irresistible. Whatever your dream trip to the islands includes, this DK Eyewitness Travel Guide is the perfect companion.

① Overlooking a cove on Kefaloniá.

② Kalamáta olives at a taverna.

③ Hiking across Crete.

④ Visitors exploring cliffside paths at Firá.

With hundreds of diverse islands to choose from, one is bound to offer the perfect escape. There are spectacular beaches, from pebble coves on Corfu to stretches of black sand on Santoríni, all lapped by crystal-clear seas. These are within reach of characterful villages, like colourful Ýdra town or artistic Folegándros.

Culture, both ancient and modern, imbues the air, too. Ancient sites and venerable monasteries are everywhere: walk in the steps of legendary heroes at the Minoan palace at Phaistos or more modern saints at the fortress-like Monastery of St John on Pátmos. The islands' culinary scene invites pilgrims of its own, with aromatic seafood served at tavernas accompanied by wine made by cult vintners from around Greece.

Besides the attractions of the well-known islands, there are numerous small islands with your new favourite beach taverna just waiting to be discovered. Often the best way to find them is by throwing your schedule to the Greek islands' famous stiff breeze, and island hopping where the wind takes you.

With so many islands begging to be explored, we've broken the region down into easily navigable chapters with detailed itineraries, expert knowledge and colourful, comprehensive maps to help you plan the perfect visit. Whether you're visiting one island, or island hopping indefinitely, this Eyewitness guide will ensure that you see and experience the very best the Greek islands have to offer. Enjoy the book, and enjoy the islands.

REASONS TO LOVE
THE GREEK
ISLANDS

Azure water, seaside tavernas frequented by friendly locals and an ancient history of mythological civilizations. There are countless reasons why people fall in love with the Greek Islands. Here, we pick some of our favourites.

1 SHIPWRECK BAY

A golden arc of sand protected by towering cliffs, with the remains of an old cargo ship rusting onshore and temptingly turquoise waters – swimming in Zákynthos' bay is what dreams are made of (p82).

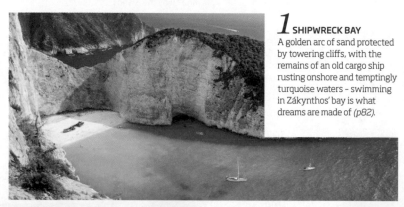

CATCHING THE BREEZE *2*

The wind defines life on the islands: when it's coming, when it's going, who's going to blow in with the breeze. Try your hand at windsurfing in Vasilikí Bay (p81) on Lefkáda.

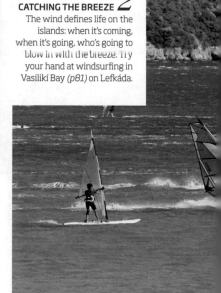

3 ANCIENT CIVILIZATIONS

The cradle of Western civilization, everyone from the Minoans to Ottomans has left their mark on the Greek Islands. Step into the past at sites such as the sun-drenched Roman ruins on Delos (p208).

THE MASTIC VILLAGES OF HÍOS 4

The plain stone fortress walls around these villages belie the black-and-white geometric patterns that adorn many of their houses. Check out Pyrgi *(p128)* for some of the best.

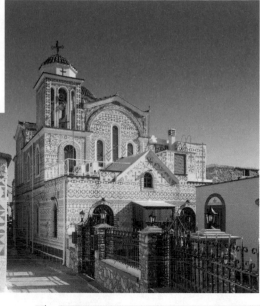

SEAFOOD RESTAURANTS 5

Whether it's fresh tender octopus cooked over coals or delicious steamed razor clams, the Greek Islands' revitalized culinary scene is worthy of Bacchanalian feasting *(p28)*.

RELIGIOUS FESTIVALS 6

Melding tradition and riotous colour, the Orthodox Christian calendar is marked by festivals. On Ýdra, Easter Sunday reaches its climax when locals light an effigy of Judas on fire *(p44)*.

THE VIEW FROM KAISER'S THRONE 7

Watching the sun set over Corfu and the Ionian Sea from Kaiser's Throne *(p75)*, so-called because it was a favourite of German Kaiser Wilhelm II, is an irresistible experience.

ENDANGERED MONK SEALS 8

With only 400 Mediterranean monk seals left in the world, and 60 in Sporádes Marine Park *(p113)*, pray to Greece's mythical gods that you see one of these rare creatures.

9 TRADITIONAL MUSIC

Every island sways to its own siren song, from gentle Zákynthian *kantades* to wild Cretan lyre music. Join the locals in a taverna for a glass of ouzo and a rousing chorus.

10 MAGNIFICENT MONASTERIES

From huge defensive monasteries to small white chapels clinging precariously to rocky outcrops, monasteries are everywhere in the Greek Islands. The towering St John on Pátmos is one of the best *(p158)*.

KALAMÁTA OLIVES 11

No trip to this part of the world is complete without a bite into a briny, savoury and incredibly moreish Kalamáta olive, so good they are found on the menu in every taverna.

HIKING THROUGH SAMARIÁ GORGE 12

The 18-km- (11-mile-) long trail through the vertiginous highs and lows of the Samariá Gorge *(p266)* is exhilaratingly beautiful. Keep an eye out for leaping *kri kri* (wild goats).

EXPLORE
THE GREEK
ISLANDS

This guide divides the Greek Islands into eight colour-coded sightseeing areas, as shown on the map below. Find out more about each area on the following pages.

Corfu Town Ioannina Lárisa

Igoumenitsa

Corfu Karditsa Vólos

Árta Skiáthos

THE IONIAN GREECE
ISLANDS Lamía **THE SPORÁDES**
p54 **AND ÉVVIA**
p102

Lefkáda Évvia

Astakos

Ithaki Halkída

Pátra

Kefaloniá **ATHENS**
p282

Kyllini Corinth

Zákynthos Égina

Póros

Ýdra

Spétses

Kalamata **THE ARGO-SARONIC**
ISLANDS
p88

Ionian Neápoli
Sea

Kýthira

Kavála

0 kilometres 100 N
0 miles 100

Keramoti

Alexandroupoli

Thásos

Samothráki

Límnos

EUROPE

RUSSIA

DENMARK

UNITED
KINGDOM

NETHER-
LANDS

BELGIUM

GERMANY

POLAND

BELARUS

CZECH
REP.

SLOVAKIA

UKRAINE

FRANCE

SWITZ.

AUSTRIA

HUNGARY

CROATIA

ROMANIA

SERBIA

ITALY

MACEDONIA

BULGARIA

SPAIN

ALBANIA

TURKEY

GREECE

CYPRUS

TUNISIA

ALGERIA

LIBYA

EGYPT

**THE NORTHEAST
AEGEAN ISLANDS**
p120

Lésvos

Mytilíni

Izmir

Skýros

*A e g e a n
S e a*

Híos

Híos Town

Ándros

Sámos

Kuşadası

T U R K E Y

Tínos

Ikaría

Sýros

Mýkonos

Pátmos

Páros

Náxos

Léros

Kálymnos

Bodrum

THE CYCLADES
p200

Íos

Kos

Marmaris

Mílos

Sými

Rhodes Town

THE DODECANESE
p152

Santoríni

Rhodes

Kárpathos

Réthymno

Iráklio

CRETE
p244

GETTING TO KNOW
THE GREEK ISLANDS

Ranging in size from uninhabited rocks to the substantial Crete and Évvia, the popular Greek Islands draw crowds to their brilliant beaches, pretty ports and renowned ruins. The islands are vastly different in character, but have in common great food, hospitable locals and the alluring Greek sea.

PAGE 54

THE IONIAN ISLANDS

Lying off the west coast of mainland Greece, the scattered Ionian islands, each culturally distinct, share dramatic coastlines of plunging cliffs and blue seas, backed by cypresses and olive groves. Most islands are reached easily from the mainland, and visitors flock here in summer for beach holidays.

Best for
West coast beaches, Italianate churches

Home to
Corfu Town

Experience
Feeling like you're in the Caribbean on Vríka beach, Andípaxi

PAGE 88

THE ARGO-SARONIC ISLANDS

The lush Argo-Saronics, easy to reach from the mainland, are extremely popular on weekends, and have cosmopolitan port towns with trendy bars and shops. Even so, these islands still feel a world apart from the capital.

Best for
The characterful port town of Égina

Home to
Égina, Temple of Aphaia

Experience
The wild (and occasionally violent) Easter celebrations on Ýdra

SPORÁDES AND ÉVVIA

The rich and the beautiful first docked their yachts on the then-deserted beaches of Skiáthos and Skópelos in the 1960s and 70s. No longer as exclusive, but even more popular, the Sporádes offer preternaturally blue seas, green countryside and achingly photogenic towns, whereas gigantic Évvia has compelling archaeological sites, museums and thermal spas.

Best for
Unspoiled mountain scenery on Évvia, yachting holidays

Home to
Halkída

Experience
Spotting wildlife on a boat tour through Sporádes Marine Park

THE NORTHEAST AEGEAN

Whatever you're looking for in a Greek island holiday, you'll find it in the Northeast Aegean. Closer to Turkey than to Greece, the seven major islands here have distinct personalities, from the isolated and brooding Samothráki to the crowded resort island of Thásos, all marked by significant ancient sites. While Sámos, Thásos and Lésvos attract the package-holiday crowd, Samothráki appeals to hardy nature lovers and Ikaria to those seeking a slower pace and more traditional life.

Best for
Ancient sites, hiking on Samothráki, beaches

Home to
Híos town, Néa Moní, Mastic Villages

Experience
Tasting the grapes of Límnos at its numerous wineries, famous since ancient times

PAGE 152

THE DODECANESE

Scattered along the coast of Turkey, the Dodecanese attracts visitors for its hot climate, fantastic beaches and lively nightlife. Each island is different in character, as well as landscape – some, like Hálki, are stark and barren, while others, such as Tílos, are green and fertile. The islands here are scattered with dramatic fortifications left by the Knights of St John, the Ottomans and the Italians, who also left an enduring taste for Italian gelato.

Best for
Charming whitewashed hilltop towns and dramatic fortifications

Home to
Pátmos, Rhodes Old Town, Rhodes New Town, Líndos

Experience
The dramatic volcanic caldera with its craters on Nísyros

PAGE 200

THE CYCLADES

With whitewashed villages, blue church domes, blonde- and black-sand beaches and incredible sunsets, the Cyclades are, to many, the ideal Greek island holiday destination – particularly postcard-ready Mýkonos and Santoríni. Made up of 56 islands, 24 inhabited, the large number of islands in the Cyclades ensures diversity. That means that while there are islands, like Íos, where staying up all night at a club is de rigueur, others, like Síkinos, are quiet and traditional.

Best for
Venetian kástra and sunset views

Home to
Delos, Santoríni

Experience
Watching a movie in the balmy Greek summer at an outdoor cinema on Mýkonos

CRETE

PAGE 244

Crete is also known as the Great Island, not just for its size, but for the space it takes up in the heart of the locals. The most southerly, and largest, of the Greek Islands, Crete is dominated by soaring mountains and sandy beaches, and is marked with a history of occupation that has not dimmed the Cretan passion for individuality and freedom. Its north coast bustles with resorts as well as historic towns, while the south-west is less developed. The island has possibly the best hiking in the region, and attracts rugged hikers bent on trekking famous Samariá Gorge.

Best for
Beaches, traditional culture, Venetian castles and urban architecture

Home to
Haniá, Réthymno, Iráklio, Palace of Knossos, Phaistos, Samariá Gorge

Experience
Live Cretan music and free-flowing tsikoudiá spirit in a taverna

ATHENS

PAGE 282

Sprawling, concrete Athens is an incredibly vibrant city. This bustling capital, overlooked by the ancient temples on the Acropolis, is the birthplace of philosophy, Classical art and democracy – a tradition that continues through lively student protests and activism. The streets here are alive with open-air markets and walls decorated with some of the best street art on the globe. While you can see the major sites, including the Acropolis, in one well-planned day, the city may tempt you to stay longer.

Best for
Lively student life, Saturday morning markets, gritty street art

Home to
Acropolis

Experience
A summer concert at the Odeon of Herodes Atticus on the Acropolis

The Setting Sun

According to ancient Greek mythology, the sun lights the world as it is pulled across the sky by the god Helios, riding a chariot. The Greek Islands, with their endless, reflective horizons of water, offer countless vistas to watch the sun god as he completes his work for the day and the sun sets. Our favourite places to catch these glorious sunsets are from west-facing Kaiser's Throne on Corfu (p75) and in Firá in Santoríni (p210), where the sun illuminates the town's famous white-washed rooftops.

→

Watching the sun setting over the sea from a terrace in Firá, Santoríni

GREEK ISLANDS FOR
SUNSEEKERS

The Greek word for sunbathing is *iliotherapía*, which translates as "sun therapy", and there are endless spots to benefit from warming rays throughout the islands, from isolated islets to pumping party beaches.

Hidden Coves

With countless coves and innumerable islets, one of the delights of any Greek island is finding a patch of sand to yourself – without the distractions of a sunbed or music pumping from the nearby bars. Go hunting for a secluded bay on the southwestern tip of Corfu (p64) or on the dramatic island of Folégandros (p219). You can also easily find an isolated spot on the 9-km (5-mile) stretch of Lésvos' famous Vatera beach.

←

Relaxing in the sea off Katergo Beach on the island of Folégandros

Resort Beaches

On some of the Greek Islands' beaches, the party started in the 1960s and hasn't stopped since. Infamous Paradise Beach on Mýkonos *(p222)* remains a popular destination for hedonists, but Íos' nightlife scene, although not as renowned as its neighbour's, is just as ebullient *(p221)*. Head to Far Out Beach Club, at Mylopotas, if you're after an energetic club on the island – it's right on the beach and attracts a young crowd from the yacht tours that call there *(www.faroutclub.com)*.

←

Walking along the wooden boardwalk to the beach at Mylopotas on Íos

→

Photographing Zákynthos' Shipwreck Bay in the golden light of sunset

TOP 5 MOST BEAUTIFUL BEACHES

Mýrtos, Kefaloniá
This curved bay is hemmed in by huge cliffs *(p84)*.

Vaterá, Lésvos
Fine shingly sand, with crystal-clear waters.

Kyrá Panagiá, Kárpathos
A small cove, presided over by a pink-domed church *(p199)*.

Elafonísi, Crete
You can only reach this beach by boat.

Beríssa, Santoríni
A vast stretch of black volcanic sand.

Most Photogenic

With twinkling turquoise seas, pristine sand, dramatic rock formations and, of course, the golden Greek sun, these beaches will have you tossing up whether to dive into the water first or snap numerous photos. Among the islands' most picturesque stretches of sand, the undoubted champion is Shipwreck Bay in Zákynthos *(p82)*, but a number of beaches come a close second, including Seychelles beach on Ikaría *(p142)*, which has the tropical vibe of Jamaica, and the smaller Bísti Bay on Ýdra *(p99)*.

Festival Fun

Time your visit with Rhodes International Festival to listen to classical music in epic surroundings. Alternatively, celebrate folk music and dance with the locals at Lefkáda's International Folklore Festival *(www.liff.gr).*

→

Dancers at Lefkáda's Folklore Festival

GREEK ISLANDS FOR
CULTURE SEEKERS

As it has been for thousands of years, the Greek Islands is a cultural hot spot. Here, it's possible to spend the morning in a local museum, the afternoon at an atmospheric and crumbling castle, and the night watching a movie under the vines at an outdoor cinema.

Ancient Footsteps

A trip to the Greek Islands provides the chance to follow the trail of Odysseus and wander in the footsteps of the Minotaur. The palaces of Knosos *(p260)* and Phaistos *(p265)* are deservedly popular, but Hellenistic or Roman ruins on Rhodes, Kos and Delos also merit a ferry ride.

←

The remains of the Doric Temple of Athena, found in Líndos, on Rhodes

Crumbling Castles

The Greek Islands are full of castles clinging to precarious rocky mountains, looming over ancient towns and peering over aquamarine seas. The ruin of Kritinía castle *(p179)* on Rhodes is particularly atmospheric, while the hilltop castle in Kefaloniá's Agios Geórgios *(p84)* is breathtaking – both for the view and the intimidating lack of safety railings.

→

Looking out over vibrant blue seas from Rhodes' Kritinía Castle

Key to the Church

With such a long religious history it's little wonder that scattered all across the Greek Islands are medieval country chapels and monasteries. Inviting exploration, they are often exquisitely located and sometimes decorated with beautiful, albeit deteriorating, frescoes. Isolated chapels may be locked for protection, especially on Crete *(p245)*, but hunting down the key warden is all part of the fun.

← A fresco depicting the Assumption of the Virgin Mary

TOP 3 ISLAND MUSEUMS

Archaeological Museum, Iráklio
An unbeatable treasure trove of Minoan art and artifacts *(p258)*, this is arguably the best museum on the islands.

Museum of Prehistoric Thera, Santoríni
Home to ancient artifacts, including ceramics, jewellery and sculpture uncovered across Santoríni *(p211)*.

Museum of Asian Art, Corfu
The only museum on the islands dedicated to Asian art *(p64)*.

A Day at the Museum

What better way to explore Greece's past than at the museum? The islands have plenty to choose from; our pick is Iráklio's Archaeological Museum *(p258)*. For something different, head to the mansion of the only female admiral to fight in the Greek War of Independence *(p96)*.

↑ Inside the Archaeological Museum on Iráklio

▷ Island Trekking

The islands once had numerous walking trails, including the magnificent cobbled *kalderímia*. Many were bulldozed during the 1980s and 90s, but local enthusiasts have protected the remaining paths, which have also been waymarked and mapped. Another option is the mountain ranges and gorges of Crete *(p244)*, or Corfu *(p64)*, with its 220-km (137-mile) trail from Corfu Town to Mount Pantokrator.

◁ Sea Swims

At their best, the aquamarine Greek seas resemble a tropical paradise: think pristine sands, glittering waters and dramatic mountain backdrops. You'll find even committed landlubbers in the water here, particularly when the temperatures soar.

GREEK ISLANDS FOR
OUTDOOR ACTIVITIES

On the Greek Islands adventures await even the most dedicated sun-worshipper. The list starts, but doesn't stop, at easy-breezy windsurfing, night-time scuba-diving and trekking on centuries-old trails.

◁ Cycle the Cyclades

Take to the Cycladic hills for steep but stunning village-to-sea ascents and descents – Mílos, Náxos and Páros provide some of the best mountain climbs. Bikes can be rented on most islands; alternatively take a bike tour – try Naxos Bikes *(www.naxosbikes.com)* or Paros Cycling *(www.paroscycling.com)*.

△ Scaling New Heights

For an adrenaline rush with a view, climbing the imposing cliffs and rocks of the Greek Islands is hard to beat. Head to rugged Kálymnos *(p192)* for a range of rock faces; the craggy west shoreline provides the perfect challenge for any climber.

▷ Catch the Breeze

The offshore breezes in this part of the world are famously strong, creating fantastic conditions for windsurfing and kiteboarding. The undisputed Greek kiteboarding capital is Poúnda on Páros *(p234)*, but other islands (with both suitable winds and equipment rental) include Kourem. énos on Crete *(p279)*, Kamári on Kos *(p189)* and Vailikí on Lefkáda *(p81)*.

△ Under the Sea

It's a weird and wonderful world under the water, with plenty of curious creatures and corals to seek out. Take a diving tour to explore more; recommended companies include Santoríni Dive Center *(www.divecenter.gr)* and Achilleon Diving Center on Corfu *(www.diving-corfu.com)*.

Enjoying wine with →
a view on Santoríni,
long known for its vintners

GREEK ISLANDS
RAISE A GLASS

There's far more to island drinking than retsína and ouzo; here, you'll drink the best wines and beers you've never heard of, all part of a gastronomic revolution in Greece that has extended to alcohol. From microbreweries to small-scale vintners, these are the tastes of the islands.

The Long Draught

Long, hot summers in the Aegean have encouraged an appetite for watery lagers and pilsners, but local microbreweries have led the charge in putting ales, dark beer and even white beer on tap and on the menu. Top microbreweries include Corfu Beer, a microbrewery producing real ale, and the Santorini Brewing Company, with its distinctive donkey logo *(p212)*. Most breweries around the islands offer tours, or at least a free tasting.

→

Unpasteurized real
ale from Corfu Beer, best
consumed on the island

From the Vine

It is unsurprising that Dionysos, the Greek god of feasting and revelry, developed a passion for wine, as the Greek Islands have been making and trading wine since Neolithic days. A taste of wine from the indigenous grape varieties is like drinking the distilled essence of each island - and there are a number of small vintners across the Greek Islands who've been busy reviving these legacy grapes, as well as planting imported varieties and combining them imaginatively. Visit one of the more well-known wineries, like Gentilini Winery on Kefaloniá *(2 km past Lassi, 26710 41618)*, which makes red, white and roses, or have fun hunting down the truly rare, like the niche wine from Andipaxí, a small island near Paxí.

← Harvesting grapes on Crete, with vines stretching as far as the eye can see

TOP 5 ISLAND VINTNERS

Nikos Gavalas, Crete
This sophisticated winery first planted vines in 1906.

Canava Roussos, Santoríni
A vintner producing wines using traditional and modern techniques.

Sigalas, Santoríni
Wines produced using old grapes from the volcanic soil.

Ariousos, Híos
A vintner reviving the wine-making tradition on Híos.

Methymneos, Lésvos
Wine from Lésvos has been famous since antiquity; this winery continues the tradition.

> **INSIDER TIP**
> ### Tisane as a Tonic
>
> Feeling worse for wear after a few glasses of *tsikoudiá* or local wine? Sip some Greek sage tea *(alisfakiá)* to say goodbye to dull headaches.

Raising the Spirits

Each island has their specialty clear spirit, which is often flavoured with a mix of local aromatics that will remain a closely guarded secret - so don't ask! Ouzo, the Greek's tipple of choice, is best from Lésvos, Sámos and Híos, and varies in strength. In west Crete, you should order the grappa-like *rakí*, whereas on eastern Crete, try *tsikoudiá*. Corfu is famous for liqueur flavoured with kumquats, which you can sample on a tour of producer Mavromatis *(www.kumquat.gr)*.

↑ Ouzo being served as an accompaniment to fresh seafood

Tasting Plate

The best way to sample an array of local specialities is to order a selection of *mezedes* (appetisers). Common dishes include *melitzánosalata* (aubergine salad) – ask for it to be served *agiorítiko*, or monastic style – but if you're feeling more adventurous then how about Cretan *marathópites* (fennel patties) or salads topped with *krítamo* (pickled rock samphire)? *Fáva* (mashed split yellow peas) is best from Santoríni, while falafel-like *revythokeftédes* can be found throughout the Aegean.

→

An array of delicious *mezedes* accompanied by glasses of raki

GREEK ISLANDS FOR
FOODIES

The Greek Islands are going through a culinary renaissance, and the resurgent pride in regional cuisines and traditional recipes makes dining out well worth writing home about – unless you want to keep one or two special tavernas to yourself.

Cheesy Delights

Here, there's a cheese for every day and every island, so is it any wonder that the Greeks eat more cheese than anywhere else in the world? Feta is a Greek staple and the undoubted king is Límnos' *kalatháki*. Soft cheeses abound: sweet *myzíthra* fills dessert turnovers such as Cretan *kalitsoúnia*, while *kopanistí*, from Mýkonos, Kýthnos and Tínos, makes a peppery, savoury spread. Refined hard cow's cheeses include *arsenikó* from Náxos, and grilled *mastéllo* from Híos.

→

Fresh cheeses being hung up at a traditional Greek cheesemakers

Eat Your Greens

A prominent part of Greek cuisine since ancient times, wild greens - especially assorted chicories - are avidly gathered throughout the countryside between October and May. Ranging in flavour from disarmingly sweet to dauntingly bitter, they liven up a host of dishes. Try mild Cretan *stamnagáthi*, which has become so popular that specialist crops are now cultivated, or pickled caper shoots *(kápari)* - leaves, thorns and all - on Nísyros *(p194)*.

← A simple salad of boiled wild greens, served with bread and lemon

TOP 5 **WEIRDEST DISHES**

Stífnos
A Cretan dish made with non-deadly nightshade greens.

Volví
Pickled narcissus bulbs, found on Crete.

Foúskes
Popular on Kálymnos and Rhodes, this marine invertebrate looks ugly but tastes delicious.

Gyalisterés
Smooth Venus molluscs, eaten alive; if they twitch when you drip lemon juice on them, they're good to go!

Tsitsírava
Pickled wild pistachio shoots on Skópelos and Alónnisos.

→ Grilled sardines served with lemon, a summer speciality

Fresh From the Sea

Those expecting basic dishes of *kalamári* or grilled octopus are in for a pleasant surprise. Dominating fish markets and taverna menus are assorted breams, especially *skathári* (black bream), *fangrí* (red porgy) and *sykiós* (corvina). Mid-summer brings *sardélles* (sardines, preferably grilled); *gávros* (big anchovies) and *atheerína* (sand smelt fried with onions and flour). Most islands have at least one excellent taverna in which to try this array, but seek out *psarotavernas* (seafood tavernas) such as Klimataria *(p74)* for something special.

Skip Across the Cyclades

Made up of numerous islands clustered relatively close together in the central Aegean, the Cyclades (p200) are ideal for those intent on serious island hopping. If you're seeking wonderful beaches, dramatic cliffs and pretty hilltop villages, try the western line linking Sérifos (p217), Sifnos (p218) and Mílos (p236). For those after a less well-trodden route, the string of minor islands between Náxos (p236) and Amorgós (p220), especially Skhinoússa and Iraklío (p239) will appeal.

→

A picturesque church perched on a clifftop on Sérifos

GREEK ISLANDS FOR
ISLAND HOPPERS

Island hopping is still the best way to see multiple Greek Islands in one trip – here, you can jump on a ferry and go to whichever island the wind takes you, where you're sure to discover brilliant beaches, quirky characters and a friendly neighbourhood taverna.

Culture and Beaches in the Ionians

Just like the legendary Sirens, the beauty and music of the Ionian islands (p54) are hard to resist – and may tempt you to stay longer. The easiest island hopping is between the major quartet of islands in the south, from half-touristic, half-wild Zákynthos (p82) to quietly stunning Lefkáda (p80) by way of sprawling Kefaloniá (p84) and tiny mythological Itháki (p86). Expect cultured capitals, rugged ridges and superb beaches, accompanied he romantic strains of tars and mandolins.

→

ird's-eye view of tiful Shipwreck on Zákynthos

→ Relaxing on Sarakíniko Beach on Mílos

TOP 5 **SEAFARING VESSELS**

Large Ferries
The most common transport for covering long distances.

Pandófles
Mainland ports and nearby islands are often linked by these smaller flat-bottomed ferries.

Catamarans
Sleek catamarans will get you to your next destination fast.

Hydrofoils
Not as common as they were, these narrow "flying dolphins" glide between certain islands.

Caïques
Used to link very close islands or islets, these small boats are quintessentially Greek.

→ The town rising above the lovely boat-filled harbour at Sými

Dive into the Dodecanese

Running deeper into the Aegean, the Dodecanese *(p152)* are barren islands with dramatic cliffs and aquamarine water. islands are spaced out here, so pick a few that are nearer. It's hard to resist the history, monasteries and towns of *(p162)*, which combine well with picturesque Sými *(p1 ged Kárpathos *(p198)*. Consider, too, the tantalizing the northern islands, including the sponge-haven o *(p192)*, holy Pátmos *(p158)*, and smaller islets like

Concerts at Ancient Sites

Whether it's a mournful classical cello or a funky jazz concert, ancient venues are made for music. Often organized by locals, these atmospheric events are held everywhere from the ancient amphitheatre of Pythagório on Sámos *(p138)* to a mosque in Réthymno *(p254)*, but the best stage is undoubtedly on the Acropolis *(p288)*.

Concerts at the ancient odeon on the Acropolis

GREEK ISLANDS
AFTER DARK

Life on the Greek Islands continues at full speed after dark, particularly in summer when the sun sets late. The climate is balmy, most places are still open, and the night is full of possibility, whether you want to ramble about ruins or rumba to *rebetiko*.

Full Moon at the Ruins

Ancient ruins and castles are magic by moonlight; but even if the moon isn't shining, most sites are atmospherically lit up by floodlights. At the full moon in August, the national archaeological service grants free admission to many major ancient cities and palaces, and there's music and dancing at numerous other sites. Find out which sites are open at *www.culture.gr.*

→

...ng on the Acropolis ...es, open late at full moon in August

Scenic Open-Air Cinemas

The *therinó sinemá* (summer movie theatre) is a much-loved Greek institution, and the venue is as much a part of the experience as the film. Some cinemas are lushly landscaped with subtropical vegetation, such as movies in a park next to the sea on Kos, whereas others take place in historical venues, like Bethlehem Cinema, in the old Venetian walls at Iraklío *(p256)*. Larger islands have at least one; the loveliest are on Sámos, Crete and Páros.

$\rightarrow$

A casual, open-air cinema during the Grecian summer

Clubbing and Bars

For those who want to dance or drink like Dionysos, the Greek Islands has resorts known to party long into the night – and sometimes into the day. Hit up the flashy jet-set crowd on Santoríni *(p110)* or the more backpacker-friendly vibes at Kávos on Corfu *(p77)*. There are even some bars – like Kavos Bach Bar on Skýros *(p116)* – where you can walk straight onto the relaxed bar terrace after taking a dip in the surrounding aquamarine waters.

↑ A buzzing bar in small seafront village of Kassiopi on Corfu

💬 INSIDER TIP
Local Sounds

Each island sways to the sound of its own traditional music, and local tavernas are the best place to hear these local melodies. These vary from soulful melodies of *kantádes* on Corfu or the louder, underground sounds of *rebetiko* in basement bars in Athens.

Nocturnal Scuba-Diving

The Greek seas are a radically different and busy world after sunset, with octopus, acrobatic squid, ghostly cuttlefish, colourful nudibranchs and spotted moray eels on the prowl amid the many shipwrecks. Most of the Greek Islands' numerous scuba-outfitters offer night dives for experienced divers. Some of the best experiences are found on Mýkonos *(p223)* and Santoríni *(p210)*.

$\rightarrow$

A pink octopus creeping along the side of a wreck in the Greek seas

At the Beach

Most Greek Islands have sheltered, gentle sandy beaches where toddlers up can safely paddle in knee- or waist-high water. Particular favourites for families include the tranquil Psilí Ámmos West on Sámos (p138), the wide expanse of water (and sun-beds with umbrellas on the sandy beach - for a fee) at Tsambíkas on Rhodes (p172), and the golden sands and turquoise sea of Elafonísi on Crete (p268).

→

The idyllic, lagoon-like beach at Elafonísi on Crete, a popular spot with families

GREEK ISLANDS FOR
FAMILIES

A culture where children are pretty much always welcome makes the Greek Islands one of the most family-friendly destinations in the Mediterranean. The islands offer sun, sand and sea - along with plenty of other attractions to keep kids entertained, from ruined castles to retro aquariums.

Under the Sea

The retro 1930s aquarium on Rhodes (p173), with its subterranean galleries, is old-fashioned fun. Beyond the vintage look, there's plenty to appeal to kids of all ages, including dolphins, sharks, seals, sea turtles, fish and crabs. The more state-of-the-art Cretaquarium near Goúrnes, on the island of Crete, houses around 2,500 sea creatures and also has educational programmes and events for children (www.cretaquarium.gr). A number of beaches have facilities for snorkelling - including Nanoú on Sými (p197) - so kids can also see underwater life in its natural habitats.

←

Getting a close-up view of a shark at the Cretaquarium

Resort Life

Three magical words: all-inclusive resorts. The Greek Islands have a number of these, many of which are explicitly aimed at families, including Mark Warner on Límnos, Kos and Rhodes; Kiani Beach or Minoa Palace on Crete; and Mayor Pelekas on Corfu. With options ranging from cheap and cheerful to super luxurious, and from beachfront hotels to inland hideaways, they take the stress out of keeping the kids entertained with childrens' pools and play areas, kids' clubs, watersports facilities and babysitting services. Perfect for relaxing, they can make a great base for venturing out to explore the local sights.

← Enjoying a swim at one of the family resorts on Kos

Bringing History into the Present

While some museums, such as Iráklio Archaeological Museum *(p258)*, have exhibitions so cool they'll captivate under-12s, most lack hands-on experiences or interactive displays. Best, then, to head for the castles dotted throughout the Greek Islands, like the Palace of the Grand Masters *(p166)*, or more dramatic ruins, such as the acropolis at Líndos *(p174)*.

Did You Know?

There are waterparks across the islands, including three on Crete and two each on Kos and Zákynthos.

→ A girl climbing through 13th-century battlements to the acropolis at Lindos

Waterworlds

Snorkelling outings can be documented with a camera that's water resistant to 6 m (20 ft) or so, although you'll need a proper underwater camera on scuba trips. There are dedicated scuba-diving photography tours that visit the top underwater ruins, artifacts and reefs in the Greek Islands, in particular Mýkonos and Corfu *(www. padi.com/courses/digital-underwater-photographer)*.

Visitor on a snorkelling trip taking a selfie with a starfish

GREEK ISLANDS FOR
PHOTOGRAPHERS

The Greek Islands just beg to be photographed, whether you're snapping their splendid seascapes, quaint villages, blue-domed churches or ancient sites. Here are a few things you need to know to get the best shots

Whitewashed Villages

Shutterbugs head to Ía at the tip of Santorini to capture the sun setting behind the blue and terracotta houses jauntily clinging to the cliff (p212). The rest of the Cyclades are also ripe with photo opportunities, including the iconic images of whitewashed villages. However, it's easy to take an underexposed photo in the blistering sun; the buildings will be right but the sky may emerge less blue than it really is. Take a tour with PhotoVoyagers to help you master the light (www.photovoyagers.tours).

$\longrightarrow$

The lovely blue and white houses of the village of Ía, Santorini

Castles at Night

From the looming Líndos acropolis to the majestic Mólyvos castle (p135) on Lésvos, all Greek Island castles are fetchingly floodlit from dusk to at least 1am. They are tempting subjects but difficult to get right. The best results come from long exposures at a moderate ISO with a tripod (or just stabilizing on top of a wall).

$\longleftarrow$

The illuminated kástro at Mólyvos (Míthymna) on Lesvos

Wild Snaps

Away from the busy beaches and bustling ports, the Greek Islands have a colourful array of wildlife just waiting to be captured on film. You'll need a hefty zoom ratio in order to capture graceful Eleonara's falcons hunting in Sporades Marine Park (p113) or strutting flamingos at the salt marshes on Sámos and the salt lake on Kos (p188).

INSIDER TIP
Best Seasons

All across the Greek Islands, spring and autumn offer more flattering illumination for photographs. Spring features greener landscapes, which include spectacular fields of wildflowers. Autumn offers prolonged, rich sunsets and vibrant golden foliage.

$\longleftarrow$

Flamingos in the salt lake at Tingkáki on Kos, in the Dodecanese

GREEK ISLANDS FOR
NATURE LOVERS

If you want to get wild in the Greek Islands, look beyond the beach bars and clubs of Mykonos and Rhodes to the abundant flora and fauna found inland and in the water. From the majestic turtles of the Ionian islands to the blooming flowers brightening Crete, there's plenty of life to explore here.

Majestic Monk Seals

The Mediterranean monk seal is Europe's most endangered mammal, with only around 400 left in the wild. At least sixty of these live in the northern Sporádes, principally in the sea caves of Alónissos, where they are protected as part of a national marine park (p113). You can take a boat tour through the marine park, but spotting one of these sleek black creatures requires a large slice of good fortune.

$\longrightarrow$

A charming Mediterranean monk seal on a rocky beach, a rare sight on the islands

Look Out For Loggerheads

The Ionian Islands, especially the southern coasts of Zákynthos *(p82)* and Kefaloniá *(p84)*, are popular breeding grounds for the beautiful loggerhead turtle. Partially successful measures, such as banning people from some breeding beaches at night, have been taken to help this protected species. If you're lucky you might meet one while swimming, but you have more chance spotting them in Argostóli harbour *(p84)*, where they are regular visitors.

←

Loggerhead turtles, spotted during a dive and *(inset)* swimming near a yacht, just offshore

TOP
4 MARINE CREATURES

John Dory
With its flat oval body and mohawk-like dorsal fins, this strange fish patrols offshore rocks.

Jellyfish
Whether translucent or orangey brown, these insidious floaters with stinging tentacles are not to be tangled with.

Octopus
More often spotted on a plate, the wily octopus catches its prey with its powerful suckers and can change colour.

Great Pipefish
Snorkellers may mistake this oddity, with its elongated body and long thin snout, for a piece of seaweed.

Step into Spring

Almost as colourful as Greek village life is the variety of flowers that bloom in spring, especially the ubiquitous yellow broom. Crete *(p244)* is a true botanist's dream, with no less than 1,700 species, including sixty different types of orchid. Go on a guided tour with Pure Crete to see the best of the blooms *(www.purecrete.com)*.

→

Passing beautiful blooms while walking to Crete's Samariá Gorge

Here We Go Again

The superlative views on Skiáthos *(p114)* and Skópelos *(p116)* are enough to make anyone burst into song – so, naturally, the islands were the perfect location for the 2008 smash hit musical *Mamma Mia!* Skópelans have eagerly used this for marketing purposes ever since, and the islands have attracted legions of fans. Most familiar of the island locations is the church of Agios Ioannis, in which Meryl Streep's Donna and Pierce Brosnan's Sam say "I do". The church requires a steep hike up numerous steps, but offers spectacular views and photo opportunities.

$\rightarrow$

The clifftop chapel on Skópelos in which *Mamma Mia!*'s Donna and Sam *(inset)* are married

GREEK ISLANDS
ON SCREEN

Forget about Meryl Streep and Pierce Brosnan, the Greek Islands were the true stars of *Mamma Mia!* The islands sparkle on the silver screen, and the numerous movies filmed here have lured visitors hoping to relive some of the magic themselves. Here are a few of our favourites.

Doing the Zorba

It's an iconic moment in Greek cinematic history when Basil and Zorba, disappointed in love, put their arms around each other and danced off the screen and into our hearts. *Zorba the Greek*, based on the eponymous book by Nikos Kazantzakis, was filmed in 1964 on Crete – such was its popularity that the "Zorba" has become a dance classic.

$\rightarrow$

Anthony Quinn as Zorba and Alan Bates as Basil in *Zorba the Greek*

→

Nicolas Cage and
Penelope Cruz in
Captain Corelli's Mandolin

HOMER'S ODYSSEY

Long before the magic
of cinema, the ancient
Greeks wove fantas-
tical tales of half-god
heroes and mythical
civilizations. The most
legendary of these is
Homer's *Odyssey*, a
sequel to the equally
epic *Illiad*, where the
bard's weary but
cunning hero took
ten long years (and
a circuitous route) to
return to his home on
Itháki after fighting in
the Trojan war. Spots
mentioned in the
famous Homeric epic
are marked through-
out the island, such as
Arethoúsa spring and
the cave of faithful
swineherd Eumaios,
friend of Odysseus.

Wartime Romance

Louis de Bernières' 1994 blockbuster novel *Captain Corelli's
Mandolin*, set on wartime Kefaloniá (p84), was a romance
between an Italian soldier and a Greek woman – but it mainly
inspired readers to fall in love with the island, where the movie
was filmed in 2000. Particularly lust-worthy locations from
the film include the beautiful beach of Antisamos and the
pastel bay village of Fiskárdo (p85). The gracious Venetian
townscapes were annihilated by the 1953 earthquake, so
sets built at Sámi (p85) stood in for 1940s Argostóli.

GREEK ISLANDS FOR
ARCHITECTURE

Reflecting a long history of conquests and occupation, the architectural style on the Greek Islands is consistent only in its variety. From cheerfully pastel-coloured villages to the ubiquitous crumbling ruins, here are a few iconic buildings to look out for.

Colourful Domestic Architecture

The history of conquest across the Greek Islands can often be seen on the homes of the locals, from the Venetian-influenced pitched tiled roofs, ornate portals and external chimneys on Crete (p245) and Corfu Town (p64) to the overhanging lath-and-plaster upper storeys that copy Ottoman style in the Northeast Aegean. And Greek homes aren't all shades of white and blue – look out for the vibrantly painted façades brightening harbours and hillsides all over the islands.

←

The picturesque old Venetian harbour of Haniá, on Crete

Wonderful Windmills

The iconic windmills found across the Cyclades (most famously on Mýkonos) used the strong Greek wind to grind wheat husks, producing the flour used by bakers across the islands. None of these windmills still function, though some have been turned into museums, but they do make for excellent photos.

←

The picture-perfect windmills of Mýkonos, iconic island landmarks

Ships of Salvation

Perched upon hilltops, island monasteries were seen as ships of salvation upon a sea of sin. The *katholikón* (main church) dominates a central courtyard, while stout perimeter walls and maybe a tower defend against sinful marauders, usually pirates. Akin to fortresses, many are still standing, including Néa Moní on Híos *(p126)* and the Monastery of St John on Patmos *(p160)*.

←

The heavily fortified Monastery of St John looming over the island of Patmos

Ageing Gracefully

Many of the island's ancient temples belong to the Doric order from around the 4th and 5th century BC. It is a style defined by its unadorned columns and tiled-roof gables, as well as three-dimensional sculptures and statues. Temples worth travelling for include the Temple of Aphaia on Égina *(p94)* and Lindos's Athena temple, which has the best view around *(p174)*.

→

The well-preserved ruins of the Temple of Aphaia on Égina

A YEAR IN
THE GREEK ISLANDS

JANUARY

Protochroniá /Ágios Vasílios (*1 Jan*). "Aï Vasíli" brings holiday gifts to children.

△ **Theofánia/Epiphany** (*6 Jan*). Church fonts are reconsecrated, *kalikántzari* (rampaging Christmas demons) are banished and boys compete to retrieve crucifixes from the Aegean for good luck.

FEBRUARY

△ **Apókries/Carnival Season** (*three weeks before Lent*). A time of colour and pageantry across the islands, from costumed processions on Réthymno to the goat dance on Skýros.

Tsikhnopémpti /"Roast-Smell" (*Thu, 66 days before Easter*). Grillhouses are booked solid; believers eat their final meat before Lent.

Kathará Deftera/Clean Monday (*55 days before Easter*). The start of Lent is celebrated with picnics and kite-flying.

MAY

△ **Protomagiá** (*1 May*). The beginning of spring is celebrated with flower shows in many cities, including Iráklio on Crete.

Análipsi/Ascension Day (*39 days after Easter*). The 40th day after the death of Jesus, when he ascended to heaven, is commemorated with the first sea swim of the season.

JUNE

Agíou Pnévmatos/Pentecost Monday (*early Jun*). A three-day weekend for the start of summer.

△ **Agioi Apostoli Petro kai Pavlos** (*late Jun*). Apostles Peter and Paul are celebrated at churches dedicated to them across the islands.

Ippokrateia Festival (*late Jun*). A long-standing summer festival on Kos, running until October.

SEPTEMBER

Rhodes Festival (*2nd week*). The Palace of the Grand Masters rings with the sound of classic music, as concerts are played on-site.

△ **Agíou Ioánni Theológou/St John the Divine** (*24 and 25 Sep*). The saint's day is celebrated at monasteries outside Nikiá on Nísyros and at Hóra on Pátmos.

OCTOBER

△ **Óhi/No Day** (*28 Oct*). Military parades commemorate General Metaxas's response to the 1940 Italian ultimatum for surrender in World War II – he said "ohi", or "no".

MARCH

△ **Independence Uprising Celebrations** (25 Mar). The anniversary of the start of the War of Independence is celebrated with military parades across the country..

Evangelismós/Annunciation (25 Mar). Orthodox Catholics rejoice the angel Gabriel appearing to Mary with the news that she was the Theotókos, or God-Bearer.

APRIL

△ **Easter Week** (Apr/May). A huge Orthodox religious festival – the most important of the year – continues for a week.

Megáli Pémpti/Maundy Thursday (Thu before Easter Sun). The abbot of the Monastery of St John on Pátmos washes his monks' feet in imitation of Christ and his disciples.

Megáli Paraskeví/Good Friday (Fri before Easter Sun). Women of each parish decorate an Epitáfios (Bier of Christ), which is paraded around before a solemn evening service marking the crucifixion of Jesus.

JULY

△ **Agía Marína** (17 Jul); **Profíti Ilía/Prophet Elijah** (20 Jul); **Agía Paraskeví/St Paraskevi** (26 Jul). Festivals for saints' days.

Paxos Festival (Jul–Sep). The island celebrates summer with a variety of cultural events hosted all over the island, including in historic sites.

AUGUST

Varkaróla Festival (2nd weekend). Fireworks light up the sky over Paleokastrítsa on Corfu as part of a weekend-long cultural festival.

△ **Kímisi tis Theotókou/Dormition of the Mother of God** (14–15 Aug). It's home time as Greeks return to their ancestral villages for a week.

Lefkáda International Folklore Festival (3rd week). Folk-dance groups from around the world perform across the island.

NOVEMBER

ton Taxiarhón Mihaíl ke Gavriíl/Taxiarch Angels Michael and Gabriel (8 Nov). The angel's feast day is celebrated with a large mass and a procession of the icon, and is attended by many pilgrims.

△ **Isódia tis Theotókou/Presentation of the Mother of God** (21 Nov). Pilgrims visit the Hozoviótissa, Amorgós, to celebrate Virgin Mary.

DECEMBER

Christoúgenna (throughout). A special time of tradition and family, Christmas is celebrat... unique style across the islands, like on K... where women burn incense outside th... doors to scare away hobgoblins.

△ **Paramoní tis Protochroniás/Ne...** (31 Dec). Adults play cards for mor... the vasilópita with a lucky coin b...

A BRIEF
HISTORY

With everyone from the Athenians to the Ottomans having occupied the Greek Islands, the region has seen a varied list of conquerors during its long history. Despite this, the Greek idea of nationhood - *éthnos* - based on shared language, religion and customs, has persisted since ancient times.

Prehistoric Greece

During the Bronze Age, three separate civilizations flourished in the region. Cycladic culture (2800–2200 BC) produced enigmatic marble figurines. The Minoans, who ruled on Crete, Melos and Thera, built technologically sophisticated palaces with complex drainage systems and light wells. After the Minoans went into decline, the Mycenaeans – known for their Linear B script (the first written Greek) – moved from the mainland to Crete. Both the Minoan and Mycenaean cultures found their peak in the Palace Periods of the second millennium, when they were dominated by a centralized religion and bureaucracy.

776 BC

The year the first Olympic Games are traditionally said to have taken place.

Timeline of events

1450–1400 BC

The Mycenaeans eclipse the Minoans in the Aegean.

800–700 BC

The first city-states and their colonies are founded.

494 BC

Statesman Solon's reforms presage Athenian democracy.

1200–1100 BC

The Sea Peoples start their invasions; Mycenaean society collapses.

00–1450 BC

...oans build technically ...¹ palaces on Crete.

The Dark Ages and Archaic Period

Between 1200 and 1100 BC Mycenaean society was harried by invaders known as the Sea Peoples, triggering the Dark Ages across the islands. This period of decline continued until the birth of city-states such as Athens and Sparta in about 800 BC. The ensuing cultural renaissance was accompanied by the founding of colonies from the Black Sea to North Africa, but, in 492 BC, Darius the Great of the Persian Empire attacked Athens and Sparta. Two years later Athens defeated the Persians at Marathon, a defining moment marking the start of a golden age.

Classical Greece

The pinnacle of Greek civilization, the Classical period saw the building of the Acropolis and other great temples; the creation of great tragedies by Sophocles, Euripides and Aeschylus; and the founding of famous schools of philosophy by Aristotle and Plato. This was also a time of bloodshed; the Peloponnesian War between Athens and Sparta began in 431 BC and ended with Sparta subjugating Athens after 27 years, only to be defeated by Thebes in 371 BC. Divided and weakened, the city-states were conquered by Philip II of Macedonia in 338 BC.

1 A 17th-century navigational chart of the Mediterranean.

2 The famous Agía Triada sarcophagus, dated to 1400 BC, with frescoes depicting Minoan funerary rituals.

3 Illustration depicting King Darius I of Persia fighting the Greeks at the Battle of Marathon.

4 Sketch illustrating the great Temple of Demeter on Naxos, built in Ionic style around 530 BC during the late Archaic Period.

461–429
Pericles reigns over Athens during its golden age.

415 BC
A disastrous Athenian expedition to Sicily leads to Sparta's eventual defeat of Athens in 404 BC.

480–79 BC
Athens and its allies finally defeat Xerxes the Great and his Persian army at the naval battle of Salamis and the land battle of Plataea.

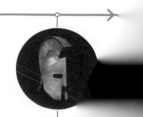

371 BC
The Theban victory at Battle of Leuktra brings an end to Sparta's power

Hellenistic Greece

Phillip II was assassinated two years after his conquest of the city-states. His son and successor, Alexander – later called "the Great" – was one of the greatest military commanders in the ancient world, and continued to expand the empire built by his father, making forays as far east as the Indian subcontinent. His reign brought in a period of Greek cultural hegemony, with the Greek language, religion and culture spreading throughout the conquered lands. After Alexander's death in 323 BC, his empire split into successor states, with the Greek Islands divided between the Egyptian Ptolemies and Kassandros of Macedonia.

Roman Greece

The rising power of Rome resulted in Greece becoming a Roman province after the sack of Corinth in 146 BC, and a period of relative calm followed. The Romans, ardent admirers of Greek culture, sent their sons to be educated in Athens, making it a cultural hub, while Roman emperors endowed the city and other parts of the land with grand monuments. Christianity was introduced to the region during this period, with St Paul travelling around the area during AD 49–61.

1 Artwork depicting Alexander the Great visiting the studio of renowned artist Apelles of Kos.

2 The courtyard of the Palace of the Grand Master of the Knights Hospitaller in Rhodes.

3 Details of a rich mosaic inside the monastery of Néa Moní on Híos.

4 Miniature from a chronicle by 15th-century French calligrapher David Aubert showing the capture of Constantinople by the Fourth Crusade in 1204.

Timeline of events

146 BC
Rome completes the annexation of Greece.

31 BC
The defeat of Antony and Cleopatra at Actium marks the start of the Roman Empire.

49–61 AD
St Paul makes evangelizing journeys around Greece to spread Christianity.

3–84 BC
...hridates VI, ...of Pontos in ...a, rebels ...omans.

117–38 AD
The philhellenic emperor Hadrian reigns over the Roman empire.

3

4

Byzantine Greece

In the 4th century AD, the Roman empire was succeeded by the Byzantine empire. This was based at Constantinople, with the Greek Islands seen as unimportant backwaters. Christianity became the official religion in 380 AD, and the famed Athenian philosophy schools closed as Christianity supplanted Classical thought. Many churches and monasteries were built across the islands in this time, leaving a wealth of Byzantine religious art and buildings. However, piracy and invasion were constant across the islands, compelling Byzantium to seek Genoese aid in return for ceding the Northeast Aegean islands to them.

Crusader and Venetian Greece

When Constantinople fell to the Crusaders in 1204, Greece was divided between the Venetians and the Franks. The Venetians fortified many islands, holding them for centuries. Their rule, which promoted Catholicism, was resented in these Orthodox lands, although it left a rich cultural and architectural legacy. The Knights Hospitaller, a military order tasked with defending the Holy Land, came to Rhodes after Jerusalem fell in 1291, eventually conquering the island and most of the Dodecanese.

RELIGIOUS ART

Religious art in 16th- and 17th-century Venetian Crete imbued Byzantine iconography with Renaissance sensibilities. Masters of the style included Mihïl Damaskinos, Theodore Poulakis, Emmanouil Tzanes and El Greco.

313 and 325 AD
Roman emperor Constantine the Great issues edicts encouraging Christianity.

1204 AD
The Fourth Crusade sacks Constantinople and deposes the Byzantine emperor.

1054 AD
The Great Schism takes place between the churches based in Rome and Constantinople.

1309 AD
The Knights Hospaller conquer Rhodes and the Dodecanese

Ottoman Greece

With the fall of Constantinople to the Ottomans in 1453 and their conquest of almost all remaining Greek territory by 1460, the Greek state effectively ceased to exist for the next 350 years. However, much of the country, including the islands, was left alone or even granted special privileges; Sými, for example, had a monopoly in supplying sponges to harems. This period profoundly affected Greek culture and everyday life, and, eventually, discontent nurtured rebellion.

The Making of Modern Greece

The Greek War of Independence against Ottoman rule started in 1821, and continued for almost ten years; this was also the beginning of the "Great Idea" to bring all Greek people under one flag. The revolution ended with the establishment of the Greek state; Ioannis Kapodistrias became its first president in 1828. Of the Greek Islands, initially only the Argo-Saronics, Cyclades, Sporades and Évvia joined this new state. Following the 1831 assassination of Kapodistrias, the London Conference of 1832 established a kingdom with Otto of Bavaria as king, followed by Danish prince George. Over the next century, the

BRITISH IONIAN PROTECTORATE

Napoleon abolished the Venetian Republic in 1797 and annexed the Ionians. They stayed under French control until 1814, except during the Septinsular Republic (1799-1807). The 1815 Treaty of Paris created a British protectorate which lasted until 1864, when the return of the Ionians to Greece was a condition of Prince George assuming the Greek throne.

Timeline of events

1523
The Knights Hospitaller surrender Rhodes to Sultan Süleyman the Magnificent in January.

1645–1669
The Ottoman conquest of Crete entails a 22-year siege of Iráklio.

1917
Greece enters World War I on the Macedonian front.

1830
Greek independence is guaranteed by the London Protocol.

1912–13
The Balkan Wars greatly enhance Greek territory, encompassing Crete and the Northeast Aegean Islands.

Greeks succeeded in doubling their national territory, and after the end of World War I, attempted to seize Constantinople. Their defeat led to a period of instability, which continued until World War II. Throughout the war, resistance towards invading powers was fierce across all the islands. After the war, the political right dominated Greece, and a 1967 coup led to military junta rule until democracy was restored in 1974.

The Greek Islands Today

Greece is now an established democracy and an integral part of the European Union (EU). The islands have been transformed beyond recognition since the start of mass tourism in the 1960s and 70s, with many villages turned into buzzing resorts. This period, however, has also been a time of economic instability, with the country rocked by multiple financial crises. The most recent, starting in 2009, resulted in a massive loan from the EU on the condition that severe austerity measures were imposed. Additional challenges arose, including the effects of climate change and the arrival of refugees. However, with a recent burst of spending on infrastructure and the gradual improvement of the economy, the future of the islands looks promising.

① Portrait of Ottoman sultan Suleiman the Magnificent by 16th-century German historian and jurist Johannes Löwenklau. ↑

② German army units invading Greece in April 1941 during World War II.

③ Former Greek prime minister Andreas Papandreou during his election campaign in June 1985.

④ Visitors watching the sunset from a popular viewpoint in Ía on Santorini island.

1919–22
The Greco-Turkish War sends over a million Orthodox refugees to Greece, including to many of the islands.

1941–44
Occupation by Germany, Italy and Bulgaria sees resistance on both the mainland and islands.

1946–49
Communist rebels lose to the Greek government during the civil war.

1974
The junta collapses, a civilian government is restored and the monarchy is abolished.

1967
A coup by hitherto unknown colonels installs a military junta in the country.

2010–11
A massive hole in public finances leads to the first of three bailouts from the IMF and EU. Harsh austerity measures prompt suffering and public unrest.

EXPERIENCE

An aerial view of a beach on Thásos

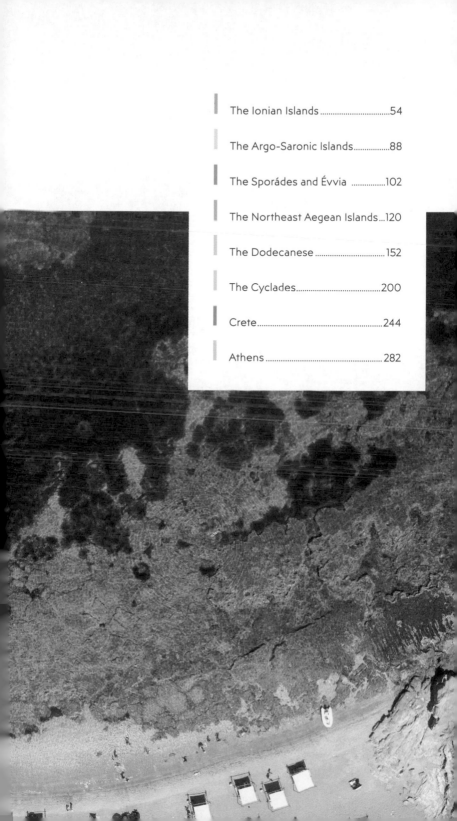

The Ionian Islands 54

The Argo-Saronic Islands 88

The Sporádes and Évvia 102

The Northeast Aegean Islands ...120

The Dodecanese 152

The Cyclades 200

Crete 244

Athens 282

THE IONIAN ISLANDS

Lying off the west coast of mainland Greece, the Ionian islands are famous as the homeland of Homer's Odysseus. The islands were colonized by the Corinthians in the 8th century BC and flourished as a wealthy trading post. But by the 5th century BC, Corfu sought independence from Corinth, and allied with Athens. The subsequent battles between Corinth and the united Athens and Corfu sparked the Peloponnesian War, and the eventual downfall of Athens. Later occupied by Venetians, whose rule began in 1363 and lasted until 1797, the islands saw a brief period of French occupation before the British took over in 1814. The islands were finally ceded to the Greek state in 1864. Evidence of the various periods of occupation can be seen throughout the islands, especially in Corfu town, which contains a mixture of Italian, French and British architecture.

The islands were not politically grouped together until Byzantine times and, as a result, each island has its own distinct character, from tiny Paxí, which is covered in the olive trees that play a major role in Greece's economy, to rocky Itháki and the rugged beauty and spectacular beaches of Kefaloniá.

Bari, Brindisi,
Venice, Ancona

Eríkousa

Othoní

Mathráki

Sidári

Kassiópi

Ágios
Stéfanos

Corfu Town

**Corfu International
Airport** ✈

Ágios
Matthéos

Corfu

See Corfu map,
below

Ionian
Sea

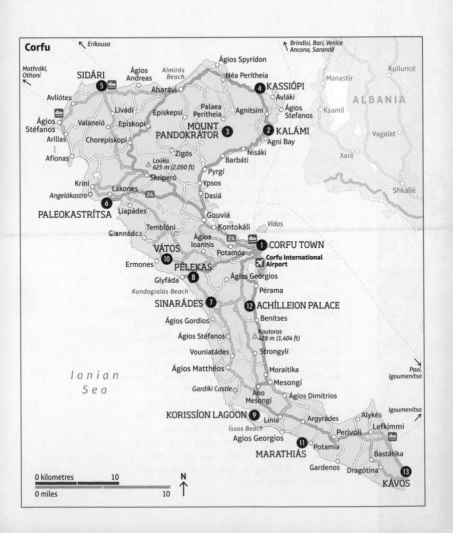

Corfu

↖ Eríkousa

Mathráki,
Othoní
↖

SIDÁRI
5

Ágios
Andreas

Almirós
Beach

Ágios Spyrídon

Néa Perítheia

↗ Brindisi, Bari, Venice
Ancona, Sarandë

Kulluricë

Manastir

ALBANIA

Avliótes

Aharávi

4 **KASSIÓPI**

Avláki

Ksamil

Livádi

Episkopí

Palaea
Perítheia

Agnitsini

Ágios
Stefanos

Valaneió

Episkopí

**MOUNT
PANDOKRÁTOR**

3

2 **KALÁMI**

Vagalat

Ágios
Stéfanos

Chorepískopi

Agni Bay

Xarè

Arillas

Afíonas

Zigós

Nisáki

Skriperó

Loúka
625 m (2,050 ft)

Barbáti

Shkallé

Krini

Angelókastro

Lákones

24

Pyrgí

Ypsos

Dasiá

PALEOKASTRÍTSA

6

Liapádes

Giannádes

Temblóni

Gouviá

Kontokáli

Vídos

Ágios
Ioannis

VÁTOS
10

PÉLEKAS
8

Potamós

24

1 **CORFU TOWN**

**Corfu International
Airport** ✈

Ermones

Glyfáda

Kondogialós Beach

SINARÁDES
7

Ágios Georgios

Pérama

12 **ACHÍLLEION PALACE**

Ágios Gordios

Benítses

Ágios Stéfanos

Kautoros
428 m (1,404 ft)

Vouniatádes

Strongylí

Ionian
Sea

Ágios Matthéos

Moraitika

Mesongí

Gardíki Castle

Ano
Mesongí

Ágios Dimítrios

Paxí,
Igoumenítsa
↗

KORISSÍON LAGOON
9

Línia

Argyrádes

Alykés

Lefkímmi

Igoumenítsa
↗

Íssos Beach

Agios Georgios

MARATHIÁS
11

Potamia

Perivóli

Bastátika

Gardenos

Dragótina

13

KÁVOS

0 kilometres   10

0 miles   10

N
↑

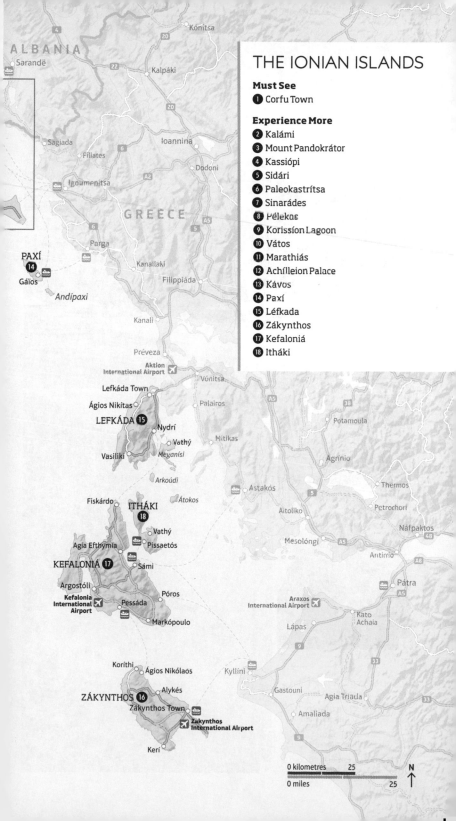

THE IONIAN ISLANDS

Must See

1 Corfu Town

Experience More

2 Kalámi
3 Mount Pandokrátor
4 Kassiópi
5 Sidári
6 Paleokastrítsa
7 Sinarádes
8 Pélekas
9 Korissíon Lagoon
10 Vátos
11 Marathiás
12 Achílleion Palace
13 Kávos
14 Paxí
15 Léfkada
16 Zákynthos
17 Kefaloniá
18 Itháki

0 kilometres 25

0 miles 25

N

→

1 Corfu town's harbourfront on a quiet afternoon.

2 The colourful exterior of Achilleion Palace.

3 The crumbling medieval fortress of Angelokastro.

4 Myrtiótissa beach, tucked away in a hidden cove.

5 DAYS
around Corfu

Day 1

Find your feet with breakfast on Corfu's French-inspired Esplanade *(p66)*, before winding through the streets to Ágios Spyrídon *(p64)*, dedicated to the island's patron saint. From here, walk along the seafront to the Byzantine Museum *(p65)* with its brooding icons. Emerge back into the sunshine for lunch at traditional Rex restaurant *(Kapodistriou 66; 26610 39649)*, before continuing to explore Corfu town and the grand Old Fortress *(p66)*, which has views back to town. Soak up the atmosphere in the buzzing Spiliá area, located between the old port and New Fortress *(p66)* before a dinner of *mezedes* and a taste of the spirit *tsípouro* at To Alato Pipero *(Kon/nou Zavitsianou 11)*.

Day 2

Take the 30-minute bus ride up to the eccentric Achilleion Palace *(p76)*, renowned for its gaudy interior and statues of Achilles. Continue the eccentricity by trying some of the local kumquat liqueur at one of the shops opposite. After lunch back in Corfu town at Ikoyenia Theotoki *(Alkiviádou Dárri; 26610 35004)*, head just outside of town to grand Mon Repos Villa *(p69)*, which has two ancient temples in its grounds. End the day with one of the best meals in town at the Venetian Well *(p66)* and a nightcap at Drops bar back on the Esplanade *(Leofóros Dimokratías 14)*.

Day 3

Rent a car to drive to the top of mighty Mount Pandokrátor *(p72)* for magnificent views in all directions – you can even see Albania on a clear day. Enjoy a taste of the traditional flavours of Corfu away from the coast at Old Perithia taverna in the atmospheric, almost-deserted village of Paleá Períthia. Afterwards, head down to the northeast coast for a dip at beautiful Agní Bay. It's a short drive from here to the popular resort village of Kassiópi *(p72)*. After a quick scout around its headland, complete with ruined castle, pick an outside table and tuck into some fish at the Old School Taverna *(26630 81211; behind the port)*.

Day 4

Drive around the scenic northwest coast, stopping for photos. It's a stiff climb up craggy and dramatic Angelókastro fortress *(p74)* for another panorama. Roll into Paleokastrítsa *(p74)* for lunch on the waterfront, followed by a swim at the town beach. Watch the sun set from iconic Kaiser's Throne *(p75)* in Pélekas, before heading to Kavos *(p77)* for a night out in Corfu's formerly notorious party town.

Day 5

Spend the morning swimming and getting an all-over tan at clothing-optional Myrtiótissa beach, then trudge back up the cliff to Myrtia taverna *(26610 94113)* for an early lunch. After, turn your wheels firmly south, stopping in Sinarádes *(p74)* to visit the folklore museum, then continue on via ramshackle Gardíki castle to the stunning dunes that separate Korissíon Lagoon from the sea. The perfect way to end your time in Corfu is relaxing by the lapping water at the friendly family-run Boukari Beach *psarotaverna (p74)*, where you can feast on fresh fish and ample local wine.

←

1 The town of Ágios Nikítas, with its stunning beach.

2 Statue of Odysseus in Stavrós' main square.

3 Windsurfing on the waves in Vasilikí Bay.

4 Tables on Vathý's seafront at twilight.

2 WEEKS
around the Southern Ionians

Day 1

Lefkáda town will be your base for the start of your time in the Ionians. After breakfast, get to know the town by popping into its venerable churches, the Folk Museum and nearby Moní Faneroménis (p80). Pick a tasty baked dish from behind the glass window for lunch at Eftyhia estiatório (off Dörpfeld; 26450 25844), then head to long Yíra beach for an afternoon relaxing on the sand. After the sun has gone down, enjoy some "soul food" in the bohemian surroundings of Ev 7in (Filarmonikís 8; 6974 641 160).

Day 2

The sandy beaches around Ágios Nikítas (p80) are perfect for a morning swim. After, stroll through the village, stopping for lunch at vine-covered Klimataria (main street; 26450 97383). In the afternoon, take the scenic coastal drive via the mountain villages of Kalamítsi and Atháni to the resort town of Yialós, where the water is temptingly clear. Watch the light fade over the coast below while tucking into authentic Armenian cuisine at John's Eatery (Atháni; 26450 33070).

Day 3

Keen windsurfers, or those willing to try, will enjoy a day on a board at renowned Vasilikí Bay (p81), while the less athletic can take a full-day boat excursion from Nydrí (p81). Grab lunch at Vasilikí harbour before more windsurfing or, if you're on a boat excursion, you'll dine on fresh bread, olives and feta on a neighbouring island or remote beach. Once you're back on dry land, Vangelaras (p81), located right on the quay at Vasilikí, is a great spot for your last meal on the island.

Day 4

Take the morning car ferry from Vasilikí to Fríkes on Itháki (p86), and stop at the tiny rock coves en route to the charming yachting harbour of Kióni (p86). Following lunch at friendly Rementzo (Fríkes port; 26740 31719), head up to Stavrós (p86) and spend the afternoon exploring the ruins of ancient Pelikáta Hill. Round off your first day on Itháki with a relaxed evening meal of spit-roasted meat and salad in the courtyard of O Tseligas (Stavrós main road, 26740 31596).

Day 5

It's a winding drive across the island to Vathý (p86), but you'll be rewarded with sweeping vistas. After arriving in the capital, which feels more like a small town, spend the morning exploring its modest museums. Enjoy some wonderful home-cooking at Nikos estiatório near the main square (26740 33039), then work off the traditional Greek dishes with a hike to the Arethousa Spring. Back in Vathý, take a stroll along the seafront and enjoy a fine fish or meat meal at To Kohili (Geogiou Gratsou; 2674 033565).

Day 6

Board an early ferry from Pisaetós to Sámi on Kefaloniá (p85); first stop after alighting is the Drogeráti cave system, where stalactites drip from the cave walls. Grab a snack for lunch at a beach bar on the splendid arc of Andísamos beach and then spend the afternoon either chilling out on the beach, or trying your hand at one of the various watersports. In the evening, meander north along Sámi's seafront and order some fresh fish and local wine at Akrogiali taverna (26740 22494). →

Day 7

To the north of Sámi, you can take a gentle boat ride into the spectacularly blue underground lake at Melissáni Cave (p85), then drive to the picture-perfect cove at Agía Efthymía. Try some of the organic produce at Oulísseas taverna (Agía Ffthymía; 26740 41133), before continuing north to explore the yachting mecca of Fiskárdo (p85) and its neighbouring coves. Choose from any seafront bar for a sundowner and eat some succulent grilled or baked meat at Lagoudera, a taverna by Fiskárdo square (26740 41275).

Day 8

Kefaloniá is known for its beaches, and today you're going to sample the best. Drive down the winding west coast road to the long curve of Mýrtos beach, pausing at picturesque Ássos for a coffee. After a swim and lunch at one of the beach canteens, carry on the Pallikí Peninsula to the magnificent Petaní beach for another dip. Watch the sunset and tuck into fresh fish on the deck of beachside Xouras taverna (26710 97458).

Day 9

The local Lixoúri–Argostóli car ferry is a useful shortcut to Kefaloniá's capital. Once in Argostóli (p84), visit the fascinating Focas-Cosmetatos Foundation. After a lunch of gigantes beans or baked pork at traditional daytime-only Tsivras restaurant (V Vandórou 1; 26710 24259), tour Ágios Gerásimos monastery, taste wine at Robola winery and ramble in Ágios Geórgios castle. After a full-on day, savour a quiet dinner of grilled meat, mezedes and Robola wine at Kastro Café (26710 69367), right beside the castle.

Day 10

After sipping your morning Greek coffee, stroll round the Botanical Gardens and along Lithóstroto, Argostóli's main shopping street. Head southeast for lunch on the spacious and stylish patio of Denis (26710 31454) on Trapezáki beach, and spend the afternoon sunbathing here. Round off your time in Kefaloniá with an exquisite seafood meal suspended above the water at Kyani Akti (p84) and maybe a bop at buzzing Bass bar.

① The azure lake in Melissáni Cave.
② Strolling through Argostóli.
③ Monastery on Zákynthos.
④ Shipwreck Bay on Zákynthos.
⑤ The harbour of Zákynthos Town.

Day 11

Board the ferry from Pessáda to Ágios Nikólaos (Skínari) in northern Zákynthos, then drive to Cape Skinári. This is the main access point to the island's famous Blue Caves *(p83)* and Shipwreck Bay *(p82);* organize a boat tour to both, and marvel at the vertiginous cliffs, hidden grottoes and hyperreal blue water. Back on land, have lunch at To Faros taverna *(Cape Skinári; 26950 31132),* before turning south to Xygiá beach. End the day dining in the tranquil courtyard of the Kaki Rahi taverna *(Pigadakia 290 90; 26950 83670).*

Day 12

Check out the array of woven materials on display in the village of Volímes, then get a bird's-eye view of Shipwreck Bay from the cliff above. Visit the Anafonítrias monastery before driving to Límni Kerioú for a late lunch at Nikolas taverna *(26950 48752).* After a lazy afternoon on the beach, head to Kerí village for an unforgettable sunset dinner in the lush garden of the Lighthouse taverna *(26950 43384),* and a nightcap at the Rock Café in Limní Kerioú.

Day 13

This morning, feel tempted to either try your hand scuba-diving, or rent a speedboat to explore the rugged coast near Límni Kerioú. After lunch, it's time to head out on the road again. Begin by touring the Vasilikós Peninsula *(p82),* which ends at the fascinating Marine Life Centre at Yérakas beach. Arrive in Zakynthos Town *(p82)* in time for a sunset cocktail on the harbour and to hear some *kantádes* (serenades) over dinner at Varkarola *(Lombárdou 78; 26950 26999).*

Day 14

Have a slow morning in town, spending an hour at both the Zákynthos Museum, which houses many Byzantine treasures, and the Solomos Museum dedicated to the poet. After lunch at Stathmos *(Filitá 42; 26950 24040),* pay your respects to the island's patron saint at Ágios Dionysios church and enjoy the view from Stráni Hill. End your trip with some soothing live acoustic music, while you enjoy the mouthwatering cuisine at Malanos Taverna *(Agíou Athanasíou 38; 45936).*

❶

CORFU TOWN
ΠΟΛΗ ΤΗΣ ΚΕΡΚΥΡΑΣ

✈ 3 km (2 miles) S of Corfu town 🚌 Xenofondos Sratigou, Corfu town 🚌 ℹ Platia Sarroko; www.corfu.gr

Corfu town is a delightful blend of European influences and historic monuments, with the Old Town a UNESCO World Heritage Site. The main hub on Corfu, it also has most of the major sites, and is packed in summer.

①
Ágios Spyrídon

🏛 Agíou Spyrídonos
🕐 6:30am-8pm daily

The holiest place on the island, Ágios Spyrídon has a distinctive red-domed tower, which guides visitors to this church. Inside, in a silver casket, is the

> 💬 **INSIDER TIP**
> **Combo Ticket**
>
> If you are planning to visit all Corfu town's major sights, buy a combination ticket for entry to the Old Fortress, Byzantine Museum, Museum of Asian Art, Archaeological Museum and Mon Repos Villa.

mummified body of the revered Spyrídon, the patron saint of the island.

Many Corfiot men are named after the saint, yet Spyrídon himself was not from Corfu but from Cyprus. He entered the church, rising to the rank of bishop. He is believed to have performed many miracles before his death in AD 350, and others since – not least in 1716, when he is said to have helped drive the Ottomans from Corfu after a six-week siege. His body was smuggled from Constantinople just before the Turkish occupation of 1453. It was only by chance that it came to Corfu, where the present church was built in 1589 to house the coffin.

The building is also worth seeing for the large amount of silver votive offerings brought by the constant stream of pilgrims. On four occasions each year (Palm Sunday, Easter Saturday, 11 August and the first Sunday in November) the saint's remains are carried aloft through the streets.

②

Palace of St Michael and St George

🏛 Platia Spianáda 📞 26610 30443 🕐 Summer: 8am-7:30pm Tue-Sun; winter 8:30am-3pm Tue-Sun
🚫 Main public hols

The Palace of St Michael and St George was built by the British between 1819 and 1824, using Maltese masons. It served as the home of Sir Thomas Maitland, the first British High Commissioner, and is the oldest official building in Greece. When the British left Corfu in 1864 the palace was used for a short time by the Greek royal family, but it was later abandoned and left to fall into disrepair.

The palace was carefully renovated in the 1950s by Sir Charles Peake, British Ambassador to Greece, and now houses the municipal art gallery, as well as the Corfu Museum of Asian Art.

↑ The pretty, sun-bathed rooftops of Corfu's Old Town

Japan, Indochina and India include statues, porcelain ware, screens, armour, silk and ceramics. In front of the building is a statue of Sir Frederick Adam, the British High Commissioner to Corfu from 1824 to 1831. He built the Mon Repos Villa (p69) south of town and was also responsible for popularizing the west coast resort of Paleokastrítsa (p74), one of his favourite spots on the island.

③ Byzantine Museum

🏛 **Prosfórou 30 & Arseníou**
🕐 **8am-2:45pm Tue-Sun**
🚫 **Main public hols** 🌐 **anti vouniotissamuseum.gr**

The Byzantine Museum, which opened in 1984, is housed in the renovated church of Panagía Antivouniótissa. One of the town's oldest buildings, it is responsible for some of the museum's finest exhibits.

The small museum takes a bit of finding but the number

First opened in 1928, the core of the museum's collection is the 11,000 items that were donated by Grigorios Manos, a Greek diplomat who had amassed the objects on his travels overseas, and wished to curate the new museum. Unfortunately he died before he could realize this ambition. The exhibits from China, Tibet,

SHOP

Agíou Spyridónos
The pedestrianized street of Agíou Spyridónos is fertile territory for buying souvenirs, with religious icons, jewellery and items made of olive wood particular specialities.

of magnificent icons on display, dating from the 15th to the 18th centuries, are worth the effort. Many are by artists from the Cretan School who worked and lived on Corfu as the island was a convenient stopping-off point on the journey between Crete and Venice from the 13th to the 17th centuries during Venetian rule, especially after Crete fell to the Ottomans.

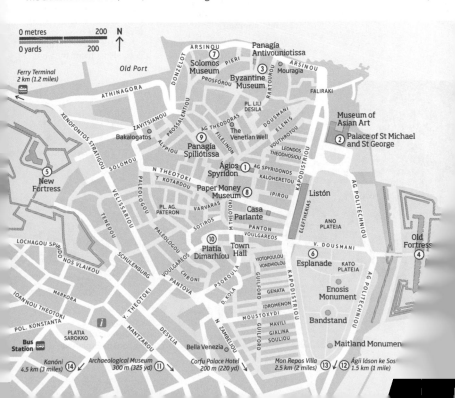

EAT

The Venetian Well
This classy bistro serves imaginative cuisine in a delightful spot beside the eponymous well.

📍 Platía Kremastí
🌐 venetianwell.gr

€€€

Mouragia
With views across the bay, this taverna offers fine meat and seafood in tasty sauces.

📍 Arseníou 15-17
📞 26610 33815

€€€

Bakalogatos
A buzzing *tsipouradiko* offering superb meat, seafood, cheese and fish *mezedes*.

📍 Alipíou 23
📞 26613 01721

€€€

Old Fortress

📞 26610 48310 🕐 8am-7:30pm daily (Nov-Mar: to 3pm) 🚫 Main public hols

The ruined Old Fortress, or Paleó Froúrio, stands on a promontory fortified by the Byzantines during the 6th century AD. The Old Fortress itself was constructed by the Venetians between 1550 and 1559 and is linked to Corfu town by an iron bridge. The very top of the fortification offers glorious views of the town and along the island's east coast. Lower down is the Neo-Classical St George church, built in 1840. Just inside the fortress is a small collection of Byzantine icons and mosaics that is well worth a look.

---

⑤

New Fortress

📍 Platía Solomoú 🕐 Apr-Oct: 9am-3:30pm daily; may stay open later in mid-summer

The Venetians began building the New Fortress, or Néo Froúrio, in 1576 to further strengthen the town's defences. It was not completed until 1589, 30 years after the Old Fortress, hence their respective names. There are a number of British buildings inside the fortress. The town's market is held in the former moat to the west.

---

⑥

Esplanade

A mixture of park and town square, the Esplanade, or Spianáda, is one of the reasons Corfu town is such an attractive place. Its grand colonnades offer relief from the packed streets in summer, as do the shady park benches and the elegant arcade known as the Listón, which is lined with many good cafés.

The Listón was built in 1807 on the orders of French imperial commissioner Mathieu de Lesseps. The name "Listón" comes from the Venetian practice of having a "List" of noble families in the *Libro d'Oro* or Golden Book – only those on it were allowed to promenade here.

Near the fountain is the Énosis Monument: the word

← Visitors enjoying the shade and graceful buildings on the Esplanade

← Flowers in bloom at a taverna near the Paper Money Museum

580 BC

The Temple of Artemis is built with Corfu's famous Gorgon frieze as part of its pediment.

énosis means "unification", and this celebrates the 1864 union of the Ionian islands with the rest of Greece, when British rule came to an end. The marble monument has carvings symbolizing each of the Ionian Islands. A statue of Ioánnis Kapodístrias, modern Greece's first president in 1827, stands at the end of the street that flanks the Esplanade and bears his name.

Solomos Museum

⌂ Theodórou Makri, off Arseníou 📞 26610 30674 🕐 9:30am–2pm Mon–Fri

Dedicated to Greece's most celebrated poet, Dionysios Solomos (who wrote the "Hymn to Liberty", two stanzas of which became the national anthem), this attractive museum is located in the house where he lived for many of his later years and died in 1857. The displays here include personal effects such as the poet's writing desk and many of his books.

Paper Money Museum

⌂ Ionikí Trápeza, Platía Iróon Kypriakoú Agóna 🕐 Hours vary, check website 🌐 alphapolitis mos.gr/en/05-Banknote-Museum

This collection of Greek banknotes traces the way in which the island's currency altered as Corfu's society and rulers changed over time. The first banknote was issued in British pounds, while later notes show the German and Italian currency of the war years. The tour ends with the last banknotes issued in drachmas, which were withdrawn in 2002 with the introduction of the euro. Another display shows the process of producing a note.

The museum, which opened in 1981, is housed on the first floor of a charming pink 19th-century building in which the first branch of the Ionian Bank opened in 1840.

Bronze memorial to the Greek resistance, New Fortress ↓

Panagía Spiliótissa, off a square in Corfu Old Town

a number of other fascinating finds from the Temple of Artemis and the excavations at Mon Repos Villa, including the Archaic Lion of Menekrates and a Classical pediment showing the god Dionysos drinking with a youth.

 ⑫

Ágii láson ke Sosípatros

🅰 Garítsa Bay

Garítsa Bay sweeps south of Corfu town, with the suburb of Anemómylo visible on the promontory. Here, in the street named after it, is the 11th-century church of Ágii láson ke Sosípatros (saints Jason and Sossipater). These disciples of St Paul brought Christianity to Corfu in the 2nd century AD. Inside are black marble columns and porous masonry blocks taken from ancient monuments.

WRITERS ON CORFU

Poet Dionysis Solomos, one of Greece's most prolific poets, lived on Corfu from 1828 until he died in 1857. Other writers who have found inspiration on Corfu include the British poet and artist Edward Lear, who visited the island in the 19th century, and Laurence and Gerald Durrell. More recently, Erikousan Yvette Manessis Corporon immortalized her islet, just off Corfu, in her novels *Something Beautiful Happened* (2017), which is set during World War II, and *When the Cypress Whispers* (2014).

 ⑨

Panagía Spiliótissa

🅰 Mitropóleos 📞 26610 39912 🕒 Daily

The Greek Orthodox church of Panagía Spiliótissa, or Virgin Mary of the Cave, was built in 1577. It became Corfu's cathedral in 1841, when the nave was extended. It is dedicated to St Theodora Avgousta, a Byzantine empress whose remains were brought to Corfu at the same time as those of St Spyrídon. Her body is in a silver coffin near the altar.

⑩

Platía Dimarhíou

26613 62700 🕒 Daily Main public hols

n this elegant square the Town Hall, a grand building that began 5 as a single-storey eeting place for the as then converted

into the San Giacomo Theatre in 1720, which was the first modern theatre in Greece. A second storey was added in 1903, after a new opera house (destroyed in 1943) was built. Adjacent to it is the Catholic cathedral Ágii Iákovos ke Hristoforos (saints James and Christopher). Consecrated in 1632, it was badly damaged by bombing in 1943 with only the bell tower surviving intact.

⑪

Archaeological Museum

🅰 Vraïla 1 📞 26610 30680 🕒 Hours vary, call ahead

The Archaeological Museum is a pleasant stroll south from the town centre along the seafront. The collection is small but a highlight is the Gorgon frieze. Dating from the 6th century BC, it originally formed part of the west pediment of the Temple of Artemis near Mon Repos Villa. The museum also displays

Mon Repos Villa

 Dairpfela 16, Kerkira
26610 41369 8am–3pm
Tue–Sun; may stay open
longer in summer

South of Anemómylo is Mon Repos Villa. It was built in 1826 by Sir Frederick Adam, the second High Commissioner of the Ionian state, as a present for his wife, and later passed to the Greek royal family. Nearby are the remains of Paleópolis, with a Doric

Did You Know?

Britain's Prince Philip, the Duke of Edinburgh, was born in Mon Repos Villa in 1921.

temple and the Kardáki spring-shrine. Opposite are the 5th-century ruins of the Iovianós basilica.

---

⑭

Kanóni

 4 km (3 miles) S of Corfu town

A short bus ride south of Corfu town is Kanóni, a town with the islands of Vlahérna and Pondikonísi just off the coast. Vlahérna has a tiny white convent that can be reached by a causeway. In summer boats go to Pondikonísi (Mouse Island), said to be where Odysseus's ship was turned to stone by Poseidon, stranding Odysseus on the island thought to be Corfu.

↓ Vlahérna's famous white convent, just off the coast of Kanóni

STAY

Bella Venezia
Classy yet welcoming hotel set in an ochre-painted Neo-Classical building behind the Esplanade, with well-appointed rooms and an airy conservatory for breakfast.

 Zambéli 4
 bellaveneziahotel.com

€€€

Corfu Palace Hotel
A grand establishment on the seafront, this luxurious hotel has splendid rooms, two pools, lush gardens and a French restaurant.

 Leofóros Dimokratías 2
 corfupalace.com

€€€

A SHORT WALK
CORFU OLD TOWN

Distance 600 m (2,000 ft) **Time** 15 minutes

The 21st century and burgeoning popularity with visitors has not spoiled Corfu town, which continues to be a charming mix of influences and buildings left by various occupiers. The Venetians ruled here for over four centuries, and elegant, often colourful Italianate buildings, with balconies and shutters, can be seen above French-style colonnades.

British rule left a wealth of monuments, public buildings and a cricket pitch, which is part of the Esplanade, or Spianáda (*p66*). This park is a focus for both locals and tourists, with park games and good walks. On its eastern side is the Old Fortress (*p66*) standing guard over the town, a reminder that Corfu was never conquered by the Ottomans.

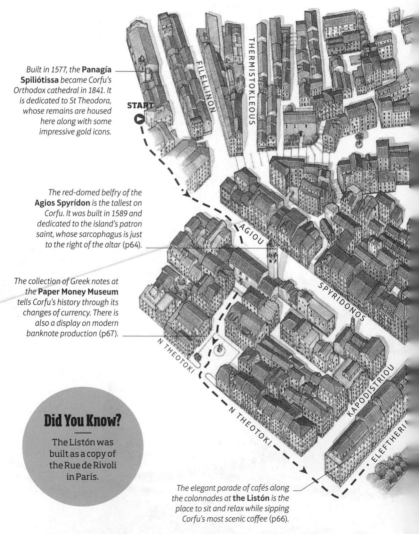

*Built in 1577, the **Panagía Spiliótissa** became Corfu's Orthodox cathedral in 1841. It is dedicated to St Theodora, whose remains are housed here along with some impressive gold icons.*

START

*The red-domed belfry of the **Agios Spyrídon** is the tallest on Corfu. It was built in 1589 and dedicated to the island's patron saint, whose sarcophagus is just to the right of the altar (p64).*

*The collection of Greek notes at the **Paper Money Museum** tells Corfu's history through its changes of currency. There is also a display on modern banknote production (p67).*

Did You Know?

The Listón was built as a copy of the Rue de Rivoli in Paris.

*The elegant parade of cafés along the colonnades at **the Listón** is the place to sit and relax while sipping Corfu's most scenic coffee (p66).*

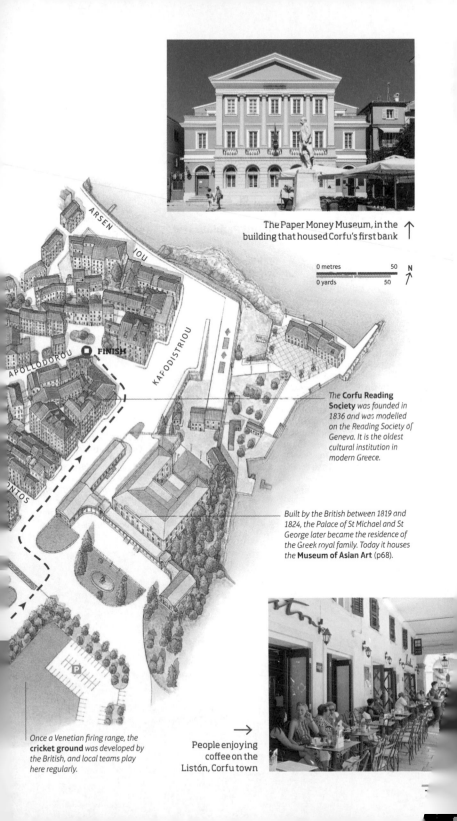

The Paper Money Museum, in the building that housed Corfu's first bank ↑

0 metres 50
0 yards 50
N ↗

The **Corfu Reading Society** was founded in 1836 and was modelled on the Reading Society of Geneva. It is the oldest cultural institution in modern Greece.

Built by the British between 1819 and 1824, the Palace of St Michael and St George later became the residence of the Greek royal family. Today it houses the **Museum of Asian Art** (p68).

Once a Venetian firing range, the **cricket ground** was developed by the British, and local teams play here regularly.

→ People enjoying coffee on the Listón, Corfu town

EXPERIENCE MORE

Kalámi
Καλάμι

 26 km (16 miles) NE of Corfu town Towards Kassiópi

Kalámi village has retained its charm despite its popularity with visitors. A handful of tavernas line its sand-and-shingle beach, while behind them cypress trees and olive groves climb up to the lower slopes of Mount Pandokrátor. The hills of Albania can be seen across Kalámi Bay. Kalámi's obvious appeal attracted the author Lawrence Durrell, who lived nearby and then in town from 1935 until 1939. Today, during in high season, when visitors throng his "peaceful fishing village", Durrell would hardly recognize this formerly quiet place.

Mount Pandokrátor
Ορος Παντοκράτωρ

 29 km (18 miles) N of Corfu town

Mount Pandokrátor, whose name means "the Almighty", dominates the northeast bulge of Corfu. It rises so steeply that its peak, at 914 m (2,999 ft), is less than 3 km (2 miles) from the beach resorts of Nisáki and Barbáti. The easiest approach is from the west, where a narrow but paved road takes you all the way to the small monastery at the very top.

The mountain has great appeal to naturalists as well as walkers, but exploring its slopes is not something to be undertaken lightly, as Corfu's weather is so changeable. The reward for those who do venture up is a view to Albania and Epirus in the north and east, of Corfu town to the south, and even west to Italy when conditions are clear.

THE DURRELLS ON CORFU

The famous literary siblings Lawrence and Gerald Durrell are forever associated with Corfu. Gerald, a noted environmentalist, described his family's arrival on the island in the early 1930s in his memoir *My Family and Other Animals*. Lawrence penned *Prospero's Cell* while living in the White House (now a hotel) in Kalámi. Their family life on Corfu is now a popular British TV series.

LAWRENCE DURRELL

Kassiópi
Κασσιόπη

 37 km (23 miles) N of Corfu town

Kassiópi has developed into one of Corfu's busiest holiday centres without losing either its charm or character. The village is set around a pretty harbour that lies between

→
The famous eroded sandstone headlands at Sidári beach

two wooded headlands. Although there is plenty of nightlife to attract younger holiday-makers, there are no high-rise hotels here to spoil the setting. Instead, tavernas and souvenir shops overlook fishing boats moored alongside motorboats from the many watersports schools. The nearest beach is at Avláki, 2 km (1 mile) south,

In the 1st century AD the Roman Emperor Nero was the first recorded tourist to come here. He most likely visited the local Zeus temple; the ancient floor of this place of worship was revealed during a recent restoration of the venerable Kassopítra church on the main shopping street, which also uncovered a fine Venetian fresco in the apse. The ruins of a 13th-century castle are a short walk further to the west.

5

Sidári
Σιδάρι

 51 km (20 miles) NW of Corfu town 🚌

One of the first settlements on Corfu, the village of Sidári has pre-Neolithic remains dating back to about 7000 BC. Today it is a bustling holiday centre with the feature twin attractions of sandy beaches and unusual rock formations. The main strip is buzzing with souvenir shops, popular cafés and restaurants.

The natural erosion of the sandstone along the coast at Sidári has formed a treasure trove of small caves and channels of turquoise sea, some leading to hidden, sandy beaches. The most famous of these passageways is a channel between two rocks known as the Canal d'Amour (Channel of Love), whose name comes from the tradition that every couple who swims in the crystal-clear waters there will remain in love forever.

💬 INSIDER TIP
Boat Trips

Northwest Corfu is a great area for taking an authentic Greek caïque trip from Sidári or Ágios Stéfanos to the laid-back outlying islands of Eríkousa, Mathráki and Othoní, or hire a boat to explore the coast from Paleokastrítsa.

←
Lawrence Durrell's famous White House next to the shingle beach at Kalámi Bay

EAT

Boukari Beach

Simply the best seafood taverna on Corfu, with tables next to the water. Pick a lobster from the tank or order a delicately prepared fish such as sea bream. Great *mezedes* and wine too.

 Boukari seafront
🌐 boukaribeach.gr

€€€

Nikolas

Excellent and welcoming taverna in a corner of the pebble beach, serving a huge range of traditional meat, fish and vegetable dishes.

 Agni Bay
🌐 agnibay.com

€€€

Pink Panther

Superb views down to the coast can be enjoyed from the terrace while you tuck into dishes like beef in a pepper sauce paired with aromatic local wine.

 Road to Vátos, Pélekas
📞 26610 94360

€€€

Klimataria

Popular *psarotaverna* known locally as Stou Bellou, which has plenty of inexpensive but tasty fish such as sardelles and gavros, as well as pricier options.

 Behind the square, Benítses
🌐 klimataria-restaurant.gr

€€€

Paleokastrítsa

Παλαιοκαστρίτσα§

🏛 26 km (16 miles) NW of Corfu town

Paleokastrítsa is one of Corfu's most popular spots. Three main coves cluster around a wooded headland, dividing into numerous other beaches, which are popular with families because swimming is safe. Watersports are available as well as boat trips out to see the nearby grottoes.

Until the early 19th century the place was noted for its beauty but was little-visited as access was difficult. The British High Commissioner Sir Frederick Adam so loved to picnic here that he had a road built between Corfu town and the area to improve the awkward journey.

On the main headland stands Moní Theotókou, which dates from the 17th century, although the first monastery stood here in 1228. The ceiling of the church features a fine carving of the Tree of Life.

Views from the monastery include Angelókastro, the ruined 13th-century fortress of Mihaíl Angelos II Komnenós, the Byzantine despot of Epirus. Situated above the cliffs west of Paleokastrítsa, the fortress was never captured, and in 1571 it sheltered locals from a determined Ottoman attempt to conquer Corfu. There is little inside the walls besides a summit chapel, some cisterns and a few rock-cut graves.

Sinarádes

Σιναράδες

🏛 13 km (8 miles) W of Corfu town

The hill village of Sinarádes has fine old houses, a fairly busy through road and the **History and Folklore Museum of Corfu**, which occupies two floors of a traditional dwelling, with one bedroom displayed as it would have been in the 19th century. It is an Aladdin's cave of vanished rural crafts and

The 17th-century Moní Theotókou, standing on a headland at Paleokastrítsa

household implements; the most intriguing exhibits are made of the local cane fennel, including a piece of a raft.

History and Folklore Museum of Corfu

 May–Oct: 9:30am–2pm Tue–Sun

Pélekas
Πέλεκας

14 km (8 miles) W of Corfu town

The village of Pélekas is unique in offering visitors a taste of fresh mountain air and island life away from the coast, while offering a range of facilities. Traditional houses line wooded slopes down to the long, narrow and secluded Kondogialós beach below. Also nearby is the more developed sandy beach of Glyfáda. Above Pélekas is its most notable feature, Kaiser's Throne, a scenic outlook from which Kaiser Wilhelm II of Germany loved to watch the sunset while staying at the Achílleion Palace (p76).

Korissíon Lagoon
Λίμνη Κορισσίων

42 km (26 miles) S of Corfu town

The Korissíon Lagoon is a 5-km (3-mile) stretch of brackish water, separated from the sea by some of the most beautiful dunes and beaches on Corfu. The lake remains a haven for wildlife, despite the Greek love of hunting. At the water's edge are a variety of waders such as sandpipers and avocets, egrets and ibis. Flowers include sea daffodils and Jersey orchids. The lagoon is artificial, set up by the Venetians as a fish nursery and joined to the sea by a sluiceway. Almost 2 km (1 mile) north lie the remains of Gardíki Castle, built in the 13th century by Mihaíl Angelos II Komnenós. The impressive towers and outer walls of this castle have undergone a lengthy restoration.

Vátos
Βάτος

24 km (15 miles) W of Corfu town

In the hillside village of Vátos, the whitewashed houses with flower-bedecked balconies offer a traditional image of Greece, largely untainted by the impact of tourism. There are a handful of shops and tavernas. From the village, a steep climb leads up Ágios Geórgios, a small church with an excellent view.

> **The village of Pélekas is unique in offering visitors a taste of fresh mountain air and island life away from the coast.**

↑ Kaiser's Throne, offering magnificent views over and beyond Pélekas

Marathiás

Μαραθιάς

🛇 33 km (20 miles) SE of Corfu town

These two adjacent beaches, separated only by a small stream, are among the best of several on the southwest coast of Corfu, looking out to neighbouring Paxí (p78).

The sand is packed rather than soft, but the water offshore is delightful for wading, if sometimes choppy by afternoon. Both beaches are well signposted from the main island road and have tavernas just inland. They attract a mixed clientele, from families and couples at Marathiás to the occasional naturist at the remoter end of the cliff-backed Agía Varvára.

Achílleion Palace

Αχίλλειον

🛇 19 km (12 miles) SW of Corfu town 🚌 🕐 8:30am–7pm daily 🌐 achillion-corfu.gr

A popular day trip from any of Corfu's resorts, the Achílleion Palace was built in 1890–91 by the Italian architect Raphael Carita for Empress Elisabeth of Austria (1837–98), formerly Elisabeth of Bavaria and best known as Princess Sisi. She used it as a personal retreat from her problems at the Habsburg court: her only son, Archduke Rudolph, had committed suicide at Mayerling and the court's pomp and ceremony was notoriously stifling. After the empress was assassinated by an Italian anarchist in 1898, the palace lay empty for a decade, until it was bought by German Kaiser Wilhelm II in 1908, only to be seized in 1919 by Greece as war reparations. It is famous as the location used for the casino scenes in the James Bond film *For Your Eyes Only*.

There have been numerous attempts to describe the Achílleion's architectural style, ranging from Neo-Classical to Teutonic. Lawrence Durrell declared it "a monstrous building" while Henry Miller derided it as the "worst piece of gimcrackery I have ever laid eyes on". Indeed, the empress was not particularly pleased with the finished building, but her fondness for Corfu made her decide to stay.

The palace contains a number of interesting artifacts. Inside, some original furniture is on display and on the walls there are a few paintings of Achilles, who was the empress's favourite Greek mythological hero, and after whom the palace is named. Another exhibit is the strange saddle-seat that was used by Kaiser Wilhelm II whenever he was writing at his desk.

After touring the palace, visitors can drop in to the Vassilakis Tastery, opposite

↓ The grand wrought-iron staircase of the Achílleion Palace *(inset)*

Did You Know?

Áï Górdis took its name from the church of Agios Gordios, which is set on the beach.

the entrance, and sample this local distiller's many products, which include a number of Corfiot wines, ouzo and the speciality kumquat liqueur.

The lush green gardens below the palace are terraced on a slope that drops 150 m (490 ft) to the coast road. The views along the rugged coast both north and south are spectacular. In the grounds the walls are draped with colourful bougainvillea and a profusion of palm trees.

The gardens are also dotted with numerous statues, especially of Achilles. A bronze of the *Dying Achilles*, by the German sculptor Ernst Herter, is rather moving. The statue is thought to have appealed to the unhappy empress after the death of her son. Another impressive statue of Achilles is the massive 15-m- (49-ft-) high cast-iron figure, commissioned by the Kaiser. It has the head of a Gorgon depicted on its shield and is said to protect the gardens.

13

Kávos

Αχίλλειον

🏛 **46 km (28 miles) SE of Corfu town**

Once notorious for its party scene, the resort of Kávos is not quite as wild as it used to be, though it is still dominated by a young British crowd looking for a good time. The long beach of packed sand is

↑ The blue waters and sandy beach at Áï Górdis, near Kávos

best visited early in the day before the crowds arrive. For a taste of genuine island life, the nearby town of Lefkími has a workaday feel and impressive churches. The real gems at the bottom of Corfu near Lefkími are the beaches of Arkoudílas and Áï Górdis.

THE LEGEND OF ACHILLES

Shortly after his birth, legendary Achilles was immersed in the River Styx by his mother, which made him invulnerable, aside from his heel where she had held him. Achilles' destiny lay at Troy, where Helen, the wife of King Menelaos of Sparta, had eloped with Paris. Menelaos and his allies laid siege to the city. A powerful warrior, Achilles killed the Trojan hero Hector, but did not live to see Troy fall, as he was struck in the heel by an arrow from Paris's bow.

→ Statue of mythological warrior Achilles

14

PAXÍ
ΠΑΞΟΙ

🚤 Gáïos, Lákka 🚌 Gáïos 🛈 Gáïos; www.paxi.gr

Green and wooded, Paxí has a number of farming hamlets and fishing ports, with row-upon-row of olive trees, which are a key part of its economy. This island is a true getaway, a small pine-covered rock that has little in the way of beaches, but is still spectacularly beautiful; its small islet of Andípaxí is particularly enchanting. While popular, Paxí has fewer visitors than many of the other Ionian islands.

① Gáïos

This lively holiday town has two harbours: the main port and the smaller fishing and yacht harbour, lined with 19th-century houses with Venetian-style shutters and balconies. This area of town is directly opposite the uninhabited Ágios Nikólaos island, which is marked by two small white churches. Fanning out from the square by the waterfront are narrow old streets, lined with bars and tavernas. The main attraction here is the seafront Folk Museum, which occupies an old school building and contains a complete 18th-century bedroom and a plethora of artifacts.

_____

② Lákka

📍 8 km (5 miles) NW of Gáïos town

At the end of a deep inlet towards Paxí's northern tip lies the town of Lákka, whose pretty harbour is backed by olive groves and pine-covered hills. Lákka and its tavernas are popular with yachts and their crews; there are also

EAT

Bella Vista
Sitting high on a cliff overlooking the beach on Andípaxí, this place is ideal for a sunset dinner of grilled fish, washed down with island wine.

📍 Voutoúmi beach
📞 26620 31766

€€€

_____

Vassilis
Situated on the harbour in Paxí, Vassilis offers a range of seafood, as well as tasty *mezedes* and refreshing salads.

📍 Longós port, Paxí
📞 26620 30062

€€€

_____

Alexandros
This welcoming family taverna is great for fresh fish, succulent meat and veggie dishes.

📍 Lákka, Paxí
📞 26620 33061

€€€

Corfu

Lákka ②
Arkoudaki Beach

Parga

Kastanítha Cave

③ Longós
Levechio Beach

Koutsi

Magaziá

Soulalenia Beach

Voïkátika

Platanós

Panagiá Islet

Paxí

Gáïos ①
Ágios Nikólaos Islet

Agrílas Bay

Makratika   Otzla

Mogoníssi

Kalkonísi

Ionian Sea

Vríka Beach   *Vatoúmi Beach*

Andípaxi ④

Andípaxi

0 kilometres   3
0 miles   3

N ↑

Níssi Daskaliá

↑ Idyllic Lákka, located on pine-covered hills overlooking the water

plentiful accommodation options for landlubbers. The two small coves of Harámi and Kanoni are the best spots around here for a swim.

③
Longós

 7 km (4 miles) NE of Gáïos town

On the northeast coast sits the attractive village of Longós. It has a pebble beach, a handful of houses and shops, and tavernas whose tables stand at the water's edge. Longós is a peaceful place where the arrival of the boat bringing fruit and vegetables every few days is a major event. Paths from the village lead through olive groves to quiet coves where you might find yourself alone, including Levrehió to the south, which has smooth slabs of rock to lie on.

④
Andípaxí

 8 km (5 miles) S of Gáïos town

Fewer than 30 people live on the island of Andípaxi, south of Paxí. Andípaxi is unusual in that olive trees are easily outnumbered by grape vines, which produce a potent, good-quality wine that is exported to other islands in the archipelago. There is little overnight tourism, although two beaches – sandy Vríka, with a touch of the Caribbean, and pebbly Voutoúmi – are busy with day-trippers.

> **Andípaxí is unusual in that olive trees are easily outnumbered by grape vines, which produce a potent, good-quality wine that is exported to other islands.**

POSEIDON'S LOVE NEST

The god of the sea Poseidon fell madly in love with the nereid Amphitrite when he saw her dancing on the Cycladic island of Náxos. The maiden hid from the deity but was discovered by a dolphin, whom Poseidon proclaimed immortal for locating her. The god promptly whisked Amphitrite off to the Ionian Sea, where he smote Corfu with his trident, and created Paxí as a love nest.

0 kilometres 6
0 miles 6

N ↑

Ionian Sea

Ágios Nikolaos

Sánta Mávra Fortress

Ágios Ioannis Beach

① Lefkáda Town

Tsoukaládhes

Monastery of Faneroménis

Karyótes

Pefkoulia Beach

GREECE

Palia Plagia

Ágios Nikítas ②
Lazareta
Káthisma
Spanohóri
Lygia

Epískopos

⑤ Karyá

Nikiana

Kalamítsi
Exánthia
Kolyvata

West Coast ②
Englouví
Dimosari Gorge

Perigialia

Hortáta
Vafkeri

Lefkáda
Komíli
Nydrí ③

Spartí

Ágios Ilías
Vlycho

Skorpiós

Drágano
Sivros
Katohóri

Katoméri

Athání
Ágios Pétros
Fternó
Spartohóri
Vathý

Yialós Beach

Egremní Beach
Vasilikí ④
Mykros Gialos
Póros
Meganísi

Megalo Limonari Beach

Sývota

Pórto Katsíki
Cavo Nira

Kithros

Cape Lefkáda

↓ Kefaloniá

Arkoudi

↓ Itháki, Kefaloniá

⑮

LÉFKÁDA
ΛΕΥΚΑΔΑ

🚗 Nydrí, Vasilikí 🚌 Dimitroú Golémi, Léfkáda town
ℹ️ Léfkáda town; www.lefkada.gr

Léfkáda, connected to the mainland by a bridge, has some of the most spectacular beaches in the islands, where mind-blowing vistas of steep cliffs tower over seas of turquoise that blend into deep azure waters.

① Léfkáda Town

While Léfkáda has suffered from repeated earthquakes, it still features interesting backstreets and provides great views of the 14th-century Sánta Mávra fortress, located on the mainland opposite. In the main square, Platía Agíou Spyrídona, is named after its 17th-century church with earthquake-proof metal bell towers. The newly revamped Archaeological Museum at the north edge of town displays ancient finds, and the Folk Museum has local costumes and old photographs of island life. There are several small churches, mostly from the 18th century, which contain important works by painters of the Ionian School, such

as its founder Panagiotis Doxaras. Above the town, Moní Faneroménis was founded in the 17th century, though the present buildings date from the 19th century, as does its famous icon of the Panagía.

② Ágios Nikítas and the West Coast

📍 12 km (7 miles) SW of Léfkáda town

The island's stunning west coast is ideal for beach hopping. It is anchored by Ágios Nikítas, the only resort, a pretty village with a pedestrianized main street and decent pebble beach.

Further south there are magnificent, unspoiled beaches beyond at Yialós and Egremní, via the towns of Kalamítsi and Atháni. Pórto Katsíki, a long sandy beach

---

KANTÁDES

Kantádes are the most popular form of folk ballad on the Ionian islands, especially on Zákynthos and Léfkáda. It was created in the 17th century by refugees from Crete, who blended Greek folk styles with Italian *bel canto* to form *kantádes*. The focus is on gentle vocal harmonies, traditionally performed by four singers in different ranges, backed by a solo acoustic guitar – or with no music, in the Cretan style. The similar *arékia* is even quieter, often performed by a singer warbling a love ballad.

→

The main resort town of Nydrí, with excellent views of offshore islands

south of Atháni, is often busier as it is visited by a large number of tour boats.

---

 ③

Nydrí and the Satellite Islands

 16 km (10 miles) S of Léfkáda town

On the east coast, Nydrí is Lefkáda's main resort; it is rather brash and very touristy, but has splendid views of the offshore islands, including Meganísi, a small island that has retained its rural lifestyle. Its main port, Vathý, is connected to Nydrí by ferry. Hordes of pleasure craft line Nydrí's quay, offering day trips to destinations further afield. You can also take boat tours from Nydrí to view, but not get onto, the other nearby islets such as Skorpiós, which used to belong to the Onassis family. A short 2-km (1-mile) walk inland will take visitors to a lovely waterfall.

 ④

Vasilikí

35 km (22 miles) SE of Léfkáda town

On the east side of a deep bay at the southern end of the island lies Vasilikí, a windsurfers paradise with a white-shingle beach. The winds and shallow nature of the bay provide the perfect conditions and the well-known resort attracts windsurfers from around the world.

---

 ⑤

Karyá

12 km (7 miles) S of Léfkáda town

It is well worth ascending the winding roads up to the island's mountainous interior. The principal town is the embroidery centre of Karyá, beautifully situated around a small flagstoned square shaded by huge plane trees

EAT

12 Gods
This excellent taverna, spread over two storeys, offers *mezedes,* such as mussel *saganáki,* and succulent grilled meat and fish dishes. There's a bar attached downstairs.

Sývota Bay seafront, Léfkáda
26450 31880

€€€

Vangelaras
Occupying a fine spot on the eastern quay in Vasiliki, this taverna serves fresh salads, tempting *mezedes* and traditional main courses such as beef in a wine sauce, plus a range of drinks.

Vasilikí harbour
26450 31224

€€€

 16

ZÁKYNTHOS

ΖΑΚΥΝΘΟΣ

🚢Zákynthos town; Ágios Nikólaos ✈Zákynthos town
ℹ️Lomvardou St, Zákynthos town; www.zanteisland.com

Lush and green Zákynthos is ripe for exploration, with mountain villages, monasteries, sandy beaches and beautiful views around nearly every corner – like that of stunning and often-photographed Shipwreck Bay.

① Zákynthos Town

Completely destroyed in the 1953 earthquake that hit the Ionian islands, Zákynthos town has now been rebuilt, with efforts to recapture its former grace. Arcaded streets run parallel to the waterfront, where fishing boats arrive each morning. Further down the waterfront the ferry boats dock alongside Mediterranean cruise ships.

At the southern end of the harbour is the church of Ágios Dionysios, the island's patron saint (1547–1622). The church, which houses the body of St Dionysios in a silver coffin, was built in 1925 and survived the earthquake. The **Byzantine Museum** houses a collection of icons and frescoes rescued from the island's destroyed churches and monasteries. North of here is the Solomos Museum, which contains the tomb of the poet Dionysios Solomos (1798–1857). A museum in Corfu town is found in his old house (p67).

Byzantine Museum
 🏛 📞26950 42714 🕐Apr-Oct: 8:30am-3pm Tue–Sat; Nov–Mar: call for times ❌Main public hols

② Laganás

🏠9 km (5 miles) SW of Zákynthos town

The growth of tourism on Zákynthos has been heavily concentrated in Laganás and its 14-km (9-mile) sweep of soft sand, where a large number of bars and dance clubs ensure the nightlife continues till dawn. The unrestricted development here has decimated the population of loggerhead turtles that nests on the beaches, and efforts are now being made to protect them. Visitors can take trips out into the bay in glass-bottomed boats to see the turtles.

③ Vasilikós Peninsula

🏠15 km (9 miles) SE of Zákynthos town

South of Zákynthos town, the vertiginous Vasilikós Peninsula is punctuated by excellent beaches. At the peninsula's southwestern tip, Yérakas beach is a breeding ground for the loggerhead turtle and home to a Marine Life Centre.

④ Shipwreck Bay

🏠30 km (19 miles) NW of Zákynthos town

On the northwest coast is Shipwreck Bay, aka Navágio Bay (p02), one of the most photographed beaches in Greece for its sheer limestone cliffs and pristine blue waters. It's named for the cargo ship

---

LOGGERHEAD TURTLES

The Mediterranean loggerhead turtle (Caretta caretta) has been migrating from Africa to Laganás Bay, its principal nesting site, for millions of years. These giant sea creatures lay their eggs in the sand, reputedly the softest in Greece, at night. With mass tourism taking its toll, environmentalists have managed to secure some protection for the turtles, with stretches of beach now off-limits.

↑ Enjoying an alfresco dinner with views over Zákynthos's waterfront

↑ Mesmerizing waters and hidden grottoes at the Blue Caves

that ran aground here in 1980, the remains of which can be seen on the beach. The only way to reach this cove is by boat, and there are frequent services from the small port of Pórto Vrómi or from Ágios Nikólaos. There is also a viewing platform above the beach. The 15th-century Anafonítrias monastery, just south, is special for locals, as it was here that the island's patron saint, Dionysios, lived.

⑤

Blue Caves

🅰 **32 km (20 miles) N of Zákynthos town**

At the northernmost tip of the island are the unusual Blue Caves, formed by waves eroding the coastline. The Blue Grotto is famous for its stunningly clear blue water. Catch a boat there from Ágios Nikólaos or from Pórto Vrómi.

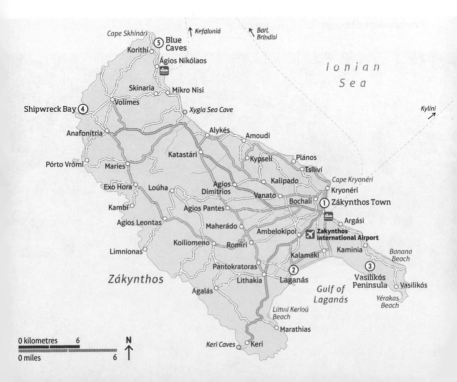

17

KEFALONIÁ
ΚΕΦΑΛΛΟΝΙΑ

🚌 Argostóli, Fiskárdo, Agía Efthimía, Sámi, Póros, Pessáda
🚌 Ioánnou Metaxá, Argostóli ℹ️ Waterfront, Argostóli;
kefallonia.gov.gr

Archaeological finds date Kefaloniá's first inhabitants to about 50 000 BC. Today this island's attractions range from busy beach resorts to Mount Énos National Park, which surrounds the Ionians' highest peak.

①

Argostóli

A big, busy town with lush surrounding countryside, Kefaloniá's capital is situated by a bay with narrow streets rising up the headland on which it stands. Its traditional appearance is deceptive, as the town was destroyed in the 1953 earthquake and rebuilt with donations from emigrants. From the waterfront you can see the Drápanos Bridge, built during British rule in 1813 and still standing.

Set on the ground floor of an old mansion, the local **Archaeological Museum** includes finds from the Sanctuary of Pan and a 3rd-century AD bronze head of a man, found at Sámi.

The **Focas-Cosmetatos Foundation** has a mixed collection of 20th-century furniture, lithographs and a notable coin collection.

Archaeological Museum
🏛️ Rókkou Vergotí 📞 26710 28300 🚫 Closed for renovation

Focas-Cosmetatos Foundation
🏛️ P Vallianoú 1 🕐 May–Oct: 10am–2pm Mon–Fri 🌐 focas-cosmetatos.gr

EAT

Kyani Akti
One of the finest tavernas in Greece, with superb seafood dishes and a view.

🏛️ A Trítsi, Argostóli,
📞 26710 26680

€€€

Lorraine's Magic Hill
An American hostess serves up delicious traditional recipes cooked by her husband.

🏛️ Lourdáta beach
📞 26710 31605

€€€

Archondiko
This cosy spot offers delights such as lamb *exohikó*.

🏛️ Rizospastón 5, Argostóli
📞 26710 27213

€€€

②
Kástro and the Central Plain

🏛 **8 km (5 miles) SE of Argostóli**

Capital of Kefaloniá until 1757, the whitewashed village of Kástro flourishes outside the ruins of the Byzantine fortress of Ágios Geórgios. The fortress was renovated in 1504 by the Venetians, but was severely damaged in the huge 1953 earthquake. The overgrown interior (rarely open) is a haven for swallowtail butterflies.

Set in impressive grounds, Ágios Yerásimos monastery is named in honour of the island's patron saint. The brave can descend into the twin cave beneath the main chapel and climb through a gap in the rock to the space where the saint meditated

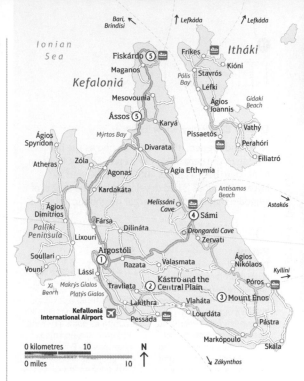

③
Mount Énos

🏛 **27 km (17 miles) NW of Argostóli**

There was once a sanctuary to the local cult of Zeus at the summit of Mount Énos. Wild horses live in Mount Énos National Park, and the slopes of the mountain are covered with the native fir tree, *Abies cephalonica*. There is a rough track up to the summit, which is 1,630 m (5,350 ft) high.

④
Sámi

🏛 **23 km (14 miles) NE of Argostóli**

A town on the east coast, Sámi has ferry services to Itháki and the Peloponnese. Drongaráti Cave, 3 km (2 miles) south-west, is the size of a large concert hall and is sometimes used as one due to its fine acoustics. The subterranean Melissáni Cave-Lake, 2 km (1 mile) to the north, was a sanctuary of Pan, the Greek god of herds and shepherds, in Mycenaean times. Part of its limestone ceiling has collapsed, creating a haunting place with deep blue water.

⑤
Fiskárdo and Ássos

🏛 **45 km (28 miles) NW of Argostóli**

Popular Fiskárdo is Kefaloniá's prettiest village, untouched by the 1953 earthquake. It has cheerfully painted Venetian houses from the 18th century, which cluster by the harbour, a popular berth for yachts.

Ássos is an unspoiled pastel-coloured village on Kefaloniá's west coast. Mýrtos Bay, south of town, has a stunning and dramatic beach.

> 💬 **INSIDER TIP**
> **Turtle Spotting**
>
> If you spend some time lingering by the water at the southern end of Argostóli's seafront, you will have a good chance of spotting a loggerhead turtle coming up to feed on the seaweed just below the surface.

↑ Looking down on the pretty houses lining the azure sea at Ássos

ITHÁKI
IΘAKH

🚢 Vathý 🚌 ℹ Vathý; www.ithaca.gr

Small and rugged, Itháki is renowned as the home of Odysseus, the hero of Homer's epic *Odyssey*. Finds on Itháki date back as far as 4000–3000 BC, and by Mycenaean times it had developed into the capital of a kingdom that included its larger neighbour, Kefaloniá.

↑ Bust of ancient king Odysseus in Stavrós

① Vathý

The capital, also known as Itháki town, is an attractive port with a lively waterfront. Its terracotta-roofed houses huddle around the bay. The surrounding hills were the site for the first settlement, and the town expanded down to the harbour in medieval times. Vathý became the capital in the 17th century. Destroyed by an earthquake in 1953, it was faithfully reconstructed to match existing styles. The only town on Itháki, Vathý has transport links to the island's villages. The Archaeological Museum has a collection of Mycenaean vases and votives. In the church of Taxiárhis is a 17th-century icon of Christ, probably painted by El Greco.

② Stavrós

🏛 16 km (10 miles) NW of Vathý

Stavrós, the largest village in northern Itháki, has only 300 inhabitants but is a thriving hill community and market centre. Nearby Pólis Bay is thought to have been the old port of ancient Itháki, and the site of an important cave sanctuary to the Nymphs. Odysseus's Palace may have stood on the hill known as Pilikáta. To find it, ask at the **Archaeological Collection of Stavrós**, which also displays a terracotta fragment from Pólis cave with the inscription "Dedicated to Odysseus". The curator here gives guided tours in several languages.

Archaeological Collection of Stavrós

🕐 📞 26740 23955
🕤 8:30am–3pm Tue–Sun
🚫 Main public hols

---

③ Fríkes and Kióni

🏛 19 km (12 miles) NW of Vathý

The tiny port of Fríkes is surrounded by diminutive pebble beaches and a series of rock coves, and is located en route to Kióni, an upmarket yachting and fishing harbour that is also a popular resort. Built around a steep bay, the village's buzzing waterfront has good tavernas and accommodation options.

↑ Lefkáda

Fríkes
Fiskárdo ③
Pólis Bay ② ③ Kióni
Lékfi
Ágios Ioannis
Pissaetós
Perahóri
Filiatró
Agia Efthymía
Kefaloniá
Antísamos Beach
Astakós
Sámi
Gidaki Beach
① Vathý
Itháki
Stavrós

0 km 6
0 miles 6
N ↑

↑ Traditional taverna at Vathý, with tables laid out beside the sea

THE LEGEND OF ODYSSEUS'S RETURN TO ITHÁKI

Homer's famous epic, the *Odyssey*, tells the story of Odyssesus, the mythical king of Itháki, who left his home to fight in the Trojan war and didn't return for 20 years, beset by all manner of detours.

Odysseus had been unwilling to leave Penelope, his wife, and their infant son Telemachos and join Agamemnon's expedition against Troy. But, forced to join the battle, his skills as warrior and speaker - and even more usefully, his exceptional cunning - meant he played a vital role in Greek victory. Upon attempting to return home, his journey was fraught with such perils as battling the monstrous one-eyed Cyclops. He blinded the creature, which angered the god Poseidon so much he ensured Odysseus lost all his companions, before the kindly Phaeacians brought him home, ten years after he left Troy. On Itháki, Odysseus found Penelope besieged by suitors. Disguising himself as a beggar, he killed them all with his famous bow and returned to his marriage bed and to power.

THE LOYAL WIFE

Penelope started weaving a shroud for Odysseus's father, and refused to marry one of her many suitors until it was finished. However, each night she secretly unpicked the day's weaving to gain time.

↑ Wood engraving depicting the moment Odysseus revealed himself and killed the unwanted suitors

A vase in the Classical Grecian style

An ancient vase, depicting Odysseus on his long journey ↑

↑ Odysseus meeting Circe, one of the obstacles on his way home

THE ARGO-SARONIC ISLANDS

Hugging the coast just off mainland Greece between Athens and the Peloponnese, the Argo-Saronic islands have a rich history. Wealth gained from maritime trading assured the islands' cultural and social development, seen today in the graceful architecture of Ýdra and in the grand houses and public buildings of Égina. Égina was particularly prosperous in the 7th century BC as a maritime city-state, minting its own coins and building the magnificent Temple of Aphaia. Scenically, Kýthira's rugged coastline has more in common with the Ionians than the Argo-Saronics, but the island's position on ancient shipping routes has today led to some major finds, such as the bronze Youth of Antikýthira, now on display in the National Archaeological Museum in Athens.

The islands were not without strife, however. The famous Battle of Salamis raged off Salamína in 480 BC, when the united Greek fleet defeated the invading Persian Empire. Hundreds of years later, Ýdra and Spétses both played important roles in the 19th-century War of Independence, producing brave fighters such as the heroic Laskarína Bouboulína, the only female admiral in the Greek fleet, and Admiral Andréas Miaoúlis.

Due to their proximity to Athens, the islands are still a major shipping route, and boats of all sizes ply the waters between the mainland and many of the big destinations here – although the main trade is now in sunseekers, rather than goods.

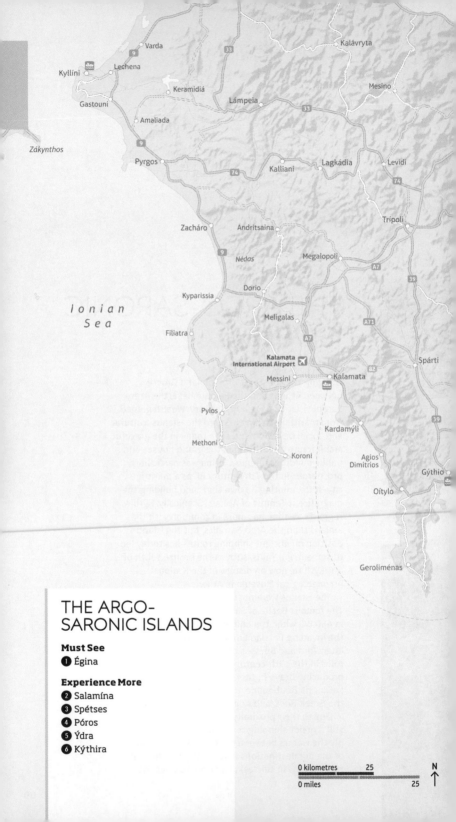

Varda
Kyllíni
Lechena
Keramidiá
Gastouni
Lámpeia
Amaliada
Kalávryta
Mesino
Zákynthos
Pyrgos
Kalliani
Lagkádia
Levidí
Zacháro
Andritsaina
Trípoli
Nédas
Megalopoli
Ionian
Sea
Dorio
Kyparissía
Filiatra
Meligalas
Kalamata
International Airport
Messíni
Kalamata
Spárti
Pylos
Kardamýli
Methoni
Koroni
Agios
Dimitrios
Gýthio
Oítylo
Geroliménas

THE ARGO-SARONIC ISLANDS

Must See

1 Égina

Experience More

2 Salamína
3 Spétses
4 Póros
5 Ýdra
6 Kýthira

0 kilometres   25

0 miles   25

N

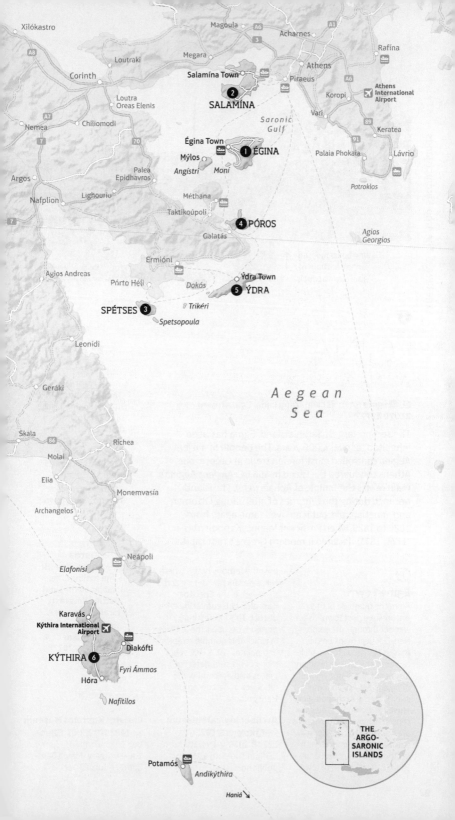

Sailing boats moored in the harbour of Égina town at dusk ↑

①

ÉGINA

ΑΙΓΙΝΑ

🚌 🚊 Égina town ℹ️ Leonárdou Ladá, Égina town; 22970 27777

The second-largest Saronic island, Égina has been inhabited for over 4,000 years. The people of ancient Aegina controlled most foreign trade in Greece, but Athens conquered the island in 456 BC. Ancient Aegina's main relic is the Temple of Aphaia (p94). The island declined during the centuries of alternating Ottoman and Venetian rule, but it enjoyed fame again from 1828 to 1029, when President Ioánnis Kapodístrias (1776–1831) declared it modern Greece's first capital.

①

Égina Town

From the quayside of this picturesque port town, visitors wander through streets of Neo-Classical mansions to Pýrgos Markéllou tower, built by Venetians. On the headland just north, the single column of an ancient Apollo temple stands by the **Archaeological Museum**. Behind the elegant central fish market, octopuses are hung out to cure along a cobbled lane crammed with seafood *mezedopolía*. Some 3 km (2 miles) north of town,

past the famous house where Níkos Kazantzákis wrote *Zorba the Greek*, is the **Christos Kapralos Museum** in Plakákia district. This interesting museum occupies the ateliers in which this notable sculptor and painter (1909–93) spent many of his summers. The pieces displayed show the influence of his contemporary Henry Moore.

Archaeological Museum

⊕ 🏛️ Kolóna 8 ☎ 22970 22248 🕐 May-Oct: 10am-5:30pm Tue-Sun 🚫 Main public hols

Christos Kapralos Museum

⊕ ☎ 22970 22001 🕐 Jun-Oct: 10am-2pm & 6-8pm Tue-Sun; Nov-May: 10am-2pm Fri-Sun 🚫 Dec

---

EAT

Agora (alias Geladakis)
The best seafood place of several in the fish market, with keenly priced octopus dishes, a wide variety of distilled spirits and efficient service.

🏠 Behind the fish market, Égina town
☎ 22970 27209

€€€

Ostria
Named for the south wind cooling diners at tables on the sand, Ostria offers tasty local *katsoúla* fish.

🏠 Marathónas, shore lane
☎ 22970 27677

€€€

② Ómorfo Ekklisía

🚩 2 km (1 mile) E of Égina town

Just east of Égina town, in Asómati district, stands the 13th-century Byzantine Ómorfo Ekklisiá church (locked; get the key from the Archaeological Museum). The interior of this church is covered in fine frescoes. Pilgrims usually continue a little bit further, to the tomb-shrine of Ágios Nektários (1846–1920), briefly a bishop but mostly a monk, canonized in 1961.

③ Paleohóra

🚩 5 km (4 miles) E of Égina town

On the hillside opposite Ágios Nektários's tomb sprawl the ruins of this deserted medieval town. Founded during Byzantine times, Paleohóra was raided by the notorious Ottoman pirate-admiral Barbarossa in 1537 but was only abandoned until three centuries later, in 1826. Several churches here, all

unlocked, preserve fine frescoes dating from the 13th to the 16th centuries.

④ Pérdika and Moní

🚩 9 km (6 miles) S of Égina town

Heading south from Égina town, the road hugs the shore, passing small beaches at Fáros, Marathónas and Fginítissa. This scenic route ends at Pérdika, near the southwestern tip of Égina. This picturesque fishing village has some excellent quayside fish tavernas and modest accommodation, which is usually packed full of Athenians on weekends.

Just ten minutes by caïque from Pérdika looms the islet of Moní, popular for its crystal waters – clearer than any around Égina itself – lapping its single beach, secluded coves and hidden caves. There are two summer-only snack bar-cafés at the beach, at least one of them open after dark. Moní has no permanent inhabitants other than a number of animals such as deer and peacocks.

↑ Snorkelling in the crystal-clear waters of Moní, a small island just off Égina

⑤ Angístri

🚩 12 km (8 miles) SW of Égina town

The small island of Angístri is accessible by caïque from Égina town. It was originally settled by Arvanítes (medieval Albanian-speaking Orthodox Christians), and is now popular for "alternative" tourism Halikiáda is Greece's oldest naturist beach. Mýlos and Skála are bustling seaside villages; the hillside settlement of Metóhi is quieter.

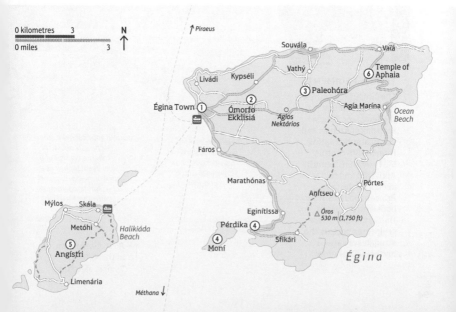

0 kilometres 3
0 miles 3

N ↑

↑ Piraeus

Souvála   Vaïá

Vathý   ⑥ Temple of Aphaia

Livádi   Kypséli

③ Paleohóra

Égina Town ①   ② Ómorfo Ekklisía   Ágios Nektários

Agía Marína   Ocean Beach

Fáros

Marathónas   Pórtes

Mýlos   Skála   Anítseo

Metóhi   Halikiáda Beach   Eginítissa   △ Óros 530 m (1,750 ft)

⑤ Angístri   Pérdika ④   Sfikári

④ Moní   *Égina*

Limenária

Méthana ↓

TEMPLE OF APHAIA

ΝΑΟΣ ΤΗΣ ΑΦΑΙΑΣ

⌂ 12 km (7 miles) E of Égina Town 📞 22970 32398 🕐 Apr–Oct: 8am–7:30pm daily; Nov–Mar: 9:30am–5:30pm daily 🚫 Main public holidays

The Temple of Aphaia is one of the best-preserved Doric temples in Greece, and was the only place of worship for the cult of Aphaia, a goddess of hunting and agriculture.

On a hilltop above the resort of Agía Marína, the ruined temple of Aphaia has a number of columns still standing and its structure largely intact. When it was built in around 490 BC, these limestone columns would have been covered in stucco and painted, as seen in this reconstruction *(right)*. This temple was initially thought to be dedicated to Athena, but in 1901 the German archaeologist Adolf Furtwängler found an inscription to the goddess Aphaia. After Athens conquered Égina, worship of Aphaia declined, and the temple became an atmospheric ruin.

TEMPLE PEDIMENTS

The famous sculptures from the pediments of the Temple of Aphaia are a mix of Archaic and Classical styles dating from the 5th century BC. They were found in April 1811 and sold at auction to the Crown Prince of Bavaria. Now housed in Munich at the Glyptothek, these sculptures portray the struggles of various mythological heroes.

The east pediment sculptures, with Athena at the centre, were replacements for an earlier set.

These large columns were made thicker for emphasis, and covered in stucco and painted.

Still in good condition, the stonework above the columns consists of a plain beam topped by a band of metopes, a type of sculpture, alternating with ornate triglyphs.

↑ A reconstruction of the 490 BC Temple of Aphaia

EXPERIENCE The Argo-Saronic Islands

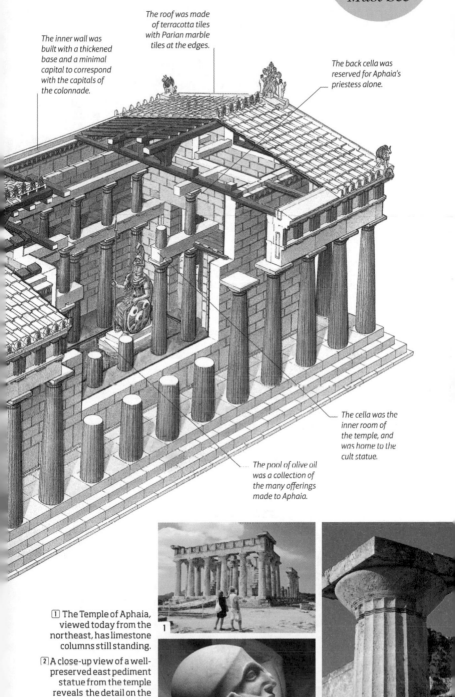

The inner wall was built with a thickened base and a minimal capital to correspond with the capitals of the colonnade.

The roof was made of terracotta tiles with Parian marble tiles at the edges.

The back cella was reserved for Aphaia's priestess alone.

The cella was the inner room of the temple, and was home to the cult statue.

The pool of olive oil was a collection of the many offerings made to Aphaia.

1 The Temple of Aphaia, viewed today from the northeast, has limestone columns still standing.

2 A close-up view of a well-preserved east pediment statue from the temple reveals the detail on the head of a Trojan king.

4 This detail of a column at the temple shows the Classical Doric style.

EXPERIENCE MORE

Salamína
Σαλαμίνα

🚢 Palóukia & Selínia
🚌 Salamína town
ℹ️ salamina.gr

Salamína is the largest (and closest to Athens) of the Saronic Gulf islands. Ancient Salamis was the site of the famous, eponymous battle in 480 BC, when the Greeks defeated the Persians. The king of Persia, Xerxes, watched his cumbersome ships being destroyed in Salamis Bay, trapped by the faster triremes of a smaller Greek fleet under command of Themistokles.

Modern Salamína island is a cheerful medley of working-class homes, whitewashed churches and tavernas; its east coast has a string of marine scrapyards and naval bases.

Salamína town, the island's charmless capital, sprawls amid vineyards. Adjacent Ágios Nikólaos has more character, with 19th-century mansions lining the quay.

Eándio, the main village of southern Salamína, has a small pebble beach; a road leads south to Peristéria

A visitor exploring the charming streets at the old port of Spétses town

5 km (3 miles) away via Peráni. Both are coastal resorts with attractive beaches.

In the north of the island, 6 km (4 miles) from town, the 17th-century Faneroméni monastery (closes 1pm) conceals vivid frescoes created in 1735 by Georgios Markou. Today, 18 nuns tend the peacock-patrolled gardens. The boathouse was used as a retreat from 1944 to 1951 by prominent modern Greek poet Angelos Sikelianos.

Spétses
Σπέτσες

🚢🚌 Spétses town
ℹ️ Spétses town; www.spetses.gr

The name Spétses is a corruption of Pityousa, or "piney", the ancient moniker for this green island. After a series of occupations, Spétses developed as a naval power, supplying a fleet for the Greek revolution. The most famous hero to be

A memorial honouring the fighters at the Battle of Salamis

produced by the island was Admiral Laskarína Bouboulina, who menaced the Ottomans from her flagship *Agamemnon* and led her fleet of ships into battle in the fierce Greek War of Independence in the early 19th century.

During the 1920s, Spétses became a fashionable resort. Vehicles are restricted, but scooters can be hired, and buses serve the beaches.

Spétses town runs along the north coast for 2 km (1 mile), but its focus is café-fringed Dápia port. The grandest of many mansions houses the **Hatzigiannis Mexis Museum**, with Bouboulina's wooden ossuary and figureheads from her ship. Her family mansion is still owned by her descendants, and now houses the **Bouboulina Museum**.

Southeast of here, the 17th-century church of Ágios Nikólaos has a fine *votsalotó* (pebble-mosaic) courtyard.

A ring road passes by all the island beaches; alternatively, use taxi boats. Going anti-clockwise, the most scenic beach is the pine-fringed arc of Agía Paraskeví. The next cove along, Ágii Anárgyri, offers watersports facilities

Did You Know?

British author John Fowles worked in Spétses and used it as the inspiration for his novel *The Magus*.

and tavernas. The pebbly beach at Xylokériza has a few palm trees and a bar.

Hatzigiannis Mexis Museum

 ⊘ 🏠 300 m (985 ft) from the port ☎ 22980 72994 🕐 8am–3pm Tue–Sun 🚫 Main public hols

Bouboulina Museum

⊛ ⊘ 🏠 Behind Platía Dápia 🕐 Late Mar–Oct: daily guided tours 🌐 bouboulina museum-spetses.gr

---

4

Póros

Πόρος

🚢🚌 Póros town 🛈 Póros town; 22983 20500

Póros takes its name from the 400-m- (1,300-ft-) long ford (*póros*) separating it from the mainland at Galatás. Póros is actually two islands, joined by a causeway: pine-swathed Kalavría to the north, and the smaller volcanic islet of Sferiá in the south, upon which Póros town was built. In spite of tourist development, Póros town is an appealing place, extending along the narrow straits to a southerly quay lined with yachts. Its 19th-century houses climb in tiers to its apex at a clock tower. Besides an attractive market hall, the only sight is the **Archaeological Museum**, with finds from the island and the Peloponnese.

Several beaches line the south-facing shore of Kalavría; the best one is Monastiriou. Zoödóhou Pigís monastery, just inland, was built around the island's only spring and is still home to monks. Near the centre of Kalavría lie the ruins of the 6th-century BC hilltop Temple of Poseidon (free access), next to which the Athenian orator Demosthenes poisoned himself in 323 BC rather than surrender to the Macedonian troops.

Archaeological Museum

⊘ 🏠 Korizi Square ☎ 22980 23276 🕐 8am–3pm Tue–Sun

STAY

Sto Roloï

Up by Poros's landmark clock tower, a centuries-old house has been sensitively converted into three apartments. Four more units – two around a pool – are located nearby.

🏠 Hatzopoúlou and Karrá 13, Póros town 🌐 storoloi-poros.gr

€€€

Poseidonion Grand

Póros's fanciest hotel, with either historic rooms in the original 1914 mansion building or modern bungalow-suites facing the garden. All-season brasserie, plus a summer-only dinner restaurant.

🏠 West of Dápia port, on the waterfront 🌐 poseidonion.com

€€€

→ Sunset over Póros town, with the pines of Kalavría in the background

ΎDRA
YΔPA

🚢 Ýdra town ℹ️ hydraislandgreece.com

A long, narrow mass of mostly barren rock, Ýdra was settled by Orthodox Albanians in the 16th century. Ýdra town was built during a brief period of prosperity in the late 18th and early 19th centuries, boosted by blockade-running during the Napoleonic Wars. Following Greece's independence, Ýdra lapsed into obscurity, until foreigners "discovered" it after World War II. By the 1960s, the trickle had become a flood of outsiders who restored the old houses, transforming Ýdra into one of the most exclusive resorts around.

①
Ýdra Town

Ýdra is charming, the result of an architectural preservation order – along with a ban on motor vehicles – that has kept the town's appearance as it was two centuries ago. The dozen or so surviving three- or four-storey *arhondiká* (mansions) around the port, built between 1780 and 1820, are particularly lovely.

On the eastern quay, the Historic Archives and Museum of Ýdra displays costumes, old engravings and memorabilia of the Independence War. Just behind the marble-paved quay towers Panagía monastic church, built between 1760 and 1770 using masonry from Póros's Temple of Poseidon (*p97*). The marble belfry was reputedly erected by a master mason from Tínos island. The Tombázi Mansion, a walk up the western hillside, hosts a School of Fine Arts, while the nearby Lazaros Koundouriotis Mansion contains an excellent ethnographic museum and art gallery. An hour's steep climb above the town, Agía Evpraxía is a convent whose nuns carry out silkwork. There is an adjacent monastery, and each has spectacular views. Both buildings shut at midday.

Picturesque houses in Ýdra town, built into the hillside overlooking the sea ↑

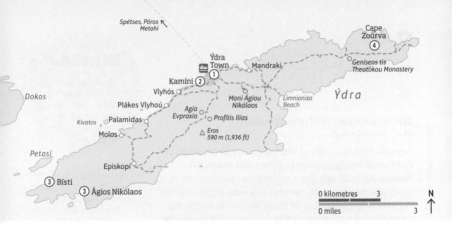

Map labels: Spétses, Póros, Metohi · Ýdra Town ① · Mandraki · Cape Zoúrva ④ · Kamíni ② · Geníseos tis Theotókou Monastery · Vlyhós · Moní Agiou Nikólaos · Limnioniza Beach · Ýdra · Dokos · Plákes Vlyhoú · Agía Evpraxía · Profitis Ilías · Kivotos · Palamidas · Molos · Eros 590 m (1,936 ft) · Petasi · Episkopí · ③ Bísti · ③ Ágios Nikólaos

0 kilometres 3 · 0 miles 3 · N

Further south along the coast from Kamíni, the village of Vlyhós has a graceful 19th-century bridge, two tavernas and a pebble beach

②
Kamíni

🏠 1 km (0.5 mile) S of Ýdra town

Visitors must walk, cycle or take a boat anywhere beyond Ýdra's town centre. Kamíni, a 15-minute walk southwest along the shore track, is a picturesque fishing port. Shingly Avláki and Kastéllo

↑ The gold interior of Profítis Ilías monastery near Ýdra town

coves are five minutes' walk from the port. A short stroll further south along the coast from Kamíni, the lovely village of Vlyhós has two tavernas, a graceful 19th-century bridge and a pebble beach with a few amenities. Continue south for another 15 minutes to Plákes Vlyhoú. Its pebble cove has a taverna and sunbeds.

③
Bísti and Ágios Nikólaos

🏠 8 km (5 miles) S of Ýdra town

Near Ýdra's southwestern tip, Bísti is considered its prettiest beach, with pines just inland

and a basic snack bar; in season boats call regularly. Nearby Ágios Nikólaos has less frequent boat service, but the southfacing shore and water are better than at Bísti.

④
Cape Zoúrva

🏠 8 km (5 miles) NE of Ýdra town

At the northeastern end of Ýdra, Cape Zoúrva is usually reached by hired boat to Lédeza dock, 636 stone steps below the isolated Geníseos tis Theotókou monastery. From there, keen hikers have a tough, often shadeless, four-hour hike back to town.

❻

KÝTHIRA

KYΘHPA

✈ 22 km (14 miles) NE of Hóra 🚢 Diakófti
ℹ www.kythira.gr

Beautiful Kýthira, one of the legendary birthplaces of Aphrodite, has unspoiled beaches and towns that feature a mix of Aegean and Venetian architecture. It is a popular holiday spot, particularly with Athenians and Italians. A large number of locals moved to Australia, and return visits are central to life here. The clumps of eucalyptus around the island, imported in the 1860s, are also a surprisingly Australian sight.

① Hóra and Kapsáli

Hóra has been Kýthira's capital since the destruction of Paleóhora in 1537. Its magnificent *kástro* was built between the 13th and 15th centuries. A multi-domed cistern lies intact near the bottom of the castle; at the summit, old Venetian cannons surround the church of Panagía Myrtidiótissa. The nearby

Avgó islet is one candidate for the birthplace of Aphrodite. The steepness of the drop to the sea here is unrivalled in the Greek Islands.

Dating from the 17th to the 19th centuries, the capital's appealing lower town has sturdy flat-roofed mansions. The Archaeological Museum, just outside Hóra, has a collection of Mycenaean, Roman and Minoan artifacts from around the island.

Only yachts and a few fishing boats anchor at the capital's harbour of Kapsáli, just east of Hóra. The beach is mediocre, but the town itself is lovely, with a selection of good cafes; better beaches are located along the coast at pebbly Fyrí Ámmos, 8 km (5 miles) north-east via Kálamos, with sea caves at its south end; and sandy Halkós, 7 km (4 miles) south of Kálamos. Like many of the Greek islands, the best way to get around Kýthira is by car, particularly as it is quite mountainous. A bus runs to the main towns once a day during summer.

② Paleohóra

🚗 22 km (13 miles) NE of Hóra

The Byzantine capital of Kýthira after 1248, Paleohóra was sited so as to be nearly invisible from the sea, but the Ottoman pirate-admiral Barbarossa detected and sacked it in 1537. The ruins of the town perch on top of a sheer 200-m (655-ft) bluff. The 13th-century Agía Varvára is the most striking of several churches in Paleohóra.

③ Káto Hóra

🚗 15 km (10 miles) NW of Hóra

The Venetian *kástro* at Káto Hóra is situated on a bluff with steep drops to the north and west. It was built in 1565

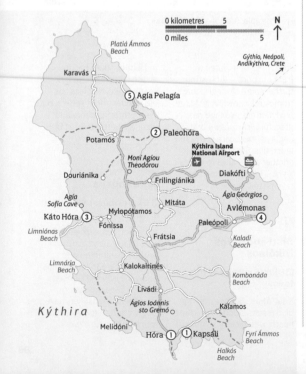

Map of Kýthira:

0 kilometres 5
0 miles 5
N ↑

Platiá Ámmos Beach

Gýthio, Neápoli, Andikýthira, Crete →

Karavás

⑤ Agía Pelagía

Potamós

② Paleohóra

Kýthira Island National Airport

Moní Agíou Theodórou

Douriánika

Frilingiánika

Diakófti

Agía Sofía Cave

Mylopótamos

Mitáta

Ágios Geórgios

Avlémonas ④

Káto Hóra ③

Fónissa

Paleópoli

Limniónas Beach

Frátsia

Kaladí Beach

Limnária Beach

Kalokairinés

Kombonáda Beach

Lívadi

Ágios Ioánnis sto Gremó

Kálamos

Kýthira

Melidóni

Hóra ① ① Kapsáli

Fyrí Ámmos Beach

Halkós Beach

An enchanting swimming spot overlooked by white washed houses in Avlémonas

> The road from Agía Pelagía goes through Karavás, an attractive oasis village where clusters of houses overhang steep banks

the latter goes through Karavás, an attractive oasis village where clusters of houses overhang the steep banks of a stream.

as a refuge for the peasantry in unsettled times. **Agía Sofía Cave**, 2 km (1 mile) from Káto Hóra and 150 m (500 ft) above the sea, has formed inside black limestone strata, with plenty of bizarrely shaped stalagmites and stalactites. At the entrance, a frescoed shrine, painted by a 13th-century hermit, depicts Holy Wisdom and her three attendant virtues, Hope, Faith and Love. A mandatory tour visits the frontmost chambers.

Agía Sofía Cave

 Mylopótamos
2736031213 Jul–Sep: 11am–6pm Thu–Tue

④

Avlémonas

20 km (12 miles) NE of Hóra

Avlémonas, with its vaulted warehouses and double harbour, forms an attractive fishing port at the east end of a stretch of rocky coast. The *Mentor*, carrying many of the Parthenon Marbles *(p290)*, sank offshore in September 1802; most of its renowned cargo was salvaged two years later by Kalymnian free-divers. The marbles are now controversially displayed in the British Museum.

Excellent beaches extend to either side of Avlémonas, in particular Kaládi. The 6th-century hilltop church of Agía Geórgios, with mosaic floors, sits high above the village.

⑤

Agía Pelagía

27 km (16 miles) N of Hóra

Ferries no longer call at Agía Pelagía, but it remains an important resort thanks to good nearby beaches like Kalamítsa and Platiá Ámmos. The road from Agía Pelagía to

EAT

Platanos
The former village *kafenío*, in an old building on the plane-tree-shaded plaza, is now a full-service taverna. Expect casseroles *(magireftá)* for lunch, and grilled dishes in the evenings.

 Mylopótamos village
2736033397

€€€

Psomoladea
This seafood spot offers a variety of dishes plus an ample wine list.

 Avlémonas port
6986520617

€€€

THE SPORÁDES AND ÉVVIA

Since ancient times, settlers and pirates alike have been lured by the pine-clad mountains dotted with villages and coastlines rich with hidden coves that are found throughout the island group of the Sporádes and the large island of Évvia. Due to their proximity to mainland Greece, these islands have been conquered numerous times throughout their history. They were initially colonized in the prehistoric era by nearby Iolkos (Vólos) and then by the Minoans, who introduced vine and olive cultivation. More than any other island, Évvia reveals its diverse history in the large number of buildings remaining from the long periods of Venetian and Turkish occupation. Susceptible to pirate raids, the inhabitants of the Sporádes lived in the safety of fortified towns until as late as the 19th century. The islanders have a rich heritage of maritime trading around the Aegean and are still noted today as sailors.

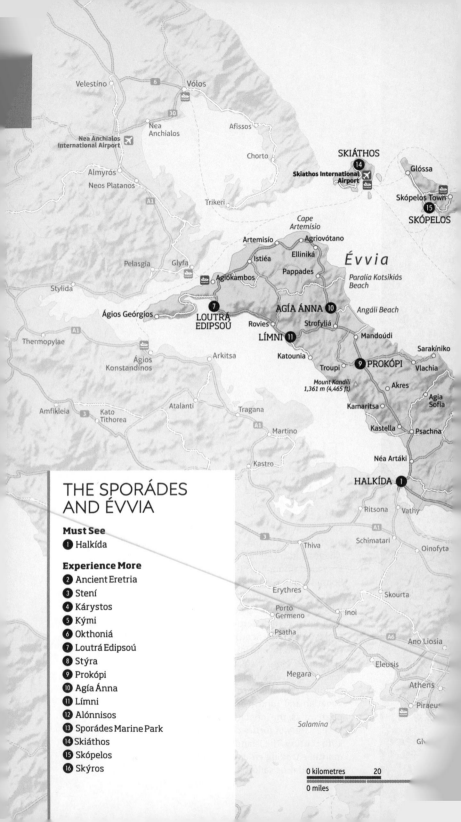

THE SPORÁDES AND ÉVVIA

Must See
1. Halkída

Experience More
2. Ancient Eretria
3. Stení
4. Kárystos
5. Kými
6. Okthoniá
7. Loutrá Edipsoú
8. Stýra
9. Prokópi
10. Agía Ánna
11. Límni
12. Alónnisos
13. Sporádes Marine Park
14. Skiáthos
15. Skópelos
16. Skýros

The Évripos Bridge illuminated at night, with Halkída in the background ↑

 1

HALKÍDA

ΧΑΛΚΙΔΑ

🚌 🚇Athinón 🚉Styrón 1, at a roundabout in the eastern part of town 🛈 dimoschalkideon.gr

The largest city on Évvia, modern Halkída is a thriving commercial port only a short distance from Athens. There are two areas of town particularly worth a visit: the waterfront and the *kástro* quarter.

💬 INSIDER TIP
Dodging the Crowds

It is a good idea to avoid Halkída - especially its seafood restaurants - at weekends, when they get crammed with escapees from Athens.

①

The Waterfront

A bridge has spanned the narrowest point of the fast-flowing Évripos channel since the 6th century BC, and connects Évvia to the mainland. According to legend, the philosopher Aristotle was so frustrated at his inability to understand the constantly reversing current that he eventually threw himself into the water and drowned.

The current swing bridge is the focus of Halkída's waterfront; in service since 1962, it opens regularly to let ships pass. The waterfront is lined with hotels, restaurants and cafés. On the mainland side of the bridge looms **Karababa Castle**, built by the Ottomans in 1684, and offering the best views of town.

Karababa Castle

📞 22210 22402 ⏱ 8am-3pm Tue-Sun

---

②

Kástro Quarter

In the medieval *kástro* quarter, southeast of the Évripos bridge, narrow streets reveal a fascinating architectural history. Many houses still bear the traces of their Venetian and Ottoman ancestry, with timbered façades or marble heraldic carving. Now inhabited partly by Thracian Muslims who settled here during the 1980s, and by the surviving members of the oldest Jewish community in Greece, the *kástro* also has a range of religious buildings, including the 19th-century synagogue at Kótsou 27; the beautiful late 15th-century Emir Zade mosque on Platía Pesónton Oplitón; and the church of Agía Paraskeví.

 On the mainland side of the bridge looms Karababa Castle, built by the Ottomans in 1684 to defend against the Venetians, and offering the best views of town.

history of Évvia better than any other building in Halkída. This huge 14th-century basilica was built on the site of a much earlier Byzantine church. Outside it resembles a Gothic cathedral but the interior mixes architectural styles, a result of years of modification by consecutive invaders. Features include a marble *témblon* (altar screen), a carved wooden pulpit, stone walls and a lofty wooden ceiling. Opposite the church, the Venetian Vaïlos House, used as an exhibition space, has a Lion of St Mark carved onto its lintel.

Occupying three galleries of the Venetian Negroponte fortress near the top of *kástro*, the **Folklore Museum** presents a scantily labelled miscellany of local costumes, rural tools and engravings.

The mosque, in the square at the entrance to the *kástro*, has been restored as an exhibition venue; the marble fountain outside bears Ottoman calligraphic inscriptions. Agía Paraskeví church traces the

Folklore Museum
Skalkóta 4
2221021817 ⏰10am–1pm & 6–8pm Wed, 10am–1pm Thu–Sun

③
Arethousa Archaeological Museum

Arethoúsis, crn Kiapékou
⏰8am–3pm Tue–Sun

This converted 19th-century distillery-winery at the eastern edge of Halkída contains not only the local archaeological collection and history of the town up to the founding of the modern Greek state, but coverage of the factory that operated here until 1980. Exhibits include an Archaic sculpture of a panther attacking a deer, and a Roman statue of Antinoös, Emperor Hadrian's lover.

EXPERIENCE MORE

②

Ancient Eretria

Αρχαία Ερέτρια

🔲 🕐 **8am–3pm (gate may be left open)**

Excavations begun in the 1890s at ancient Eretria, 22 km (14 miles) southeast of Halkída, have revealed a sophisticated ancient city-state that was destroyed by the Persians in 490 BC and by the Romans in AD 198. At the height of its power, Eretria had colonies in both Italy and Asia Minor. The ancient harbour is silted up, but evidence of its maritime wealth can be seen in the ruined agora, temples, gymnasium, theatre and sanctuary, located in the north of modern Eretria town.

Artifacts from the ancient city (and elsewhere in Évvia) fill the town's **Archaeological Museum**. Tomb finds include some bronze cauldrons and funerary urns. There are also votive offerings from the Temple of Apollo, gold jewellery and terracotta Eros figures from a 4th-century BC Macedonian tomb.

Archaeologists have also restored the early 4th-century BC House with Mosaics (ask for the key at the museum). Inside, pebble floor mosaics show sphinxes and panthers, and lions attacking horses.

At Lépoura, east of modern Eretria, the island trunk road divides. The southerly turning leads to the hill village of Stýra, with an engagingly decorated *kafenío* (café) at the central junction; from here, a side road leads down to the seaside resort of Néa Stýra. This town offers the cheapest, shortest and most scenic ferry route to or from the mainland and plenty of tavernas to eat at before departure or after arrival.

Archaeological Museum

⊛ 🔲 Arhéou Theátrou 1, near main archaeological site 📞 22290 62206 🕐 8am–3pm daily

③

Stení

Στενή

📍 **31 km (20 miles) NE of Halkída** 🔲

Despite appearances on maps, the 51-km (32-mile) inland road between Kými and the mountain resort of Stení is paved and passable to any car, offering an impressive passage through forested mountains, high above the Aegean. Much loved by Greeks who come for its cool climate and fine scenery, Stení is also popular with hikers bound for Mount Dírfys. This mountain is the island's highest peak at 1,744 m (5,720 ft), offering spectacular views from the summit. A brisk seven- to eight-hour round-trip walk followed by a late lunch or early carnivorous dinner at one of Stení's many grill tavernas is the usual programme. Shops sell local specialities like wild herbs, honey and candied nuts.

DRAGON HOUSES

From the main road at Stýra, a signpost points the way to the enigmatic *drakóspita*, or dragon houses. Constructed with huge slabs of stone, they are named after the only creatures thought capable of carrying such weight. There are similar sites on Mount Óhi and Mount Ymittós. All three are near stone quarries, and it is believed that Carian slaves from Asia Minor built them as temples around the 6th century BC.

④

Kárystos

Κάρυστος

📍 **130 km (80 miles) SE of Halkída** 🔲 🔲

Kárystos, overlooked by Castel Rosso (always open), the original castle built in the 13th century, and the village of Mýli, where plane trees surround several tavernas, has existed since ancient times. The modern town dates from the 1840s, and the grid of streets is still lined by many fine Neo-Classical buildings. One of these, the Mégaro

The refuge situated near to the summit of Mount Dirfys, near Steni

Giokálio, houses the small two-room archaeological museum, which also doubles as an information resource for all of southern Évvia. Star exhibits include a statue of Herakles reclining while feasting with a satyr, and a grave-stele base showing, in relief, athletes training. All that is visible of ancient Kárystos is a Roman mausoleum in the town centre and old stones worked into the walls of the Venetian Boúrtzi fortress on the waterfront.

The Kárystos region is famed for its lovely, if often windy, beaches. Psilí Ámmos, just behind the Apollon Suites Hotel in town, is the most sheltered. Alykés, a further 4 km (2 miles) to the southeast, has a taverna and sunbeds. A more strenuous 30-km (18-mile) drive, via Platanistós village and its photogenic waterfall, leads to the enormous Potámi beach, with a picturesque riverside taverna just inland.

Mount Óhi is the backdrop to Kárystos, but the premier hike is not to the 1,398-m (4,586-ft) peak, but the three-hour descent north along the spectacular Dimosári Gorge to the turquoise Aegean. Easiest as an organized outing, you can arrange this with agencies in Kárystos.

Monument to sailors lost at sea, Kárystos

5

Kými

Κύμη

90 km (56 miles) NE of Halkída

The thriving town of Kými is 4 km (2 miles) above the port. With a commanding view of the sea, this remote settlement once did very well out of silk production and maritime trading; in the 1880s, 45 ships from Kými plied the Aegean sea routes. Narrow streets lined with elegant Neo-Classical houses testify to the past wealth here. It is known today mainly for the bottled spring water from nearby Choneftikó and for Dr Geórgios Papanikoláou, Kými's most famous son and inventor of the cervical Pap smear test, who has a statue in the town's main square. A well-organized Folklore Museum contains exhibits from Kymian life. Some 4 km (2.5 miles) north of Kými, Metamórfosis tou Sotíros, a 17th- century convent, perches on the cliff edge.

6

Okthoniá

Οχθωνιά

90 km (56 miles) E of Halkída

The north road at the town of Lépoura leads past a few Venetian towers towards the villages of Okthoniá and nearby Avlonári, which seem more like Italian hill-towns than anywhere in Greece.

A Frankish castle overlooks the village of Okthoniá, while west of Avlonári stands the distinctive 14th-century basilica of Agios Dimítrios, the largest Byzantine church in Évvia. Beyond the fertile fields that surround these villages are wild beaches, such as Agios Merkoúris and Mourterí.

7

Loutrá Edipsoú

Λουτρά Αιδηψού

 100 km (62 miles) NW of Halkída ⬛ 🛈 22260 23500

Loutrá Edipsoú is Greece's largest spa resort, popular since antiquity for its cure-all sulphurous waters. These waters bubble up all over the town, and many hotels are built directly over hot springs that supply their treatment rooms. In the rock pools of the public baths by the sea, steam rises in winter, scalding the red rocks. Dominating the town is the luxurious belle-époque Thermae Sylla, which offers wellness and medical treatments that use the

STAY

Thermae Sylla Hotel and Spa

An "anti-stress" hotel, this renovated belle-époque monument has every imaginable therapeutic treatment at its hot-springs spa.

🏠 Loutrá Edipsoú
🌐 thermaesylla.gr
€€€

natural, mineral-rich spring waters. These luxuries are reminders of the days when the rich and famous came to take the cure. Other Neo-Classical hotels along the seafront also recall the town's glory days of the late 1800s. Today, Loutrá Edipsoú, with its relaxed atmosphere, is popular with Greek families. Across the

bay at Loutrá Giáltron, more warm spring water mixes with the shallow sea at a quiet and lovely beach, which is edged by a number of tavernas.

8

Stýra

Στύρα

🏠 88 km (55 miles) SW of Halkída

The hill village of Stýra has an engagingly decorated *kafenío* at its central junction, from where a side road leads down to the seaside resort of Néa Stýra. From there, a ferry offers the cheapest, shortest and most scenic route to or from the mainland.

9

Prokópi

Προκόπι

🏠 52 km (32 miles) NW of Halkída ⬛

Sleepy at most hours, Prokópi only wakes when buses arrive full of devout Orthodox Christians coming to worship the relics of St John the Russian (Agios Ioánnis o Róssos), housed in an otherwise unmemorable 1950s church. As a Ukrainian soldier, John (1690–1730) was captured in 1711 by the Ottomans and taken to Prokópi (present-day Ürgüp) in central Turkey. After his death, his miracle-working remains were brought over to Évvia by Orthodox Christians during their exodus from Asia Minor in 1923. Souvenir shops and hotels around the village square cater fully for the visiting pilgrims.

Prokópi is also famous for the English Noel-Baker family, resident since the 19th century, who own the nearby Kandíli (Candili) estate. While the family has done much for the region, local feeling is mixed about the once-feudal status of this estate. Many locals, however, now accept the important role Kandíli plays by bringing money into the economy in its latest incarnation as a specialist seminar centre.

The only other sight around Prokópi, just off the riverside road 3 km (2 miles) before

A waterfront café at the seaside resort of Néa Stýra ↑

Mandoúdi, is one of the most venerable trees in Greece, supposedly over 2,000 years old. This huge oriental plane tree, *Platanus orientalis*, has a circumference of over 11 m (36 ft), but sadly is in poor condition. Take the marked path opposite the Kímisi tis Theotókou chapel to get to it.

 10

Agía Ánna
Αγία Άννα

🚗 70 km (43 miles) NE of Halkída

Beyond Prokópi, a right fork at Strofyliá junction leads to the substantial village of Agía Ánna, known for its nearby beaches and an excellent Folklore Museum. Displays include intricate local weavings, tools of vanished trades and photographs of old festivals.

Among the beaches, the most famous are Angáli, which is 4 km (2 miles) below, and Paralía Kotsikiás, just north, both with a cult following with Athenians. Still further north is the small but picturesque Elliniká. The coastline finishes at Cape Artemísio, where the Persians defeated the Greeks in 480 BC.

 11

Límni
Λίμνη

🚗 87 km (54 miles) NW of Halkída 🚌 ℹ️ 22270 32111

A wealthy seafaring power during the 19th century, the pleasant town of Límni has elegant houses, cobbled streets and a charming seafront. The local museum contains archaeological finds, including a Roman mosaic, and a rich ethnographic and historical collection.

Just south of Límni, **Agíou Nikoláou Galatáki** dates from the 13th century and is the oldest monastery on Évvia. Perched on Mount Kandíli, and inhabited by nuns since the 1940s, its porch is covered with vivid 16th-century frescoes. One stand-out is the *Entry of the Righteous into Paradise*, with virtuous souls climbing the ladder to heaven being crowned by angels upon arrival, while wicked ones stumble and fall into Leviathan's jaws.

Agíou Nikoláou Galatáki
🏛️ Beyond Katoúnia coastal hamlet, on Mount Kandíli 📞 22270 31489 🕐 Summer: 9am–noon & 5–8pm; winter: 9am–noon & 2–5pm

← Límni, home to the oldest monastery on the island, Nikoláou Galatáki *(inset)*

Tavernas lining the colourful backstreets of the old town of Alónnisos

⑫

Alónnisos

Αλόννησος

🚢🚌 Patitíri ℹ alonissos.gr

Similarly to the other islands in the Sporádes, Alónnisos has a history of attacks by the Ottoman pirate-admiral Barbarossa. It also sustained severe damage in the earthquake of 1965. However, the island is relatively unspoiled by tourism, with most development centred in the main towns of Patitíri and Paleá Alónnisos. There are many beaches – though none as spectacular as those on Skiáthos or Skópelos – and a good network of maintained, marked hiking paths.

The port of Patitíri is a hive of activity, and is the place to hire boats for day trips to islands in the Sporádes Marine Park. Picturesque backstreets display typical Greek pride in the home, evident in the immaculate whitewashed courtyards and pots of flowers. Rousoúm Gialós and Vótsi, 3–4 km (2–2.5 miles) north of Patitíri, are quieter alternatives with their natural cliff-faced harbours and tavernas.

The old capital of Paleá Alónnisos, west of Patitíri, perches precariously on a clifftop. The ruins of a 15th-century Venetian castle here offer superb views across the straits to Skópelos. Paleá Alónnisos was seriously damaged by the earthquake of 1965, and the inhabitants were forced to leave their homes. They were rehoused initially in makeshift concrete shelters at Patitíri. During the 1970s and 80s, the wrecked houses of Paleá Alónnisos were bought and restored by foreigners and Athenians; there is now little genuine village flavour here. The road across the island, northeast from Patitíri, reveals a fertile land of pine, olive and arbutus trees. At popular Kokkinó-kastro, a pebble beach edged by red cliffs and pines, are the scattered remains of the ancient city of Ikos, the name of Alónnisos in antiquity. Further north, Tzortzí Gialós and Leftó Gialós are scenic, east-facing beaches, good for swimming. Leftó Gialós has two tavernas.

Stení Vála beyond attracts many yachts and has a scuba operator; it also hosts the main local station of the Hellenic Society for the Study and Protection of the Monk Seal, where any orphaned or injured seals are rescued and treated before being released. Nearby Kalamákia has a more pronounced fishing-port feel, with some seafood tavernas.

At the end of the paved road is the last beach on the east coast, Ágios Dimítrios. This shadeless south-facing pebble beach has a basic bar and sunbed rental.

300

The number of endangered monk seals that live in the Aegean.

→

A glimpse of the stunning natural beauty at Sporádes Marine Park

13

Sporádes Marine Park
Θαλάσσιο Πάρκο

From Skiáthos, Skópelos, Alónnisos **alonissos-park.gr**

Founded in 1992, the National Marine Park of Alónnisos and the Northern Sporádes is an area of great environmental importance. The only such park in the Aegean, it includes not just Alónnisos but also its uninhabited outlying islands of Peristéra, Skántzoura, Gioúra, Pipéri and Kyrá Panagiá. Boat trips to most of these are offered daily in season from Patitíri.

The park was created to protect an important breeding colony of the Mediterranean monk seal and a fragile marine ecosystem of other rare flora and fauna. Thanks to the pioneering efforts of marine biologists from the University of Athens, who formed the Hellenic Society for the Study and Protection of the Monk Seal in 1988, Greece's largest population of this elusive marine mammal – estimated at around 60 seals – is now scientifically monitored. Fewer than 400 monk seals exist worldwide, making it one of the most endangered species in the world. A campaign to promote awareness of the endangered status of the

MARINE WILDLIFE IN THE SPORÁDES

Visitors can see a wide range of other wildlife in the Sporádes while looking for monk seals. Spring and autumn are good for several species of gulls and terns, and when venturing close to sea cliffs, keep an eye out for the Eleonora's falcons, which are breathtaking acrobats.

Out at sea, look for jellyfish and the occasional group of common dolphins. Cory's shearwaters fly near the waves and towards the shore in high winds and as dusk falls.

seals and restrictions on fishing in the area seem to be paying off. Local fishermen are beginning to concede that they can coexist with the seals, which they formerly killed as competitors. The best way to visit the park is by organized tour, although sightings of seals are not always guaranteed. There are a number of restricted areas across the islands covered by

the marine park that only scientists are allowed to visit, so check the website before your visit.

The marine park is also an important route and staging post for many migratory birds during spring and autumn. Land birds, from tiny warblers to elegant pallid harriers, pass through in large numbers to and from breeding grounds in northeastern Europe.

14

SKIÁTHOS
ΣΚΙΑΘΟΣ

✈2 km (1 mile) NE of Skiáthos town 🚌🚌Harbourfront, Skiáthos town ℹskiathos.gr

An unashamedly hedonistic island since the 1960s, when it attracted the rich and famous with its beaches, Skiáthos now balances its role as a bucket-and-spade paradise for family package tours with being a summer mecca for hipsters.

① Skiáthos Town

Skiáthos's oldest quarter is a charming place with red-tiled roofs and a maze of cobbled streets. It covers two small hills, dominated by the 19th-century cathedral of Trión Ierarhón, and the nearby church of Ágios Nikólaos at the district's highest point, where you can climb to the belfry balcony for 360-degree views. Southwest of Trión Ierarhón, lanes wind through a quiet district of restored sea captains' houses, festooned in bougainvillea and trellised vines. The newer quarter – destroyed by the Germans in 1944 – is undistinguished, but it provides some decent shopping opportunities.

The new and old ports are separated by the Boúrtzi, a pine-covered islet reached by a narrow causeway. The islet hosts a summer cultural festival, with venues including an amphitheatre and the Neo-Classical former school, guarded by a statue of writer Alexandros Papadiamantis.

Life in the town centres on the long quayside. In the summer, it attracts people for a stroll in the after-dark cool; by day, there is the spectacle of arriving and departing ferries and hydrofoils. The old fishing port marks the western end of the quay; this is where small boats depart for day trips around the island, calling at famous northcoast beaches difficult to reach by land, such as Kástro, Lalária,

and coves on Tsouvgriá or Árkos islets. Just off the main street is the **Papadiamantis Museum**, in the former house of the island-native writer. The upper floor, left as it was when he lived here, reflects his religiously ascetic lifestyle; he spent several years in Athens as a *psáltis* (church chanter) and officiated at a church.

Papadiamantis Museum
⊘ ☎24270 22240
🕐9:30am–1:30pm & 5:30–7:30pm daily

0 kilometres 2

0 miles 2

N ↑

Skiáthos

Kástro

Laláría Beach

Moní Agíou Haralámbou

Panagía Kardási

Evangelistrías Monastery

Panagía Kehreás

Taxiárhis

Kehriá Beach

Profítis Ilías

Asélinos Beach

Eliá Beach

Ágios Ioánnis

Mandráki Beach

Skiáthos Town

Skiáthos International Airport

Panagías Kounístras

Koukounariés

Zorbades

Fteliá

Árkos

Koukounariés Beach

Plataniás

Achladias

anana each

Máratha Beach

Troúllos

Skýros, Skópelos Thessaloníki

Kalamáki

Tsoungriá

Tsoungriáki

Vólos ↙

④
Kástro

🏛 8 km (5 miles) N of Skiáthos town

At the northwesternmost tip of Skiáthos, this fortified town was abandoned after 1830, when the abolition of Aegean piracy made the present site of Skiáthos town viable. There are four churches remaining among the rubble of houses; one, Génnisis tou Hristoú, still has vivid frescoes.

Circum-island boat trips anchor below at Kástro beach, and visitors must climb up to the headland ruins, where a stone stairway has replaced the old drawbridge.

EAT & DRINK

Amfiliki
Creative seafood dishes like monkfish in spicy red sauce, plus a high-quality wine list.

🏛 Southwest edge of town
📞 24270 22839

€€€

Ergon
Offerings at this chain deli might include black noodles with marinated tuna, capers and dill.

🏛 Papadiamándi Lane
🌐 ergonfoods.com/skiathos/

€€€

Rock and Roll
Patrons sit on squishy sofas under the plane trees, listening to a rock and Latin soundtrack.

🏛 Old port
🌐 skiathos-rocknroll.gr

€€€

②
Evangelistrías Monastery and the Northern Monasteries

🏛 4 km (2 miles) N of Skiáthos town

The island's lush interior of pine, olive and shrubbery is decorated with notable monasteries and country chapels. Founded in 1775, Evangelistrías Monastery, a decent walk from town, sheltered many fighters during the Greek War of Independence. Below Evangelístrias stands Taxiárhis Chapel, covered in plates in the shape of a cross. Look out for an adjacent tap – it yields the island's best spring water.

Panagía Kehreás is the island's oldest surviving monastery, with vivid frescoes from 1745 under its bright pink-and-blue cupola. Most easily reached by paved road

←

Looking over the tiled rooftops of the beautiful harbour of Skiáthos

from Troúllos on the south coast, Moní Panagías Kounístras was founded by a 17th-century monk who discovered a miraculous icon in a nearby tree. The icon is now kept in Trión Ierarhón.

③
Koukounariés

🏛 12 km (7 miles) W of Skiáthos town

Named after the thick stand of pines just inland, this is the beach that kick-started tourism on 1960s Skiáthos. Koukounariés is merely the focus for several excellent sandy coves at this end of the island, where the efficient bus (and occasional taxi-boat) service from town ends.

A short distance west lie the two Banana beaches, "Big" and "Little": the former is a serious party spot, the latter completely naturist. Nearby Mandráki, accessed through a path in the pine forest, has a popular taverna. Eliá beach, just around the coast, also has a taverna and a bit of surf.

⑮

SKÓPELOS
ΣΚΟΠΕΛΟΣ

🚌 🚢 Skopelos town ℹ Harbourfront, Skópelos; www.skopelos.gr

Skópelos has a gorgeous main town, many good beaches and a lush interior. It has recently been celebrated as the main filming location for the movie *Mamma Mia!*, starring Meryl Streep. You can visit the idyllic beaches and wedding chapel from the film on the island, which, until recently, has flown somewhat under the radar compared to nearby Skiáthos.

① Skópelos Town

This charming town proudly reveals its rich history with over 120 churches, many fine mansion houses and myriad shops selling local delicacies such as honey and prunes. Among the churches, Panagía Papameletíou (Kímisis tis Theotókou), built in the cruciform style in 1662, is particularly splendid, with a carved altar screen by craftsman Andonios Agorastos. The landmark Panagía tou Pýrgou church, with its glinting fish-scale roof, overlooks the old harbour. Follow the winding cobbled streets, covered with intricate designs made from sea pebbles and shells, up from the waterfront. Just behind the

harbour sits the Folklore Museum. Housed in a 19th-century mansion, it exhibits embroidery, local weaving and costumes.

At the top of town is the *kástro*, the oldest and highest quarter. Here, the remains of the 13th-century Venetian Ghisi castle were erected atop the 5th-century BC acropolis of ancient Skópelos.

---

② Mount Paloúki Monasteries

📍 7 km (4 miles) SE of Skópelos town

On Mount Paloúki, across the bay from Skópelos town, are several monasteries. Most have immaculate churches with carved altar screens and icons. Evangelistrías, the lowest, was built in 1712 and is one of the largest on the island, but it is now home to just two elderly nuns. Continue up the road to Metamórfosis tou Sotíros, one of the oldest monasteries on Skópelos. Built in the 1500s, it is now inhabited by a solitary monk.

← The statue that stands at the end of the old harbour in Skópelos town

---

INLAND KALÝVIA

Skópelos's interior is covered with beautiful *kalývia* (farmhouses). Some of these traditional stone buildings are occupied year round, while others are used as weekend retreats only around important holidays. They all have distinctive outdoor prune-drying ovens – a legacy from the days when Skópelos prunes were widely exported. The *kalývia* provide a rare insight into a rural lifestyle that has essentially disappeared.

Timíou Prodrómou suffered badly in the 1965 earthquake but musters three nuns. The last monastery, deserted Taxiarhón, is reached by a tough hike up the mountain.

---

③ Stáfylos

📍 4 km (2 miles) S of Skópelos town

The main road traverses the island, and is the easiest way to reach the beaches on the developed southern coast. Stáfylos, a one-taverna beach just south of Skópelos town, can get a bit cramped and is sometimes windy. Velanió, a short walk east from here (there is no road access), is a long stretch of pebbles favoured by naturists. It has a sometimes noisy bar.

---

④ Agnóndas

📍 8 km (5 miles) SW of Skópelos town

Agnóndas is the alternative commercial port of Skópelos, and is used when storms close the town harbour. People

An outcrop with the picturesque *Mamma Mia!* chapel (inset)

come here for the taverna, shaded by plane trees, beside the pebble beach. Nearby Limnonári has a stunning pebble beach and is reached by boat or via a clifftop road.

---

⑤
Glóssa

📍 5 km (3 miles) E of Skópelos town

Glóssa is Skópelos's second largest village, and has tavernas, cafés and a small pebble beach. Most of the seagoing transport stops at nearby Loutráki, as well as at Skópelos town. Nearby Glystéri beach has routes up Mount Délfi, which has views towards Alónnisos.

---

⑥
Pánormos

📍 5 km (3 miles) E of Skópelos town

This huge gulf is a favourite with yachters, though there is a fair-sized resort onshore too. Just beyond is Miliá pebble beach and sandy Kastáni. Opposite both lies the verdant Dassía islet.

> 📷 PICTURE PERFECT
> **High Point**
>
> Fans of *Mamma Mia!* can't miss seeking out the famous wedding chapel atop a cliff near Ágios Ioánnis Kastrí beach, some 7 km (4 miles) east of Glóssa.

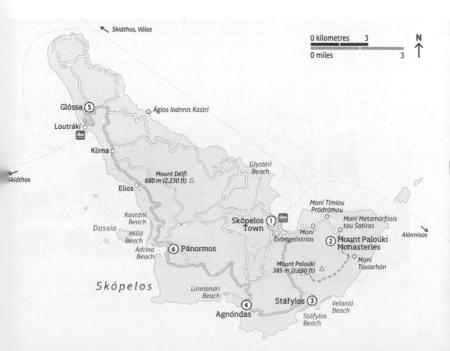

 Glóssa ⑤
Loutráki
Klima

Skiáthos, Vólos

Skiáthos

Ágios Ioánnis Kastrí

Glystéri Beach

Mount Délfi 680 m (2,230 ft) △
Elios

Kastáni Beach
Dassía
Miliá Beach
Adrína Beach

⑥ Pánormos

Skópelos Town ①

Moní Evangelístrias

Moní Timíou Pródromou
Moní Metamórfosis tou Sotíros
② Mount Paloúki Monasteries

Alónnisos

Mount Paloúki 385 m (1,260 ft) △
Moní Taxiarhón

Skópelos

Limnonári Beach

Agnóndas ④

Stáfylos ③
Stáfylos Beach
Velanió Beach

0 kilometres 3
0 miles 3
N ↑

⑯

SKÝROS
ΣΚΥΡΟΣ

✈18 km (11 miles) NW of Skýros town ⛴Linariá 🚌Skýros town ℹwww.skyro.gr

Renowned in myth as the hiding place of Achilles and the home-in-exile of the hero Theseus, Skýros has played an important role in Greek history. Its unique heritage, landscape and architecture bear more resemblance to the Dodecanese than the Sporádes.

① Skýros Town

Skýros's main town – a fascinating mix of cube-shaped houses, medieval churches and arcades – is architecturally unusual in the Aegean. Although its main street is crowded with scooter traffic and jarring signage, many backstreets allow glimpses into Skýrian homes, where traditional ceramics, woodcarving, copperware and embroidery are on display.

Topping the old town's impressive mansion houses are the remains of the Castle of Lykomedes, site of both an ancient acropolis and a later Venetian fortress. It is reached through a tunnel underneath the whitewashed Agíou Georgiou monastery, which contains a fine painting of St George killing the dragon. The view west from the summit over the rooftops below is quite breathtaking. Nearby are the remains of a 9th-century church and three tiny chapels with colourful interiors.

The Archaeological Museum displays Bronze Age and Geometric-era finds from around the island, including a rhyton in the shape of a Skýrian pony.

Housed in an old mansion owned by the Faltaïts family, the excellent **Faltaïts Museum** was opened in 1964 by one of their descendants, Manos Faltaïts. Visits entail a guided tour by his widow Anastasia through a diverse collection of folk art, including rare manuscripts and books, paintings and photographs, plus a recreated medieval Skýrian house interior.

Flanking the museums, Platía Rupert Brooke is notorious for its statue of a naked man by Mihail Tombros. Erected In 1931 In memory of

THE SKÝROS GOAT DANCE

One of several modern Greek rites rooted in pagan times, the goat dance is the centrepiece of the pre-Lenten festivities in Skýros town. Groups of men parade noisily around the streets, each led by three central characters: the *géros* (old man), with a shepherd's outfit, goatskin mask and heavy bells; the *korélla*, a young man in Skýrian women's clothes; and the comic *frángos*, or Westerner.

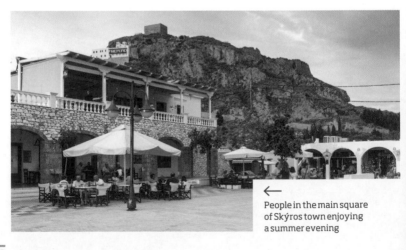

← People in the main square of Skýros town enjoying a summer evening

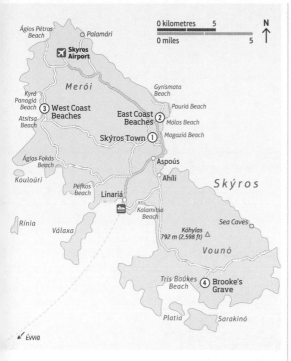

few good tavernas and lots of accommodation. Boat trips depart from here to visit the sea caves of Pendekáli and Diatryptí, as well as the beach-islet of Sarakinó.

---

④ Brooke's Grave

🏠 **20 km (12 miles) E of Skýros town**

At Tris Boúkes, which has a natural deep-water harbour, is poet Rupert Brooke's elaborate grave, signposted in an olive grove. Brooke (1887–1915) died of a mosquito bite on a ship bound for the fighting at Gallipoli in World War I.

EAT

Istories tou Barba
Excellent menu focusing on seafood ensures full tables here most days. Best sea-view terrace on the island.

🏠 Magaziá/Mólos beach boundary 【 22220 91453

€€€

Lambros
Grilled chops, seafood and home-style casserole dishes make this a favourite for locals and visitors.

🏠 Through road, Aspoús
【 22220 91388

€€€

Eleónas
Tzitzírafa (lentisc shoots), *ftéri* (fern sprouts) and marinated tuna are prepared by all-female chefs in the olive-grove.

🏠 Leftó Gialós beach
🖥 eleonas-alonissos.gr

€€€

the notable British poet Rupert Brooke, who died on the island, the statue is known as *Immortal Poetry*.

On another edge of the town the main branch of the Skýros Centre runs summer courses in yoga, reflexology, music, creative writing and windsurfing. There is an annexe of the centre at Atsítsa, on the west coast.

Faltaïts Museum
🏠 Paleópyrgos, Platía Rupert Brooke 【 22220 91232 🕐 Summer: 10am–2pm & 6–9pm daily; winter: 5:30–8pm daily

---

② East Coast Beaches

🏠 **1 km (0.5 mile) N of Skýros town**

Just above Skýros town are the east coast's best beach resorts. From south to north, they are Magaziá, with a few pottery studios inland; Mólos, with better sand; and Pouriá, with weird rock outcrops on the cape. Around the coast is big, sandy Gyrísmata.

---

③ West Coast Beaches

🏠 **14 km (9 miles) W of Skýros town**

West of Skýros town, past the Bronze Age site of Palamári and the airport turning, are the more sheltered beaches of Ágios Pétros and Kyrá Panagiá on the coast of Merói (the northern half of Skýros), though neither have facilities. The nearest are at the village of Atsítsa, which has no beach.

Continuing along the Merói loop road leads to sandy Péfkos on the west coast, the island's most scenic and wind-protected beach. This is just before Linariá, the ferry port settlement, which is not without charm and offers a

THE NORTHEAST AEGEAN ISLANDS

Although the islands in the Northeast Aegean are neighbours, all with lively fishing industries and sharing a common history of rule by the Genoese, they are culturally distinct, encompassing a range of landscapes and lifestyles. Sámos and Híos were prominent in ancient times, although few traces of that former glory remain. Sámos became a major maritime power, conquering the surrounding islands – and making inroads into the Cyclades – under the tyrant Polykrates in the 6th century BC. Ruled by the Byzantine Empire, followed by the Genoese and then the Ottomans, Híos became rich off the production of mastic resin. Its preeminent monastery, Néa Moní, was one of the most influential in the Greek Islands, accruing wealth and power over hundreds of years. Similarly, Límnos was ruled by both the Genoese and Ottomans. Its volcanic topography led to mythology labelling it as the landing place of Hephaistos, the metalworking god cast out of Olympus by Zeus. Nearby Lesvos, the third-largest Greek island, was a popular holiday destination for ancient Romans, as well as home to Sappho, one of the greatest poets produced by ancient Greece. Today, the islands remain distinct, with some islands – like Lesvos – particularly known for the eccentricity of its residents.

↑ Kavála
Keramotí
Alexandroúpoli

Thracian
Sea

Enez

Thásos Town
Potamiá
23
THÁSOS
Alykí

Hóra
Ano Meria
25
SAMOTHRÁKI

Kaleköy
Geliboluí

Eceabat
Gökçeada
Çanakkale

LÍMNOS
Panagía
24
Limnos
International Airport
Mýrina

Kumkale

Ezine

Ágios
Efstrátios

Ayvacık

Behram

See Lésvos map,
right

Míthymna
Kalloní
Sigrí
Mytilíni Town
Mytilene
International
Airport
Lésvos

THE NORTHEAST AEGEAN ISLANDS

Must Sees
1 Híos Town
2 Néa Moní
3 Mastic Villages

Experience More
4 Avgónyma
5 Volissós
6 Moní Moundón
7 Inoússes
8 Psará
9 Mytilíni
10 Agiásos
11 Sykaminiá
12 Plomári
13 Mandamádos
14 Mólyvos (Míthymna)
15 Pétra
16 Kalloní
17 Ándissa
18 Moní Ypsiloú
19 Sígri
20 Skála Eresoú
Sámos
...aría
...ásos
...nos
...thráki

Karaburun

PSARÁ
8
Andípsara

Kardámyla
Inoússes

Híos Town
Çeşme

Kómi
Híos

See Híos map,
right
← Piraeus

Aegean
Sea

Évdilos
Agios
Kírykos
Foi
22
IKARÍA
Pátmos

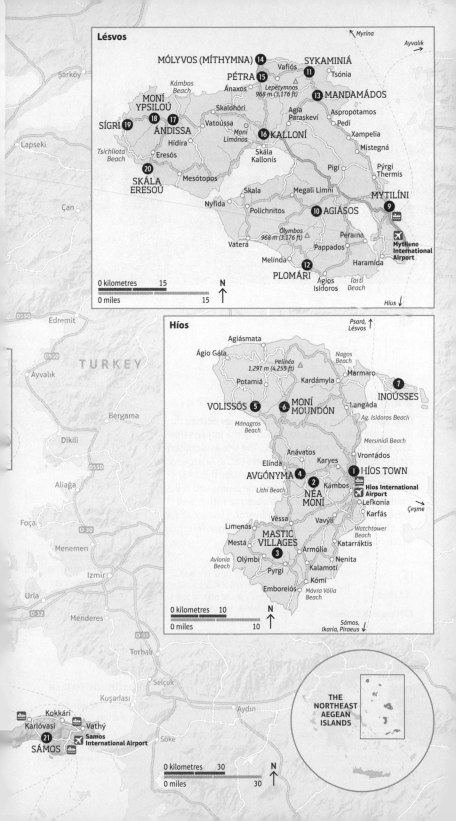

❶

HÍOS TOWN
XIOΣ

🚌 🚢 Egéou 41; Dimokratías 𝒊 Kanári 18; 22713 50514

Híos town, like the eponymous island, was settled in the Bronze Age and was colonized by the Ionians from Asia Minor by the 9th century BC. The site was chosen for its convenient position for travel to the Anatolian mainland opposite. Few buildings predate the 1881 earthquake, but there are several museums and relics from the town's past, which includes the rather well-preserved Byzantine *kástro*, the bustling bazaar at the top of Roidou, as well as the ornate Ottoman fountain, which dates from 1768.

①

Kástro

🏠 Maggiora 🕐 Daily

The most prominent medieval feature of the town is the *kástro*, a Byzantine fortress improved by the Genoese after they acquired Híos in 1346. Today the *kástro* lacks the southeasterly sea rampart, which fell prey to developers after the deadly earthquake in 1881. Its most impressive gate is the southwesterly Porta Maggiora; a deep dry moat runs from here around to the northwest side of the walls. Behind the walls, Ottoman-era houses line the narrow lanes of what were once the Muslim and Jewish quarters of the town; after the Ottoman conquest in 1566, Orthodox Christians and Catholics were required to live outside the walls. Also inside are a disused mosque, restored Turkish baths and a small Ottoman cemetery, which contains the grave of Ottoman Admiral Kara Ali, who commanded the massacre of locals on Híos in 1822. He was later killed aboard his flagship.

②

Giustiniani Palace

🏠 Kástro 🕐 Closed for renovation

This small 13th-century building is now a museum primarily showcasing frescoes and icons.

 Windmills at the shoreline of Híos town, with the sun low on the horizon

③
Byzantine Museum

🏠 Plateía Vounakíou
📞 22710 26866 🕐 8am–3pm Tue–Sun

This museum is housed within the former Mecidiye Cami, one of the few mosques to have survived intact in the east Aegean; it still retains its minaret. Inside are 18th-century frescoes by Mihaïl Homatzas, rescued from the rural church of Panagía Kchrína, and a Genoese marble relief of St George and the Dragon.

④
Filippos Argentis Folklore Museum

🏠 Koraís 2 📞 22710 44246
🕐 8am–3pm Mon–Fri (also 5–8pm Fri), 9am–2pm Sat

Endowed in 1932 by one of the members of the leading Argentis family, and occupying the floor above the Koraís library, this museum's collection features rural wooden implements, plus examples of traditional embroidery and costumes. Also on view, alongside a number of portraits of the Híot family, are rare engravings of islanders

and numerous copies of the *Massacre at Chíos* by Delacroix (1798–1863). The main core of the Koraís library, on the ground floor, consists of books and manuscripts bequeathed by the cultural revolutionary and intellectual Adamantios Koraís (1748–1833); these include works given to Koraís by Napoleon.

⑤
Kámbos

📍 6 km (4 miles) S of Híos town

This fertile plain is crossed by a number of unmarked lanes that stretch between high stone walls, betraying nothing of what lies behind. However, through an open gateway, you may catch a glimpse of what were once the summer estates of the medieval Híot aristocracy. Several of the

mansions were devastated by the 1881 earthquake, but some have been restored. Many of these still have their own waterwheels.

> ### THE REFUGEE CRISIS
>
> Since 2015, there have been tens of thousands of refugees, escaping the Syrian civil war and other trouble spots, who have made the short but often perilous crossing from the Turkish coast to the nearest Greek islands. Híos, Lésvos, Kos and Sámos have seen the greatest influx. The refugees have not always been warmly welcomed by the locals on these islands.

2 M3

NÉA MONÍ
NÉA MOVH

🏛 15 km (9 miles) W of Híos Town ☎ 22710 79370 🚌
🕐 8am–1pm & 4:30pm–sunset daily

The monastery of Néa Moní is a World Heritage Site, listed and best known for its mosaics, which are spectacular examples of Byzantine art. Prior to the Ottoman massacre of 1822, this monastery was one of the richest and most powerful in the Aegean islands.

🔍 HIDDEN GEM
Cistern Complex

A key part of Néa Moní's infrastructure, the cistern, or *kinsterna*, is a well-preserved underground complex of marble columns, arches and vaults, which was designed to collect and hold rain water for the monks.

Hidden in a wooded valley 15 km (9 miles) west of Híos town, Néa Moní and its mosaics – some of Greece's finest – date from the 11th century. The monastery was established by Byzantine Emperor Constantine IX Monomahos in 1042 on the site where three hermits found an icon of the Virgin hanging from a tree. Built in the cross-in-a-square architectural style, Néa Moní has a number of buildings within a defensive wall, including the main domed church, or *katholikon*. Granted a number of privileges, tax exemptions and land, Néa Moní at one time controlled a third of the land on Híos and reached the height of its power after the fall of the Byzantine Empire. It remained influential until the Greek War of Independence, when a horrific massacre occurred. Néa Moní has now been a convent for decades, but when the last nun dies it is to be taken over again by monks.

The belfry is a modern structure, added after the 1881 earthquake.

Well-preserved Néa Moní, constructed in the octagonal church style ↑

→ A detail of one of the fine mosaics, showing the Descent into Limbo

THE MASSACRE AT CHÍOS

After 250 years of Ottoman occupation, the Chians joined the War of Independence uprising in March 1822. Enraged, the Sultan sent an expedition that massacred 30,000 Chians, enslaved almost twice that number and brutally sacked most of the monasteries and houses. Many Chians fled to Néa Moní for safety, but they and most of the 600 monks were also killed. Just inside the main gate of the monastery stands a chapel containing the bones of those who died here *(right)*. There are axe-wounds visible on many skulls, including those of children.

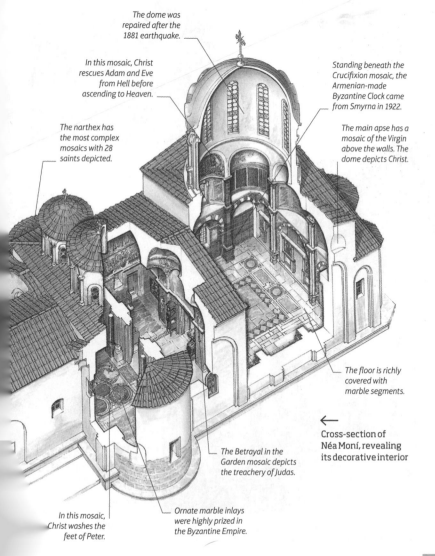

The dome was repaired after the 1881 earthquake.

In this mosaic, Christ rescues Adam and Eve from Hell before ascending to Heaven.

Standing beneath the Crucifixion mosaic, the Armenian-made Byzantine Clock came from Smyrna in 1922.

The narthex has the most complex mosaics with 28 saints depicted.

The main apse has a mosaic of the Virgin above the walls. The dome depicts Christ.

The floor is richly covered with marble segments.

← Cross-section of Néa Moní, revealing its decorative interior

The Betrayal in the Garden mosaic depicts the treachery of Judas.

In this mosaic, Christ washes the feet of Peter.

Ornate marble inlays were highly prized in the Byzantine Empire.

MASTIC VILLAGES
ΜΑΣΤΙΧΟΧΩΡΙΑ

📍 28 km (17 miles) SW of Híos town 🚌 Mestá

The mastic villages, 20 remarkable settlements situated in southern Híos, were founded by Genovese occupiers in the 14th and 15th centuries to protect the immensely lucrative production of mastic resin, which formed the basis of paints, cosmetics and medicine.

Situated well inland to protect against pirate attack, the mastic villages are almost fortress-like in their unique defensive features, made all the more necessary by Híos's proximity to Turkey. Key defensive features were perimeter walls with guarded fortification towers, flat roofs to facilitate escape and deliberately confusing streets designed to an intricate grid. Though they were the only villages to be spared in the 1822 massacre *(p126)*, most have had their architecture compromised by ill-advised modernization and earthquake damage. The most photogenic of the villages is Pyrgi, with its distinctive decorated houses.

↑ Locals outside a taverna in Olýmbi, part of continuing traditional life here

↑ The church of Taxiárhis in the village of Mesta, with its glittering chandelier *(inset)*

TOP 5 — TOP FIVE MASTIC VILLAGES

Olýmbi
Locals winnow mastic at the well-preserved central tower.

Vávili
The 13th-century Byzantine church of Panagía Krína here is famed for its frescoes.

Mestá
The best-preserved village, Mestá still has all its perimeter towers.

Pyrgí
Renowned for houses decorated with *xystá*, a geometric pattern.

Armólia
A smaller village known for its pottery.

A church in Pyrgi village, ↑
decorated with the striking
traditional geometric pattern

EXPERIENCE MORE

④ Avgónyma
Αυγώνυμα

20 km (12 miles) W of Híos town

This is the closest settlement to Néa Moní (p126) and the most beautiful of villages in central Híos, built in a distinct style: less labyrinthine and claustrophobic than the Mastic Villages (p128), and more elegant than the houses of northern Híos. Virtually every house has been tastefully restored by Greek-Americans with roots here. The medieval pýrgos (tower) on the main square, with its interior arcades, is home to the excellent central taverna.

Few local villages are as striking when glimpsed from a distance as Anávatos, 4 km (2 miles) north of Avgónyma. Unlike Avgónyma, Anávatos has scarcely changed since the 19th century; shells of houses blend into the palisade on which they perch, over-looking pistachio orchards. The village was the scene of a dramatic incident during the atrocities of 1822. Some 400 Greeks threw themselves into a ravine from the 300-m (985-ft) bluff above Anávatos, choosing suicide rather than death at the hands of the besieging Ottomans.

---

⑤ Volissós
Βολισσός

40 km (25 miles) NW of Híos town

Volissós was once the primary market town for the 20 smaller villages of northwestern Híos, but nowadays the only vestige of its previous commercial standing is a saddlery on the western edge of town. Its now-crumbled hilltop castle, erected in the 11th century by the Byzantines and repaired by the Genoese three centuries later, shows the strategic importance of medieval Volissós. The town's stone houses stretch along the south and east flanks of the fortified hill; many of them have been bought and restored by Volissós's growing expatriate population.

Close to the village of Ágio Gála, 26 km (16 miles) northwest of Volissós, two 15th-century chapels can be found lodged in a deep cavern near the top of a cliff. The smaller, hindmost chapel is the more interesting of the two; it is built entirely within the grotto and features a sophisticated and mysterious fresco of the Virgin and Child. The larger chapel, at the entrance to the cave, boasts an intricate carved témblon (altar screen). Ágio Gála can be reached by bus from Volissós, but admission hours are fairly limited, as it is only open in the summer months.

> Some 400 Greeks threw themselves into a ravine from the 300-m (985-ft) bluff above Anávatos, choosing suicide over death at the hands of the besieging Ottomans.

↑ Stone houses on the hillside of the town of Volissós, overlooked by castle ruins

A charming, pastel-coloured Orthodox church on the island of Inoússes

reprisal for its producing one of Greece's greatest heroes, Admiral Kanaris. As a result, the single town here, built in a pastiche of island architectural styles, is a product of the 20th century. The landscape is still desolate and infertile, though there are good beaches east of the harbour, especially Límnos. In the far north, Moní Koímisis tis Theotókou is a deserted, atmospheric monastery.

EAT

Hotzas
The capital's oldest taverna has a courtyard where you can enjoy local sausages and stuffed cabbage leaves.

🏠 Georgíou Kondýli 3, Híos town
📞 22710 42787

€€€

Psarokokkalo
An excellent place for fish, seafood and meat dishes, as well as pizza, pasta and a large choice of tasty *mezedes*.

🏠 Corner of beach access road, Agía Fotiní
📞 22710 51596

€€€

Fabrika
A converted olive press with a leafy courtyard, serving succulent meat on the spit, as well as baked dishes.

🏠 Behind Volissós square
🌐 chiosfabrika.com.gr

€€€

 6

Moní Moundón
Μονή Μουνδών

🏠 35 km (22 miles) NW of Híos town 🚌 Towards Volissós 🕐 Ask for key at first house in Diefhá village

Founded late in the 16th century, this picturesque monastery was once second in importance to Néa Moní (p126). The *katholikón* (central church) has a number of interesting murals, the most famous being the *Salvation of Souls on the Ladder to Heaven*. The church is only usually open to the public during a festival (29 August), but the setting makes the stop worthwhile.

 7

Inoússes
Οινούσσες

■ 20 km (12 miles) NE of os town

domestic architecture on eaceful islet of Inoússes,

a short ferry ride east of Híos town, is deceptively humble; it's the wealthiest territory in Greece. This is because the diminutive islet was home to several of the most successful shipping families, with famous seafaring names such as Lemos, Livano and Pateras.

The main attraction in town is the Marine Museum, while the lovely beaches of Biláli, Kástro and Zepága lie west of the port, and the deserted Fourkeró to the east.

In the northwest of the island is the Evangelismoú convent, endowed by the Pateras family.

 8

Psará
Ψαρά

🏠 20 km (12 miles) W of Híos town

Much of the island of Psará, reached by a long ferry ride from Híos town, was destroyed during the Greek War of Independence, as a

9

Mytilíni
Μυτιλήνη

✈ 8 km (5 miles) S
🚌 Pávlou Kountourióti
ℹ Aristárchou 6; 22510 37040

Lésvos' capital Mytilíni, on the site of ancient Mytilene town, is a scenic town on a slope bracketed by twin harbours. The main street, Ermoú, has a lively bazaar and, at the south end of the street, a fish market selling species rarely seen elsewhere. At the north end the roofless shell of the Gení Tzamí mosque and the restored bathhouse (now an art gallery) mark the edge of the former Turkish quarter. The Ottomans ruled here from 1462 to 1912 and houses of that era still line the narrow lanes between Ermoú and the castle. The silhouettes of belle époque churches, such as Ágii Theodóri and Ágios Therápon, pierce the tile-roofed skyline.

Surrounded by lush pine groves, **Kástro Mytilínis**, the Byzantine castle of Emperor Justinian (527–65), has huge, impressive curtain walls, but these were even larger during the Genoese era. Many of the ramparts and towers were destroyed during the siege by the Ottomans in 1462 – an Ottoman Turkish inscription can be seen at the south gate. Over the inner gate the initials of Maria Paleologina and her husband Francesco Gatelluzi – a Genoan who helped John Paleologos take back the Byzantine throne – complete the resumé of the castle's various occupants. The site also includes the remains of a Gatelluzi palace, an Islamic *medrese* (theological school) and a dervish cell.

Lésvos's **Archaeological Museum** occupies a belle époque mansion and, in a modern building nearby, is its **New Archaeological Museum**. Star exhibits at the newer gallery are vast mosaics from 2nd- and 3rd-century Roman villas. Neolithic finds from the British excavations (1929–33) at Thermí, just north of town, are in the original building.

Devoted almost entirely to exhibiting icons, the ecclesiastical **Byzantine Museum** has a collection ranging from the 13th to the 18th centuries and also has a more recent, folk-style icon by Theophilos Hatzimihail, (1873–1934), who was a prominent Mytilíni-born artist.

The **Theophilos Museum**, 5 km (3 miles) south, offers four rooms of canvases by Theophilos Hatzimihail. All were commissioned by his patron Tériade in 1927 and created over the last seven years of the painter's life. Theophilos detailed the fishermen, harvesters and bakers of rural Greece and executed creditable portraits of personalities he met on his travels. For his depictions of historical episodes or landscapes beyond his experience, Theophilos relied purely on his imagination. The only traces of the modern age are occasional aeroplanes or steamboats in the background of his landscapes.

A few steps beyond this museum stands the **Tériade Museum**, housing the collection of Stratis Eleftheriadis – a local who emigrated to Paris in the early 20th century, adopting the new surname of Tériade. He became a noted publisher of avant-garde art and literature. Miró, Chagall, Picasso, Léger and Villon were some of the artists who took part in his projects.

Kástro Mytilínis
♿ 📞 22510 27790 🕐 8am–3pm daily 🚫 Main public hols

Archaeological Museum
♿ 📍 Argýris Eftaliótis 7 📞 22510 28032 🚫 Closed for renovation

New Archaeological Museum
♿ 📍 Corner of 8 Noemvríou & Melínas Merkoúri 📞 22510 40223 🕐 8am–3pm Tue–Sun 🚫 Main public hols

Byzantine Museum
♿ 📍 Agios Therápon 📞 22510 28916 🕐 9am–1pm Mon–Sat

Theophilos Museum
♿ 📍 Variá 📞 22510 41644 🕐 8:30am–2:30pm Mon–Fri

Tériade Museum
♿ 📍 Variá 🕐 8:30am–3pm daily 🌐 museumteriade.gr

←
A small boat moored in the clear, reflective waters at Mytilíni's old harbour

OLIVE GROWING IN GREECE

A symbol of peace since ancient times, the first olive tree was said to have been planted by the goddess Athena on the Acropolis in Athens.

The Cretan Minoans are thought to have been the first people to have cultivated the olive tree, in around 3800 BC. The magnificent olive groves of modern Greece date back to 700 BC, when olive oil became a valuable export commodity. The 11 million or so olive trees on Lésvos are reputed to be the most productive oil-bearing trees in the Greek islands; Crete produces more and better-quality oil, but no other island is so dominated by olive monoculture. The best olives on Lésvos come from the hillside plantations between Plomári and Agiásos, founded in the 18th century by local farmers The fruits can be cured for eating throughout the year, or pressed to provide a nutritious and versatile oil. Further crushing yields oil for soap and lanterns, and the pulp is used as fertilizer.

TYPES OF OLIVES

From the mild fruits of the Ionians to the small, rich olives of Crete, the Greek islands are a paradise for olive lovers.

Elítses are small, sweetly flavoured olives from the island of Crete.

Tsakistés are picked young and lightly cracked before curing in brine.

Throúmpes are a true taste of the countryside, very good as a *mezedes* with olive-oil bread.

Kalamáta, the most famous Greek olive, is glossy-black, almond-shaped and cured in red-wine vinegar.

Thásos olives are salt-cured and have a strong flavour that goes well with cheese.

Ionian greens are mild, mellow-flavoured olives, lightly brine-cured.

↑ Shaking olives from the trees, the traditional method of harvesting

Olives fresh after harvesting on Lésvos, ↑ renowned for its olive oil

10

Agiásos
Αγιάσος

🚗 28 km (17 miles)
W of Mytilíni 📞 22530
71313 💬

Hidden in a forested ravine beneath Mount Olympos, Agiásos is possibly the most beautiful hill-town on Lésvos. It began life in the 12th century as a dependency of the central monastic church of the Panagía Vrefokratoússa, which was constructed to enshrine a miraculous icon said to have been painted by St Luke.

The town expanded rapidly in the 18th century due to the Ottoman Sultan exempting the town from taxes. Little has changed in its narrow, cobbled lanes since then, except for the arrival of numerous stalls of souvenirs, which now line the way to the church and its surrounding bazaar.

The presence of shops built into the church's foundations, with rents going towards its upkeep, is an ancient arrangement. It echoes the country fair element of the traditional religious *panigýria* (festivals), where pilgrims once came to buy and sell as well as perform devotions.

Agiásos musicians are hailed as the best on Lésvos, and they are out in force during the 15 August festival of the Dormition of the Virgin, considered one of the liveliest in Greece. The pre-Lenten carnival is also celebrated with verve here.

↑ The charming village of Plomári, arrayed around a central harbour

11

Sykaminiá
Συκαμινιά

🚗 46 km (29 miles) NW of Mytilíni 💬

Flanked by a deep valley and overlooking the straits to the Asia Minor coast, Sykaminiá is endowed with the most spectacular position of any village on Mount Lepétymnos, which stands at a height of 968 m (3,176 ft).

The novelist Efstratios Stamatopoulos (1892–1969), known as Stratis Myrivilis, was born close to the village's atmospheric central square. The jetty church, which featured in his novel *The Mermaid Madonna*, can be seen down in nearby Skála Sykaminiás on

the coast. One of Skála's tavernas is named after the *mouriá* or mulberry tree in which Myrivílis slept on hot summer nights.

12

Plomári
Πλωμάρι

🚗 42 km (26 miles)
SW of Mytilíni 📞 22520
32200 💬

Plomári's attractive houses spill off the slope above its harbour and stretch down to the banks of the usually dry Sedoúndas River. The houses date predominantly from the 19th century, when Plomári became wealthy as a major shipbuilding centre. Today, it is known as the island's "oúzo capital", with five distilleries in operation, the most famous being Varvagiannis, which runs regular tours.

The best and longest beach on Lésvos, composed of sand and light shingle, Vaterá occupies a 7 km (4 miles) stretch of the southern coast, fringed by verdant green hills. The water is crystal clear and shallow, making it good for families.

→

Tavernas and cafés lining the cobbled back streets of Mólyvos

---

| **LOCAL LIQUEUR**

Oúzo is the Greek version of a spirit found throughout the Mediterranean. The residue of grape skins left over from wine-pressing is boiled in a still to make a distillate called rakí. The term oúzo means rakí flavoured with star anise or fennel. The alcohol content varies from 38 to 48 per cent, with 44 per cent considered the minimum for a quality product.

Mandamádos
Μανταμάδος

 36 km (22 miles) NW of Mytilíni 🛈 **22530 61203**

This attractive village is known for its pottery industry and the adjacent Moní Taxiarhón. The existing monastery dates from the 17th century and houses a black icon of the Archangel Michael, reputedly made from mud and the blood of monks slaughtered in an Ottoman raid. A bull is sacrificed here on the third Sunday after Easter and its meat eaten in a communal stew. Mantamádos ceramics come in a range of sizes and colours, from giant *pythária* (olive oil containers) to smaller *koumária* (ceramic water jugs).

Mólyvos (Míthymna)
Μόλυβος (Μήθυμνα)

61 km (38 miles) NW of Mytilíni 🛈 **22530 71313**

Mólyvos was the birthplace of Arion, the 7th-century-BC poet, and the site of the grave of Palamedes, the Achaian warrior buried by Achilles. According to legend, the Greek hero besieged the city until the king's daughter fell in love with him and opened the gates – though Achilles killed her for her treachery. There is little remaining of the ancient town, apart from the tombs excavated near the tourist office, but its ancient name, Míthymna, has been revived and is used as an alternative to Mólyvos.

Before 1923 over a third of the population was Muslim, who built many sumptuous town houses and graced Mólyvos with a dozen street fountains. The mansions, or *arhondiká*, are influenced by Eastern architecture; the living spaces are arranged on the top floor around a central stairwell, or *hagiáti*. One, the Komninaki-Kralli mansion, has fine murals upstairs, and may be visited.

Overlooking the town, with splendid views of the Turkish coast, is a Byzantine *kástro*. Modified by the Genoese adventurer Francesco Gatelluzi in 1373, the castle fell to the Ottomans in 1462. Restored in 1995, it still retains its wood-and-iron medieval door and a calligraphic inscription over the lintel. In summer, it often serves as a concert venue.

A boatyard operates at the fishing harbour, which remains from the days when Mólyvos was a major port.

EAT

Ermis
A great place to taste ouzo and feast on *mezedes* such as stuffed courgette flowers.

 Ermou, Mytilíni
📞 22510 26232

€€€

Balouhanas
Grilled fish is the speciality at this taverna, which has a deck over the water.

 North end of the seafront, Pérama
📞 22510 51948

€€€

The Captain's Table
A huge range of grilled meat and fish, plus plenty of local wine.

 Volissós harbour
📞 22530 71241

€€€

Zorba the Buddha
A sociable place, with a tasty range of meals.

 Eastern seafront, Skála Eressoú
📞 22530 53777

€€€

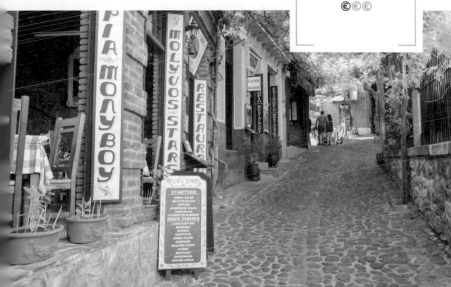

HIDDEN GEM
Quiet Beach

Dune-backed Kámbos beach, near Gavathás on the coast north of Andíssa, stays quiet even in mid-summer.

 15

Pétra
Πέτρα

⌂ **55 km (34 miles) NW of Mytilíni** 🚌 *i* **22530 42222**

This village takes its name (meaning "rock") from the volcanic monolith at its centre. The 16th-century basilica of Ágios Nikólaos still has its original frescoes, while a flight of 103 steps climbs to the 18th-century Panagía Glykofiloúsa church. Catch a glimpse of 18th-century Greek life inside the preserved **Arhondikó Vareltzídenas**, an Ottoman-era dwelling.

Arhondikó Vareltzídenas
📞 22530 41510 ⊙ 8am–3pm Tue–Sun 🗓 Main public hols

 16

Kalloní
Καλλονή

⌂ **40 km (25 miles) NW of Mytilíni** 🚌 *i* **22530 22288**

The important crossroads and market town of Kalloní lies

2 km (1 mile) inland from its namesake gulf. The area is renowned for its sardines, known as *sardélles kallonís*, which are seasoned with salt and herbs, then either baked or grilled, and often served split open. Sardines are netted in the gulf offshore from Skála Kallonís.

In 1527, the abbot Ignatios founded **Moní Limónos**, the second most important monastery on Lésvos. You can still view his cell, maintained as a shrine. A carved wood ceiling, interior arcades and a holy spring distinguish the central church. Moní Limónos also has various homes for the infirm, a mini zoo and two museums: one ecclesiastical and the other focused on folkloric miscellany.

Moní Limónos
⌂ **5 km (3 miles) NW of Kalloní** 📞 22530 22289 ⊙ Museum: daily; folk museum: on request

 17

Ándissa
Αντισσα

⌂ **76 km (47 miles) NW of Mytilíni** 🚌 *i* **22530 53600**

The largest village in this part of Lésvos, Ándissa merits a stop for its fine central square alone, in which a number of cafés and tavernas stand overshadowed by

three huge plane trees. Most people, however, visit here for its proximity to the ruins of its eponymous ancient city, destroyed by the Romans in 168 BC, which lie just outside of town, 8 km (5 miles) below by road. Nearby the ruins are the remains of the Genoese Ovriókastro. This castle stands on the shore, east of the tiny fishing port of Gavathás and the long, if exposed, sandy beach of Kámbos.

Vatoússa, 10 km (6 miles) east of Ándissa, is the area's most attractive village, even though it has no view of the sea. Tiered Skalohóri, another 3 km (2 miles) north, does overlook the north coast and – like most local villages – has a ruined mosque dating to the days before the 1923 Treaty of Lausanne.

Hidden in a lush river valley, 3 km (2 miles) east of Ándissa, is the 16th-century Moní Perivolís, standing in the middle of a riverside orchard. The narthex features three 16th-century frescoes, restored in the 1960s: the apocalyptic *Earth and Sea Yield Up Their Dead*, the *Three Magi Approaching with Gifts* and *Abraham, Virgin and Penitent Thief*. The interior is lit by daylight, so plan to visit the monastery well before dusk.

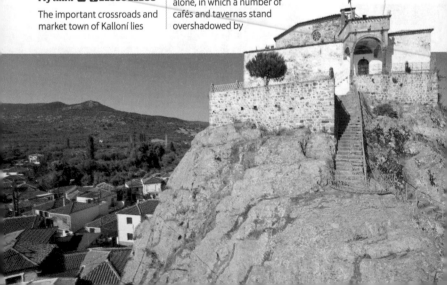

The stone base of a tree at Lésvos Petrified Forest →

18
Moní Ypsiloú
Μονή Υψηλού

🏠 **62 km (39 miles) NW of Mytilíni** ✉ ☎ 22530 56259

Spread across the 511-m (1,676-ft) summit of Mount Órdymnos, an extinct volcano, Moní Ypsiloú was founded in the 12th century and is now home to just four monks. It has a handsome double gate, and a fine wood-lattice ceiling in its *katholikón* (main church), plus a rich exhibition of ecclesiastical treasures. In the courtyard outside stand a number of fragments of petrified trees. The patron saint of the monastery is John the Divine (author of The Book of Revelation).

The main entry to Lésvos's petrified forest is just west of Ypsiloú. Some 15 to 20 million years ago, Mount Órdymnos erupted, beginning the process whereby huge stands of sequoia trees that were buried in the volcanic ash were transformed into stone. The **Natural History Museum of the Lésvos Petrified**

←

The church on the volcanic monolith in the middle of the coastal village of Pétra

Forest, based in Sígri, was established to promote this area. It is actually strongest on Aegean geology and seismic activity.

Natural History Museum of the Lésvos Petrified Forest
📍 Sígri 🕐 8:30am–4:30pm daily (from 9am Sun) ⊗ Main pub hols 🖥 lesvosmuseum.gr

19
Sígri
Σίγρι

🏠 **93 km (58 miles) NW of Mytilíni** ✉

An 18th-century Ottoman castle and the church of Agía Triáda dominate this sleepy port, protected by long, narrow Nisópi island. Sígri's continuing status as a naval base and occasional ferry port has discouraged tourist development, though it has a couple of small beaches; emptier ones are only a short drive away.

20
Skála Eresoú
Σκάλα Ερεσού

🏠 **89 km (55 miles) W of Mytilíni town** ✉

Extended beneath the acropolis of ancient Eresos, the long beach at Skála Eresoú is Greece's prime lesbian resort, and is popular with families. From the

acropolis hill, you can spot the ancient jetty submerged in the fishing anchorage. Little remains at the summit, but the Byzantine era is represented in the ancient centre by the foundations of the basilica of Ágios Andreás; its 5th-century mosaics still await restoration.

The village of Eresós, 11 km (7 miles) inland, grew up as a refuge from medieval pirate raids; a fertile plain extends between the two settlements. Two of Eresós's most famous natives were the philosopher and botanist Theophrastos, known for associating with Plato, and Sappho, one of the ancient world's greatest poets.

SAPPHO, THE POET OF LÉSVOS

Sappho (c 615–562 BC) was born into an aristocratic family. In her day, her poetry was known across the Mediterranean, though it now survives only in short quotations. Much of her work was inspired by female companions: discreet homosexuality was unremarkable in her time. Legend asserts that she fell in love with a younger man. Assured that unrequited love could be cured by leaping from a cliff, she did so and drowned: an unlikely end for a poet reputed to be the first literary lesbian.

SÁMOS
ΣΑΜΟΣ

⊠ 4 km (2 miles) W of Pythagório ⛴ Vathý, Karlóvasi, Pythagório 🚹 Themistoklí Sofoúli 107; www.samos.net

Sámos is a major hub for the Northeast Aegean, with a bustling capital, good beaches, charming ports and a major archaeological site at Heraion, a remainder of ancient times when Sámos was a maritime power.

① Vathý

🚌⛴ Gefyráki junction, waterfront

Though the original hillside village of Áno Vathý already existed in the late 1600s, today's lower town is recent; the harbour quarter grew up only after 1832, when the town became the capital of Sámos. Above the harbour quarter, charming cobble-laned Áno Vathý carries on, oblivious to the commerce below, whereas lower Vathý, large enough to provide all amenities, caters to tourists and locals alike. Here you'll find the Sámos **Archaeological Museum**, which contains artifacts from the excavations at the Heraion sanctuary *(p141)*. Because of the far-flung origins of the pilgrims who visited the shrine, the collection of small votive offerings is one of the richest in Greece – among them are a bronze statuette of an Urartian god and a miniature of Perseus and Medusa. The largest surviving freestanding sculpture from ancient Greece is the star exhibit: a 5-m- (16-ft-) tall marble *koúros* from 580 BC, dedicated to Apollo.

Archaeological Museum

⊛ 🅰 Platía Dimarhíou
☎ 22730 27469 🕒 8am–3pm Tue–Sun 🚫 Main public hols

② 🚲
Efpalínio Órygma

🅰 15 km (9 miles) SW of Vathý 🕒 Mid-Feb–Nov: 8:30am–2:40pm (prebook by phone: 22730 62813) 🌐 eupalinos-tunnel.gr

Efpalínio Órygma (Eupalinos's tunnel) is a 1,036-m (3,400-ft) section of an aqueduct, ranking as one of the premier engineering feats of the ancient world. Designed by the engineer Eupalinos and built by hundreds of slaves between 529 and 524 BC, the tunnel guaranteed ancient Sámos a water supply in times of siege, and remained in use until the 7th century AD. Eupalinos's surveying was so accurate that when the work crews met, having begun from opposite sides of the mountain, their vertical error was nil. Visitors may walk along the ledge used to remove waste

Small boats lining the shore at the harbour of the colourful town of Vathý ↑

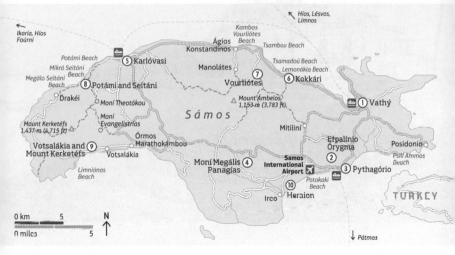

from the channel far below. Half the total length is open to the public, with grilles to protect against the drop.

---

③
Pythagório

📍 **13 km (8 miles) SW of Vathý** 🚌🚖 🅸 **Lykoúreou Logothéti**

Cobble-paved Pythagório, named after the philosopher Pythagoras, who was born here in 580 BC, has long been one of the lodestones of Samian tourism. The extensive foundations and walls of ancient Sámos act as a brake on tower-block construction; the only genuine tower is the fortified 19th-century Lykourgos Logothetis, named for the local chieftain who organized a decisive naval victory over the Ottomans on 6 August 1824, Transfiguration Day. Next to this are the church of the Metamórfosis, built to celebrate the victory, and a Byzantine basilica.

Near the main crossroads is the **Archaeological Museum**, exhibiting local Roman and Byzantine finds, where star displays include a huge hoard of Byzantine gold coins and statues of Roman emperors.

At the western edge of town are ruins of a 2nd-century AD Roman baths.

Archaeological Museum
♿ 📞 22730 62813 🕐 8am–3pm Tue-Sun

---

④
Moní Megális Panagías

📍 **27 km (17 miles) W of Vathý** 🚌 22730 41249 🕐 10am–noon daily (subject to caretaker)

Founded in 1586 by Nílos and Dionýsios, two hermits from Asia Minor, the monastery of Megális Panagías is the second

↑ A modern mural at the Megális Panagías monastery

oldest on Sámos and contains the island's best surviving frescoes from that period. The central church was probably built directly above a temple of Artemis, which it replaced. The unoccupied monastery is still visited by pilgrims each year for its festival on 22–23 August.

 ⑤
Karlóvasi

📍 **32 km (20 miles) W of Vathý**

Sprawling Karlóvasi, gateway to western Sámos and the island's biggest town, has several districts. Néo Karlóvasi was a major leather centre from the 1880s to the 1950s; abandoned tanneries can be seen by the sea in Ríva. Meséo Karlóvasi, on a hill across the river, is attractively arrayed around its plaza, but most visitors stay near the waterfront at Limín harbour, with its tavernas and lively boatyard. Above the port, Paleó (Áno) Karlóvasi is tucked away in a wooded ravine, overlooked by the church of Agía Triáda.

---

⑥
Kokkári

📍 **11 km (6 miles) W of Vathý** **ℹ️ Agíou Nikoláou; 22730 92333**

Built on and behind twin headlands, the charming fishing port of Kokkári takes its name from the shallot-like onions once cultivated just inland. Today it is Sámos's third resort after Pythagório and Votsalákia, its wind-blown location turned to advantage by a nearby windsurfing school. The main west beach, covered in coarse pebbles, is often surf-battered; Calma cove on the east side of town is more sheltered. Nightlife clusters along the north quay.

---

⑦
Vourliótes

📍 **34 km (21 miles) W of Vathý**

Southwest of and inland from Kokkári, several hill villages perch on the northern slopes of Mount Ámbelos. Though many have been deserted, Vourliótes is an exception, thriving thanks to nearby orchards and vineyards. The central square is among the most beautiful on Sámos, and has several tavernas.

Vourliótes straddles a major junction in the area's mapped and maintained network of hiking trails; paths come up from Kokkári, descend to Agios Konstandínos, and cross to Manolátes, the trailhead for the ascent to Profítis Ilías peak (1,153 m/3,783 ft) on Mount Ámbelos, a five-hour round trip. Manolátes itself is decidedly tourist-geared, with upmarket souvenirs and two very good tavernas.

---

⑧
Potámi and Seïtáni

📍 **34 km (21 miles) W of Vathý**

Some 3 km (2 miles) west of Limín, Potámi beach is the site of a Byzantine port settlement. Its most substantial traces include the 11th-century church of Metamórfosis, the oldest on the island, and a castle immediately above, which can be climbed to. Half of Karlóvasi decamps to Potámi at weekends, but there are better beaches for those who continue past the town, off the road heading west. Visitors park near a trailhead and walk 25 minutes to pebbly Mikró Seïtáni cove, or 1 hour to long, sandy Megálo Seïtáni. There are no facilities at either of these beautiful beaches, but in season there may be taxi boats from Limín.

> **Built on and behind twin headlands, the charming fishing port of Kokkári takes its name from the shallot-like onions once cultivated just inland.**

↑ Boats on the pebbly beach of the lovely port town of Kokkári

THE SAMIAN CULT OF HERA

Hera was worshipped as the main cult of a number of Greek cities, and always at out-of-town sanctuaries. Before the 1st millennium BC, she was venerated in the form of a simple wooden board *(xoana)*, later augmented with a copper statue. The annual Heraia festival, which saw the copper statue dressed in wedding finery, celebrated Hera's union with Zeus, and was accompanied by concerts and athletic contests. Housed in a special shrine after the 8th century, the statue of Hera was flanked by a number of live peacocks and sprigs from an osier tree. Both are shown on Samian coins of the Roman era, stamped with the image of the richly dressed goddess.

⑨
Votsalákia and Mount Kerketéfs

🏠 50 km (31 miles) W of Vathý 🚌 to Marathókampos

Sandy Votsalákia (Kámbos Marathokámbou) has the longest, calmest-water beach on Sámos. Overhead, dominating the western tip of Sámos, 1,437 m (4,715 ft) Mt Kerketéfs is the second-highest peak in the Aegean after Fengári on Samothráki. On an island composed of smooth sedimentary rock, this partly igneous mountain with its jagged formations and bottomless chasms is an anomaly. Kerketéfs acquired prominence during Byzantine times, when religious hermits occupied some of its caves. Today, two uninhabited convents remain: 16th-century Evangelistrías, perched on the south slope, and Theotókou (1887), tucked into a north-westerly valley.

---

⑩ ⓢ
Heraion

🏠 21 km (13 miles) SW of Vathý 📞 22730 95277 🚌 Iréo 🕐 8am–3pm Tues–Sun ✷ Main public hols

A fertility goddess was worshipped here from Neolithic times, though the cult only became identified with Hera after the arrival of Myccnaean colonists, who brought their worship of the Olympian deities with them.

A 30-m- (98-ft-) long temple built in the 8th century BC was replaced in the 6th century BC by an Ionic stone one, planned by local architect Rhoikos. This collapsed during the reign of Polykrates, who ordered a grand replacement designed by Rhoikos's son, Theodoros. He began the new temple in 525 BC, but the vast structure was never completed.

Most of the finds on display at the Archaeological Museum in Vathý *(p138)* date from the 8th to the 6th centuries BC, when the sanctuary was at the height of its prestige. Byzantine and medieval masons removed ready-cut stone for reuse, leaving only one column untouched, still standing on the site today.

↑ The lone remaining column amid the ruins at the sanctuary of Heraion

22

IKARÍA

IKAPIA

🛫 🏠 12 km (7 miles) NE of Ágios Kýrikos 🚌🚢 Ágios Kýrikos
ℹ️ Citizen Service Centre, Ágios Kýrikos; 22753 50521

Lying little over 20 km (12 miles) west of Sámos, wild Ikaría is named after the Ikaros of legend who flew too near the sun on artificial wings and plunged to his death. Perhaps the offbeat nature of its mythological namesake has imbued the character of the island's inhabitants, who have a reputation for eccentricity.

AUGUST PANEGÝRIA

The annual festivals that celebrate the saints' days of many churches in Greece, known as *panegýria*, are famous for being particularly wild on Ikaría. They reach their peak in August, when there are celebrations for the Holy Mother and other saints. In the Ráhes villages, especially, there is all-night live traditional music, dancing, feasting on roast goat and prodigious amounts of wine, beer and ouzo.

① Ágios Kírykos

Ágios Kírykos, the island's capital and main port, is a pleasant town with a modest archaeological museum as its only tourist attraction. It is flanked by two spas, one of them dating to Roman times and still popular with an older Greek clientele. A number of hot baths can be visited at Thérma, a short walk to the northeast, while at Thérma Lefkádas, to the southwest, the springs still well up among the boulders in the shallows of the sea. Twelve km (7 miles) to the east, towards lonely Cape Drákano and its deserted Hellenistic watchtower, Fáros is a lovely sandy stretch of beach.

② Évdilos

🏠 32 km (20 miles) W of Ágios Kírykos

It is a heart-in-mouth ride across the massive spine of the island, which is often shrouded in cloud even in high summer, to the other main port of Évdilos. About 2 km (1 mile) west of here lies the village of Kámbos. It boasts a broad, sandy beach, a ruined 12th-century church and the remains of a Byzantine manor house, remaining from a time when the island was considered a humane place of exile for

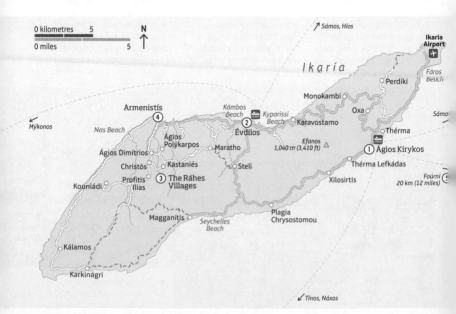

↑ Rocky cove with crystal-clear waters on the island of Ikaría

disgraced noblemen. A small museum contains artifacts from the town of Oinoe, Kámbos's ancient predecessor. A further 5 km (3 miles) inland is Kosoíki village, which has the looming remains of Byzantine castle Nikariás, built during the 10th century to guard the road to Oinoe.

---

③
The Ráhes Villages

 43 km (28 miles) SW of Ágios Kírykos

One of the most unique areas in the whole of Greece is the conglomeration of four tiny villages – Ágios Dimítrios, Ágios Polýkarpos, Kastaniés and Christós – a few kilometres inland from Armenistís. Collectively called the Ráhes villages, they are best known for the eccentric nocturnal hours kept by their inhabitants. Nothing happens around here until at least lunchtime and the locals still manage to fit in a siesta after that, but all the tavernas and shops then stay open through the night until dawn or later in summer.

④
Armenistís

 38 km (23 miles) W of Ágios Kírykos

Tiny Armenistís, with its forests and fine beaches, such as Livádi and Messaktí to the east, is Ikaría's main resort. The foundations of a temple dedicated to the goddess Artemis Tavropolos, who was the patroness of bulls, lie a further 4 km (2 miles) west.

A far more alternative and laid-back place to hang out is Nas, 3 km (2 miles) west of Armenistís, whose beautiful beach lies where a river cuts through a ravine into the sea.

---

⑤
Foúrni

 20 km (12 miles) E of Ágios Kírykos

Home to the most active fishing fleet in the East Aegean, the island of Foúrni, due east of Ikaría, is populous and lively. Kambí, Áspa and Pelekánia beaches lie within walking distance of the port.

EAT

Klimataria
Tucked in a pedestrianized alley beneath vines, this friendly spot has great barrelled wine to wash down the juicy grilled meat and fresh salads.

Two blocks in from the seafront, Ágios Kírykos
22750 23686

Thea's
Boasting stunning views down the ravine to the sea, Thea's offers some rare vegetarian dishes such as chickpea purée and pita bread filled with pumpkin, as well as a range of meat and fish dishes.

East cliff, Nas
22750 71491

23

THÁSOS

ΘΑΣΟΣ

 Liménas bus station 🔲 thassos.gr

Thásos has been inhabited since the Stone Age, with settlers from Páros colonizing the east coast during the 7th century BC. Spurred by revenues from gold deposits near modern Liménas, ancient Thasos became the seat of a seafaring empire, though its autonomy was lost to the Athenians in 462 BC. The town thrived in Roman times, but lapsed into medieval obscurity. Today, the island's last source of mineral wealth is delicate white marble, cut from quarries whose scars are prominent on the hillsides south of Liménas.

 INSIDER TIP
Ferry Crossings

Although there are some ferries travelling to Thássos from the city of Kavála, there are far more frequent (and cheaper) crossings from the port of Keramotí, located just under 40 km (25 miles) east of Kavála.

① **Liménas**

Modern Liménas, also known as Thásos town, is a rather undistinguished resort on the coastal plain which has been settled for nearly four millennia. One of the more interesting sights in town is seeing the vestiges of the ancient city blend into the modern town. The remains of a Byzantine basilica take up part of the central square, while the road to Panagiá cuts across a vast shrine of Herakles before passing a monumental historic gateway.

Established in the 7th century BC, **ancient Thasos** had a complex series of buildings, only the remains of which can be seen today. French archaeologists have conducted excavations here since 1911; digs have continued at a number of locations in Liménas. Well defined by the ruins of four stoas, which were colonnaded walkways, the Hellenistic and Roman agora covers a large area behind the ancient military harbour, today the picturesque modern *limanáki* (fishing port). Though only a few columns have been re-erected, you can trace the essentials of ancient civic life, including several temples to gods and deified Roman emperors, plus the remains of heroes' monuments and an extensive drainage system.

Foundations of a Temple of Dionysos, where a 3rd-century BC marble head of the god was found, mark the start of the path up to the

acropolis. Partly overgrown by oaks, the Hellenistic theatre has spectacular views out to sea. The Romans adapted the stage area for their bloody spectacles; it is now being excavated with the intent of complete restoration.

The ancient citadel, once the location of an Apollo temple, was rebuilt during the 13th century by the Venetians and Byzantines. It was then ceded by Emperor Manuel II Paleologos to the Genoese Gatelluzi clan in 1414, who enlarged and occupied it until 1455. By the late 5th century BC, substantial walls of more than 4 km (2 miles) surrounded the city, the sections by the sea having been mostly wrecked on the orders of victorious besiegers in 492 and 462 BC.

Foundations of a Temple to Athena Poliouhos, who was patroness of the ancient city, dated to the early 5th century BC, can be seen just below the acropolis summit; massive retaining walls support the site terrace.

A cavity hewn in the rocky outcrop beyond served as a shrine to Pan, the god of wild places, shepherds and herds,

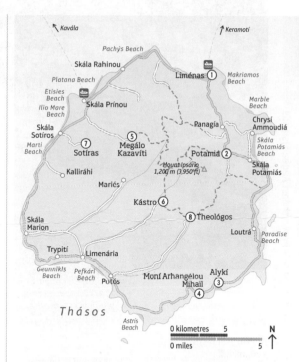

in the 3rd century BC; he is depicted in faint relief playing his pipes.

Behind the summit point, a steep 6th-century BC stairway descends to the Gate of Parmenon in the city wall. The gate retains its lintel and takes its name from an inscription "Parmenon Made Me" (denoting its mason), on a nearby wall slab.

Next to the agora at the entrance to the site, the Archaeological Museum has numerous treasures from the site, including a magnificent *kouros* dating from 600 BC.

Ancient Thasos

⊗ ⌂ Liménas ☎ 25930 22180 ⌚ Apr-Oct: 8am-8pm Tue-Sun; Nov-Mar: 8:30am-3pm Tue-Sun ⌚ Main public hols

←
Ruined walls and a few columns remaining at ancient Thasos

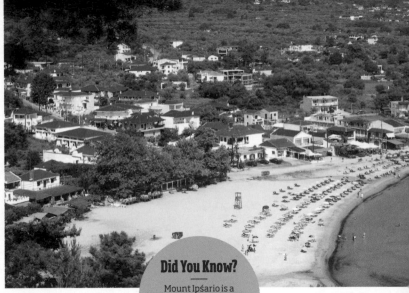

Did You Know?

Mount Ipśario is a nature zone and protects species of wild chicken, as well as other birds.

 ②

Potamiá

🏛 9 km (6 miles) S of Liménas 🚌

Potamiá is a small village, but home to a popular hiking path leading to the 1,200 m (3,950 ft) summit of Mount Ipśário. Following bulldozer tracks upstream brings you to the trailhead for the ascent, which is a 7-hour excursion; although the path is way-marked by the Greek Alpine Club, it is in poor condition.

The sculptor and painter Polygnotos Vagis (1894–1965) was a native of the village, although he emigrated to America at an early age. Before his death, the artist bequeathed most of his works to the Greek state and they are now on display at the small **Polygnotos Vagis Museum**, situated in the village centre. His work has a mythic, dreamlike quality; the most compelling sculptures are representations of birds, fish, turtles and ghostly faces, which he carved onto boulders or smaller stones.

Many visitors stay at Skála Potamiás, a popular resort lining the harbour 3 km (2 miles) east of Potamiá.

This village is noted for its great tavernas serving traditional Greek food, as well as its proximity to beautiful Golden Beach. Nearby Panagía, 2 km (1 mile) further north, is the most visited of the inland villages. It is situated above a sandy bay, has a lively square and many of its 19th-century houses have been preserved or restored.

Polygnotos Vagis Museum
♿ 📞 25930 61400
🕐 May-Sep: 10am-1pm & 6-9pm Tue-Sun 🚫 Main public holidays

 ③

Alykí

🏛 29 km (18 miles) S of Liménas 🚌

Perhaps the most scenic spot on the Thasian shore, the headland at Alykí is tethered to the body of the island by a slender spit, with beaches to either side. The westerly cove is fringed by the hamlet of Alykí, which has well-preserved vernacular architecture from the 19th-century due to its official classification as an archaeological zone. A Doric temple stands over the eastern bay, while behind it are two fine Christian basilicas from the 5th century, with a few of their columns re-erected.

The local marble was highly prized in ancient times; now all that is left of Alykí's quarries are overgrown depressions on the headland. At sea level, "bathtubs" (trenches scooped out of the rock strata) were once used as evaporators for salt-harvesting.

 ④

Moní Arhangélou Mihaïl

🏛 34 km (21 miles) S of Liménas 📞 25930 31500
🚌 🕐 Daily

Overhanging the sea 3 km (2 miles) west of Alykí, Moní Arhangélou Mihaïl was established as a monastery early in the 12th century by a hermit called Luke, on the spot where a spring was said to have appeared at the behest of the Archangel.

Now a dependency of Moní Filothéou on Mount

 View across the water to Skála Potamiás, fringed by mountains

Athos in northern Greece, the monastery's most treasured relic is a Holy Nail from the Cross. Nuns have occupied the grounds since 1974.

 ⑤

Megálo Kazavíti

⌂ 22 km (14 miles) SW of Liménas ▣

Greenery-shrouded Megálo Kazavíti (officially Ano Prínos) surrounds a central square, which is a rarity on Thásos. There is no better place to find examples of traditional domestic Thasian architecture, with its characteristic mainland Macedonian influence: original

 Sheep on the wall of a house in the mountain village of Kástro

house features include narrow-arched doorways, balconies and overhanging upper storeys, with traces of the indigo, magenta and ochre plaster pigment that was once commonly used across the Balkans.

 ⑥

Kástro

Κάστρο

⌂ 45 km (28 miles) SW of Liménas

At the centre of the island of Thásos, 500 m (1,640 ft) up in the mountains, the village of Kástro was extremely secure from pirate attacks. Founded in 1403 by Byzantine Emperor Manuel II Paleologos, the village became a stronghold of the Genoese, who fortified the local hill, where the cemetery is now located. Kástro was slowly abandoned after 1850, when the establishment of a German mining concession created jobs at Limenária, on the coast below.

Kástro has now been reinhabited on a seasonal basis by sheep farmers. The *kafenío* occupies the ground floor of the former school, beside the church. Many house restorations since the 1990s have finally brought mains power to the village.

⑦

Sotíras

⌂ 23 km (14 miles) SW of Liménas ▣

Facing the sunset, Sotíras has the most alluring site of all the inland villages – a fact not lost on the many foreigners who have made their homes here. Under huge plane trees watered by a fountain, the tables of a small taverna fill the relaxed, balcony-like square. The ruin above the church was a lodge for miners, whose exploratory shafts still yawn on the ridge opposite.

 ⑧

Theológos

⌂ 50 km (31 miles) S of Liménas ▣

Well inland, secure from attack, Theológos was the Ottoman-era capital of Thásos. A traditional village, development here is restricted, and tiered houses still have their typically large chimneys and slate roofs. Generous gardens and courtyards give the village a green and open aspect. A ruined tower and low walls on the hillside opposite are evidence of Theológos's original 16th-century foundation by Greek refugees.

EAT

Archodissa
An enjoyable all-round taverna, with attractively priced fish dishes and wine, as well as great views.

 Hillside beyond eastern cove, Alykí
☎ 25930 31552

€€€

Iatrou
At this delightful taverna, the aroma of goat and suckling pig being roasted wafts in the fresh mountain air.

 Theológos village, Thásos
☎ 25930 31000

€€€

Pigi
Located near a spring, this decades-old eatery is particularly atmospheric at night.

 Southwest corner, main square, Liménas
☎ 25930 22941

€€€

⑳ LÍMNOS
ΛΗΜΝΟΣ

✈ 22 km (14 miles) NE of Mýrina 🚢 Mýrina 🚌 Plateía Kída, Mýrina ℹ Town Hall, on the waterfront, Mýrina; 22543 50000

The mythological landing place of Hephaistos, the god of metalworking cast out of Olympus, volcanic Límnos prospered under various occupiers and has long been famous for its excellent wine and beaches. Although there is a military presence on the island, it's an incredibly peaceful place.

① Mýrina

Sprawling between two sandy bays at the foot of a rocky promontory, Mýrina is a pleasant island capital, with cobbled streets and imposing, late-Ottoman houses, a reminder of the long period of Ottoman occupation. The most ornate of these cluster behind the northerly beach, Romeïkós Gialós, which is also a nightlife hub. The only explicitly Turkish relic is a fountain on Kydá, inscribed with Ottoman calligraphy, from which delicious potable water can still be drawn.

Housed in a 19th-century mansion behind Romeïkós Gialós, the Archaeological Museum displays artifacts from the four main cities of ancient Límnos. The most prestigious items, however, have been sent to Athens, leaving a collection made up of compelling ceramic exhibits, including a pair of votive lamps in the form of sirens from the temple at Hephaistia. Metalwork from the nearby town of Poliohne is represented by a number of decorative articles and some bronze tools.

The town is overshadowed by the formidable *kástro*, spread across the headland. This fortress was, in turn, an ancient acropolis and a Byzantine fort, fought over and refurbished by Venetians and Genoese until the island was taken by Ottomans in 1478. Though dilapidated, the *kástro* makes a rewarding evening climb for beautiful views over western Límnos.

The south beach in the town, Néa Máditos extends beyond the port with its quayside tavernas.

---

② Kondiás

🏠 11 km (7 miles) E of Mýrina 🚌 ℹ 22260 23500

Southeast from Mýrina, the road leads to Kondiás, the third-largest settlement on Límnos, sited between two volcanic outcrops supporting pine woods. Sturdy, red-tiled houses combine with the landscape to make this an appealing inland village.

The bay of Moúdros was the Commonwealth headquarters during the ill-fated 1915

Dusk falling on Mýrina's *kástro* and the beach of Romeïkós Gialós

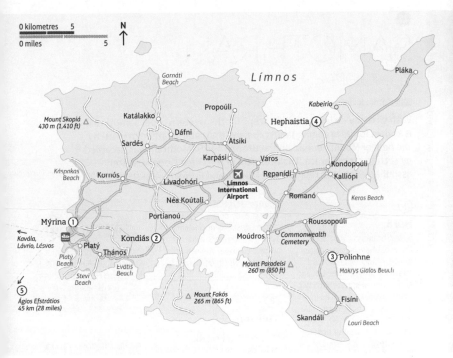

Gallipoli campaign, when Allied forces invaded Turkey. Casualties were evacuated to the hospital here; the unlucky ones were laid to rest in the Commonwealth cemetery a short walk east of town, on the road to Roussopoúli. With 887 graves, this ranks as the largest from either world war in the Greek Islands.

---

③ Poliohne

🏛 37 km (23 miles) SE of Mýrina 🚌 ℹ 22260 23500

Founded just before 3000 BC, the town of Poliohne pre-dates famous Troy, just across the water on the coast of Asia Minor. Like Troy, it was levelled in 2100 BC by an earthquake and never resettled. Poliohne was noted for its metalsmiths, who refined and worked raw ore from Black Sea deposits. A hoard of gold jewellery, now displayed in Athens, was found in one of the houses.

④ Hephaistia

🏛 28 km (17 miles) NE of Mýrina 🚌 ℹ 22260 23500

The patron deity of Límnos was honoured at Hephaistia, on the shores of Tigáni Bay. This was the largest city on the island until the Byzantine era. Most of the site has yet to be uncovered; all that is visible are outlines of the Roman theatre, parts of a necropolis and remains of the temple. Grave offerings found on the site can be seen in the Mýrina Archaeological Museum.

The ancient site of the Kabeirio (*Kavírio* in modern Greek) lies across Tigáni Bay from Hephaistia and has been more thoroughly excavated. This was a sanctuary to the Great Gods, but little remains of the former shrine and its adjacent stoa other than a number of column stumps.

---

⑤ Ágios Efstrátios

🏛 45 km (28 miles) S of Mýrina 🚌 ℹ 22260 23500

The loneliest outpost of the North Aegean, tiny, oak-covered Ágios Efstrátios – Aï Strátis for short – has scarcely a handful of tourists even in summer. The single port town was damaged by an earth-quake in 1968, with dozens of islanders killed; some pre-quake buildings survive above the jetty. Deserted beaches can be found 90 minutes' walk to either side of the port.

> **The loneliest outpost of the North Aegean, tiny, oak-covered Ágios Efstrátios - Aï Strátis for short - has scarcely a handful of tourists even in summer.**

㉕

SAMOTHRÁKI

ΣΑΜΟΘΡΑΚΗ

🚢🚌 **Kamariótissa**

With virtually no level terrain except for the western cape, Samothráki is known for its brooding landscape and dramatic weather, marked by the bulk of Mount Fengári. In the Bronze Age Samothráki was occupied by settlers from Thrace. Their religion of the Great Gods was later assimilated into the religions of Hellenic and Roman colonists.

① Hóra

Samothráki's capital, Hóra is the most handsome village on the island, with cobbled streets, a labyrinthine bazaar and a central square with two good tavernas. Located in a pine-flecked hollow, Hóra is invisible from the sea, but the square has excellent ocean views beyond the ruins of the Genoese castle, adapted from an earlier Byzantine fort. More fortifications can be found downhill at Paleópoli, Hóra's predecessor, where three towers from 1431 protrude above the extensive walls of the ancient town.

Samothráki has several villages worth visiting on its southwest flank, hidden in olive groves or poplars. The north coast has abundant springs and rivers, and waterfalls meet the sea at Kremastá Nerá to the south.

② Thérma

🏛 **12 km (7 miles) NE of Hóra**

Thérma has been the island's premier resort since the Roman era, due to its hot springs and lush greenery. You can choose from two rustic outdoor pools (which reach temperatures of 34° C or 93° F) under shelters, a very hot tub of 48° C (118° F) in a

> **Did You Know?**
>
> Legend has it that if you scale Fengári at full moon – not advisable – your wishes will be granted.

cottage for groups, and a bathhouse that has temperatures of 39° C (102° F).

After the hot springs, visitors can walk 2 km (1 mile) east to plunge into the chilly rock pools and low waterfalls at Gría Váthra. These are not as impressive as the ones in the Foniás canyon, a further 5 km (3 miles) east of Thérma.

↑ The imposing ruins of the Sanctuary of the Great Gods, surrounded by flowers

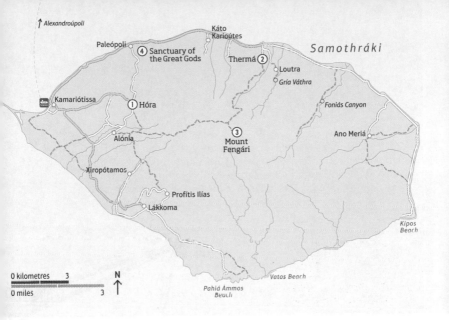

↑ Alexandroúpoli

Paleópoli

Káto
Karioútes

④ Sanctuary of
the Great Gods

Samothráki

Thermá ②

Loutra

Gría Váthra

Kamariótissa

① Hóra

Foniás Canyon

Alónia

③
Mount
Fengári

Ano Meriá

Xiropótamos

Profítis Ilías

Lákkoma

Kípos
Beach

Vatos Beach

0 kilometres   3
0 miles   3

N ↑

Pahiá Ammos
Beach

③
Mount Fengári

□ 11 km (7 miles) SE of Hóra

The highest summit in the Aegean, at 1,611 m (5,285 ft), this granite mass serves as a seafaring landmark. The views from the top are superb; in legend, the god Poseidon watched the Trojan War from this mountain. The peak is usually climbed from Thérma as a 6-hour round trip, though there is a longer and easier route up from Profítis Ilías village on its southwest flank.

④
Sanctuary of the Great Gods

□ 3 km (2 miles) NE of Hóra
▦ Towards Paleópoli
⊙ May–Oct: 8am–8pm Tue–Sun; Nov–Apr: 8am–3pm

The Sanctuary of the Great Gods on Samothráki was, for almost a millennium, the major religious centre of ancient Aeolia, Thrace and Macedonia. There were similar shrines on Límnos and Ténedos, but this

DEITIES AND MYSTERIES OF SAMOTHRÁKI

When Samothráki was colonized by Greeks around 700 BC, the settlers combined their Olympian deities with those they found here, who had been introduced by occupiers from Thrace, like the Nike of Victory *(right)*. The principal deity of Thrace was Axieros, the Great Mother, an earth goddess whom the Greeks identified with Demeter, Aphrodite and Hekate. Her consort was the fertility god Kadmilos, and their twin offspring were the *kabiri*. The cult was open to allcomers of any age or gender, free or slave, Greek or barbarian. Details of the cult's mysteries remain unknown, as adherents honoured a vow of silence.

site had the largest following, and each of the shrines performed different rites. Its position in a canyon at the base of savage, plunging crags on the northwest slope of Mount Fengári was perhaps calculated to inspire awe; today, though thickly over grown, it is scarcely less impressive. The sanctuary was expanded and improved in Hellenistic times by Alexander the Great's successors, and most of the ruins visible today date from that period. It has remarkable sights like the Arsinoeion, or rotunda, the largest circular building constructed by the Greeks.

THE DODECANESE

Scattered along the coast of Turkey, the diverse Dodecanese are the most southerly group of Greek Islands. Distant from Athens and the mainland, these islands were the last territories to be incorporated into modern Greece. The Dodecanese have been subject to a number of fierce invasions, with traces of occupation left behind on every island. The crusading Knights of St John were the most famous invaders, arriving in 1309 after being forced out of Jerusalem and staying until they were defeated by Süleyman the Magnificent in 1522. The long period of Ottoman occupation that followed marked the islands with Ottoman-style houses and mosques, most prominent on larger, wealthier islands such as Kos and Rhodes. After centuries of Turkish rule, the Italians arrived in 1912 and began a regime of persecution that lasted throughout World War II. Italian dictator Mussolini built many imposing public buildings, most notably at Lakkí on Léros, which is made unique by its Italian modernist structures. After years of occupation, the islands were united with the Greek state in 1948.

The most cosmopolitan archipelago, the islands here are separated by both long distances and by geography. While some ancient trades are dying out, such as sponge-harvesting on Kálymnos, many of the islands continue to thrive on industries other than tourism, such as mineral-rich and fertile Nísyros.

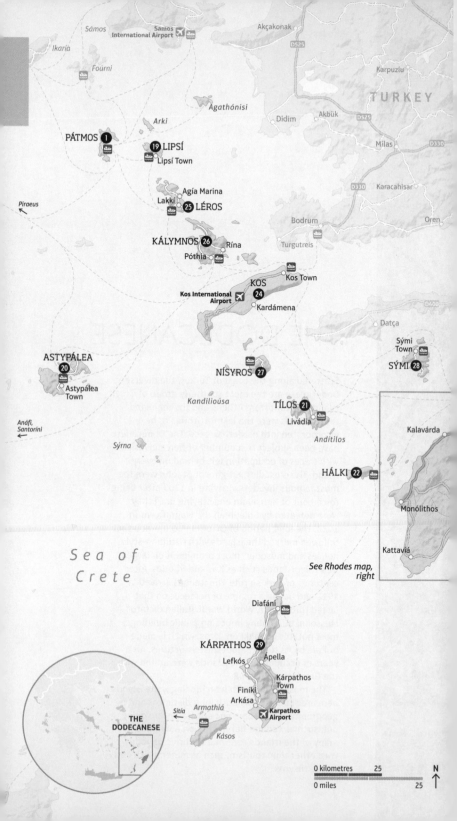

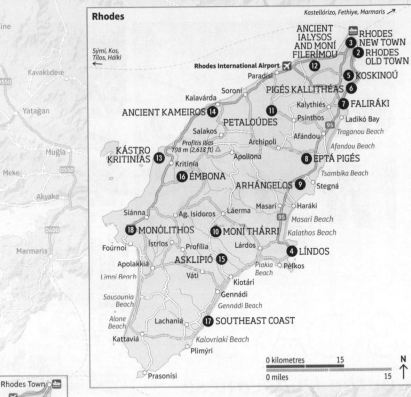

Rhodes

Kastellórizo, Fethiye, Marmaris ↗

Síncir, Kos, Tílos, Hálki ←

ANCIENT IALYSOS AND MONÍ FILERÍMOU

RHODES NEW TOWN ③
RHODES OLD TOWN ②

Rhodes International Airport ✈

Paradísi

PIGÉS KALLITHÉAS ⑥
KOSKINOÚ ⑤

Kalavárda

Soroní

Kalythiés

FALIRÁKI ⑦

ANCIENT KAMEIROS ⑭

PETALOÚDES ⑪

Psínthos

Ladikó Bay

Salakos

Traganou Beach

Profítis Ilías 798 m (2,618 ft) △

Archipoli

Afándou

Afandou Beach

KÁSTRO KRITINÍAS ⑬

Kritiniá

Apóllona

EPTÁ PIGÉS ⑧

ÉMBONA ⑯

Tsambíka Beach

ARHÁNGELOS ⑨

Stegná

Siánna

Masari

Haráki

Ag. Isidoros

Láerma

Masari Beach

95

MONÓLITHOS ⑱

MONÍ THÁRRI ⑩

Kalathos Beach

Foúrnoi

Ístrios

Profília

Lárdos

LÍNDOS ④

Apolakkiá

ASKLIPIÓ ⑮

Váti

Plakia Beach

Péfkos

Limni Beach

Kiotári

Sousounia Beach

Gennádi

Gennádi Beach

Alone Beach

Lachaniá

SOUTHEAST COAST ⑰

Kattaviá

Kalovriaki Beach

Plimýri

0 kilometres   15
0 miles   15

N ↑

Prasonísi

KASTELLÓRIZO ㉓

Ro ▷

Strongylí

Rhodes Town

Rhodes International Airport ✈

Faliráki

Rhodes

Arhángelos

Líndos

THE DODECANESE

Must Sees

① Pátmos
② Rhodes Old Town
③ Rhodes New Town
④ Líndos

Experience More

⑤ Koskinoú
⑥ Pigés Kallithéas
⑦ Faliráki
⑧ Eptá Pigés
⑨ Arhángelos
⑩ Moní Thárri
⑪ Petaloúdes
⑫ Ancient Ialysos and Moní Filerímou
⑬ Kástro Kritinías

⑭ Ancient Kameiros
⑮ Asklipió
⑯ Émbóna
⑰ Southeast Coast Beaches
⑱ Monólithos
⑲ Lípsi
⑳ Astypálea
㉑ Tílos
㉒ Hálki
㉓ Kastellórizo
㉔ Kos
㉕ Léros
㉖ Kálymnos
㉗ Nísyros
㉘ Sými
㉙ Kárpathos

8 DAYS
in the Dodecanese

Day 1

Start with a coffee in the main square of Rhodes Old Town *(p162)*, then head to the Crusader Palace of the Grand Masters *(p166)*. After a morning of exploration, make your way up to the medieval walls and follow them as far as the Kókkini Pórta – it's a great way to orient yourself. Have lunch at Ta Petaladika *(p163)*, then visit the Nestoridion wing of the Modern Greek Art Museum in New Town *(p173)* before a swim at Élli beach. Return to the Old Town for dinner in the charming courtyard of Marco Polo Café *(p163)*.

Day 2

Catch the ferry from Mandráki port to the picturesque Panormítis monastery on Sými *(p197)*. After your visit, hop back on the boat and continue to Sými's main town, Gialós, for some retail therapy, then climb the stair-paths to Horió village to catch the museum before its 2:30pm closure. Have lunch back down on the shoreline at To Spitiko *(Akti Pavlou)*, which specializes in seafood. Return to Rhodes for the evening; Mezes *(Akti Kanari 9)* in New Town is a good choice for dinner.

Day 3

Board the 8:30am catamaran to Mandráki on Nísyros *(p194)*, where you can fit in a visit to the archaeological museum and the Knights' Castle before lunch. Hire a scooter, car or bike to reach Emborió for lunch at To Balkoni (in the village centre), which has stunning views over Nísyros' volcanic zone – you can visit it after your meal. Continue on to Nikiá village for an afternoon coffee, then descend to the coast for a sunset dip at Hohláki. Dine at a seaside taverna in Mandráki, where fresh fish will undoubtedly be on the menu.

Day 4

Have a leisurely morning wandering around town before catching the midday catamaran to Kos port *(p186)*. Pay a visit to the harbour and the nearby ruins of Neratziá Knights' castle before riding a rented scooter up to Platáni for lunch at Hasan tavern *(main road)*. Afterwards, tour the nearby Asklepion archaeological site *(p188)*, then have a dip at the Bros Thermá *(p187)* seaside hot springs. More fresh fish is on the menu for dinner back in town at Barbouni *(26 G. Averof street, Kos)*.

1 Palace of the Grand Masters, Rhodes.

2 The pretty village of Nikiá, Nísyros.

3 Asklepion archaeological site, Kos.

4 The Byzantine castle on Léros.

5 Exploring the narrow roads of Skála on Pátmos by scooter.

Day 5

Island hop aboard the early ferry from Mastihári port to Póthia port on Kálymnos (p192). After you've settled into your hotel, head to Platýs Gialós – Kálymnos' best sandy beach – and relax for the rest of the morning. Have lunch at friendly, family-run Kafenes (near Christós church) before popping into the Archaeological Museum, which showcases finds from the island's long history of human occupation. Have supper at Giorgios in nearby Linária, or alternatively get a taxi to Anna's in Melitsáhas further north.

Day 6

After a short but sweet stay in Kálymnos, jump on the catamaran to Léros (p190), where the Italian occupation in World War II is marked by the surreal 1930s modernist Italian buildings of Lakkí port. Have lunch above Vromólithos at Dimitris O Karaflas (Marcopoulo St) – ask for a balcony table – then pop to the beach for a swim. If you still have energy, climb to the looming hilltop castle built by the Knights of St John, before having supper in Álinda resort at To Steki tou Dimitri (p191).

Day 7

Spend a relaxing morning in Lakkí before catching the midday catamaran to the upmarket port town of Skála on historic Pátmos (p158). Hire a scooter for a quick zip over to Livádi Geranoú beach in the north for lunch, followed by a leisurely swim. After a lazy afternoon, return to Skála in time to enjoy the beautiful sunset view from nearby Hóra's Platía Lótza. Dinner tonight is on the water-front at Skála port – Votrys taverna is particularly good.

Day 8

Spend the morning exploring Pátmos' Monastery of St John (p160), a UNESCO World Heritage-listed religious fortress that dominates the town of Hóra. For your final afternoon, go on an adventure to one of the small islands close by – choose from either Maráthi's sheltered sandy beach and lunch tavernas, or quirky Lipsí town and nearby crescent-shaped coves (p182). Say goodbye to the Dodecanese with – what else? – a fine seafood dinner back in the main town at Chiliomodi (main road, Skála).

① PÁTMOS
ΠΑΤΜΟΣ

🚌 Skála 🛈 Main square, Skála; patmos.gr

Known as the Jerusalem of the Aegean, Pátmos has been a place of religious significance since St John arrived in AD 95 and wrote the Book of Revelation. Famous for the dramatic monastery founded in St John's name, rugged, volcanic Pátmos today caters for both pilgrims and tourists.

①
Skála

Ferries, yachts and cruise ships dock at Skála, the island's port and main town, which stretches around a wide sheltered bay. Upmarket and smart, Skála has a number of exclusive gift shops and boutiques. Social life centres on café-bar Aríon, in a Neo-Classical building that doubles as a meeting place and also a waiting point for ferries. From the harbourfront caïques and small cruise boats leave daily for the island's main beaches.

Above Skála lie the remains, primarily Hellenistic walls, of the ancient acropolis at Kastélli. The walls surround Agios Konstandínos, the little chapel whose sunset views are worth the hike from Skála's westernmost neighbourhood.

The sandy town beach of Theológos can get very crowded. Head instead one bay north of Skála to the coarse-sand, tamarisk-shaded beach of Melói, which has a campsite and long-running taverna. The next cove on, Agriolivádi, is shadeless but has finer sand.

KYNOPS VS JOHN

In legend, the wizard Kynops challenged St John to a duel of miracles. Kynops' trick was to retrieve effigies of the dead from the bottom of the sea. John responded by begging God to petrify Kynops while he was submerged, and so it was.

②
Hóra

🏠 3 km (2 miles) S of Skála 🚌

A maze of white narrow lanes with over 40 monasteries and chapels, Hóra, the capital of Pátmos, is a gem of Byzantine architecture and has views to Sámos and Ikaría. Many of the buildings here have distinctive window mouldings, known as *mandómata*, decorated with a Byzantine cross. Along the twisting alleys, some doorways lead into vast sea captains' mansions *(arhontiká)* built to keep marauding pirates at bay. The Monastery of St John *(p160)* looms above Hóra.

Near Plateía Xánthou, is the **Simantiris Mansion** is the town's Folk Museum. Built in 1625 by Aglaïnos Mousodakis, a wealthy merchant, it still has the original furnishings and objects from Mousodakis's travels. Nearby, the tranquil convent of Zoödóhou Pigís, built in 1607, has some fine frescoes and icons and is set in peaceful gardens.

About halfway between Skála and Hóra, the chapel of Agía Ánna forms the anteroom to the **Holy Cave of the Apocalypse**, where St John saw the vision of the end of days and dictated the Book of Revelation, the final book in the Bible, to his disciple,

↑ Cheerful white Hóra underneath the looming Monastery of St John

Próchoros. Here you can see the rock that served as the desk for the task, and the indentation where the saint rested his head. St John is said to have heard the voice of God coming from a cleft in the rock that is divided into three, symbolizing the Holy Trinity.

Simantiris House
♿ 📞 22470 31360 🕐 9am–1:30pm & 5–7:30pm daily

Holy Cave of the Apocalypse
📍 Between Skála and Hóra 🕐 Daily

---

③
Gríkou
📍 4 km (2 miles) S of Skála 🚌

The main southerly resort of Gríkou fringes a vast bay east of Hóra, and has a sand beach with fishing boats, water-sports facilities and a few tavernas. From here, the bay curves south through Pétra pebble beach to bizarre Kallikatsoú rock, perched on a sand spit. The rock, whose name is formal Greek for cormorant, had chambers hollowed out of it in 1100 BC, and may later have served as the hermitage mentioned in the 11th-century writings of the Blessed Christodoulos

The island's only pure-sand beach, Psilí Ammos, lies well southwest of Gríkou, reached by boat or a short hike from

Diakófti. The southern part of the beach is a naturist haunt and popular camping spot. There's also a good seasonal taverna here.

---

④
Lámpi
📍 8 km (5 miles) N of Skála 🚌

A windy village on the north coast, Lámpi is famous for its colourful, multipatterned volcanic pebbles – irresistible to many, but signs forbid gathering them. On the beach with tables on the pebbles is one of the oldest tavernas on Pátmos, well worth a stop.

EAT

Votrys
Med-fusion dishes like pesto squid, with an enormous wine list.

📍 Main yacht anchorage, Skála
📞 6988 807376

€€€

Despina & Thanasis
Best seafood spot on the island, with grilled fish at a bargain price.

📍 Approach road, Livádi Geranoú 📞 6977 279259

€€€

Arion Café-Bar
Wood-panelled Wild West saloon look, with breakfast and snacks.

📍 Excursion-boat quay, Skála 📞 22470 31595

€€€

Léfkes Beach
Kámbos
Kámbos Beach
Vagiá Beach
Livádi Geranoú Beach
Agriolivádi Beach
Etia
Meloí Beach
Sámos, Ikaría, Agathonísi
Kastélli
Skála ①
Holy Cave of the Apocalypse
Hóra ② ⑤ Monastery of St John
③ Gríkou
Kallikatsoú rock
Petra Beach
Cape Génoupas
Diakófti
Psilí Ámmos Beach
Mount Prásino 775 m (2,540 ft)
④ Lámpi
Pátmos
Lipsí, Léros, Piraeus

0 kilometres 2
0 miles 2
N ↑

⑤ 🏛

MONASTERY OF ST JOHN

MONH TOY ΑΓΙΟΥ ΙΩΑΝΝΟΥ ΤΟΥ ΘΕΟΛΟΓΟΥ

🏛 Hóra, 4 km (2 miles) S of Skála 🕑 8am–1:30pm daily;
4–6pm Tue, Thu & Sun 🌐 patmosmonastery.gr

St John was said to have written the Book of
Revelation on Pátmos, and the Monastery of St John
was founded in his name in 1088. A UNESCO World
Heritage Site, it remains rich and influential.

A spectacular example of Byzantine religious architecture, the
Monastery of St John looks more like a fortress than a holy
building. It looms over Hóra with defensive walls and fortifications of towers and buttresses protecting its religious
treasures; its treasury, containing over 200 icons, 300 pieces
of silverware and a dazzling collection of jewels, is the star
attraction for the thousands of pilgrims and tourists who visit
the site every year. Particularly revered is the 12th-century icon
of St John, housed in the complex's *katholikón*
(main church). The walls of the monastery
encircle a number of buildings, including the
tomb of the Blessed Christodoulos, who
founded it in the name of St John.

*The Hospitality of
Abraham is one of the
most important
frescoes in the chapel
of the Panagía.*

*The monks'
refectory has two
marble tables
from the Temple
of Artemis.*

NIPTÍR CEREMONY

The Orthodox Easter celebrations on
Pátmos are some of the most important
in Greece. Hundreds of people pack Hóra
to watch the Niptír (washing) ceremony
on Maundy Thursday. The abbot of the
Monastery of St John publicly washes
the feet of 12 monks, re-enacting
Christ's washing of his disciples' feet
before the Last Supper. The rite was
once performed by the head of the
church, the Byzantine emperors, as
an act of humility.

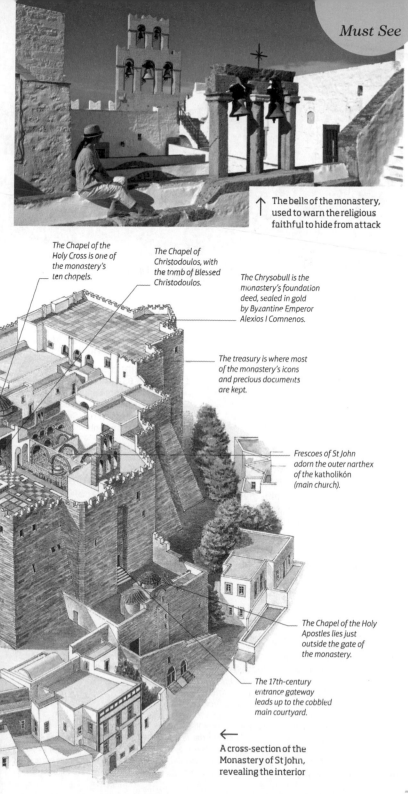

↑ The bells of the monastery, used to warn the religious faithful to hide from attack

The Chapel of the Holy Cross is one of the monastery's ten chapels.

The Chapel of Christodoulos, with the tomb of Blessed Christodoulos.

The Chrysobull is the monastery's foundation deed, sealed in gold by Byzantine Emperor Alexios I Comnenos.

The treasury is where most of the monastery's icons and precious documents are kept.

Frescoes of St John adorn the outer narthex of the katholikón (main church).

The Chapel of the Holy Apostles lies just outside the gate of the monastery.

The 17th-century entrance gateway leads up to the cobbled main courtyard.

← A cross-section of the Monastery of St John, revealing the interior

↑ Strolling at dusk in a pedestrianized square in Rhodes's Old Town

2
RHODES OLD TOWN
ΠΑΛΙΑ ΠΟΛΗ ΡΟΔΟΥ

✈ Paradísi 15 km (9 miles) SW of Rhodes town
⛴ Kolóna and Akandiá ports 🏪 New Market

Dominated by the Palace of the Grand Masters, this medieval citadel is surrounded by moats and 4 km (2 miles) of walls. Eleven gates give access to the Old Town, which is divided into the Collachium (Kollákio) and the Bourg (Boúrgos). The former was the Knights' quarter and dates from the mid-1300s. The Bourg housed the rest of the population, which after 1523 included Jews and Turks instead of Greeks, who were expelled. As one of the finest walled cities in existence, the Old Town is now a World Heritage Site.

①
The Collachium

This magnificent stone section in the walled Old Town traditionally housed the buildings of the Knights of St John, including the Street of the Knights (p168) and the Palace of the Grand Masters (p166). Today, the best way into the Collachium from Rhodes New Town are d'Amboise gate and the Elefherías (Liberty) gate

in the medieval walls. The former was built in 1512 by Grand Master Pierre d'Amboise, who famously resisted the first Ottoman assault on the town, and led from Dimokratías to the palace. Designed for defensive purposes, the Elefherías gate was built by the Italians and leads from Elefherías to Plateía Sýmis. This is a fantastic area to wander, soaking up the atmosphere.

②
Archaeological Museum

🏛 Platía Mousíou 📞 22413 65256 🕐 Apr-Oct: 8am-7:40pm daily (from 1:30pm Mon); Nov-Mar: 8am-2:40pm Tue-Sun 🔒 Main public hols

Rhodes's Archaeological Museum is located in the New Hospital of the Knights, built in 1440–89. Most famous among the exhibits is the 1st-century-BC marble of Aphrodite Bathing. Other gems in the collection include a 2nd-century-BC head of Helios the sun god, discovered at the Temple of Helios on the nearby hill of Ágios Stéfanos (Monte Smith). The grave stelae unearthed at the necropolis of Kameiros provide a good insight into 5th-century-BC life. Exhibits also include coins, jewellery and ceramics retrieved from the Mycenaean graves at nearby Ialysos.

③
Medieval City Walls

A masterpiece of military architecture, these huge walls run for 4 km (2 miles) and display 151 escutcheons of Grand Masters and Knights. The walls can be accessed from the Palace of the Grand Masters and walked all the way to the Agíou Ioánnou Gate, where you will have to pay a charge. They provide unrivalled photo opportunities over the Old Town.

4
Panagía tou Kástrou

🕐 Apéllou 🔒 Closed for renovation

Dating from the 11th century, this Byzantine church became the Knights' cathedral, but was converted by Ottomans into the Mosque of Enderun, or the Red Mosque. It used to be the Byzantine Museum, but this closed some years ago, with exhibits moved to the Palace of the Grand Masters, which has excellent displays on Rhodes's history.

EAT

Marco Polo Café
Offerings at this courtyard diner vary seasonally, but expect delicious platters, such as grilled octopus. Booking is mandatory.

📍 Agíou Fanouríou 42, Old Town 📞 22410 25562

€€€

Ta Petaladika
Fair-priced fish dishes served in a courtyard shaded by a giant ficus tree. There's a good list of distilled grape spirits.

📍 Menekléous 8, Old Town 📞 22410 27319

€€€

Mezes
Excellent mains include grilled smoked mackerel and steamed mussels. Tables on the sea-view terrace need reserving.

📍 Aktí Kanári 9, Psaropoúla district, Neohóri 📞 22410 27962

€€€

To Steno
Tuck into stuffed courgette flowers or octopus in several guises. Book ahead for the courtyard.

📍 Agíon Anargýron 29, SW of Ágios Athanásios Gate 📞 22410 35914

€€€

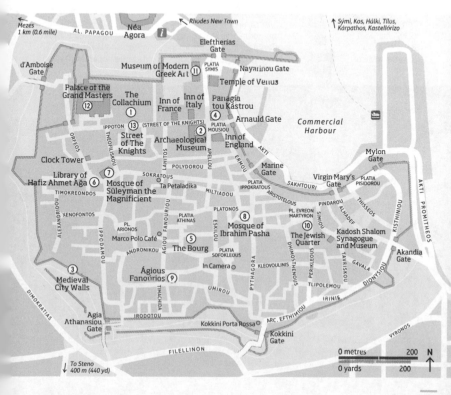

The Bourg (Boúrgos)

The section of the Old Town housing the Jewish, Turkish and Greek populations under the Knights of St John's rule, this labyrinth of streets begins at Sokrátous, the "Via Turista" of bazaar-style shops, off which lie shady squares with cafés and tavernas.

One of the main entrances to the quarter is through the d'Amboise gate in the medieval walls. The restored clock tower nearby, which was built in 1852 on the site of a Byzantine tower and marks the southwest corner of the Collachium (Kollákio), has excellent views.

The architecture here is a mix of medieval, Neo-Classical and Levantine. Many of the houses have distinctive Ottoman overhanging wooden rooms, and mosques can be found throughout these streets. For those exploring the streets, the Hospice of the Tongue of Italy (1392) on Ippotón is worth a visit, as is the apse of

Panagía tou Boúrgou (All Holy of the Bourgos), just inside the Mylon (Jews') Gate, built by the Knights but mostly obliterated during World War II.

Library of Hafiz Ahmet Ağa

44 Orféos **22410 74090** **9:30am–3pm Mon-Sat** **Main public hols**

The Library of Hafiz Ahmet (1794) houses a chronicle of the 1522 siege of Rhodes. This is the stand-out of a collection of very rare Arabic and Persian manuscripts, including many beautifully illuminated 15th- and 16th-century Qur'ans. These Qur'ans were stolen in the 1990s, and discovered in London before being restored to the library. The library was the collection of an 18th-century diplomat, who was born to a wealthy Ottoman family. He donated the books to the city. While casual visitors can only access the front room, this free library offers a quiet retreat from the hustle and bustle of Rhodes.

Mosque of Süleyman the Magnificent

Orféos, corner Sokrátous **Closed to the public**

This pink mosque was first constructed soon after 1523 to commemorate the Sultan's victory over the Knights, and it is the oldest mosque in all of Rhodes. Rebuilt in 1808, using material from the original, it remains one of the town's major landmarks. The mosque's superb, but unsafe, minaret was pulled down and rebuilt during the 1990s, and the rest of the building was subsequently restored. It is still not open to the public.

Mosque of Ibrahim Pasha

Plátanos, corner Sofokléous **Daily**

Built in 1531 in honour of Süleyman the Magnificent's conquering of Rhodes, and refurbished in 1928, this mosque has an exquisite

↑ The Square of the Jewish Martyrs, in the heart of Rhodes's Old Town

interior. A new minaret was added in 1999. It is still an operating mosque, used regularly by local Muslims.

Ágious Fanoúrios

 Agíou Fanouríou, corner Omírou

The tiny, partly subterranean, frescoed Byzantine (dated 1335) church of Ágios Fanoúrios is close to the Mosque of Ibrahim Pasha. It is much loved locally, as Phanourios is the saint of lost objects, unrequited love and prostitutes. The traditional red-light district is scarcely a block away.

The Jewish Quarter

East from Platía Ippokrátous, the Bourg embraces Ovriakí. This was the Jewish Quarter from the 1st century AD until German occupation in 1944 (with a brief gap when one

← The pink-hued Mosque of Süleyman the Magnificent, with its rebuilt minaret

Grand Master expelled all the Jews), when Rhodian Jewry was transported to Auschwitz. East along Aristotélous is Platía Evréon Martýron (Square of the Jewish Martyrs), named for all those who perished in the extermination camp. A multilingual memorial of black granite dominates the square. The sole remaining synagogue, **Kadosh Shalom Synagogue and Museum**, stands nearby on Simíou, and has a good museum on the local Jewish community.

Kadosh Shalom Synagogue and Museum
 Simíou crnr Dosiádou ⏰ Apr–Oct: 10am–3pm Sun–Fri 🌐 rhodesjewish museum.org

Museum of Modern Greek Art

 Platía Sýmis 2 ⏰ 9am–2pm & 5–9pm Mon–Fri 🌐 mgamuseum.gr/en/ info.php

This museum is dedicated to 19th- and 20th-century art, and displays engravings, paintings and sculptures by local artists.

PALACE OF THE GRAND MASTERS
ΠΑΛΑΤΙ ΤΟΥ ΜΕΓΑΛΟΥ ΜΑΓΙΣΤΡΟΥ

⌂ Ippotón ☎ 22413 65270 🕐 Apr–Oct: 8am–8pm daily;
Nov–Mar: 8am–3pm Tue–Sun 🚫 Main public holidays

A fortress within a fortress, the Palace of the Grand Masters was the centre of power of the Knights of St John, a military religious order from Jerusalem who conquered Rhodes in 1309. They built epic fortifications and ruled the island for 200 years.

The Palace of the Grand Masters is the best-preserved of all of the castles built by the Knights. It was the seat of the 19 Grand Masters of the order, until the Knights were ejected from Rhodes by the Ottomans in the 16th century. The palace was the heart of the Collachium, or Knights' Quarter, and the last refuge for the population in times of danger.

Built in the 14th century, it survived siege and earthquakes, but was blown up by an accidental explosion in 1856.

The grand entrance, with twin horseshoe shaped towers ↓

💬 INSIDER TIP
Real Rhodes

Medieval Rhodes and Ancient Rhodes, two permanent exhibitions in the Palace of the Grand Masters, showcase historical finds from around the island and can be seen as part of a tour of the building.

1 The palace, built around a central courtyard, with paved geometric tiles, is lined with Hellenistic statues from Kos.

2 A mosaic featuring the mythical Gorgon Medusa is found in the Medusa Chamber.

3 The grand interior of the palace is inlaid with intricate mosaic floors and furnished with opulent gold objects.

Did You Know?

The castle was restored in the 1930s for use by Italian dictator Mussolini.

THE FIRST GRAND MASTER

The Knights were drawn from noble Roman Catholic families. Those who entered the Order of the Knights of St John swore vows of chastity, obedience and poverty. The first Grand Master of the Knights, the leader of the order who was elected for life, was Foulkes de Villaret (1305–19), a French knight. He negotiated to buy Rhodes from Genovese Admiral Vignolo de Vignoli. This left the Knights with the task of conquering the island's populace. The Knights of Rhodes, as they became known, remained here until defeat by the Ottomans in 1522. The Villaret name lives on in Villaré, one of the island's white wines.

The Street of the Knights, running through Rhodes Old Town for 610 m (2,000 ft)

> The Knights fortified the Dodecanese with around 30 castles, some of the best examples of medieval military architecture in Greece.

←

An arched bridge connecting two of the Knights' meeting places

STREET OF THE KNIGHTS

ΟΔΟΣ ΤΩΝ ΙΠΠΟΤΩΝ

Ippoton 1-9 **Daily**

The dramatically stone Street of the Knights, with nary a tree in sight, runs from the harbour to the Palace of the Grand Masters. It was the artery of the Old Town during the Knights' 200-year rule over Rhodes.

The medieval street is one of the most famous sights in Rhodes Old Town, and is lined by the Inns of the Tongues, or nationalities, of the Order of St John. Founded in the 11th century, the Order of Hospitallers of the Knights of St John guarded the Holy Sepulchre and tended Christian pilgrims in Jerusalem. They became a military order after the First Crusade (1096–9), but had to take refuge in Cyprus when Jerusalem fell in 1291. They bought Rhodes from the Genoese pirate Admiral Vignoli in 1306, but only conquered the town in 1309.

A Grand Master (p167) was elected for life to govern the Order, which was divided into seven Tongues, or nationalities: France, Italy, England, Germany, Provence, Spain and Auvergne. Each Tongue protected an area of city wall. Built in the 14th century in Gothic style, the Inns that line the Street of the Knights were used as meeting places for the military order, particularly in times of attack, when the Knights would muster here. The site of the German Inn is still unknown, but the others were largely restored in the early 20th century.

The Knights did not just conquer Rhodes, but many of the surrounding islands. They fortified the Dodecanese with around 30 castles, some of the best examples of medieval military architecture in Greece.

↑ A coat of arms on the exterior of an Inn of the Tongues

THE SEIGE OF RHODES

The Ottoman Empire attacked Rhodes in 1522, after an initial failed seige in 1480, when they were fought off by Grand Master D'Aubusson (right). Led by Sultan Süleyman the Magnificent with a force of 75,000 troops and over 300 ships, the Ottomans blockaded the citadel over the course of six months. From a garrison of 650 Knights, only 180 survived. They negotiated a safe departure, and seven years later found sanctuary on the island of Malta. Their final defeat came in 1798, when Malta was annexed by Napoleon.

A SHORT WALK
RHODES
OLD TOWN

Distance 3 km (2 miles) **Time** 30 minutes

The town of Rhodes has been inhabited for
more than 2,400 years. A city was first built
here in 408 BC, and when the crusading
Knights of St John conquered Rhodes in 1309
they built their citadel over these ancient
remains. The Knights' medieval citadel,
dominated by the Palace of the Grand Masters,
encircles the Old Town, which was entered
through one of the 11 gates built into the
defending wall. Koskinoú (St John's) gate,
which leads into the Bourg quarter, has the
best view of the city's defences.

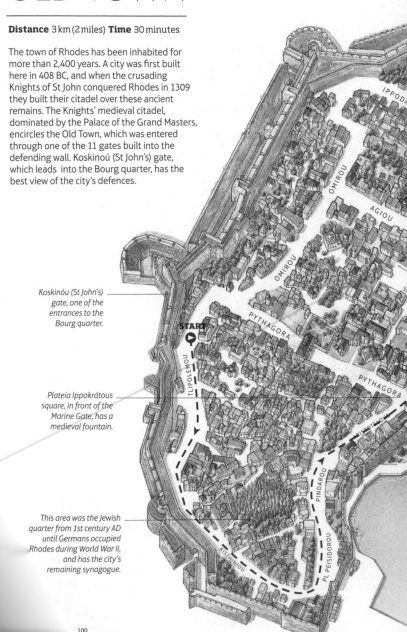

*Koskinóu (St John's)
gate, one of the
entrances to the
Bourg quarter.*

START

*Plateía Ippokrátous
square, in front of the
Marine Gate, has a
medieval fountain.*

*This area was the Jewish
quarter from 1st century AD
until Germans occupied
Rhodes during World War II,
and has the city's
remaining synagogue.*

IPPODAM

OMIROU

AGIOU

OMIROU

PYTHAGORA

TLIPOLEMOU

PYTHAGORA

PINDAROU

PL PEISIDOROU

KISTHINIOU

100

→N

Did You Know?

The Knights of St John were Crusaders who conquered Rhodes after leaving the Holy Land.

A collection of exquisite and rare Arabic and Persian manuscripts is kept at the Library of Ahmet Havuz (p164).

First built in 1523, the Mosque of Suleiman the Magnificent commemorates the Sultan's conquest of Rhodes (p164).

The final line of defence for the Knights, the Palace of the Grand Masters (p166) now has two permanent exhibitions.

Lining the Street of the Knights (p168) are the various Inns of the Knights, one for Germany, Spain, France and Italy.

Housed in the flamboyant Gothic Knights' hospital, built in 1481, the Archaeological Museum has a large collection (p162).

This Marine gate (Pýli Agías Aikaterínis), with twin towers, is the main route into the Old Town from the harbour.

The walls, dating from 1330, are up to 12 m (40 ft) thick and 4 km (2 miles) long.

APOLLONION

IPPODAMOU

ORFEOS

FINISH

SOKRATOUS

RIOU

TOUS

PPOLTON

APELLOU

RHODES NEW TOWN

NEA ΠΟΛΗ

The New Town (Neohóri) grew steadily after the Ottoman conquest, and it expanded even more during the Italian colonial period. Architecture here is marked by buildings from every era, running the gamut from old Greek cottages to modern high-rises, by way of Neo-Classical villas and Art Deco public buildings.

Did You Know?

Rhodes New Town actually dates from the Ottoman period, when it was created by displaced Greeks.

...ndráki Harbour

...rbour, lively with yachts ...rsion boats, is the ...in Rhodes, the link ...New and nearby ...e, locals take ...oll, or *vólta*. ...g statues ...trance, ...he

Nikólaos, now a lighthouse, which rises from the promontory past the three medieval windmills. Elegant public buildings, built by the Italians in the 1920s, line Mandráki harbour: the post office, law courts, town hall, police station and the National Theatre all stand in a row.

Nearby, on Plateía Eleftherías, the splendid church of the Evangelismós (Annunciation), a 1925 replica of the Knight's Church of St John has superb frescoes by the neo-Byzantine painter

Photis Kontoglou. Further along, the mock-Venetian-Gothic Government House (Nomarhío) has ornate decorations and is surrounded by grand vaulted arcades. Unfortunately there is no access to the general public.

At the north end of 7 Martíou is the Mosque of Murad Reis, with its graceful minaret. It was named after a Turkish admiral serving under Süleyman who was killed in the 1522 siege of Rhodes. Situated in the grounds is Villa Kleoboulos, which was home to the British writer Lawrence Durrell (*p72*) between 1945 and 1947. Also in the grounds is a cemetery for Ottoman notables.

Heading north from the area around Mandráki harbour,

The view across the shoreline of Rhodes New Town and out to sea

a pleasant stroll along the waterfront via crowded Élli beach leads to the northern tip of Rhodes town and island. The Hydrobiological Institute here houses the retro 1930s **Aquarium**. Set in a subterranean grotto, this contains nearly 40 tanks of sea life.

Aquarium

 Hydrobiological Institute, Ko Apr-Oct: 9am-8:30pm daily; Nov-Mar: 9am-4:30pm daily Main public hols rhodes-aquarium.hcmr.gr

---

②

Modern Greek Art Museum

100 Palms (Georgíou Harítou) roundabout 22410 43780 8am-2pm Tue-Sat, 5-8pm Fri

Housed in the Nestorideion Mansion, this contains Greece's best collection of 20th-century paintings outside Athens. All the big-name Greek artists are represented, including Spyros Vassiliou, Níkos Hatzikyriakos-Ghikas and Yiannis Tsarouhis.

---

③

Néa Agora

Mandráki is backed by the New Market, or Néa Agora, with its Ottoman domes and lively cafés. The most notable structure is a whimsical Art Deco gazebo where fish were once sold, now popular as a meeting place for people coming from outlying villages.

---

④

Monte Smith

Monte Smith (Ágios Stéfanos), a hill to the southwest of town, offers panoramic views over Rhodes town and the coast. It is named after the English Admiral Sir Sidney Smith, who in 1802, kept watch from there for Napoleon's fleet. The hill is the site of a 3rd-century-BC Hellenistic city that was excavated by the Italians.

THE COLOSSUS OF RHODES

One of the Seven Wonders of the Ancient World, the Colossus was a huge statue of Helios, the sun god, standing 32-40 m (105-130 ft) tall and made of marble and steel. It most likely stood at the harbour entrance, and was built to commemorate a military victory. An earthquake toppled it in 227 BC and the rubble lay there until 654 AD, when it was sold for scrap.

⑤

Rodíni Park

This beautiful park, around 3 km (2 miles) south of New Town, is now home to the Rhodian deer sanctuary, a perfect spot for a break from the crowded centre. Sights include a 3rd-century-BC necropolis with several Hellenistic, rock-cut tombs.

④

LÍNDOS
ΛΙΝΔΟΣ

🏠 50 km (31 miles) S of Rhodes Old Town 🚌🚌 From Rhodes
ℹ️ Platia Eleftherias; 22440 31900

Líndos was first inhabited in 3000 BC, and became a rich naval power. Now a National Historic Landmark, Líndos's pretty white village, Crusader castle and acropolis attracts visitors in large numbers.

The charming, pedestrianized village of Líndos is mainly visited for its historic sites, but it also has a wide stretch of beach, which curves around Líndos bay. Best visited in autumn or spring, when the streets aren't as crowded with visitors, the most pleasant way to arrive is by boat from Rhodes.

The village's winding lanes are fronted by imposing doorways which lead into the flower-filled courtyards of the unique Líndian houses, mainly *arhontiká* (mansions) built by rich sea captains between the 15th and 18th centuries; older houses mix Byzantine and Arabic styles. A few of these houses are open to the public for viewing. In the centre of the village lies the Byzantine church of the Panagía, complete with graceful bell tower and excellent frescoes by Gregory of Sými in 1779.

The Acropolis

Perched on a sheer precipice 125 m (410 ft) above the village, the spectacular acropolis here is a sign of Líndos's early wealth. The complex is crowned by the 4th-century-BC Temple of Líndian Athena, its remaining columns etched against the sky. The temple was among the most sacred sites in the ancient world, visited by Alexander the Great and supposedly by Herakles and Helen of Troy. This temple was joined by the Roman temple of Diocletian in the 3rd century AD. In the 13th century the Knights of St John fortified the acropolis with much higher walls, still looming over the town today.

The acropolis is open daily throughout summer, and closed on Mondays in winter.

INSIDER TIP
Líndos Lace

...ath up to the
...re women
...ace for
...s well

...ht

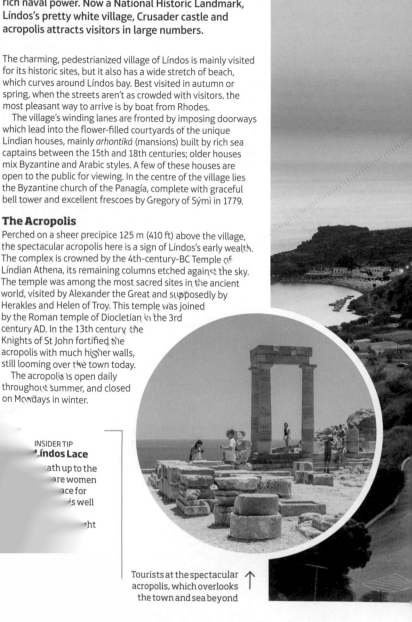

Tourists at the spectacular acropolis, which overlooks the town and sea beyond ↑

Did You Know?
—
Traditional mansions called *arhontiká* have distinctive carvings of ship's cables on the stonework.

↑ Th
I

EXPERIENCE MORE

5

Koskinoú
Κοσκινού

 10 km (6 miles) S of Rhodes town

This old village features traditional Rhodian houses with *votsalotó* (pebble-mosaic floors) and courtyards. The church of Isódia tis Theotókou has a multitiered bell tower. Nearby, Réni Koskinoú is the closest resort strip to Rhodes town, though beaches here are not the best.

6

Pigés Kallithéas
Πηγές Καλλιθέας

 Leoforos Kallitheas 80
 8am–8pm daily (closes earlier in winter)
 kallitheasprings.gr

South of Koskinoú lies Pigés Kallithéas, a former spa built in 1929 that has been restored to its former Art Deco glory. It's a wonderfully atmospheric spot with two rotundas, one fringed with palm trees. Fashion and film shoots, as well as weddings, occur here regularly. In the large rotunda

there's a small photo exhibit on the history of the place. The lido is used for beginners' scuba dives. Through the pines towards the south there are rocky coves with tavernas.

7

Faliráki
Φαληράκι

 15 km (9 miles) S of Rhodes town

Faliráki, one of Rhodes's most popular beach resorts, comprises two zones: Faliráki North, with its luxury hotels and a family-friendly vibe, and the southern zone, which was a young clubbers' resort in the 1980s and 90s. The party has now moved to other islands, but there are still fine beaches. For the more adventurous, there's bungee-jumping. The northern sector also offers the huge **Faliráki Water Park**.

South from Faliráki, rocky Ladikó Bay is worth a visit. It was used as a location for the Gregory Peck film *The Guns of Navarone*. Continuing in the same direction brings you to Afándou, with a good sandy beach and a pebbly

bay, lined with olive groves, at Traganoú. Near the start of the main road down to the sea sits the medieval chapel of Panagía Katholikí, with frescoes that include an almond-eyed Virgin Enthroned.

Faliráki Water Park
 Faliráki May–Oct: 9:30am–6pm daily (to 7pm Jun–Aug) water-park.gr

8

Eptá Pigés
Επτά Πηγές

 26 km (16 miles) S of Rhodes town

Eptá Pigés, or Seven Springs, is one of Rhodes's leading woodland beauty spots. Peacocks strut beside streams and waterfalls, and the springs feed a central reservoir. The springs were harnessed by the Italians to irrigate the orange groves of Kolýmbia to the east. The lake can be reached either by a woodland trail, or you can shuffle ankle-deep in water through a 185-m (605-ft) tunnel.

Further east along the coast, the 17th-century Moní Tsambíkas sits on a mountaintop at 300 m (985 ft). Legend has it that the 11th-century

Did You Know?

Feraklós castle was originally built as a pirate fortress before becoming a prison.

← The elegant, palm-fringed entrance to the spa complex at Pigés Kallithéas

The ruined pirate stronghold of Feraklós looming over Charáki

icon in the chapel was found by an infertile couple, who later conceived a child. The chapel subsequently became a place of pilgrimage for childless women to come to pray to the icon of the Virgin. They also pledge to call their child Tsambika for a girl or Tsambíkos for a boy, names unique to the Dodecanese.

Below the monastery lies Tsambíka beach, a superb stretch of sand that becomes very crowded in the tourist season. Various watersports are practised in the gentle water. The closest tavernas lie 2 km (1 miles) inland along the access road.

Arhángelos
Αρχάγγελος

📍 33 km (20 miles) S of Rhodes town 🚌

The Rhodes's largest village, Arhángelos lies in the Valley of Éthona, which is renowned for its oranges. The town itself is long famous for its colourful pottery, produced using time-honoured methods and featuring traditional Rhodian motifs. Only two workshops remain active, with sales outlets on the main highway.

In the centre, the church of Arhángeli Mihaïl and Gavriïl,

the village's patron saints, features a tiered bell tower and pebble-mosaic courtyard. Above the town sits a ruined Crusader castle, built by Grand Master Giovanni Battista Orsini in 1467 as part of the Knights' defences against the invading Ottomans. To the east lies the bay of Stegná, a low-key resort with an average sandy beach, but striking scenery and good tavernas.

Driving south towards Malóna, there are more, denser citrus groves and, closer to the sea, Feraklós castle. Now a ruin, it was built on the site of an ancient acropolis. The fortress has fantastic views over Agathi Bay and Charáki, once Malóna's port but now a low-key resort hugging a bay with a pebble beach and a taverna-lined promenade.

Moní Thárri
Μονή Θάρρι

📍 40 km (25 miles) S of Rhodes town 🚌 To Laérma, then walk ⏰ Daily

From the inland resort of Lárdos follow signs, or catch the bus, to Láerma, which is just north of Moní Thárri, famous for its 14th- to 15th-century frescoes. Reached by walking through a forest, the

monastery was hidden well inland to escape the attention of marauding pirates. Legend has it that the monastery was built by a Byzantine princess, who had been kidnapped by pirates; the Archangel Michael, now patron of Thárri, came to her in a dream promising deliverance, and in gratitude she founded the monastery upon her ransom.

The nave, apse and dome of the main church are covered with frescoes. In the transept are the most distinct frescoes, of the Evangelists Mark and Matthew, plus the Archangel Gabriel in an *Annunciation*. In the nave are scenes from the life of Christ, such as the *Storm on the Sea of Galilee*, *Meeting with the Samaritan Woman* and *Healing the Cripple*. The monastery offers accommodation, albeit quite basic, for visitors.

🔍 HIDDEN GEM
Panagía Katholikí

Just off the main from Afándou the 16th-cent Panagía Kat *votsalotó* mosaic) fresco a Pan att a

The lush green Butterfly Valley, famous for its Jersey tiger moths *(inset)* ↑

11

Petaloúdes

Πεταλούδες

⌂ 26 km (16 miles) SW of Rhodes town
☎ 22410 91998 📟

Petaloúdes, or Butterfly Valley, is a narrow leafy valley with a stream crisscrossed by wooden bridges. It teems not with butterflies, but with Jersey tiger moths from June to September. Thousands are attracted by the sap of the local oriental sweetgum (*Liquidambar orientalis*) trees, still extracted for industrial and medicinal use in Turkey. and pleasant, this pop-valley attracts walkers as lepidopterists, and it is peaceful in the ing before all the rive.

12 🕸

Ancient Ialysos and Moní Filerímou

Αρχαία Ιαλυσός and
Μονή Φιλερήμου

⌂ 11 km (7 miles) SW of Rhodes town 📟 Towards Trianda ⏰ May-Oct: 8am-8pm Tue-Fri, 8am-3pm Sat-Mon; Nov-Apr: 8am-3pm Tue-Sun

Ialysos fused with two other Doric city-states, Lindos and Kameiros, to create one capital, Rhodes, in 408 BC. As this new centre grew, Ialysos, Lindos and Kameiros lost their former importance. However, Ialysos proved a much fought-over site: the Byzantines were besieged by the Genoese there in 1248; the Knights of St John used it as a base before taking Rhodes town in 1309; and it was the headquarters of the Ottomans before their assault on the Knights in 1522. It was also used defensively by the Italians, as gun positions during World War II.

The only remnant of the acropolis is the 3rd-century BC Temple of Athena Polias and Zeus Poliefs on the hill-sides of beautiful Mount Vounára, by the church of Agios Geórgios Hostós. Inside the temple, the holder of the statue of Athena can be seen. To the south, the restored lion-head fountain is from the 4th century BC.

The mountain is home to cypresses and pines. Among the lush trees near the ruins

teems not with butterflies, y tiger moths from June to usands are attracted local oriental sweetgum *talis)* trees

replacement for the one the Italians themselves pulled down in 1941 to deprive Allied pilots of a navigational aid.

13

Kástro Kritinías
Καστρο Κρητινιας

🏛 **52 km (31 miles) SW of Rhodes town**

Boasting superb views west towards various islets, Kástro Kritinías was erected by the Knights during the 14th century, in visual line-of-sight with their forts on Hálki and Alimiá.

The vaulted chapel has been restored, but otherwise the fortification is ruined, with half-intact walls. To the east of the Kástro spread the white houses of Kritinía village.

14

Ancient Kameiros
Αρχαία Κάμειρος

🏛 **36 km (22 miles) SW of Rhodes town** ☎ **22413 65200** 🚌 🕐 **May-Oct: 8am-8pm daily; Nov-Apr: 8am-3pm Tue-Sun** 🔒 **Main public hols**

Discovered in 1859, this Doric city thrived during the 5th century BC. Founded by Althaemenes of Crete, it was probably destroyed in a

large earthquake in 142 BC, yet it remains one of the best-preserved Classical Greek cities.

Here you'll find the remains of a 3rd-century BC Doric temple, an altar to the Greek sun god Helios, public baths and a 6th-century BC cistern, which supplied 400 families with fresh water. The 6th-century BC Temple of Athena Polias is on the top terrace, below which are the remains of the Doric stoa, a covered walkway, 206 m (675 ft) long.

of the ancient city sits Moní Filerímou, its domed chapels decorated with the cross of the Knights and the coat of arms of Grand Master Pierre d'Aubusson. Moní Filerímou has been a place of worship for 2,000 years, and layers of history and traditions can be seen here from numerous occupiers and eras.

The main attraction is Our Lady of Filérimos, the Italian reconstruction of the Knights' 14th-century church of the Virgin Mary. It is a complex of four chapels: the main one was built in 1306, and leads to three others. The innermost chapel has a Byzantine floor decorated with a red mosaic fish. The Italians laid out a Calvary from the entrance of the monastery: a walkway passing the Stations of the Cross, ending at a huge cross, 18-m (60-ft) tall, which visitors can climb. This is a 1995

→

Visitors strolling the well-preserved ruins of Ancient Kameiros

 Stone steps leading
to the ruins of a castle
at Asklipió

⑮
Asklipió
Ασκλήπιο

🏛 62 km (39 miles) SW
of Rhodes town

A quiet hill village just inland
from the coast, Asklipió's
central, 11th-century church
Kímisi Theotókou is its pride
and joy. Nearly every surface
of the interior is decorated
with lively 15th-century
frescoes in cartoon-like
sequence. These depict
traditional New Testament

WINDSURFING AT PRASSONÍSI

The unique geography
of isolated Prassonísi
has created fairly
constant winds, and
the bay has long been
known as the major
windsurfing venue on
Rhodes. As a result, a
number of schools and
rental facilities have
sprung up here.
Among the best for
instruction
and rent equip-
ment Wind4Fun
(wind4fun.pl/
en), as kite-

episodes, plus the entire Old
Testament Book of Genesis
from the Creation to the
Expulsion from Eden.

Kímisi Theotókou
⊘ ⏰ 9am–5pm daily; fee
includes entry to small
adjacent folklore museum

⑯
Émbona
Έμπωνας

🏛 55 km (34 miles) SW
of Rhodes town 🚌

On the western flanks of
Mount Attávyros, the
atmospheric village of Émbona
has been associated with the
Rhodian wine industry since
the still-extant CAIR co-op was
founded by the Italians in
1928. Now, however, there are
other better and smaller
private microwineries to tour
and taste wines at, including
Kounakis and **Alexandris**,
which offers an excellent red
(Citizen of the World) and rosé

(Apiro). The village itself is
exceedingly popular with
coach tours, especially on
"Greek nights", which usually
feature dancing and singing.

Alexandris Winery
⊘ 🏛 Émbona 📞 2246 041349

⑰
Southeast Coast Beaches

🏛 60 km (37 miles) S
of Rhodes town

Between Glýstra cove and
the far southwestern tip of
Rhodes, a string of excellent
sandy beaches beckons,
developed to lesser or greater
degrees. Kiotári has some of
the busiest, with tavernas
across the beach-front road,
thanks to several mega-hotels
just inland. Gennádi, next up,
has a few tavernas and music
bars right on the beach but
otherwise endless coarse
sand in both directions.
Plimýri Bay has lovely, finer

sand but can get very windy. Sugar-sandy Kórakas can be reached from the Ágios Pávlos Italian agricultural colony by a dirt track; it is so pristine that sea turtles are rumoured to nest there. The final beach on the tip is wild Prassonísi; windy conditions have made it a popular windsurfing spot.

18

Monólithos
Μονόλιθος

 80 km (50 miles) SW of Rhodes town

Monólithos is the most important village in the southwest, and is named after its monolith, a crag with a dramatic 250-m (820-ft) drop to the sea. Situated at the foot of Mount Akramýtis, the village is 2 km (1 mile) from Monólithos castle. This impregnable 15th-century fortress, built by Grand Master d'Aubusson, has a spectacular position on top of the vast grey rock. Its massive walls enclose two small 15th-century chapels, Agios Panteleïmon and Agios Geórgios, both decorated with frescoes. Views from the top of the walls are impressive.

Down a mostly paved road south from the castle lie several secluded beaches at Foúrni; these are some of the best on this coast, though the only facility is a seasonal drinks-and-sandwich shack.

Between Émbona and Monólithos, the hill village of Siánna is famous for its honey and fiery *soúma* – a grape-pomace spirit, like Cretan *raki* or Italian *grappa*. The villagers were granted a licence by the Italians to make the spirit; you can sample both the firewater and honey at roadside cafés. The village houses have clay roofs, and Ágios Panteleïmon has 18th-century frescoes.

↓ Monólithos castle, dating from the 1400s, perched atop a huge rocky hill

EAT

Mavrikos
This family-owned spot serves creative baked dishes and seafood, with a limited meat menu. Excellent wines.

 Main taxi square, Líndos **22440 31232**

€€€

Paraga
Honest rural food is prepared here by friendly folk who clearly love what they do.

Apóllona village **paraga-apollona.gr**

€€€

Platanos
Dine at the most idyllic tables on Rhodes, under plane trees and beside two gushing fountains.

Lower platía, Lahaniá village **lachania platanostaverna.com**

€€€

Lipsí

Λειψοί

🚤 Lipsí town 🛈 Town hall, Lipsí 🌐 lipsi-island.com

Only 10 sq km (4 sq miles) long, Lipsí is a magical island of green hills dotted with blue and white chapels, and colourfully painted village houses. It is one of many islands claiming to be the place in legend where the nymph Kalypso beguiled Odysseus, keeping him from his wife Penelope for seven years. Officially owned by the monastery at Pátmos since Byzantine times, Lipsí is a haven for traditional Greek island life, producing some good local wines and cheeses. It has excellent beaches, and is popular for day excursions from Pátmos and Léros.

The main settlement of Lipsí town is wrapped around the harbour, where the main attraction is the blue-domed church of Agios Ioánnis. Inside, the unique icon of the Panagía is known for the lilies that miraculously bloom within the frame on 23 August, the date of the Virgin's reception into paradise in Orthodox belief, and when the island's main religious festival is held. In the town hall, on the main square, the interesting **Ecclesiastical and Folklore Museum** features an odd collection of finds, from neatly labelled bottles of holy water to traditional costumes. These sights are all signposted from the harbour.

There are good, sandy beaches easily walkable from town at Liendoú and Kámbos, with an informal taxi service to the more distant beaches of Platýs Gialós, Monodéndri, Kímisi and the twin sandy

... Folklore ...

Astypálea

Αστυπάλαια

🚤 11 km (7 miles) E of Astypálaia town 🚤 Astypálaia town 🛈 Near Kástro, Astypálaia town; astypalaia.gr

With its dazzling white fortified maze of the old capital, Hóra, and its scenic coastline, the island of Astypálea is charming. The westernmost spot in the Dodecanese, it is a remote island with high cliffs and a hilly interior. There are many coves and sandy bays along the coast, which was once the lair of Maltese pirates. A backwater in Classical times, Astypálea flourished in the Middle Ages from 1207 to 1537, under the rule of the Venetian Quirini family.

Astypálea town, the island's capital, grew up around the island's original centre, Hóra, which still forms the maze-like upper town. Equally well-preserved is the splendid Venetian *kástro* of the Quirini family, on the site of the ancient acropolis. Houses were built into the *kástro*'s walls for protection, and the Quirini coat of arms can still be seen on the fortification's gateway. Within its walls are two churches: the silver-domed, 14th-century Panagía Portaïtissa (Madonna of the Castle Gates), and the 14th-century Agios Geórgios (St George), built on the site of an ancient temple.

Livádi, the main resort, lies west of Astypálea town in a fertile valley with citrus groves

600 BC

The year soldiers were caught in a volanic eruption at Agios Antónis and petrified.

and cornfields. It has a long beach. From Livádi a dirt track leads west to remote but gorgeous Kaminakia cove, with two tavernas and protection from most winds.

North of Astypálea town, on the narrow land bridge between the two sides of the island, lies Maltezána (also known as Análipsi), named after the marauding pirates who once frequented it. On the northeastern peninsula is the "lost lagoon", a deep inlet at the hamlet of Vathý.

Tílos

Τήλος

🚤🚤 Livádia 🛈 Megálo Choriό; tilos.gr

Remote Tílos is a tranquil island, more known for its good walking and bird-watching than its beaches. Away from the barren beaches, Tílos has a lush hinterland, with farms growing everything from citrus to almonds. Its hills are scattered with chapels and ruins of castles left by the Knights of St John, who ruled here from 1309 until 1522.

The maze-like old capital of Astypálea, with the *kastró* lit up above

Livádia, the main settlement, has a tree-fringed pebble beach sweeping round its bay, with the picturesque blue and white church of Agios Nikólaos dominating the waterfront.

Built on the site of the ancient city of Telos, Megálo Horió is 8 km (5 miles) uphill from Livádia, and is reached by bus. Its *kástro* was built by the Knights of St John, who incorporated a Classical gateway and stone from the ancient acropolís. The town's Palaeontological Museum has the fossilized bones of miniature elephants found in the Harkadió cave across the valley from Megálo Horió; the castle of Messariá above it marks the spot.

The most interesting, and likely to be open, of several medieval churches in and around Megálo Horió is Ágios Ioánnis Theológos, with appealing 16th- and 17th-century frescoes.

West of Megálo Horió is the little fishing village of Ágios Antónios, with at least one taverna open in summer. For those who wish to swim, Pláka beach, 2 km (1 mile) west, is an ideal spot.

High above on the west coast, the Byzantine Moní Agíou Pandelímonos is the island's main attraction. Set in a spring-fed oasis, this fortified monastery is famous for its sunset views. Founded in 1470 it has circular chapels, a pebble-mosaic courtyard and medieval monks' cells. The dome of the church has a version of Christ *Pandokrátor* (1776) by Gregory of Sýrni, who also executed the Holy Trinity in the apse, a carved *témblon* (icon screen) that dates from 1714.

Mikró Horió, below castle at Messariá, roofless abandon Those resident stone roofs to Livádia wh abandon 1950s. night nat re

STAY

Ilidi Rock
This hillside apart-hotel is the poshest on the island.

Livádia, Tílos
ilidirock.gr

€€€

Kilindra Studios
The island's first, and still the best, boutique lodging.

Southwest slope of Hóra, Astypálea
astipalea.com.gr

€€€

Aretanassa Hotel
Hotel in a historic former sponge-factory.

Emborió quay, Hálki
aretanassa-hotel.gr

€€€

Nefeli
A comfortable bungalow hotel with cheerful decor.

Behind Kámbos beach, Lipsí
lipsinefelihotel.com

€€€

22

Hálki
Χάλκη

🚢 Emborió 🚹 Piátsa, Emborió; www.dimosc halkis.gr

> Its Crusader castle, perched high on a crag, is worth a visit for the coat of arms and Byzantine frescoes in the ruined chapel. On a clear day you can see Crete.

Hálki was once a thriving sponge-fishing island, but was virtually abandoned when its sponge divers emigrated to Florida in search of work in the early 1900s. Tourism has steadily replaced the trade as the island has been smart-ened up. While it used to be a fertile island, the water table was infiltrated by sea water and it is now barren, with fresh water shipped in by tanker and produce imported from Rhodes.

Hálki's harbour and only settlement, Emborió is a quiet and picturesque village with a Neo-Classical flavour. The main sight in Emborió is the church of Ágios Nikólaos with its elegant bell tower, the highest in the Dodecanese, tiered like a wedding cake. The church is also known for its magnificent black-and-white *votsalotó*, a pebble-mosaic courtyard depicting birds and the tree of life. The watchful eye painted over the main door is to ward off evil spirits.

A row of restored windmills stands above the harbour, which also has an Italianate town hall and post office, plus a fine stone clock tower. Nearby is the small and sandy Póndamos beach, which is suitable for children as it is protected and shallow.

The island is almost traffic-free, so it is ideal for walkers. An hour's walk uphill from Emborió is the abandoned former capital of Horió. Its Crusader castle, perched high on a crag, is worth a visit for the coat of arms and Byzantine frescoes in the ruined chapel. On a clear day you can see Crete. The Knights of St John built the castle on an ancient acropolis, using much of the earlier stone.

The Byzantine church of the Panagía (Virgin Mary) below the castle has interesting frescoes, and is the hub of an annual festival held on 14–15 August, the only time the building opens. Clinging to the mountainside opposite is the church of Stavrós (the Cross).

From Horió you can follow the road west to the 18th-century Moni Agíou Ioánnou Prodrómou (St John the Baptist). The round-trip walk takes about four hours, or is a 20-minute drive. The mon-astery courtyard is shaded by a giant juniper tree. It is best to visit in the early morning or to stay overnight: the care-takers will offer you a cell.

Did You Know?

Sponge divers used to descend to depths of 30 m (99 feet) – without using any diving equipment.

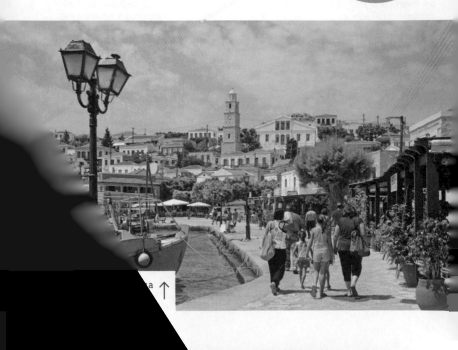

→
A unique tomb
cut into the rock
at Kastellórizo

 INSIDER TIP
Day Trip to Turkey

The Kastellórizans do their shopping and even get their haircuts in Kaş, just across the water in Turkey. The most reliable boat making the crossing is the Meis Express (*www.meis express.com/en/home*).

You can walk from the settlement Emborió to the pebbly beaches of Trahía and Gialí, below Horió, or more ambitiously to Aréta on the north coast. Occasional excursions go east to deserted Alimiá island, where Germany berthed some submarines in World War II. There are several small chapels in the derelict village – abandoned in the 1960s – and a ruined castle.

 23

Kastellórizo

Καστελλόριζο

🔹 3 km (2 miles) S of Kastellórizo town
🔹 Kastellórizo town
🔹 500 m (1,640 ft) N of port; 22460 49269

Remote Kastellórizo is the most far-flung Greek island, just two nautical miles from Kaş in Turkey but over 70 nautical miles from Rhodes. Known locally as Megísti (the biggest), it is the largest of 14 islets. It was isolated until the airport opened up tourism in 1987. Kastellórizo has no beaches, but its clear seas, full of marine life, are excellent for snorkelling. The local population has declined from 12,000 in the 19th century to just under 500 today. It was shelled from Anatolia during World War I (when the French held the island), enjoyed a brief 1930s revival as a seaplane stop on routes to the Middle East. It was evacuated during World War II and devastated by looting and a July 1944 fuel dump explosion. Fortunes only really revived in 1991 after Kastellórizo served as the location for Oscar-winning film *Mediterraneo*, attracting numerous visitors. Now the quay of this back-water bustles with tavernas and impromptu celebrations.

Kastellórizo town (including little Mandráki suburb) is the island's only settlement, with reputedly the best natural harbour between Mílos and Beirut. Above the town, the half-ruined Knights' castle (completed during the 15th century) enjoys spectacular views over nearby islets and the Turkish coast. It was nicknamed the Red Castle (Kastello Rosso) due to its reddish masonry, and the moniker quickly got applied to the entire island. Today, the museum inside the castle displays lighthouse parts, frescoes and pottery.

A rubber-raft trip southeast from Kastellórizo town to the spectacular Perastá Cave should not be missed; the large cave is famed for its stalactites and the eerie and strange light effects on the water. On a tour, you can sometimes hear (but not see) monk seals in an adjacent, but inaccessible grotto.

VOTSALOTÓ MOSAICS

These mosaics were used for floors in the Dodecanese from Byzantine times onwards. An exquisite art for well as a functional piece of architecture, they we made from sea pebbles wedged together to form kaleidoscope of raised patterns. Kept wet, the n also helped to keep houses cool. Early exampl abstract, formal and mainly geometric desig circles. Later on the decorations became mo boyant, with floral patterns and symbol lives of the householders with ships, fis

↑ Dusk at the harbour of Kos's old town, with boats and yachts moored for the night

24

KOS

ΚΩΣ

27 km (16 miles) W of Kos town 🚌Aktí Koudouriótou, Kos town 🚍Kos town 🛈Kos town; 2242360400

The second largest island in the Dodecanese, Kos has attracted settlers since 3000 BC with its pleasant climate and fertile land. This also attracted occupiers throughout history, including the Knights of St John, Ottomans and the British, until Kos's unification with Greece in 1948. Kos is now a popular holiday resort, with some of the best beaches in the Dodecanese.

Kos Town

🏖 🚌Aktí Koudouríotou 🛈Artemisías, corner of Epiharmoú

s town is arrayed around the
r. The harbour bristles
oats and pavement
ave with tourists dur-
h season. There are
pines and gardens
.
ed by its Castle
uch of old Kos
d during an
This
ent ruins,
d

Ancient and modern sit side by side here: Nafklírou, or "Bar Street", runs beside the ancient agora, but is now a shadow of its former self, with many premises permanently shut. Hippocrates's ancient plane tree, in Platía Platánou, is said to have been planted by him 2,400 years ago. Despite its 14 m (46 ft) diameter, the present tree is only about 700 years old, though possibly a descendant of the original. The adjacent fountain was built in 1792 by Gazi Hasan Pasha, to serve the nearby Loggia Mosque; the water gushed into the ancient marble sarcophagus that is still there. A bridge from Platía Platánou leads over a busy boulevard to the **Castle of the Knights** (Kástro Neratziá), finished in 1514; the gateway is carved with the coat of arms of Fernández de Heredia, Grand Master of the Order from 1376 to 1396. The inner keep and battlements were built between 1450 and 1478 from stone and marble, including blocks from the Asklepion (p188). The fortress was an important defence for the Knights Hospitaller in the event of any Ottoman attack.

South of Platía Platánou, the site of the ancient agora is a series of ruins from every era, from the original Hellenistic city to Byzantine buildings. Built over by the Knights, the ancient remains were revealed in the 1933 earthquake. Highlights include the ruins of the Temple of Pandemos Aphrodite and mosaic floors depicting ancient heroes Orpheus and Herakles. A 5th-century Christian basilica was also discovered.

The town's **Archaeological Museum** has an excellent collection of the island's Hellenistic and Roman finds, including a 4th-century-BC marble statue of Hippocrates welcoming Asklepios to Kos and 2nd-century statues of Dionysos with Pan and a satyr.

> **Bros Thermá hot springs are a wonderful spot, created by scalding water emerging from a sluice in the hillside.**

The most impressive of the Roman remains is the **Casa Romana**. This was the villa of a wealthy family and inside are superb mosaic floors depicting a lion and a leopard attacking stags. A gallery of small artifacts rounds off what is essentially a museum of 3rd- to 4th-century domestic Roman life.

Set back off the road down an avenue of cypresses is the ancient *odeion* (theatre). It has rows of marble benches (first-class seats) and limestone blocks for non-aristocats. It is now frequently used as a concert venue.

The excavations opposite reveal a mix of historical periods. There are Mycenaean remains, a tomb dating from the Geometric period and Roman houses with some fine mosaics, now mostly covered for protection.

Despite all the historic sites, most visitors come for Kos's sandy beaches. Those on the southwest shore are some of the finest in the Dodecanese, while the northwest bays are ideal for water sports.

Castle of the Knights
⊕ 🏛 Platía Platánou
📞 22420 27927 🕐 Apr-Oct: 8am-8pm daily; Nov-Mar: 8am-3pm Tue-Sun

Archaeological Museum
⊕ 🏛 Platía Eleftherías
📞 22420 28326 🕐 Apr-Oct: 8am-8pm Tue-Sun; Nov-Mar: 8am-3pm daily

Casa Romana
🏛 Grigoríou tou Pémptou, corner Vasiléos Pávlou
📞 22420 23234 🕐 8:30am-3pm Tue-Sun

Bros Thermá

🏛 11 km (7 miles) S of Kos town

Bros Thermá hot springs is a wonderful spot, created by scalding water emerging from a sluice in the hillside. It is very popular in the evenings, especially on moonlit nights. Take sturdy footwear; the carpark is some distance away.

EAT

Ampeli
Mezedes-only taverna with a good wine list.

🏛 2 km (1 miles) E of Tingáki central crossroads
🌐 ampelirestaurant.gr

€ € €

Pote tin Kyriaki
Lots of veggie dishes and assorted seafood.

🏛 Pisándrou 9, Kos Old Town 📞 22420 48460

€ € €

Hasan
Hasan serves savoury kebabs and veggies.

🏛 Crossroads, Platáni village 📞 22420 20230

€ € €

Palia Pigi
Basic but impeccable fare in an idyllic spot.

🏛 Modern Pylí village 📞 22420 41510

€ € €

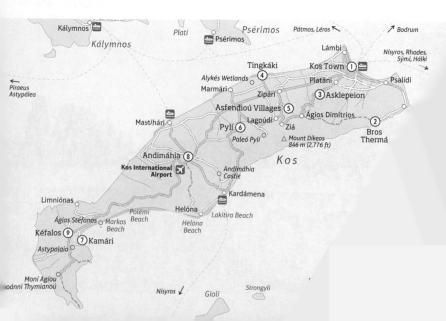

③

Asklepion

📍 4 km (2 miles) NW of Kos town ☎ 22420 28326 🚌 🕐 May-Oct: 8am-8pm Tue-Fri, 8am-3pm Sat-Mon & public hols; Nov-Apr: 8am-3pm Tue-Sun

One of Greece's most important Hellenistic sites, Asklepion was a sanctuary, school and medical centre combined. With its white marble terraces cut into a pine-clad hill with spectacular views, the site was chosen in the 4th century BC to encourage rest and recuperation and it still exudes an air of tranquillity. It was built in the 4th century BC after the death of Hippocrates and was the most famous of ancient Greece's 300 *asklepieia* dedicated to Asklepios, god of healing. The doctors, priests of Asklepiados, were practitioners of famous Hippocrates's methods. and the cult's symbol of the snake, once used to seek healing herbs, is now the emblem of modern Western medicine.

There are three levels: the first has a 3rd-century-BC porch and 1st-century-AD Roman baths; the second has a 4th-century-BC Altar of Apollo and Temple of Apollo from the 2nd- to 3rd-century-AD; and on the third level is the Doric Temple of Asklepios from the 2nd century BC.

___

④

Tingkáki

📍 12 km (7 miles) W of Kos town 🚌

The popular coastal resorts of Tingkáki and neighbouring Marmári have long white sand beaches and steady breezes ideal for windsurfing. The nearby Alykés Saltmarsh is perfect for bird-watching. The numerous wetland species here include small waders like the avocet and the black-winged stilt, with its long pink legs; flamingos are frequent visitors, as well.

___

⑤

Asfendioú Villages

📍 14 km (9 miles) W of Kos town

The Asfendioú villages of Zía Asómatos, Evangelístria, Ágios Dimítrios and Lagoúdi are a cluster of picturesque hamlets on the craggy and wooded slopes of Mount Díkeos. These mountain villages have all managed to retain some traditional character, with whitewashed houses and attractive churches. The highest village, Zía, has become the epitome of a traditional Greek village, at least to the organizers of the many coach tours that regularly descend upon it, especially towards sunset. A paved road leads from the Asklepion, via Ágios Dimítrios and Asómatos, to Zía. Alternatively, Lagoúdi, the lowest village, is less commercialized and is home to the unmissable hilltop church of Génnisis Theotókou, which has a festival on 8 September. It is renowned for the frescoes created by Nikos Vlahogiannis, an iconographer, in the 1980s. The road continues from Lagoúdi to Palaió Pylí.

___

⑥

Pylí

📍 15 km (9 miles) W of Kos town 🚌

The deserted Byzantine town of Paleó Pylí is perched on a crag 4 km (2 miles) above the farming village of Pylí, with the remains of its castle walls built into the rock. Just below, the 11th-century church of the

A white church
on Kastrí islet, in the
midst of turquoise sea

⑨
Kéfalos

🚗 38 km (23 miles) SW
of Kos town

Kéfalos, on the mountainous
peninsula inland from Kamári,
is known for its thyme, honey
and cheeses. Sights include
a tiny ruined fortress of the
Knights Hospitaller and a line
of derelict windmills on the
ridge above.

More interesting, south of
Kéfalos, are the ruins of
Panagía Palatianí, a 9th- or
10th-century chapel built of
ancient masonry, probably
pilfered from Astypalaia,
Hippocrates's birthplace.
Some 7 km (4 miles) beyond
Kéfalos is Agíou Ioánni
Thymianoú monastery.

Ypapandí (Presentation of
Jesus) was built by Blessed
Christodoulos using ancient
columns, before he went to
Pátmos (p158).

In modern Pylí lies the
Harmylio, the purported grave
of king of legend Harmylos –
but actually a Hellenistic
family tomb with 12 underground niches. On top, built
reusing ancient masonry, sits
Stavrós chapel.

---

⑦
Kamári

🚗 30 km (19 miles) SW
of Kos town 🚌

Kamári is a good base for
exploring the southwest coast
where the island's best
beaches can be found. A half-
dozen of these in a row are
signposted just east of
Kamári, down steep tracks
(part paved) from the main
highway. With its golden sand,
Magic (Polémi) is the best of
the lot and has a naturist
section, followed by Markos
(Langádes), with its juniper-
stablized dunes. At the far
east end of Kamári bay itself
stands the 5th-century
Christian basilica of Ágios
Stéfanos, once Kos's premier

The steps and niches
at the archaeological
site of Asklepion

Byzantine monument but
now in deplorable condition,
its mosaics of peacocks and
ducks covered in thick gravel
and its columns knocked over.
Still, it's an atmospheric spot,
right opposite Kastrí islet, a
small island with the church of
Ágios Nikolaos, now popular
as a wedding destination.

---

⑧
Andimáhia

🚗 25 km (16 miles) W of
Kos town 🚌

Andimáhia village is best
known for its restored central
windmill, now a small museum,
and eponymous nearby castle,
4 km (2 miles) southeast.
Constructed by the Knights
Hospitallers during the 14th
century atop Byzantine foundations, this castle served as a
vital lookout, as the island was
bombarded by pirates in the
same era. In the early 2000s,
the massive crenellated battlements and entry gatetower
were restored. The inner
gateway still bears the coat of
arms of the Grand Master
Pierre d'Aubusson (served
1476–1503), known for his
defence of Rhodes against the
Ottomans, and there are two
small chapels within the walls.
Well worth the detour, it also
has good views over resort
town Kardámena. The road
north from the town leads to
the port town of Mastichari.

HIPPOCRATES

The first holistic healer
and "father of modern
medicine", Hippocrates
was born in 460 BC on
Kos and died in about
375 BC on Thessaly. He
was the first physician
to classify diseases,
and he introduced new
methods of diagnosis
and treatment. He
taught on Kos, and the
Asklepion was set up
using his methods. His
disciples wrote the
Hippocratic Oath, to
cure rather than harm.

25

LÉROS
ΛΕΡΟΣ

EXPERIENCE **The Dodecanese**

🚩 Parthéni 🚌 Lakkí, Agía Marína 🚌 Plateía Plátanos, Plátanos 🛈 Harbourfront, Lakkí; www.leros.gr

Léros is marked by a varied history of occupation – including by the Italians from 1912 until 1943, who left a unique collection of modernist buildings. United with Greece in 1948, Léros was subsequently used as a prison for political dissidents by the junta. Tourism is low-key, but life here is traditional and the locals are friendly and very welcoming.

①

Lakkí

Lakkí, the main port and former capital when Léros was occupied by Italians, has one of the best natural harbours in the Aegean, and it served as an anchorage point in turn for the Italian, German and British fleets. Today the town resembles a disused film set, full of 1930s buildings, the legacy of Italian attempts to rebuild Lakkí to Mussolini's vision of a Fascist dream town. Around the bay at Teménia,

site of the former Italian naval base, sit huge dry docks, which remain some of the busiest in the Aegean.

Housed in an Italian-dug underground gallery, the **War Museum** at nearby Merikiá tells the story of a battle that took place here in November 1943 with histrionic recordings, military debris and interesting archival footage from the aftermath.

War Museum

🚇 Tunnel, Merikiá 📞 22470 28199 🕙 10am–1pm daily

②

Plátanos

🚶 4 km (2 miles) N of Lakkí

Expelled by the Italians, native Lerians moved north to Plátanos, now the island capital. Straddling a hilltop, the town's houses spill down

descending from
ne *kástro* above
ge of Plátanos ↑

to the little port of Pandéli and to the fishing village of Agía Marína. Perched above the village, the Byzantine *kástro* offers fine views. Renovated by the Venetians and Knights of St John, it houses Panagía tou Kástrou (the Madonna of the Castle), a church that is famous for its miraculous icon.

---

③
Pandéli

 3 km (2 miles) NE of Lakkí

Pandéli, located near Lakkí, is a fishing port with a tree-fringed pebble beach and several tavernas. Immediately south, the Vromólithos bay has a number of sandy coves

Did You Know?

In Léros, property passes down the female line, a remnant of the early worship of Artemis.

facing Agía Kyriakí islet, more tavernas and accommodation.

The road north from Plátanos, lined with Neo-Classical mansions built from 1880 and 1920, leads to Agía Marína, the main port for local excursion boats. Here, too, are more whimsical-looking Italian-built public buildings, in particular the customs house, the fish market and the post office.

---

④
Krithóni

 5 km (3 miles) NW of Lakkí

From Agía Marína, the coastal road heads west to Krithóni, with the Commonwealth War Graves Commission's well-maintained cemetery for the 184 Allied casualties of the 1943 Battle of Léros. Beyond the cemetery, Álinda is the main Lerian resort, with a long, narrow pebble beach.

The Historical and Folklore Museum highlights the Battle of Léros, and has costumes and musical instruments.

Little remains of the once-powerful Temple of Artemis. These ruins, a few carved blocks of stone and fragments of pillars, now overlook the airport further north from the resort at Álinda.

---

⑤
Xirókambos

 4 km (2 miles) S of Lakkí

The sleepy fishing port of Xirókambos is in a shored southeaste surrounded by o overlooked by 3rd-century Lepída, with preserve contain Pana mo ci

↑ Agía Saavas on a rocky spur overlooking the island of Kálymnos

26

KÁLYMNOS
ΚΑΛΥΜΝΟΣ

🚌 Póthia, Myrtiés 🚍 Behind the market place, Póthia
ℹ️ Town hall, Póthia; www.kalymnos-isl.gr

Famous as a sponge-fishing island, Kálymnos's history can be traced back to Bronze Age times, though most surviving monuments are of the Byzantine era. Today, Kálymnos is known as one of the top rock-climbing destinations in the world thanks to the rocky landscape and breathtaking views of the Aegean Sea.

①

Póthia

The capital and main port of the island is a busy working harbour. Wedged between two mountains, the town's pastel-hued houses extend a long way inland from the quay. The waterfront is lined with and tavernas, and the landmarks are the named Italian like the adminis-g (1926–34), the –4), which is covered ver-domed hrist). edral d by e

mermaid on the quay is one of 43 works donated to the island by local sculptors Irene and Mihalis Kokkinos.

The state-of-the-art Archaeological Museum, features the *Lady of Kalymnos*, a 3rd- or 2nd-century BC bronze retrieved by fishermen in 1994. The Maritime and

Folklore Museum offers fascinating photos showing the history of Póthia and a miscellany of old specialized seafaring equipment.

An hour's ride east of Póthia, the islet of Psérimos has a sandy beach in its port town, Avlákia; if it's crowded, you'll have to hike to one of three more remote beaches; the best is Grafiótissa.

②

Chrysoheriás

🏛️ Póthia 🕐 Daily

A well-preserved fortress built by the Knights to defend the town, the Knights of St John castle at Chrysoheriás looms over Póthia. Inside the walls are two churches, one with Byzantine frescoes.

The Byzantine citadel of Péra Kástro is just to the

SPONGE FISHING

Kálymnos has been a sponge-fishing centre from ancient times, although fishing restrictions and two blights since the 1960s have all but wiped out the trade. Men diving for natural sponges, which were used for cosmetic and industrial purposes, were weighed down with rocks or used crude air apparatus. Many men were drowned or died of the bends. Now most of the former sponge fleet is engaged in commercial deep-sea fishing.

 hamlet, has a huge plane tree, a fountain with drinkable water and the remains of ancient walls. It is also the start of a popular walk to the Evangelístria district in Póthia.

---

 ⑤

Télendos

🚗 11 km (7 miles) NW of Póthia

Served by frequent shuttle-boat from Myrtiés, Télendos is perfect for a hideaway holiday, with a few rooms to rent, one proper hotel, tavernas and beaches. It is also a popular spot on the island for rock climbing. There are Roman ruins, the remains of the Agía Triáda basilica, a ruined 13th-century monastery and a trail up to the Byzantine chapel of Ágios Konstandínos.

---

northeast, immediately above Horió, the former capital. Péra Kástro was inhabited from the 11th to the 18th centuries, but is now an atmospheric ruin with several churches, some with frescoes, still standing.

---

③

Brostá

🚗 5 km (3 miles) NW of Póthia

After passing the Byzantine basilicas of Limniótissa and Agía Sofía, the road descends to the line of west-coast resorts collectively known as Brostá (meaning "forward"). This area has craggy cliffs and walls, and thrives on rock-climbing tourism, as well as beach holidays.

The first remarkable beach is sandy Platýs Gialós. Further along, the view of the sunset over the islet of Télendos from tourist town Myrtiés is one of Kálymnos's most famous sights. This coast ends at fortified Kastélli, the refuge of

survivors from an 11th-century Turkish raid. The coast road from here is spectacular, passing fish farms and inlets. The paved road ends at the northernmost resort of Emboriós, with decent beaches nearby and a shuttle-boat service back to Myrtiés.

---

④

Vathýs Valley

🚗 15 km (9 miles) NE of Póthia

Heading out of Póthia in the easterly direction leads to the citrus-lush Vathýs valley, which has three hamlets just inland from Kálymnos' fjord, unique in the islands.

The yacht and fishing port of]Rína, a pretty hamlet with a working boatyard, is backed by citrus trees. Excursion caïques from Rína visit the Daskalió Cave in the side of the fjord, or the beaches of Armyrés, Drasónda and Paliónisos on the east coast.

Plátanos, the main Vathýs

EAT

Stukas
Expect large portions of meat and fish served at waterside tables.

📍 Yacht marina, Póthia
📞 6970 802346

€ € €

Plaka
Fair prices for fresh tuna and swordfish, plus some meat dishes.

📍 East shore promenade, Télendos
📞 22430 47921

€ € €

Kafenes
A wonderf
central fish

📍 Platí
📞 2

27

NÍSYROS
ΝΙΣΥΡΟΣ

🚢 🚌 Mandráki harbour ℹ www.nisyros.gr

Nísyros, an almost circular island, is on a volcanic line that passes through Méthana, Santoríni, Póros and Mílos. Its 1,400-m- (4,594-ft-) high peak erupted and collapsed around 27,000 years ago, leaving a huge caldera. Everything flourishes in the volcanic soil here, and Nísyros is incredibly lush and green with terraces of olives, figs and almond trees contrasting with the strange grey and yellow moonscape of the craters.

①
Mandráki

By day, the island is swamped with visitors from Kos *(p186)*; but it becomes quiet once the excursion boats have left. Boats dock at Mandráki, the capital, which has tavernas, accommodation, ticket agencies and buses shuttling visitors to the caldera. The town's narrow two-storey houses have brightly painted wooden balconies, often hung with strings of drying onions, octopus and tomatoes. A maze of lanes converge at Platía Iróön, with its war memorial. Other roads go south, away from the sea, past the *kípos* (public orchard) to Platía Ilikioménon, the main square, which is shaded by a giant ficus. Shops often resemble houses but traditional painted signs depicting their wares mark them out. Back down on the shoreline, the hub of nightlife is Lefkándio district, which has several bars.

The main attractions in the town are the dramatic Castle of the Knights Hospitaliers, built in 1325 atop a cliff, and the gleamingly white Panagrías Spilianís monastery, perched on a hilltop and dating from around 1600. Inside the latter, a finely carved *témbion* holds a Russian-style icon, decked in gold and silver, of the Panagía and Christ. The **Folklore Museum**, on the way up to the castle, has a reconstructed traditional island kitchen, a collection of local photographs and embroideries. The Archaeological Museum,

ghts
ks
s ↑

recently reopened, comprises two well-organized storeys of local artifacts from the Archaic to Byzantine eras.

In the nearby Langádáki district, the streets are so narrow the balconies on facing houses almost touch. Just beyond lies Paleókastro, the acropolis of ancient Nísyros, dating back 2,600 years. You can safely clamber up onto the massive walls via a broad stairway inside the still-intact gate.

Folklore Museum
 Kástro 🕒 May–Sep: hours vary

_____

②
Pálli

🚶 5 km (3 miles) SE of Mandráki

East of Mandráki, Pálli is a pretty fishing village and yacht port with good tavernas and a string of dark volcanic-sand beaches. During summer, the famed _meltémi_ breeze blows fiercely and beaches here can be littered in debris. A short stroll west of Pálli stands the Dimotiká Loutrá (Municipal Baths) where you can enjoy a relaxing soak for a small charge.

Nísyros's best sandy beaches lie beyond Pálli, at Liés, which has a summer snack bar, and Pahiá Ámmos, where grey-pink sand and pristine sea are a ten-minute walk along a path beyond the final parking area. Expect naturists and rough campers. Pahiá Ámmos is partly protected from the summer winds that buffet other island beaches.

_____

③
Emboriós and Nikiá

🚶 9 km (6 miles) SE of Mandráki

High above Pálli, Emboriós, which was abandoned in

favour of the coast during the 1950s, has excellent views over the volcanic zone. The derelict houses here are being bought up for restoration, and new owners often discover that they have their very own volcanic steam vent in the basement.

The nearby village of Nikiá has more life than Emboriós,

and great views over the caldera. The highlight is the round "square" with a _votsalotó_ (pebble-mosaic surface), which has a couple of _kafenía_ to enjoy it from.

Avláki, in the south of the island, has a stunning black-pebbled beach that is a bit tricky to get to, but is well worth the effort.

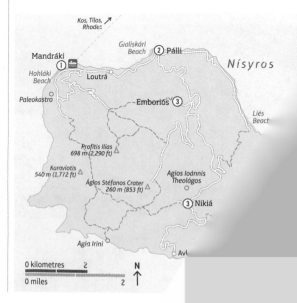

Kos, Tílos, Rhodes

Mandráki ①

Gialiskári Beach ② Pálli

Nísyros

Hohláki Beach

Loutrá

Paleokastro

Emboriós ③

Liés Beach

Profitis Ilías 698 m (2,290 ft) △

Karaviotis 540 m (1,772 ft) △

Ágios Stéfanos Crater 260 m (853 ft) △

Agios Ioánnis Theológos

③ Nikiá

Agia Irini

Avl

0 kilometres   2

0 miles   2

N ↑

28

SÝMI
ΣΥΜΗ

🚢 🚌 Gialós, Sými town ℹ️ Sými town; www.symis.gr

In Classical times, rocky, barren Sými thrived on the success of its sponge-diving fleet and boat-building industry. By the 17th century it was the third-richest island in the Dodecanese. The Italian occupation in 1912 and the arrival of artificial sponges and steam power ended Sými's good fortunes. While the island's population has fallen, Sými remains a beautiful island that attracts visitors to its charming main town.

Did You Know?

Sými doesn't have a supply of fresh water, so the islanders have it shipped in by tanker.

①

Sými Town

The harbour area, Gialós, is one of the most beautiful in Greece, surrounded by Neo-Classical houses and elaborate churches built on the hillside, and is often busy with day trippers. A clock tower (1884) stands on the northwestern side of the harbour where the ferries and catamarans dock. Next door to the town hall, the Maritime Museum has an interesting record of Sými's seafaring past.

Gialós is linked to the upper town, Horió, by a road and also by 375 marble steps. The road from Gialós to Horió passes the hill of Noúlia, also known as Pondikókastro. On the hill are the remains of an ancient tomb monument believed to have been erected by the Spartans in 412–411 BC.

Horió comprises a maze of lanes and distinctive houses, often with traditional interiors. The Sými Museum, high up in Horió, has a collection of Byzantine frescoes and folk art. Beyond the museum is the ruined *kástro* from Crusader days, and medieval walls. Megáli Panagía church,

the jewel of the *kástro*, has an important post-Byzantine icon, the *Last Judgment*, by 16th-century Cretan-School iconographer Geórgios Klontzás.

②

Moní Taxiárhi Mihaïl Roukounióti

🚗 6 km (4 miles) W of Sými town

Just west of Sými town is the 18th-century church of Moní Taxiárhi Mihaïl Roukounióti, which was built like a desert fortress using Gothic and folk architecture. It shelters naive 18th-century frescoes and a rare 15th-century semicircular icon of the *Hospitality of Abraham* by Cretan artist Stylianós Génis.

↑

Hondrós

Nímos

Platí

Kos, Tílos,
Rhodes →

Oxía

Emboriós

Nos
Beach

Agía
Marína
Beach

Agíos
Nikólaos
Beach

Moní Taxiárhi
Mihaïl Roukounióti

Sými Town

Pédi

Cape
Kefála

△ Bígla
617 m (2,024 ft)

East Coast
Bays

Ágios
Vasílios
Beach

Nanoú Beach

Pídima

Gialesíno

Megalonísi

Sými

Marathoúnda
Beach

Panormítis
Beach

 Moní Taxiárhi
Mihaïl Panormítis

0 kilometres   3

0 miles   3

N
↑

Sesklí

③

Moní Taxiárhi
Mihaïl Panormítis

**☐ 19 km (12 miles) S
of Sými town**

Sými's most popular sight is
the enormous Moní Taxiárhi
Mihaïl Panormítis in Panormítis
bay, a place of pilgrimage for
Greek sailors worldwide. An
icon of Archangel Michael,
Sými's patron saint and guard-
ian of seafarers, was found
here; despite being removed
to Gialós, it kept returning to
Panormítis so the monastery
was founded. Its white buildings, spanning the 18th to
20th centuries, sit slightly
back from a horseshoe-
shaped harbour. The rather
elaborate mock-Baroque
belfry is a 1905 copy of the
famous, now vanished, bell
tower of Agía Fotiní in Smýrna.
    According to tradition, if
you ask a favour of St Michael,
you must vow to give something in return. As a result, the

interior is a dazzling array of
votive offerings, or *támata*,
from pilgrims, including model
ships in silver and gold. The
walls and ceiling are covered
in smoke-blackened 18th-
century frescoes by the two
Sýmiot brothers Nikítas and
Michaïl Karakostís.
    The sacristy museum is full
of treasures, including a post-
Byzantine icon of the Ágii
Déka (The Ten Holy Martyrs)
by Creto-Venetian master
Theodoros Poulakis. There are
prayers in bottles, which have
floated miraculously into
Panormítis; if they arrived
safely, the sailor would get
his prayer answered.

---

④

East Coast Bays

**☐ 4 km (2 miles) E
of Sými town**

Sými's most popular beaches
are on the east coast. East of
Horió, an avenue of eucalyptus

trees leads through farmland
to Pédi bay, a beach popular
with fishermen, visiting yachts
and local families. From here
taxi boats run to Ágios Nikólaos
beach and there are marked
paths to sandy Ágios Nikólaos
and shingly Agía Marína.
Nanoú, with mixed gravel,
sand and small pebbles, a
scenic backdrop, good snorkelling and a snack bar.
Marathoúnda, the most
south, is reached from
woodlands. It has a
pebble beach
water and a
and can be
a turning
road. Be
goats

STAY

Thea Apartments
In a colourful house in
the centre of town, this
hotel offers charming
rooms with views and a
friendly host.

**☑ Egialos, Sými
◲ symi-thea.gr**

€€€

Iapetos Village
Self-catering bungalow
complex around a
covered pool and
landscaped grounds.

**☐ Gialós, Sými, 100 m
(328 ft) from the
main square
◲ iapetos-village.gr**

€€€

Aliki
This 1895 mansion
right on the water is
now Sými's most
exclusive hotel.

**☐ Harani quay, Gialós,
Sými ◲ symi-hotel-
aliki.gr**

€€€

KÁRPATHOS
ΚΑΡΠΑΘΟΣ

✈ 17 km (11 miles) S of Kárpathos town 🚢 Kárpathos town, Diáfani 🚌 Corner of 28th Oktovríou & Dimokratías, Kárpathos town 🛈 Kárpathos town; www.karpathos.gr

Wild, rugged Kárpathos is dramatically beautiful and has remained largely unspoiled. Like most of the Dodecanese, it has had a chequered history. Along with Astypálea, it was the only Dodecanese seized by the Venetians during medieval times, rather than the Knights of St John.

①
Kárpathos Town

Kárpathos town, also known as Pigádia, is the island's main port and capital, sheltered in the southeast of Vróndi bay. Once an ordinary working town, it now has hotels strung out all around the bay. The waterfront bustles with cafés and tavernas. An archaeological museum occupies one wing of the county authority building, displaying finds from both Kárpathos and Kásos.

South of Kárpathos town, beyond groves of olive trees, lies the main resort of Amopí, 7 km (4 miles) away. This consists of hotels, apartments and tavernas arrayed around three sand-and-gravel coves. Above Amopí, the village of Menetés, nestling 350 m (1,150 ft) up the slopes of Mount Profítis Ilías, has quaint vine-covered streets. The traditional pastel-coloured houses have attractive court-yards and gardens.

②
Diafáni and Ólymbos

🚗 50 km (31 miles) N of Kárpathos town

Diafáni, a small, colourful village on the northeast coast, has several tavernas and hotels, and both sand and shingle beaches.

HIKING IN THE NORTH OF KÁRPATHOS

Since the millennium old paths have been rehabilitated in northern Kárpathos and decent maps are now available. The canyon walk from Diafáni to Ólymbos is an easy classic; for a bit of culture, Ólymbos to Vrykoúnda via Avlóna hamlet ends at a major archaeological site.

A 20-minute bus ride (or hour's walk along the path) away is Ólymbos, a village that spills down from a bleak ridge 600 m (1,950 ft) up. Founded during the 8th century AD, and virtually cut off from the rest of the island for centuries by its remote location, this village is now a mix of medieval and modern. The painted houses huddle together in a maze of steps and narrow alleys. One of these traditional houses is open to visitors and has a single room displaying bric-a-brac and embroideries. Customs and

EAT

Porto Paradiso

A vibrant café directly on the waterfront. The coffee is good, and it becomes a bar at night.

Near the marina, Kárpathos town
☎ 22450 22232

€€€

Corali (aka Mihalis & Popi)

Meat grills, fish, salads with home-grown veggies and Cretan *tsikoudiá* are served by a lovely couple.

South end of quay, Diafáni ☎ 22450 51332

€€€

Orea

This is the best all-rounder in the port, with dishes such as spinach pie, to pair with local wine.

Southeast end of the quay, Kárpathos Town
☎ 22450 22501

€€€

Under the Trees (Kostas)

Dine under the tamarisks at this rural taverna. On the menu are expertly grilled swordfish, racks of chops and courgette chips.

West coast, a short walk north of Finí
☎ 6977 9847?

€€€

---

village life have been carefully preserved and traditional dress is daily wear for the older women who still bake their bread in outdoor ovens.

---

③ Central Kárpathos

8 km (5 miles) NW of Kárpathos town

Apéri, north of Kárpathos town, was the island's capital until 1892, and is said to be one of the richest villages in Greece, owing to money sent back from islanders who immigrated to North America. It sits 300 m (985 ft) up Mount Kalí Límni and has fountains and fine 19th-century houses with exquisite gardens.

Othos, just to the west of Apéri, is the highest village on the island, at 450 m (1,500 ft) above sea level. It is also one of the oldest, with traditional Karpathian houses. One of the houses is a **Folk Museum** with textiles and pottery on show. There is also a family loom and tools for traditional crafts. Lefkós, a west coast resort, is considered by the Karpathians to be the jewel of the island, with its three horseshoe bays of white sand. Kyrá Panagiá, on the east coast, is a lovely cove of fine white sand with a pink-domed church.

Folk Museum

Othos village ☎ 22460 49283 Apr–Oct: Tue–Sun

Pink-d...
eleva...
co...

THE CYCLADES

The 56 islands that comprise this archipelago formed the cradle of the Cycladic civilization from around 3000 BC. Early Cycladic culture developed in the Bronze Age during which the arts flourished, with numerous distinctive marble figures discovered from this era. The island group, like many of those in the region, experienced one ruling group after another, each marking the territory with diverse architectural styles: the Minoans from Crete colonized the islands during the middle Cycladic era, then followed by the Mycenaeans, the Romans and the Egyptians. The Venetians, who ruled for over two hundred years from 1204, left medieval *kástra* that still form the centre of many towns. The Ottomans conquered most of the Cyclades in the 16th century, although Venetian-ruled Tínos didn't fall until 1715. The far-flung islands of the Cyclades were difficult to govern, let alone protect against the large number of pirate raids and incursions, and much of the populace left. Although some islands, like Ándros, became rich off the success of local shipping families, the fortunes of the Cyclades as an island group didn't revive until the advent of mass tourism in the 1960s. Tourism is the lifeblood of most of the mainly rocky and arid islands today, as they are considered the ultimate islands for sun, sea and sand holidays.

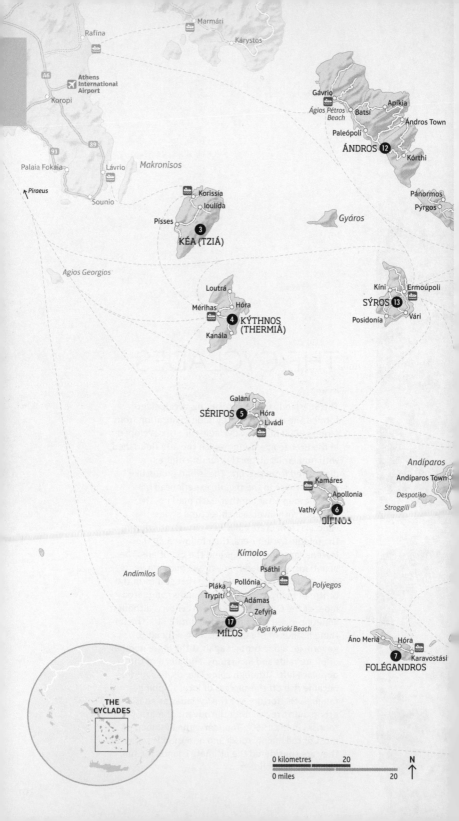

CYCLADES

Must Sees

1 Delos
2 Santoríni

Experience More

3 Kéa (Tziá)
4 Kýthnos (Thermiá)
5 Sérifos
6 Sífnos
7 Folegandros
8 Síkinos
9 Amorgós
10 Íos
11 Mýkonos
12 Ándros
13 Sýros
14 Páros
15 Náxos
16 Tínos
17 Mílos

Kolymbíthra

16 TÍNOS

Tínos Town

Ágios Ioánnis

Ikaría →

Mýkonos Town

11 MÝKONOS

Áno Merá

Ríneia

Mykonos International Airport

1 DELOS

Kos →

Agía   Apóllonas

Akrotíri   Koronída

Náxos Town   Mélanes   Moní

Náoúsa   Moutsoúna

Parikía   Donoússa

14   Léfkes   Filóti   Kinaros

PÁROS   Píso Livádi   15 NÁXOS   △ Mount Zas 1,000 m (3,280 ft)

Alykí   Pyrgaki   Panermos   Megalo Livodi

Koufoníssi   Egiáli

Hóra   9 AMORGÓS

Iraklía   Skhinoússa   Katápola   Hóra

SÍKINOS   Kalotaritissa

8   Íos   Psáthi Beach   Ast

Áno Horió   10 ÍOS

Aloprónia   Manganári Bay

Ánidro

SANTORÍNI

2 Firá

Santorini International Airport

Athiniós   Kamári   Anáfi

Vlyháda   Anáfi

Crete ↓

8 DAYS
in the Western Cyclades

Day 1

It's a four-hour trip from Athens to Livádi port on beautiful Sérifos (*p217*), so catch the 8:30am ferry and you'll arrive to the breathtaking view of the hillside town and bay just in time for lunch. Enjoy the remaining daylight – which in the summer stretches on and on – at superb local beach, Livadáki. As the heat abates, walk up the old cobbled path to dazzlingly white Hóra for dinner and drinks on central Platía Agíou Athanasíou.

Day 2

Sérifos is criss-crossed with numerous old paths, which are numbered and marked. Take the route from Hóra towards Panagía, which has shady tavernas where you can ~~stop~~ for lunch. Carry on hiking to Galaní, ~~Pý~~rgos village, where you can rest ~~at a~~ peaceful, white and fortress-like ~~nun~~ monastery near Galaní. From ~~here a p~~aved road leads to the hillside ~~village of Ké~~ndarhos, where the trail ~~leads~~ back to Hóra. Return to ~~sup~~per at a seaside taverna ~~for a la~~te-night swim.

Day 3

Catch a ferry to Kamáres port on Sífnos, the most popular island in the west Cyclades (*p218*). Above the port is the pretty capital Apollonía, where you can stop for lunch and a quick visit to the charming Museum of Popular Arts and Folklore. Spend the afternoon swimming at Apokoftó beach further down the east coast, a desert paradise overlooked by picturesque Chrysopigí monastery. Have dinner in Kastro village, at traditional Leonidas tavern.

Day 4

Hop over to neighbouring Mílos island (*p242*), a dramatic volcanic rock, and rent a car for the drive to picturesque Klíma, with its white shacks marked by colourful doors right on the waterfront. After a swim, head to the Christian Catacombs near Pláka village (*p243*), the only such complex in Greece. In the village itself, climb to the Venetian *kástro*'s summit for the best sunset in the western Cyclades, framed by Mílos Bay. Dine at a taverna in Trypití village, en route back to Klíma.

1 Overlooking Sérifos from a hilltop.
2 A picturesque street on Sífnos.
3 The volcanic coastline of Mílos.
4 Enjoying a harbourside dinner in Pollónia, Mílos.
5 Hóra village on Folégandros.

Day 5

Point the car towards the southern coast of Mílos, and make your way to one of the excellent beaches at either Paleohóri or Firipláka. After a late-morning swim and a spot of lunch, head back to Adámas to embark on a pre-arranged cruise along the coast, which features stunning formations of volcanic rock. On your return, have supper at an Adámas taverna before spending another night in Klíma.

Day 6

Drive to Pollónia port at the northeastern tip of Mílos. Leaving the car here and making a note of the time of the last boat back, hop on a ferry to Kímolos islet immediately opposite. Have lunch on arrival at Psathí port, then walk for 15 minutes up to the fascinating hilltop town of Hóra, which has a 16th-century Venetian *kástro* at its core. The rest of the afternoon can be spent hiking back down to the south coast, with a swim at either Skála or Kalamítsi. Catch the last ferry back to Pollónia and enjoy dinner there before returning to your hotel in Klíma.

Day 7

Take a ferry or catamaran to beautiful Folégandros (p219) and transfer up to Hóra. After dropping your things off, walk a short way west of town for lunch and a swim at protected Angáli beach or adjacent Ágios Nikólaos. Return to Hóra in time to ascend the zig-zag steps up to landmark Kímisi Theotókou church, stopping to savour the amazing views over the steep cliff on which the village is built. As the light begins to fade, descend back to the centre to partake in Hóra's lively evening shopping and café scene.

Day 8

Walk along the ridge lane to Áno Meriá, the island's other, straggling settlemen sometimes there's a bus service, spar the walk in at least one direction. H lunch at Kafenío Irini, before desce to Livadáki beach for a lazy after its sheltered sands. Return to H or by bus for a final evening a buzzing bars and tavernas. Y transport back to Piraeus, c eastern Cyclades, will be th

8 DAYS

in the Eastern Cyclades

Day 1

Catch a morning catamaran or ferry from Athens to the holy island of Tínos (p240). Upon arrival in Tínos town, hire a scooter to tour the villages around Exóbourgo, stopping for lunch at fabled Drosia in Ktikádos and calling in to Vólax to browse the wares of the local basket weavers. Descend to Porto for a late swim at one of its beaches, then make a pilgrimage to fabled Panagía Evangelístria before it shuts. For dinner, head to seafood-strong Marathia (Ágios Fokás) by the beach.

Day 2

Point your scooter at the pretty village of Pýrgos in northern Tínos and its museum of marble-carving, pausing en route at photogenic villages of Kardianí and [...]ja. End the morning with a lunch of [...] cuisine at Thalassaki in Órmos [...], then choose an afternoon swim [...] the locals do it – depending on [...] stiff breeze. Skhináki at Órmos [...]res are both good options. [...] town for dinner at charm-[...] Elenis (Gafou 5).

Day 3

Take an early-morning catamaran from Tínos to Mýkonos (p222), arriving in time to grab some picnic supplies from a local deli before hopping onto a late-morning excursion boat to ancient Delos (p208), which is the ruin of a Roman town. Take your time to have a thorough wander around the archaeological ruins and museum, soaking up the fascinating history of this impressive site, before having a picnic on the island. Return to Mýkonos for dinner at Joanna Niko's on Megáli Ámmos beach, before joining the famous party scene and bar-jumping your way along the waterfront.

Day 4

Have a lazy start on a Mýkonos beach, before catching a catamaran to Náxos (p236). Make your way to Agía Ánna for lunch, and then pass the rest of the day on its superb beach under a beach umbrella. Make your way to the nearby village of Ágios Prokópios for dinner at Stelida in the Kavos Naxos Hotel, a hillside oasis serving delicious food.

① The small village of Vólax on Tinos.

② Seafront coffee shops and restaurants on Mýkonos.

③ Náxos Town, illuminated at dusk.

④ Ágios Prokópis beach, Náxos.

⑤ Summer sunset over Santoríni.

Day 5

Pick up a rental car to explore Náxos. Stop first at the restored Demeter temple at Gyroúla, then pop into the ancient church of Panagía Drosianí between Halkí and Moní villages. After lunch in Moní or Halkí, proceed to Apiráthou for a wander and a coffee before heading to the impressive tower-monastery of Photodoti. If time and weather permit, take a quick dip at Moutsoúna before returning to the west coast via the Mélanes valley, admiring the unfinished Archaic *koúros* left in its quarry. Follow dinner in Náxos Town with a Domus Festival event in the *kástro*.

Day 6

Travel by catamaran to Santoríni *(p210)*, picking up a pre-arranged rental car at Athiniós port before checking into accommodation in Pýrgos, Imerovígli or Ía. After lunch at Giorgaros *(p213)*, tour the ruins of Minoan Akrotiri and then cool off with a swim nearby, perhaps at famous Kókkini Ámmos. Head up to Ía in time to view one of its jaw-dropping sunsets, followed by dinner at Melitini *(p213)*.

Day 7

Start the day with a visit to the colourful frescoes at the engaging Prehistoric Musem in Firá town, then drive out to the ruins of Ancient Thera *(p214)*, scenically located on a blufftop above Kamári beach. Backtrack slightly for lunch at Metaxy Mas *(p213)* in Éxo Goniá, enjoying the great views across to Anáfi island while you eat. After lunch, descend to Perívolos, the best east-coast beach, for a relaxing afternoon swim. Make your way to Pýrgos by dinnertime, for some designer cuisine at Selene *(p213)*.

Day 8

Take an organized cruise to the Kaméni islets of the caldera, which offer striking volcanic landscapes and the novelty of swimming in a thermal spring. Most tours provide for a lunch stop on Thirasiá islet, beyond. Follow the cruise with a tasting tour of some of the many excellent wineries at Megalohóri, Episkopí Goniás and Vourvoúlos, ending the day with dinner at Psaraki in Vlyháda marina, watching the sun set over the Hristiána islets.

Did You Know?

Delos had a number of temples dedicated to foreign gods, including those from Egypt and Syria.

❶ ⌖ Ⓜ 🖵

DELOS
ΗΛΟΣ

🏛16 km (10 miles) SW of Mýkonos town 【22890 22259 🚢From Mýkonos town 🕐May-Oct: 10:30am-7:30pm Tue-Sun; Nov-Apr: 9am-5pm Tue-Sun

Tiny, uninhabited Delos is one of the most important archaeological sites in Greece and is a UNESCO World Heritage Site. First settled in the third millennium BC, Delos was a major port in the eastern Mediterranean, and home to a thriving Roman town.

According to legend, Leto, pregnant by Zeus, gave birth to goddess Artemis and god Apollo here. This legend resulted in Delos becoming a major religious centre by 700 BC, and the Delia Festival celebrating Apollo occured every four years until 316 BC. From a place of pilgrimage, Delos became a thriving commercial port in the 3rd and 2nd centuries BC. The resulting wealth led to opulent houses and large public spaces, such as the theatre and temples of Apollo. But this wealth also attracted enemies of Rome; the town was sacked in 88 BC and 69 BC, and eventually abandoned. It is now an open-air archaeological museum.

↑ Lion statues, replicas of the originals, guarding the Sacred Lake

↑ The House of Dioscourides and Cleopatra, who lived on Delos in the 2nd century BC

Timeline

1000 BC
△ Ionians arrive on Delos and introduce the worship of Apollo.

550 BC
Polykrates, tyrant of Sámos, conquers the Cyclades, but respects sacred Delos.

478 BC
Athenians make Delos the centre of the first Delian League.

422 BC
Athens exiles Delians to Asia Minor; Delians return the following year.

314 BC
Delos declares independence from Athens.

250 BC
◁ Romans settle in Delos.

69 BC
△ Romans fortify Delos after sack by pirates.

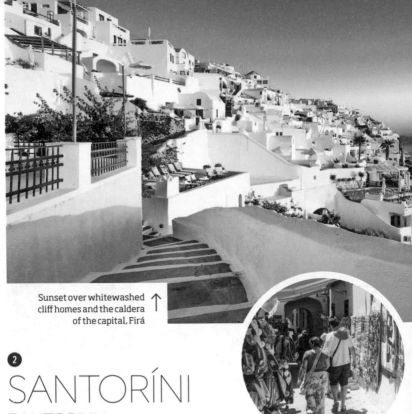

Sunset over whitewashed cliff homes and the caldera of the capital, Firá ↑

2

SANTORÍNI
ΣΑΝΤΟΡΙΝΗ

✈ 5 km (3 miles) SE of Firá 🚢 Athiniós 🚌
ℹ Firá; www.santorini.gr

Originally colonized by the Minoans in 3000 BC, this volcanic island erupted in 1620 BC, forming Santoríni's crescent shape and outlying islands. Named Thera by the Dorians when they settled here in the 8th century BC, it was renamed Santoríni, after St Irene, by the Venetians who acquired the island in the 13th century. Extremely popular with tourists, Santoríni is simply stunning, with white villages clinging to volcanic cliffs above black-sand beaches.

①
Firá

🚌 🚌 50 m (165 ft) S of main square ℹ 22863 60100

Firá, or Thera, overlooking the caldera and the island of Néa Kaméni, is the island's capital. It was founded in the late 18th century, when islanders moved from the Venetian citadel of Skáros, near present-day Imerovígli, to the clifftop plains for easier access to the sea. Devastated by an earthquake in 1956, Firá has been rebuilt, terraced into the volcanic cliffs with domed churches and barrel-roofed cave houses.

The terraces are packed with hotels, bars and restaurants in good positions along the lip of the caldera to enjoy the magnificent views, especially at sunset. The tiny port of Gialós (Skála Firón) is 270 m (885 ft) below Firá, connected by cable car or by 580 steps. Firá is largely pedestrianized with winding cobbled alleys. The town's main square, Platía

Theotokopoúlou, is the hub of the road network and the bus terminal is nearby. All the roads running north from here and Athiniós harbour eventually merge in Platía Firostefáni. The most spectacular street, Agíou Miná, runs south along the edge of the caldera to the 18th-century church of Ágios Minás. With its distinctive blue dome and its white bell tower, it has become the symbol of Santoríni.

The **Archaeological Museum** houses finds from the ancient

Despite the 1956 earthquake you can still see vestiges of Firá's architectural glory from the 17th and 18th centuries, on Nomikoú and Erythroú Stavroú where several mansions have been restored.

In the northeasterly suburb of Kondohóri, the **Lignos Folklore Museum** offers a fascinating glimpse at pretourism island life. The 19th-century cave-house features reconstructed workshops of bygone trades, including a *kánava* (dugout winery), showing the age of the wine trade here. The pretty ochre chapel of Agios Stylianós, clinging to the edge of a cliff, is a worthwhile detour on the way to the Frankish quarter, with its maze of streets.

↑ Pottery on display in the Archaeological Museum in Firá

city of Thera on Mésa Vounó *(p214)*, including early Cycladic figurines found in local pumice mines. The **Prehistoric Museum** contains colourful frescoes of blue monkeys and elegant women, discovered during the excavation at ancient Akrotíri *(p214)*.

Housed inside the former Catholic episcopal palace, the **Megaro Gyzi Cultural Centre**, in the northern part of the town, displays manuscripts from the 16th to 19th centuries, maps, engravings, and photographs of Firá before and after the earthquake. Nearby, the still-functioning Catholic cathedral of Ágios Ioánnis Pródromos (John the Baptist) is well worth a look inside.

Archaeological Museum
⊛ 🏛 Opposite cable car
☎ 22860 22217 🕐 8am–3pm Tue–Sun 🚫 Main public hols

Prehistoric Museum
⊛ 🏛 Near Firá main square
☎ 22860 23217 🕐 8am–3pm Wed–Mon 🚫 Main public hols

Megaro Gyzi Cultural Centre
⊛ 🏛 Near cable car 🕐 May–Oct: 10am–4:30pm Mon–Sat
🌐 gyzimegaron.gr

Lignos Folklore Museum
⊛ ⊛ 🏛 Kondohóri ☎ 22860 22792 🕐 May–Oct: 10am–2pm daily

📷 PICTURE PERFECT
Classic Church

To capture the idyllic blue-domed roof of a whitewashed cliff church in Firá, find Mama Thira's taverna in town, proceed up past the carpark, and look for a dome with three bells, overlooking the caldera.

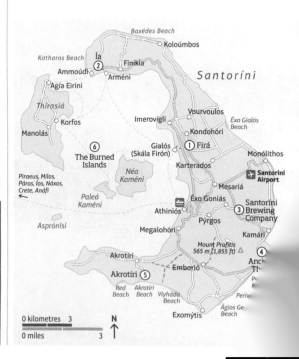

Baxédes Beach
Koloúmbos
Katharos Beach
Ía ②
Finikia
Ammoudi
Arméni
Agía Eirini
Santoríni
Thirasiá
Vourvoulos
Imerovigli
Éxo Gialós Beach
Korfos
Kondohóri
Manolás
Gialós (Skála Firón)
① Firá
Monólithos
⑥ The Burned Islands
Néa Kaméni
Karterados
Santoríni Airport
Piraeus, Milos, Páros, Ios, Náxos, Crete, Anáfi ←
Mesariá
Paleá Kaméni
Éxo Goniás
Santoríni ③ Brewing Company
Asprónisi
Athiniós
Pýrgos
Megalohóri
Kamári
Mount Profitis 565 m (1,855 ft) △
Akrotíri
Emborió
④
Akrotíri ⑤
Red Beach
Akrotíri Beach
Vlyháda Beach
Perív
Ágios Ge
Exomýtis
Beach

0 kilometres 3
0 miles 3
N ↑

THE ISLAND OF ATLANTIS

The myth of Atlantis dates from around 360 BC, when legendary Athenian philosopher Plato told the story of an advanced civilization founded by people who were half-god, half-humans. They established a progressive, wealthy society, set on a concentric island, that embodied the ideals of a utopian city – at least at first. But the citizens of Atlantis grew in hubris and greed, and at some point the island was completely destroyed in an unknown disaster, possibly as a result of the gods punishing the society. The original shape of Santoriní – and the fact that it was partially destroyed by a volcanic explosion in 1450 BC, creating a massive caldera that filled with water – has led scholars to suggest the island might have been the location of the mythical civilization. Other scholars posit that it seems more likely Plato made up Atlantis as an allegory for the ideal city-state.

churches, along with some still-standing Neo-Classical mansions built by wealthy shipowners. There are staircases leading down to Arméni and the nearby fishing harbour at Ammoúdi with its floating pumice stones and pebbly ochre beach. Here, the tradition of boatbuilding continues at Arméni's small ferry dock at the base of the cliff, although the port is now mainly used by tourist boats departing daily for the inhabited islet of Thirasiá. You can walk along a caldera-edge footpath all the way from Ía to Firá in about three hours.

② Ía

 11 km (7 miles) NW of Firá

At the northern tip of the island, the beautiful town of Ía is famous for its spectacular sunsets. A popular island pastime is to gather at the far western end of Ía, phones at the ready as the sun sinks behind the caldera.

Reached by one of the most spectacular roads in all of the Cyclades, Ía is the island's third port and was an important and wealthy commercial centre before it was badly damaged in the earthquake of 1956.

Today Ía is a designated traditional settlement, having been carefully reconstructed after the earthquake. Its white- and pastel-coloured houses with red pebble walls cling to the cliff face. The mix of architecture styles here also includes the famous *skaftá* cave houses and blue-domed

③ Santoríni Brewing Company

 Mésa Goniá Noon-5pm Mon-Sat Sun santorinibrewing company.gr

Although the village of Mésa Goniá used to be known for its winemaking, it is now home to

the island's only brewery, the Santorini Brewing Company, founded in 2011 by a Serb, a Greek, an American and a Brit. The brewery has since produced a number of what they call "Hip Hoppy Kick-Ass Ale", including the Yellow Donkey label. The brewery doesn't offer tours, but you can enjoy a small tasting of its selection

↑ The only brewery on Santoríni, producing "Donkey" beers

of beers. "Donkey" beers are unfiltered and unpasteurized, which means they don't travel very far. It's best to try them while you're on site, or at a bar on the island.

> Although the village of Mésa Goniá used to be known for its winemaking, it is now home to the island's only brewery, the Santorini Brewing Company.

↑ The colourful homes of Ía, peppered across the volanic cliffs

EAT

Melitini
This *tsipourádiko* is popular thanks to sharing dishes like lamb *loukániko* (sausage) and *pastourmadópita* (cured-beef turnovers). There is a roof terrace.

🏠 Ía, main through road
🌐 melitinioia.com

—

Metaxy Mas
Scrumptious dishes such as bulgur with lamb covered in yogurt sauce can be enjoyed on the terrace facing Anáfi island, or inside the old vaulted house.

🏠 Éxo Goniá (take stairs from the church)
🌐 santorini-metaximas.gr

—

Giorgaros
A reliable bet for cheap, fresh, locally caught fish and the usual fried *mezedes*, with jaw-dropping views north to the caldera-rim villages.

🏠 Near Akrotíri lighthouse
📞 22860 83035

—

Selene
Both the posh upstairs restaurant and the informal downstairs "Meze and Wine" bistro are run by a team dedicated to the revival of Aegean cuisine.

🏠 Pýrgos village
🌐 selene.gr

STAY

Esperas Traditional Houses

Studios, houses and suites are dug into the cliff, arranged around a central pool. Excellent on-site restaurant.

Ía, western end of village esperas-santorini.com

€€€

Voreina Gallery Suites

There are compelling views from the giant suites and four villas. In most of the suites, breakfast is delivered to your plunge-pool patio.

Pýrgos village, north-flanking road voreinasuites.gr

€€€

Afroessa

This small boutique hotel offers panoramic views, a bar-side pool, helpful staff and a restaurant with an affordable snack menu.

Imerovígli, 2 km (1 mile) from Firá afroessa.com

€€€

④

Ancient Thera

11 km (7 miles) SW of Firá
To Kamári 8:30am–2:30pm Tue–Sun Main public hols

On the rocky headland of Mésa Vounó, 370 m (1,215 ft) on the southeast coast, the ruins of the Dorian town of Ancient Thera are visible on terraces above the sea. The ancient town was recolonized in the 8th century BC after the great eruption. Most of the ruins date from the rule of the Egyptian Ptolemies. The 7th-century Santoríni vases that were discovered here are now housed in Firá's Archaeological Museum (p210).

A path through the site passes an early Christian basilica, remains of private houses (some with mosaics), the agora, or marketplace, and a theatre with a view down to the sea. On the far west is a 3rd-century-BC sanctuary cut into the rock. It features relief carvings of an eagle, a lion, a dolphin and a phallus symbolizing the gods Zeus, Apollo, Poseidon and Priapus.

To the east, on the Terrace of Celebrations, is graffiti that dates back as far as 750 BC. The messages praise the competitors and dancers of the *gymnopediés* – festivals where boys danced naked and sang hymns to Apollo, or competed in feats of physical strength. The main access point for the

Did You Know?

Néa Kaméni was formed over thousands of years from erupted lava and ash.

site, Kamári beach is situated to the north and is the island's main resort. The beach, a mix of stone and black volcanic sand, is backed by tavernas and apartments.

⑤

Akrotíri

12 km (7 miles) SW of Firá
10am–5pm daily

Akrotíri was once a Minoan outpost on the southwest tip of the island and is one of the most inspiring archaeological sites in the Cyclades. After an eruption in 1866, French archaeologists discovered Minoan pots at Akrotíri, though

→

A visitor reading about the well-preserved ruins of Ancient Thera

←
Pleasure crafts moored off the coast of Néa Kaméni, one of the Burned Islands

it wasn't until 1967 that the complete city was unearthed. Akrotíri was wonderfully preserved after some 3,650 years of burial under volcanic ash. The highlight was the discovery of frescoes such as *The Young Fisherman*, depicting a youth holding blue and yellow fish, and *The Young Boxers*, showing two sparring partners. These are are now displayed at the Prehistoric Museum in Firá *(p211)*.

Now covered by a modern roof, the excavations include late 17th-century BC houses on the Telkhines road, two and three storeys high, many still containing huge *pithoi*, or ceramic storage jars. The lanes were covered in ash and it was here that the fresco of the two boys boxing was uncovered.

Further along there is a mill and a pottery. A flyover-style bridge enables you to see the town's layout, including a storeroom for *pithoi* that held

grain, flour and oil. The House of the Ladies is named after its fresco of two voluptuous women. The Triangle Square has large houses that were decorated with frescoes of fisherboys and ships, now also displayed in Firá's Prehistoric Thera Museum. No human remains were ever discovered, suggesting that the inhabitants were probably warned by tremors and left.

The Burned Islands

From Ammoúdi or Gialós, boats run to the neighbouring islands. The nearest are Paleá Kaméni and Néa Kaméni, known as the Burned Islands. You can take a hot mudbath at Paleá Kaméni and walk up the crater at Néa Kaméni. The most southerly island in the group, Anáfi is a true retreat.

GEOLOGICAL HISTORY OF SANTORÍNI

Santoríni is one of several ancient volcanoes lying on the southern Aegean volcanic arc. It was a circular volcanic island before a massive eruption during the Minoan era, around 1450 BC, blew out its middle. Clouds containing molten rock extended for 30 km (19 miles). The eruption left a huge crater, and the rush of water into the void created a tsunami, which devastated the Minoan civilization. A huge volume of lava was ejected, burying Akrotíri. The Burned Islands, Paleá Kaméni and Néa Kaméni, in the middle of the sunken caldera, now part of the sea, emerged after subsequent volcanic activity in 197 BC and 1707.

EXPERIENCE MORE

Kéa (Tziá)

Κέα

🚌🚢 **Korissía** 🛈 www.kea.gr

Kéa, also known as Tziá, was first inhabited around 3000 BC and later settled by Phoenicians and Cretans. Mountainous with fertile valleys, Kéa has been known since ancient times for its wine, honey, oak trees and almonds. Today, the island is favoured by Athenians escaping from the city for a weekend break.

Kéa's port of Korissía can be packed with Greek families on holiday. From Korissía, catch a bus or ferry to the capital, Ioulída, perched on a hillside 5 km (3 miles) above Korissía. A maze of winding alleyways, Ioulída was founded in Classical times. Its centrepiece is a spectacular 1902 Neo-Classical town hall with statues of Apollo and Athena. In the entrance is a sculpture of a woman and child found at Karthaia. Inside a fine Neo-Classical house, the **Archaeological Museum** displays finds from around the island, including a collection of Minoan artifacts from Agía Iríni. The legendary 6th-century BC Lion of Kéa is carved into the rock 400 m (1,300 ft) north of the town.

The *kástro* quarter is reached through a white archway, and stands on the site of the acropolis. Built by the Venetians in 1210 using stones from the ancient walls and Temple of Apollo, it has panoramic views.

Just north of the port of Korissía is the archaeological site of Agía Iríni. The Bronze Age settlement was destroyed by an earthquake in 1450 BC, and was excavated from 1960 to 1968. First occupied at the end of the Neolithic period, the town was fortified twice in the Bronze Age. There are remains of the great wall with a gate and a tower. The most spectacular monument on Kéa is the Hellenistic tower at Moní Agías Marínas, 5 km (3 miles) southwest of Ioulída.

Archaeological Museum
♿ 📞 22880 22079 ⏰ Apr–Oct: 8am–3:30pm Tue–Sun
🚫 Main public hols

> ### Did You Know?
>
> The Lion of Kéa myth tells that jealous gods sent a lion to destroy the island and its beautiful nymphs.

Kýthnos (Thermiá)

Κύθνος

🚌🚢 **Mérihas** 🛈 www. kythnos.gr

Barren Kýthnos attracts more Greek visitors than foreign tourists, although it is a popular anchorage for flotilla holidays. Known locally as Thermiá because of its hot springs, the island attracts visitors to the thermal spa at Loutrá. Its dramatic, rugged interior, which has excellent walking trails, is fringed by some good beaches.

The local clay, traditionally used for pottery and ceramics, is also used to make the red roofing tiles that characterize all the island's villages.

→ Taverna tables outside the town hall in Kéa's historic capital, Ioulída

Dotting the hillside, the whitewashed village of Hóra on Sérifos

Kythnos's picturesque capital Hóra, also known as Mesaria, is a charming mix of red roofs, narrow streets and Cycladic cube-shaped houses. Also worth visiting is the church of Ágios Sávvas, which was founded in 1613 by the Venetian Gozzadini family, and is marked with their coat of arms. The oldest church is Agía Triáda (Holy Trinity); this is considered the "protector" of the village.

Kýthnos's road network is limited, but buses connect the port of Mérihas with Kanála in the south and Loutrá in the north. The remaining areas of the island are mostly within a walkable distance of these points. Mérihas, on the west coast, has a small marina and tree-fringed beach, lined with small hotels and tavernas. Just to the north, the sandy beach of Martinákia is popular with families. Further along the coast are the lovely beaches at Episkopí and Apókrousi, overlooked by Vryókastro, the Hellenistic ruins of ancient Kýthnos. You can walk to Dryopída, a good hour south of Hóra, down stretches of the ancient cobbled way, which has dramatic views.

At Kanála, 5 km (3 miles) to the south, holiday homes have sprung up by the church of Panagía Kanála, the island's patron saint. Set in attractive shaded picnic grounds, the church houses Kýthnos's most venerated icon of the Panagía. Legend states that it was miraculously found by fishermen in the sea nearby.

Loutrá is a straggling resort on the northeast coast with windswept beaches. Its spa waters are saturated with iron, and the springs of Kákavos and Ágii Anárgyri have been used as a cure for ailments such as rheumatism since ancient times. Since the late 1990s, Loutrá has been "freshened up" with new accommodation, though the 19th-century hydro-therapy centre, designed by noted Danish architect Christian Hansen, remains. A Mesolithic settlement to the north, is the oldest in the Cyclades, dating from 7500–6000 BC.

 5

Sérifos

Σέριφος

🚌🚢 Livádi *i* www.serifos-island.com

In mythology, the infant Perseus and his mother Danae were washed up on the shores of rocky Sérifos. Once rich in iron and copper mines, the island is renowned for its beauty and has bare hills with small fertile valleys, and long sandy beaches.

Ferries dock at Livádi on the southeast coast, which is on a sandy, tree-fringed bay buzzing with hotels and tavernas. Follow the stone steps up from Livádi or use the sporadic bus service to reach the dazzling white village of Hóra high above on the steep hillside, which is dotted with chapels and windmills, and topped by the ruins of a 15th-century Venetian *kástro*. Many of its medieval houses, some built using stones from the castle and all with breathtaking views, have been renovated as holiday homes by Greek architects and artists.

> **Kýthnos' picturesque capital Horá, also known as Mesaria, is a charming mix of red roofs, narrow streets and Cycladic cube-shaped houses.**

↑ Local crafts for sale displayed outside the charming white houses of Apollonia, Sífnos

EAT

Leonidas

This basic, but very delicious, spot is the place for tasty *magirevtá*, such as *revythokeftédes* (like falafel), rabbit stew and *mastélo* (lamb stew). On top of this, the views from the veranda are more than match the impressive food.

🏠 Entrance to Kástro, Sífnos 📞 22840 31153

Irini

A heart-warming traditional shop and *kafenío* (café) where Mrs Irini whips up comforting meals for hungry diners. On the menu, you'll find local noodles with various toppings, including delectably tender stewed goat.

🏠 Folégandros 📞 22860 41436

⑥
Sífnos
Σίφνος

🚌🚢 Kamáres ℹ️ www. sifnos.gr

Famous for its pottery, poets and chefs, Sífnos has become the most popular destination in the western Cyclades. Visitors in their thousands flock to the island in summer, lured by its charming villages, terraced countryside dotted with ancient towers, a few Venetian dovecotes and long, sandy beaches. A small, hilly island, it is also a magnet for walkers. In ancient times Sífnos was renowned for its gold mines, and the islanders paid yearly homage to the Delphic sanctuary of Apollo with a solid gold egg. One year they cheated and sent a gilded rock instead, incurring Apollo's curse. The gold mines were flooded, the island ruined and from then on it was known as *sífnos*, meaning "empty".

The capital, Apollonía, is east of Kamáres port. A labyrinth of white houses, flowers and belfries, it is named after the 7th-century BC Temple of Apollo, which overlooked the town, now the site of the 18th-century church of the Panagía Ouranofóra. The **Museum of Popular Arts and Folklore** in the main square has a good collection of embroideries and local pottery.

Artemónas is Apollonía's twin village. The second largest on Sífnos, it has impressive Venetian houses. The 17th-century church, Ágios Geórgios tou Aféndi, contains several fine icons from the period. The church of Panagía Kónhi, with its cluster of domes, was built on the site of a temple of Artemis.

Kástro village overlooks the sea 3 km (2 miles) east of Artemónas. The backs of its houses form massive outer walls, and some buildings in the narrow, buttressed alleys bear Venetian coats of arms. There are ruins of an ancient acropolis in the village, and the **Archaeological Museum** has a collection of Archaic and Hellenistic sculpture, and Byzantine pottery.

The port of Kamáres is an old-fashioned resort, with waterside cafés and tavernas. Buses from Kamáres port connect it with Apollonía and Kástro, on the east coast. The north of the harbour was once lined with studios making Sífnos's distinctive blue and brown ceramics, but only two remain. Taxi boats go from Kamáres to the funnel-shaped bay and beach at Vathý, in the south. An hour's walk to the east Is the busy resort of Platýs Gialós, with its long sandy beach. This is also connected by bus to Apollonía and Kamáres.

Museum of Popular Arts and Folklore

⊛ ♿ Platía Iróön 📞 22840 33730 🕐 Jun-Sep: 7am-11pm daily

Archaeological Museum

♿ Kástro 📞 22840 31022 🕐 Apr-Oct: 8am-3pm Tue-Sun (limited in winter) 🚫 Main public hols

---

❼ Folégandros

Φολέγανδρος

🚢🚌 Karavostási 🚉 Hóra; www.folegandros.gr

Bleak and arid, Folégandros is one of the smallest inhabited islands in the Cyclades and, with its towns perched on vertiginous cliffs, aptly takes its name from the Phoenician for "rocky". This remote island was often used as a place of exile, and suffered from the threat of pirate attack.

Popular with photographers and artists, Folégandros can be busy in peak season. It's also a good place for walkers, offering a wild beauty and unspoiled beaches.

Folégandros town, or Hóra, perched 300 m (985 ft) above the sea to avoid pirates, is

→

Taverna next to a pretty white church in Karavostási harbour, Folégandros

spectacular, divided into the fortified *kástro* quarter and main village surrounding it. The *kástro*, built in the 13th century by Marco Sanudo, Duke of Náxos, is reached through an arcade. Within its maze of crazy-paved alleys full of geraniums are two-storey cube houses with brightly painted wooden balconies and white steps up. It is rimmed with tall stone houses backing onto the sea, forming a stronghold along the ridge of the cliff. Village life here centres on four squares with craft shops, lively tavernas and bars. The stair-path from the central bus stop leads to the church of Kímisi tis Theotókou (Assumption of the Virgin Mary), which dominates the village. It was built after a silver icon was miraculously saved by a villager from medieval pirates who drowned in a storm.

Ferries dock at Karavostási on the east coast, a tiny harbour with a tree-fringed pebble beach, restaurants, hotels and rooms. There is a bus to Hóra, and Livádl beach is a short walk from the port. In season there are excursions available to the western beaches at Angáli, Ágios Nikólaos and Latináki, as well as to the Island's most popular sight, the Chrysospiliá or Golden Cave. Named after the golden shade of its stalactites and stalagmites, the grotto lies just above sea level in the northeasterly cliffs.

Áno Meriá, 5 km (3 miles) to the west of Folégandros town,

is a string of farming hamlets on either side of the road, surrounded by terraced fields. There are wonderful sunset views here and on a clear day you may be able to see Crete in the distance.

The excellent **Ecomuseum** presents the way of life in a rural homestead in days gone by. Displays include farming implements, grape and oil presses, a threshing floor and reconstructions of traditional peasant life. On 27 July a major local festival is held here for Ágios Pandelímon. From Áno Meriá steep paths weave down to the remote beaches at Ágios Geórgios bay and Livadáki, which is wildly beautiful.

Ecomuseum

♿ Áno Meriá 📞 22860 41370 🕐 Jun-Sep: 5-8pm daily

8 Síkinos

Σίκινος

 Aloprónia 🚌 Síkinos town 🛈 Kástro, Síkinos town; www.sikinos.gr

Quiet Síkinos is one of the most ruggedly beautiful islands in the Cyclades. Known in Classical Greece as Oinoe (winey island), it has remained a traditional backwater throughout history. Fishing and farming remain the main occupations of the 300 or so islanders and, although there are some holiday homes, there is little mass tourism.

Síkinos town is divided into twin villages: Kástro and the pretty and unspoiled Áno Horió perched high up on a ridge overlooking the sea. Kástro is a maze of lanes and *kafenía*. At the entrance to the village is Platía Kástrou, where the walls of 18th-century stone mansions formed a defensive bastion. The church

of the Pandánassa forms the focal point of Kástro. Among the ruined houses is a huge marble portico.

The partly ruined Moní Zoödóhou Pigís, fortified against pirate raids, looms down from the crag above Áno Horió and its church can be visited in the evening.

In medieval Áno Horió there is a private **Folk Museum**, which is in the family home of an American expatriate. It has an olive press and a wide range of local domestic and agricultural artifacts.

Episkopí is a good hour's trek south of Áno Horió, past ancient ruined Cycladic walls. With Doric inscriptions and columns it is thought to be a 3rd-century AD mausoleum, converted during the 7th century to a church of Kímisi tis Theotókou. Little remains of the church's monastery.

On the east coast 3 km (2 miles) southeast of Síkinos town, the port of Aloprónia, also known as Skála, has a few tavernas and cafés, several places to stay (including a luxury hotel) and a wide sandy beach that is safe for children. A bit further east, the sandy beach at Ágios Georgios is a favourite with locals for its golden sands, clear waters and fish taverna.

Folk Museum

🏠 Áno Horió, Síkinos town
☎ 22860 51228 🕐 May–Sep: daily (normally evenings)

📷 PICTURE PERFECT
Moní Panagías Hozoviótissas

On Amorgós island, the gleaming fortress-like Moní Panagías Hozoviótissas, precariously built into a craggy cliff face, is incredibly photogenic. Snap it as you climb the stairs.

---

9 Amorgós

Αμοργός

🚢 Katápola & Egiáli 🚌 Harbours at Katápola & Egiáli 🛈 Katápola quay; www.amorgos.gr

Dramatically rugged, the small island of Amorgós is narrow and long with a few beaches. Inhabited as early as 3300 BC, its peak was during the Cycladic civilization, when there were three cities: Minoa, Arkesini and Aegiale.

The capital, Hóra, or Amorgós town, is a dazzling clutch of whitewashed houses with windmills nearby. Above the town is Apáno Kástro, a fortress built by the Venetian Ghisi clan in 1260. Hóra also has the smallest church in Greece, the two-person Ágios Fanoúrios.

The star attraction on the island is the spectacular Byzantine Moní Panagías Hozoviótissas, below Hóra on the east coast, which is accessible by bus or on foot. The stark white monastery clings to the cliffs. It is a huge fortress housing a miraculous icon of the Panagía. Founded in 1017 but renovated in 1088 by the Byzantine Emperor Alexios I Komnenos, the monastery has a fine library with a collection of ancient manuscripts. The best way to get around the island is on foot, as buses are limited. There is a

→ A windmill perched at the edge of the rugged cliffs on the island of Amorgós

from Gialós to Manganári bay in the south and Psáthi bay in the east.

Homer's tomb is supposedly in the north at Plakotós, an ancient Ionian town that has slipped down the cliffs over the ages. In legend, Homer died on the island after his ship was forced to dock en route to Athens. The tomb entrance, as well as remains of the Hellenistic Psarópyrgos tower, can be seen today.

↑ A white-walled and blue-domed church overlooking Íos town

⑩

Íos

Ιος

🚌 Gialós 🚌 Íos town 🚍 Ano Hóra, Íos town; www.ios.gr

well-marked path system. The main port of Katápola in the southwest is in a horseshoe-shaped bay with tavernas, *pensions*, fishing boats and a shingly beach. The harbour area links three villages: Katápola in the middle where the ferries dock, quieter Xylokeratidí to the north and Rahídi on the hillside above. A track leads from Katápola to the hilltop ruins of ancient Minoa.

The northern port of Egiáli Aegiáli is the island's main resort, popular for its sandy beach. Head north, via the cobbled paths, to Tholária, a hill village with tavernas and an ecclesiastical museum, and Langáda, the largest settlement in the northeast, and the prettiest.

In ancient times Íos was covered in oak woods, later used for building ships. The Ionians built cities at the port of Gialós and at Íos town, later to be used as Venetian strongholds. Íos is also supposedly the burial place of Homer, and in mid-May the Homer festival takes place. A local speciality is *myzíthra* cheese, similar to a soft cream cheese.

Íos is known for its serious nightlife and attracts a party-ready crowd. Away from the clubs, Íos is a beautiful island. Its mountainous coastline has over 400 chapels, as well as beaches with some of the finest sands in the Cyclades.

Íos town, also known as the Village, is a dazzling mix of white houses and blue-domed churches interspersed with bars and clubs. There are ruins of the Venetian fortress, built in 1400 by Marco Crispo, remains of ancient walls and 12 windmills above the town.

The port of Gialós, or Órmos, has a busy harbour, with yachts and fishing boats, good fish tavernas and low-key places to stay. A 20-minute walk west leads to the sandy cove at Koumpará. A bus service runs from Gialós to Íos town and the superb Mylopótas beach, which has two campsites. Excursion boats run

STAY

Ios Palace
This hillside hotel above the beach has rooms for all budgets; some have unobstructed sea views. There is a spa with a full range of treatments.

🏠 Mylopótas beach, Íos
🌐 iospalacehotel.com

€€€

Porto Sikinos
Overlooking the beach with Cycladic-style buildings, this is the best accommodation on the island.

🏠 Aloprónia, Síkinos
🌐 portosikinos.gr

€€€

Aegialis
Built in tiers on the hillside above Amorgós's bay, this comfortable hotel has predictably amazing views. Facilities include a pool and spa.

🏠 Ormos Egiális, Amorgós
🌐 amorgos-aegialis.com

€€€

MÝKONOS

ΜΥΚΟΝΟΣ

✈ 3 km (2 miles) SE of Mýkonos town 🚌 Mýkonos town
🚏 Polykandrióti, Mýkonos town (for north of island);
on road to Ornós, Mýkonos town (for south of island)
ℹ Harbourfront, Mýkonos town; www.mykonos.gr

Although Mýkonos is dry and barren, its sandy beaches and dynamic nightlife make it one of the most popular islands in the Cyclades. Under Venetian rule from 1207, the islanders set up the Community of Mykonians in 1615 and flourished as a self-sufficient society. Visited by intellectuals in the early days of tourism, today Mýkonos, a premier gay resort, thrives on its reputation as one of the glitziest islands in Greece.

① Mýkonos Town

Also known as Hóra, Mýkonos town is the supreme example of a Cycladic village – a tangle of dazzling white alleys and cube-shaped houses. Built in a maze of narrow lanes to defy both wind and pirate raids, the old port is one of the most photographed in Greece and excursion boats for the island of Delos (p208) leave from the quayside. The island's mascot, Pétros the Pelican, may be seen near the quay, hunting for fish. Adjacent to the harbour is Platía Mavrogénous, overlooked by the bust of Mando Mavrogenous (1796–1848), a revolutionary heroine. The **Archaeological Museum**, facing the old harbour, has a large collection of Geometric and Archaic pottery, whose painted detail is notable. There are also many finds from the ancient site on Delos.

The *kástro*, the oldest part of the village, sits high up above the waterside district. Built on part of the ancient castle wall is the **Folk Museum**. Housed in an elegant sea captain's mansion, it has a fine collection of ceramics, embroidery and ancient and modern Mykonian textiles. Among the more unusual exhibits is the original Pétros the Pelican, now stuffed, who was the island's mascot for 30 years (the current mascot is a substitute). The 16th-century Voní s Windmill is a remote annexe of the Folk Museum and has been re-stored to full working order. It was one of the 30 windmills that were used by families all over the island to grind grain.

The most famous church on the island, familiar from postcards, is the extraordinary Panagía Paraportianí, in the

> **Mýkonos town is the supreme example of a Cycladic village - a tangle of dazzling white alleys and cube-shaped houses.**

Mýkonos

Piraeus, Rafina, Sýros, Pátmos, Ikaría →

Faros Armenistis

Ágios Sóstis Beach

Fókos Beach

Ágios Stéfanos

Pánormos Bay

Toúrlos

Moní Palaiokástrou

Klouvás

Páros, Náxos, Delos →

Mýkonos Town ①

③ Ano Merá

Megáli Ámmos Beach

Mýkonos International Airport

Kalafáti

Ágios Ioannis

Ornós

Elia Beach

Kaló Livádi Beach

Platýs Gialós ②

Agrári Beach

Delos

Ágia Anna Beach

Paradise Beach

Super Paradise Beach

0 kilometres   4

0 miles   4

N ↑

beaches further east. Backed by hotels and restaurants, this is the main family beach on the island, with watersports and a long sweep of sand.

 Ano Merá

📍 **9 km (6 miles) NW of Mýkonos town**

The inland village of Ano Merá, east of Mýkonos town, is unspoiled by tourism. The 16th-century Panagía Tourlianí, dedicated to the island's protectress, is just off the central *platía*. Founded by two monks from Páros, the red-domed monastery has an ornate marble tower, as well as some fine 16th-century icons.

kástro. Built on the site of the postern gate *(parapórti)* of the medieval fortress, it is made up of four chapels at ground level with another above. Part of it dates from 1425, while the rest was built in the 16th and 17th centuries.

From the *kástro*, the lanes run down into Venetía, or Little Venice (officially known as Aléfkándra), the artists' quarter. The tall houses have painted balconies jutting out over the sea. The main square, Platía Aléfkandras, is home to the large Orthodox church of Lozária; originally a 17th-century Catholic shrine, it still bears a Bourbon crest.

The Maritime Museum of the Aegean, in the Tría Pigádia district, features model ships from pre-Minoan times to the 19th century, maritime instruments, paintings and 5th-century BC coins with nautical themes. The museum's restored traditional sailing boat is moored in the harbour for visits in the summer.

←
Sunset over the whitewashed village of Mýkonos town

Next door, Lena's House, a 19th-century mansion, evokes the life of a Mykonian lady, Lena Skrivanou. Everything is preserved, from her needlework to her chamber pot.

Works by international and Greek artists are on show at the Municipal Art Gallery, also in Tría Pigádia, including an exhibition of paintings by Mykonian artists.

Archaeological Museum
🏛 📍 Old Harbour 📞 22890 22325 🕐 9am–4pm Tue–Sun (Apr–Oct: to 8pm Fri–Sat) 🚫 Main public hols

Folk Museum
📍 Harbourfront, near Paraportianí 📞 22890 22591 🕐 Apr–Oct: 5–8pm Mon–Fri

---

 Platýs Gialós

📍 **3 km (2 miles) S of Mýkonos town**

Mýkonos is popular primarily for its beaches, with the best ones along the south coast. At stylish Platýs Gialós, regular taxi boats are available to ferry sun-worshippers to the other

EAT

Joanna's Niko's
Unpretentious taverna with great sunset views and a cosy interior.

📍 Megáli Ámmos beach, Mýkonos
📞 22890 24251

€€€

To Ma'ereio
This hole-in-the-wall is popular with locals for its home-style dishes.

📍 Kalogéra 16, Hóra, Mýkonos
📞 22890 28825

€€€

To Steki tou Proedrou
The broad menu here of various roast meats includes spit-roast goat.

📍 Main plaza, Áno Méra, Mýkonos
🕐 22890 71925

€€€

ÁNDROS

΄ΑΝΔΡΟΣ

🚌 Gávrio 🚌 🛈 www.andros.gr

First colonized by the Ionians in 1000 BC, Ándros retains its traditional charm while playing host to international holiday-makers. The northernmost of the Cyclades, Ándros is dotted with many white dovecotes built by the Venetians, and has a number of unspoiled sandy beaches backed by wild mountains.

①

Ándros Town

The capital, Ándros town, or Hóra, is located on the east coast of the island, 20 km (12 miles) from the main port at Gávrio.

An elegant place with magnificient Neo-Classical buildings, it is the home of some of Greece's wealthiest shipowners. The pedestrianized main street is paved with marble slabs and lined with old mansions converted into public offices, as well as *kafenía* and small shops.

Platía Kaïri is the main square in the town's Ríva district and is home to the **Archaeological Museum**. The museum's most famous exhibit is the 2nd-century BC *Hermes of Andros*, an excellent marble copy of the 4th-century BC bronze original. Other exhibits here include the *Matron of Herculaneum*, which was found with the *Hermes*, as well as finds from the 10th-century BC city at Zagorá. There are also discoveries from Ancient Paleópoli, located near Batsí, architectural illustrations and a large collection of ceramics.

The town's **Museum of Contemporary Art** has an excellent – and somewhat surprising – collection of paintings by 20th-century artists such as Picasso and Braque, plus leading Greek artists such as Alekos Fasianos. The sculpture gallery features works by Mihalis Tombros (1889–1974).

From Platía Kaïri an archway leads into the maze of streets that form the medieval city, Káto Kástro, wedged between Parapórti and Nimporió bays. The narrow lanes twist down to windswept Platía Ríva at the end of the peninsula, jutting into the sea and dominated by the statue of the *Unknown Sailor* by Mihalis Tombros. Just below, a precarious stone bridge connects to the islet opposite, with its Venetian castle, Mésa Kástro, built between 1207 and 1233. The **Maritime Museum**, situated inside the town hall, has model ships and a collection of nautical

Garlands across a sunny street in Ándros town

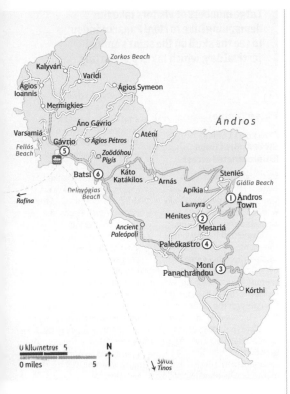

Kalyváni
Zorkos Beach
Varídi
Ágios Symeon
Ágios
Ioánnis
Mermigkiés
Áno Gávrio
Ándros
Varsamiá
Aténi
Gávrio
Ágios Pétros
Fellós
Beach
Zoödóhou
Pigis
Batsí (6)
Káto
Katákilos
Arnás
Steniés
Delινγógias
Beach
Apíkia
Giália Beach
← Rafína
Lamyra
(1) Ándros
Town
Ménites (2)
Ancient
Paleópoli
Mesariá
Paleókastro (4)
Moní
Panahrándou (3)
Kórthi

0 kilometros 5
0 miles 5
N ↑
Sýros,
↓ Tínos

instruments on display. On the way back to the centre of the town stands the church of Panagía Theosképasti, built in 1555 and dedicated to the Panagía (Virgin Mary). Legend has it that when the ship delivering the wood for the church roof arrived, the priest could not pay for the goods – so the ship set sail again. It ran into a storm and the crew prayed to Panagía for help, promising to return the cargo to Ándros. The seas were calmed and the church became known as Theosképasti, meaning "sheltered by God".

Steniés, 6 km (4 miles) northwest of Ándros town, is very beautiful and popular with wealthy shipping families. Below Steniés is Giália beach.

Archaeological Museum
⊕ ⬛ Platía Kaïri ☎ 22820 23664 ⬛ Apr-Oct: 9am-4pm Tue-Sun; Nov-Mar: 9am-4pm Fri-Sun ⬛ Main public hols

Museum of Contemporary Art
⊕ ⬛ Platía Kaïri ☎ 22820 22444 ⬛ Jun-Sep: 11am-3pm Mon, 11am-3pm & 6-9pm Wed-Sun; Oct & Apr-May: 10am-2pm Wed-Mon; Nov-Mar: 10am-2pm Tue-Sat ⬛ Main public hols

Maritime Museum
⊕ ⬛ Platía Ríva ☎ 22823 22275 ⬛ 8am-10pm daily ⬛ Main public hols

___

Mesariá

⬛ 8 km (5 miles) SW of Ándros town ⬛

From Ándros town the road passes through the medieval village of Mesariá with ruined tower-houses and the restored Byzantine church of Taxiárhes, built by Emperor Manuel I Komnenos in 1158. Springs

gush from marble lion's-head fountains in the leafy inland village of Ménites, just above Mesariá on the slopes of Pétalo mountain.

Ménites is known for its nightingales, its decorated wells and for the taverna overlooking a stream. From here, steps lead up to the restored church of Panagía Koúmoulos (the Virgin of Heaped Abundance), thought to be built on the site of an ancient Temple of Dionysos.

③ Moní Panachrándou

📍 12 km (7 miles) SW of Ándros town ☎ 22820 51090 🕐 Daily

Offering incredible views over the valley, this monastery is perched 230 m (755 ft) above sea level in the mountains southwest of Ándros town. It can be reached either by a 2-hour steep walk from Mesariá or a 3-hour trek from Ándros town, both of which are fairly strenuous.

The fortified monastery was founded in 963 AD by Nikephoros Phokas, who had just become Byzantine Emperor as a consequence of his liberation of Crete from Arab occupation. It is built in Byzantine style and today houses just three monks. The church holds many treasures, such as the skull of 4th-century St Pandeleimon, who was thought to have healing powers. Large numbers of visitors and pilgrims make the hike to Moní Panachrándou to see the skull on the saint's annual festival day, which takes place in July.

> Large numbers of visitors take the demanding hike to Moní Panachrándou to see the skull on the saint's annual festival day, which takes place in July.

④ Paleókastro

📍 18 km (11 miles) SW of Ándros town 🕐 Unrestricted access

Standing high on a rocky plateau inland is the ruined Venetian Paleókastro, which was built between 1207 and 1233. Its alternative name, the Castle of the Old Woman, commemorates a woman who betrayed her Venetian overlords during the 16th century. After tricking her way inside the castle, she opened the gates for the Ottoman Turks. Appalled by the bloody massacre that followed, she hurled herself off the cliffs near Kórthi, 5 km (3 miles) to the southeast, in remorse. The rock from which she jumped is known as Tis Griás to Pídima, or Old Woman's Leap.

⑤ Gávrio

📍 32 km (20 miles) NW of Ándros town

Gávrio is a pleasant enough, though rather characterless, port that becomes packed with Athenians heading for their holiday homes on week-ends. Set in an oval bay, Gávrio has a beach, a good camp site and several tavernas. During the high season it can be the only coastal place with rooms available at short notice, as Batsí is often pre-booked.

From Gávrio, it takes an hour or so to walk up to the tower of Ágios Pétros, the island's best-preserved ancient monument. Dating from the Hellenistic era, the tower stands 20 m (66 ft) high in an olive grove below the hamlet of Káto Ágios Pétros. Its upper storeys were reached by footholds and an internal ladder, and its inner hall was once crowned by a corbelled dome. The purpose of the tower remains a mystery, although it may have been built to serve as a watchtower to guard the nearby mines from attack by marauding pirates.

Just north of Gávrio there are good beaches beyond the village of Varsamiá, which has two sandy coves. Fellós beach (fine sand and pebbles combined) is the best, although it has been encroached upon by a few holiday villas that are set inland.

A turnoff from the coastal road, 8 km (5 miles) south of Gávrio, leads to the imposing 14th-century convent of Zoödóhos Pigís, the Spring of Life. Formerly a monastery occupied by 1,000 monks, in 1928 it became a convent. Only a handful of nuns now remain but they are always happy to show visitors their collection of icons and Byzantine tapestries.

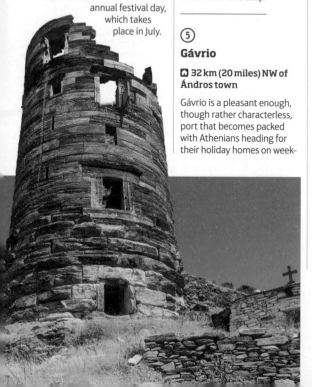

← The well-preserved tower of Ágios Pétros, an hour's walk from Gávrio

Batsí

🏛 8 km (5 miles) S of Gávrio 🚌

Built around a sweeping sandy bay, Batsí is a pretty and increasingly popular resort. It has a small fishing harbour and a maze of narrow lanes reached by white steps from the café-lined seafront. Despite the lively nightlife, Batsí has retained its village atmosphere. The main beach is popular with families, while Delavógias beach, south along the coastal track, is a favourite with naturists. Agía Marína, further along, has a friendly, family-run taverna.

South of Batsí the original capital of Ándros, **Ancient Paleópoli**, was inhabited until around 1000 AD when the people moved to Mesariá (p211). It was largely destroyed in the 4th century AD by an earthquake, but part of the acropolis is still visible, as are the remains of some of the temples under the sea.

Inland lies Káto Katákoilos village, known for its island music and dance festivals.

A rough track leads north from here to remote Aténi, a hamlet at the head of a lush valley. Two beautiful beaches, worth seeking out, lie further to the windy northeast, in the bay of Aténi. The village of Arnás, high on the slopes of the Kouvára mountain range, has flowing springs and is one of the island's greenest spots. With charming dry-stone walls and slate bridges, this is attractive walking country.

Ancient Paleópoli
🏛 9 km (6 miles) S of Batsí
🕐 Unrestricted access

CYCLADIC ART

With their simple geometric shapes and purity of line, Cycladic marble figurines are the legacy of the Bronze Age civilization of these islands and the first real expression of Greek art.

The figurines come from graves and are thought to represent, or be offerings to, an ancient deity. The earliest figures, from before 3000 BC, are slim and violin-shaped. By 2700–2300 BC, the forms were recognizably human and usually female. They range from palm-sized up to life-sized, with the proportions remaining consistent. Obsidian blades, marble bowls prefiguring later Greek art, abstract jewellery and pottery (including the unusual "frying pans") also survive. Excellent examples of Cycladic art can be seen in the Museum of Cycladic Art in Athens (p294); Cycladic artifacts are also found in museums throughout the world.

INFLUENCE ON MODERN ART

Cycladic art was considered ugly and crude when first discovered in the 19th century, but the simplicity of its form and decoration exerted a strong influence on several 20th-century artists and sculptors. These included Picasso, Modigliani, Constantin Brancusi and Henry Moore.

The figure is playing a harp and is one of the earliest musicians ever found.

The head is tipped back, and arms and legs are minimally marked.

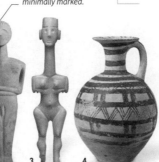

① This Early Cycladic figurine dates from 2800–2700 BC.

② A male figure is depicted in this highly stylized statuette.

③ This female figurine has folded arms and an incised headdress.

④ A Melos tomb held this terracotta vase from 2300–1900 BC.

13

SÝROS
ΣΥΡΟΣ

🛫 1 km (0.5 miles) SE of Ermoúpoli 🚢 Ermoúpoli 🚌
ℹ️ Ermoúpoli; www.syrosisland.gr

Rocky Sýros, or Sýra, is the commercial, administrative and cultural centre of the Cyclades. It became a rich and powerful port in the 19th century, and as a result the capital has richly decorated churches and grand squares. Tourism is not the main industry here, although the island becomes more popular every year.

MARKOS VAMVAKARIS

One of the greatest exponents of *rembétika*, the Greek blues, Markos Vamvakaris (1905-72) was born in Áno Sýros, and was a composer as well as a musician. Synonymous with hash dens, *rembétika* was the music of the urban underclass. With strong Byzantine and Islamic influences, it is often played on the *baglamá* or the bouzouki, both stringed guitar-like instruments. There are hundreds of recordings of Vamvakaris's music, the earliest dating back to 1932. A bust of the musician looks out to sea from the small square named after him in Sýros.

①

Ermoúpoli

 🚢 Aktí Ethnikís Antístassis ℹ️ Thymáton Sperhíon 11; 22810 82500

Elegant Ermoúpoli, named after Hermes, the god of commerce, is the largest city in the Cyclades. In the 19th century it was Greece's leading port and a major coaling station with a huge natural harbour and thriving shipyard. Crowned by the twin peaks of Catholic Áno Sýros to the north and the Orthodox Vrontádo to the south, the city is built like an amphitheatre around the harbour.

The central Platía Miaoúli in the lower town is one of the glories of Ermoúpoli. Paved with marble and lined with palm-shaded cafés and pizzerias, the grand square is the city's hub and meeting place, especially for the evening stroll, or *vólta*. There is also a marble bandstand and a statue dedicated to the revolutionary hero Admiral Andréas Miaoúlis. The square is dominated by the vast and impressive Neo-Classical town hall (1876). Designed by the German architect Ernst Ziller, the building is now a National Historical Landmark.

The **Archaeological Museum**, up the steps to the left of the town hall, houses bronze and marble utensils from the 3000 BC Cycladic settlement at Halandrianí. Also on display are Cycladic statuettes and Roman finds. Left of the town hall is the Historical Archives Office.

Nearby, on Platía Vardáka, is the Apollo Theatre, designed in 1864 by Italian architect Pietro Sampo as a copy of La Scala in Milan. The first opera house in Greece, it is noted for its fine paintings of Mozart and Verdi and is still used for plays and concerts.

Across the street the 1871 Velissaropoulos Mansion, now housing the Labour Union, has an elaborate marble façade and splendid painted ceilings and murals. Beyond here is the church of Ágios Nikólaos (1848) with a marble iconostasis by the 19th-century sculptor Vitális. Also by Vitális is the world's first monument to the unknown soldier, in front of the church.

In the upper town, the twin bell towers and distinctive blue and gold dome of Ágios Nikólaos mark the start of the Vapória district. Here Sýros's shipowners built Neo-Classical mansions, with some of the

finest plasterwork, frescoes and marble carvings in Greece. The houses cling to the coastline above the city's quays and moorings at Tálira, Ágios Nikólaos and Evangelístria.

The charming district of Vrontádo, on the hillside, has a number of excellent tavernas spread out on its slopes.

A half-hour's climb along Omiroú street, or a brief bus ride, brings you to the fortified medieval Catholic quarter of Áno Sýros. Also known as Apáno Hóra or Kástro, Áno Sýros is a maze of white-washed passages, arches and steps weaving through a huddle of interlinking houses. The main entrance is Kamára, an ancient passageway leading into the main road, or Piatsa.

The **Vamvakaris Museum**, dedicated to the life and work of the famed singer Markos Vamvakaris, is just off this road. At the top of Áno Sýros, the Baroque Aï-Giórgis, known as the cathedral of St George, contains fine icons. The Jesuit cloister was founded in 1744 around the church of Panagía Karmílou (1581), and has 6,000 books and manuscripts in its library. Below it, the Capuchin convent of Ágios Ioánnis was a meeting place and a refuge from pirates.

Archaeological Museum

⌂ Platía Miaoúli 📞 22810 88487 🕑 Apr–Oct: 9am–4pm Tue–Thu, 9am–9pm Fri–Sun; Nov–Mar: 8am–3pm Tue, Wed & Fri–Sun 🕑 Main public hols

Vamvakaris Museum

⌂ Platía Vamvakári, Áno Sýros 📞 22810 84762 🕑 10am–3:30pm Mon–Tue, 11am–6pm Wed–Sun

←

Looking over the bright and busy harbour from Ermoúpoli's upper town

EAT

Iliovassilema

The most innovative taverna in this resort, with creative renditions of local dishes, like fennel pie, squid-ink risotto and crunchy fish, plus oddities like Mesolóngi eel.

Galissás beach, Sýros
May–early Oct
22810 43325

€€€

Apano Hora

By day a popular *kafenío* thanks to its terrace, after dark this becomes a *mezedopolío*, with live acoustic music at weekends. Platters might be carrot-and-cheese turnovers, sausages and a dish of the day or two. You will have to fight for a terrace table.

Piátsa, Áno Sýros town
22810 80565

€€€

Stin Ithaki tou Aï

The narrow lanes east of Platía Miaoúli are packed with tavernas and mezedopolía. This is perhaps the best, specializing in meat medleys with quick, friendly service, even when busy.

Stefánou Kyparíssou 1, Ermoúpoli, Sýros
22810 82060

€€€

Kíni

9 km (6 miles) NW of Ermoúpoli

The fishing village of Kíni is set in a horseshoe-shaped bay with two good sandy beaches, making it a popular meeting place for watching the sunset over a glass of ouzo. It also has some excellent fish tavernas.

North, over the headland, extends Delfíni beach, the longest on Sýros and among the best, with pristine water well sheltered from most winds. It used to be a naturist haven with no facilities, but now there is a beach bar with a sunbed concession.

Between Ermoúpoli and Kíni, set in pine-covered hills, is the red-domed convent of Agía Varvára. With spectacular views to the west, this attractive Orthodox convent was once a girls' orphanage. The nuns run a weaving school and their knitwear and woven goods are on sale at the convent. The frescoes in the church depict St Barbara's martyrdom, killed by her father for being a Christian.

Boat services run from Kíni to some of the island's remote northern beaches. Grámmata Bay is one of the most spectacular, a deep sheltered inlet with golden sands where sea lilies grow in autumn. Some of the rocks here have a Hellenistic inscription carved on them, with the writers seeking protection for ships on the deadly seas.

A boat trip around the tip of the island past Cape Diapóri to the east coast takes you to Sykamiá beach. Here there is a cave

where the Syriot philosopher Pherekydes is thought to have lived during the summer months. A physicist and astronomer in the mid-6th century BC, Pherekydes was one of the first philosophers, and invented the heliotrope, an early sundial. From the beach you can see the remains of the Bronze Age citadel of Kastrí with six towers perched on a steep rock.

→

Panagía Gorgona statue at Kíni, a memorial to sailors drowned at sea

↑ Boats moored in the shallow, clear waters at Althea beach near Vári

③ Galissás

 7 km (4 miles) W of Ermoúpoli 🚌

Lively Galissás has the most sheltered beach on the island, fringed by tamarisk trees. It is particularly popular with families. Across the headland, a short walk to the west, Armeós beach is a haven for nudists. Galissás has both the island's campsites, making it popular with backpackers. In high season it can be a noisy place to stay, and is often full of motorbikers. To the south of the bay looms the Catholic chapel of Agía Pákou, occupying the site of the Classical city of Galissás.

Fínikas, 3 km (2 miles) further south on the coast, was originally settled by the Phoenicians. The town is now a popular resort, home to more than 1,000 people, with a pier and moorings for yachts and fishing boats.

④ Posidonía

 12 km (7 miles) SW of Ermoúpoli 🚌

Posidonía, or Dellagrázia, south of the capital, is one of the largest tourist sites on the island, with cosmopolitan hotels and restaurants. It was named for Poseidon, the sea god. The island's first main road was built in 1855 from Ermoúpoli through Posidonía to Fínikas. The affluent village contains some Italianate mansions, which are the country retreats of wealthy islanders.

Only a short walk to the southwest, quieter Agathopés is one of the island's best beaches, with safe, shallow waters for swimming, created by the protective islet opposite. It has amenities including sun-loungers and cafés. Mégas Gialós, 3 km (2 miles) further down the south coast, is a pretty beach shaded by tamarisk trees.

Did You Know?

The inhabitants of Sýros converted to Catholicism under the French Capuchins in the Middle Ages.

⑤ Vári

 8 km (5 miles) S of Ermoúpoli 🚌

Quaint, sheltered Vári has become a major resort, but it still has traditional houses lining its hills and a small castle. The town's main beach is a curved bay with turquoise water that doesn't get too crowded. It has some good amenities. The Hontrá peninsula, east of Vári, is the site of the island's oldest prehistoric settlement, dating from 4000–3000 BC.

PÁROS
ΠΑΡΟΣ

🛫 Alykí 🚢 Parikiá 🛈 22843 60100

Fertile, thyme-scented Páros is famous for its white marble, which ensured the island's prosperity from the early Cycladic age through to Roman times. Páros is the hub of the Cycladic ferry system and its resorts are busy in high season, but it is still a charming island with hill-villages, vineyards and olive groves.

① Parikiá

🚢🚌 Harbour 🛈 22843 60100

The port of Parikiá, or Hóra, owes its foundations to the marble trade. Standing on the site of a leading early Cycladic city, it became a major Roman marble centre. Traces of Byzantine and Venetian rule remain, although earthquakes have caused much damage.

Today it prospers as a resort town, with a waterfront that is crammed with ticket agencies, cafés and bars. The area behind the harbour is a historic Cycladic town, with medieval archways, narrow paved alleys and white houses overhung with cascading jasmine.

Ekatondapylianí, (Church of a Hundred Doors) in the west of town, is the oldest in Greece in continuous use and is a major Byzantine monument. It is dedicated to the Dormition of the Virgin. According to legend, the church was founded by St Helen, mother of Constantine, the first Christian Byzantine emperor. After having a vision here showing the path to the True Cross, she vowed to build a church on the site but died before fulfilling her promise. In the 6th century AD the Emperor Justinian carried out her wish, commissioning the architect Ignatios to design a cathedral. Ignatios was the apprentice of Isidoros of Miletos, master builder of Agía Sofía in Constantinople (Istanbul). The result was so impressive that Isidoros, full with jealousy, pushed his pupil off the roof. Ignatios grabbed his master's foot and they both fell to their deaths. The pair are immortalized in stone in the north of the courtyard in front of the church.

Ekatondapylianí is made up of three interlocking buildings,

Charming Parikiá village, home to Ekatondapylianí church with its beautiful iconostasis *(inset)*

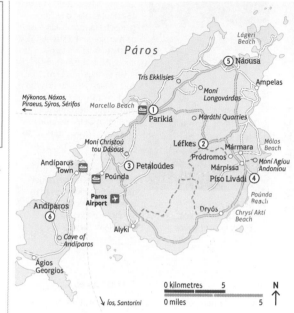

INSIDER TIP
Trendy Neighbour

For decades those in the know have regarded Páros's smaller neighbouring island of Andíparos - with its relaxed and stylish café scene - as a much cooler hangout.

and is meant to have 99 doors and windows. According to legend, when the hundredth door is found, Constantinople will return to Greek rule.

Numerous earthquakes have forced much reconstruction of the church, and the main church was restyled in the 10th century in the shape of a Greek cross. The sanctuary columns date from the pre-Christian era and the marble screen and capitals are of Byzantine origin. A footprint, set in stone, is claimed to be that of Agía Theoktísti, Parikia's patron saint. Also displayed is her severed hand.

From the back of the church a door leads to the chapel of Ágios Nikólaos, an adapted

4th-century-BC Hellenistic building, which has a double row of Doric columns, along with a marble throne and a 17th-century iconostasis.

Given Paros's geology, marble artifacts unsurprisingly dominate the displays at the **Archaeological Museum**. One of its main exhibits is part of the priceless Parian Chronicle, a historical record of the artistic achievements of ancient Greece up to 264 BC. It is carved on a marble tablet and was discovered in the kástro walls during the 17th century. Also on display are discoveries from the Temple of Apollo.

Built in 1260 on the site of the ancient acropolis, the Venetian kástro lies on a small hill at the end of the main street of the town. The marble remains from the temples of Apollo and Demeter at the acropolis were used to construct the eastern fortification of the Venetian kástro. These ancient columns have also been partially used to form the walls of houses neighbouring the site.

THE LEGEND OF AGIA THEOKTÍSTI

Parikia's patron saint, Theoktísti, was a young nun captured by pirates in the 9th century. She escaped to Páros and lived alone in the woods for 35 years, leading a pious and frugal life. Found by a hunter, she asked him to bring her some Communion bread. When he returned with the bread, he found she had died. Realizing she was a saint, the hunter cut off her hand to take as a relic, but found he could not leave Páros until he reunited her hand with her body.

Ekatondapyliani
⌂ Western Parikiá ▯ 22840 21243 ◷ Dawn-dusk daily

Archaeological Museum
⊘ ⌂ Behind the Ekatondapyliani ▯ 22840 21231 ◷ 8am-3pm Tue-Sun

↑ Whitewashed cottages in Léfkes, the capital of Páros

② Léfkes

🏠 10 km (6 miles) SE of Parikiá 🚌 🛈 22840 41617

The mountain road to Léfkes, the island's highest village, passes the abandoned marble quarries at Maráthi, last worked for Napoleon's tomb. They are now inaccessible.

Léfkes, which is named after long-vanished local poplar trees, was the capital under Ottoman rule. It is a charming, unspoiled village with medieval houses covered in pink and red bougainvillea, a labyrinth of paved alleys, cafés in the lovely lower *platía* and restaurants with terraces overlooking the green valley below. Visitors must explore on foot; parking is at the village entrance. Shops stock local weaving and ceramic handi-crafts and there is a tiny Folk Museum (key is available from the town hall).

From the white windmills overlooking Léfkes, a Byzantine marble pathway leads 3 km (2 miles) southeast to Pródromos, an old fortified

→ Fishermen repairing their nets at a sunny fishing port on Páros

farming village. Walk a further 15 minutes past olive groves to reach Mármara village with its marble-paved streets. The pretty hamlet of Márpissa lies about 2 km (1 mile) south.

On Kéfalos hill, 2 km (1 mile) east of Márpissa, stands the 16th-century Moní Agíou Andoníou. The monastery is built from Classical remains and has a 17th-century fresco of the Second Coming, rarely visible as the place is kept firmly locked. Beyond lies Cape Kéfalos, with a ruined 14th-century fortress that was the last Parian-Venetian stronghold to fall to the Ottomans in 1537.

③ Petaloúdes

🏠 6 km (4 miles) SW of Parikía 🚌
🕐 Jun–20 Sep daily

Petaloúdes, or the Valley of the Butterflies, is easily reached from Parikiá. This lush green oasis is home to swarms of Jersey tiger moths from May to August, which flutter from the foliage when disturbed.

About 2 km (1 mile) north of Petaloúdes, the 18th-century convent of Moní Christoú tou Dásous, Christ of the Woods, is worth the walk, although only

women are allowed into the sanctuary. Páros island's patron saint, Ágios Arsénios, a 19th-century confessor and miracle-worker, is buried here.

④ Píso Livádi

🏠 15 km (9 miles) SE of Parikiá 🚌 Towards Márpissa

Situated below Léfkes on Páros's east coast, the former fishing village of Píso Livádi, with its sheltered sandy beach of Logarás, has grown into a lively small resort. It was once the port for the island's hill villages and marble quarries; there are no longer seagoing services from here. The small harbour has a wide range of bars and tavernas, with occasional local activities and entertainments.

Mólos, 6 km (4 miles) north, has a long sandy beach with dunes, tavernas and a wind-surfing centre. Just to the south lies Poúnda (not to be confused with the village of Poúnda on the west coast), one of the best and most fashionable beaches in the Cyclades with a relaxed and trendy beach bar. The island's most famous east coast beach, 3 km (2 miles) south,

↑ Caïques lining up at the attractive fishing harbour at Náousa

is Chrysí Aktí (Golden Beach). With 700 m (2,300 ft) of golden sand it is perfect for families. It is also a well-known centre for water sports and has hosted the world windsurfing championships.

Dryós, 2 km (1 mile) further southwest, is an expanding resort but at its heart is a pretty village with a duck pond, tavernas, a small harbour with a pebbly beach and a string of sandy coves.

Náousa

 12 km (7 miles) NE of Parikiá ⬜ ℹ 2284051220

With its brightly painted fishing boats and winding white alleyways, Náousa has become a cosmopolitan destination for the jet set, with expensive boutiques and relaxed bars. It is the island's second-largest town and the place to sit and watch the rich and the beautiful parade in chic designer clothes along the waterfront. The colourful harbour has a unique break-

water in the half-submerged ruin of a Venetian castle that has slowly been sinking with the coastline.

Every year, on the evening of 23 August, 100 torch-lit fishing caïques assemble to re-enact a victory over an Ottoman fleet during the War of Independence, ending with music and dancing.

⑥
Andíparos

The island of Andíparos is separated from Páros by a narrow channel too shallow for large ferries to negotiate. A shuttling Ro-Ro ferry links the two from the west coast kitesurfing resort of Poúnda and there is also a seasonal caïque service from Parikiá. Andíparos town has a relaxed if increasingly trendy scene in its tavernas, cafés and boutiques. Most activity in town happens on the main commercial street and the Venetian *kástro* area. The *kástro* is a good example of a 15th-century fortified neighbourhood, with the backs of

houses forming the defensive perimeter. The village also has two charming 17th-century churches, Ágios Nikólaos and Evangelismós.

The island has fine beaches, but the star attraction is the massive **Cave of Andíparos**, with a breathtaking array of stalactites and stalagmites, said to have been discovered by Arilohos of ancient Páros around the time of Alexander the Great. It is cheap and easy to take a vehicle across the straits to Andíparos and drive right up to the cave entrance. Unfortunately, only the topmost layer of this deep cave system is open to visits. This caves have been often-visited throughout history: Lord Byron and others have carved their names on the walls and in 1673 the French ambassador, the Marquis de Nointel, held a Christmas Eve Mass here for 500 friends. The church outside, Ágios Ioánnis Spiliótis was built in 1774.

Cave of Andíparos

◈ ◷ Summer: 10am–6pm daily; spring/autumn: 10am–3pm daily ◷ Nov–May

15

NÁXOS
ΝΑΞΟΣ

✈ 2 km (1 mile) S of Náxos town 🚌 Náxos town
🚢 ℹ️ Náxos town; www.naxos.gr

The largest of the Cyclades, Náxos was first settled in 3000 BC and became a major centre of the Cycladic civilization, famed for its marble. Náxos fell to the Venetians in 1207, and numerous fortified towers (*pýrgoi*) were built across the island; many are still standing today. Náxos's landscape is rich with grazing flocks of sheep and olive groves. The island is also spoken of in mythology as the place where the hero Theseus abandoned Cretan princess Ariadne.

💬 INSIDER TIP
Cultural Events

In summer, Náxos is alive with festivals. The Náxos Festival, held in historic fortified Bazeos Tower, celebrates contemporary culture through art, music and plays (*www. bazeostower.gr/eng*).

①
Náxos Town

🚌 🚢 Harbourfront
ℹ️ Harbourfront; www. naxos.gr

There are four distinct areas that make up Náxos Town, or Hóra: the harbour, Ágios Geórgios, *kástro* and Boúrgos. The harbour, bustling with cafés and fishermen at work, is dominated by the huge marble Portára gateway on the islet of Palátia. North of the port and reached by a causeway, the gateway was constructed in 530 BC and was designed as the entrance for the unfinished Temple of Apollo.

To the south of the harbour, Ágios Geórgios is a concrete mass of hotels, apartments and restaurants. Above the harbour, the old town divides into the Venetian *kástro* district, once home to the

Catholic nobility, and the medieval Boúrgos, where the Orthodox population lived. The twisting alleys of the Boúrgos market area are lined with restaurants and gift shops. The 18th-century Orthodox cathedral, with the ancient agora revealed in its courtyard, is dedicated to Ágios Nikódimos, the island's patron saint. A festival is held in his honour on 14 July.

Uphill lies the imposing medieval north gate of the fortified *kástro*, built in 1207 by Marco Sanudo. Only two of

the original seven gate-towers remain. Little is left of the 13th-century outer walls, but the inner walls still stand, protecting 19 impressive houses, which each bear the coats of arms of the Venetian nobles who lived there. The nobles' remains are housed in the Catholic cathedral in the *kástro*, which dates from the 14th century, beneath marble slabs dating back to 1619. In the *kástro*, many of the current residents are still descended from these same families. In the square is a tower, all that remains of the Sanudo Palace, former seat of the dukes of Náxos.

During the occupation by the Ottomans, Náxos was famous for its schools. The French Commercial School, founded by Jesuits in 1627, provided education to Orthodox and Catholic alike. The most famous pupil was Níkos Kazantzákis, a Cretan novelist who described his time here

←

The ancient Portára gateway to the Temple of Apollo, Náxos town

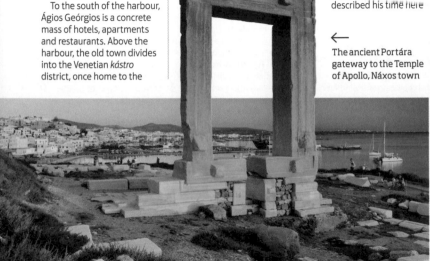

in his book *Report to Greco* (1961). The **Archaeological Museum** is now housed in the building, and has a notable collection of Cycladic marble figurines, as well as some beautiful Roman mosaics.

The lagoon-like bay of Ágios Geórgios, to the south, is Náxos town's main resort area, with golden sands and shallow water. The best beaches are out of town, along the west coast. Agía Ánna is a pleasant small resort with silver sands and watersports. For more solitude, head south 3 km (2 miles) over the dunes to remote and beautiful Pláka, the best beach on the island. Still further south, the pure white sands of Mikrí Vígla and Kastráki, which is named after a ruined Mycenaean fortress, are good for watersports.

Archaeological Museum

French School **C** 22850 22725 **8am–3pm Tue–Sun** Main public hols

---

②
Mélanes Valley

10 km (6 miles) E of Náxos town To Kinídaros

The road southeast of Náxos town passes through the Livádi valley, the heart of ancient marble country, to the Mélanes villages. In Kouroúnohori, the first village, stands the 14th-century Venetian Frangópoulos-Della Rocca tower, the oldest of several such structures on Náxos. At Mýli, near the ancient marble quarry at Flerió, lie two 6th-century BC *koúroi*, huge marble statues. One, 8 m (26 ft) long, lies in a private garden that is open to visitors. The other, slightly smaller statue, 5.5 m (18 ft) long, lies up on a hillside, reached by a graded walkway.

Southwest of the Mélanes villages is Glinádo, home to the Belónia Tower, built around the 1600s, which is the best-preserved of the fortified

mansions on Náxos. Beyond Sangrí village at Gyroúla, the reconstructed Temple of Demeter is well worth the trip out. The grounds are always open, but the museum is closed on Mondays.

---

③
Trageá Valley

15 km (9 miles) SE of Náxos town

From Ano Sagrí the road twists to the Trageá valley. The first village in the valley, Halkí, is the most picturesque, with Neo-Classical architecture including the Venetian Barozzi-Grazia Tower. Just off the road from Halkí to Moní, Panagía Drosianí is the oldest and most artistically significant church on Náxos. Built between the 4th and 12th centuries, the interior shelters damaged but discernible 5th-century frescoes. Filóti is a traditional village and is the largest in the region. The

attractive small settlement sits on the slopes of towering Mount Zas, which, at 1,000 m (3,300 ft), is the highest peak in the Cyclades.

↑ A charming street displaying Venetian architecture at Halkí

④

Apírathou

📍 25 km (16 miles) SE of Náxos town

Apírathou (formerley known as Apíranthos) was established by Cretans fleeing Muslim oppression after the Ottoman conquest of Crete. It is the island's most atmospheric village, featuring marble-paved streets, two tower-mansions built by the Zevgoli and Bardanis clans, and a vast pedestrian terrace with some excellent cafés.

Among several small museums in Apírathou, the most noteworthy is the **Folklore Museum**, which showcases the village's weaving tradition, and the **Geological Museum**, covering the local emery industry. There are also displays on other Aegean minerals.

Below the village is the port of Moutsoúna, where ships were once loaded with emery before the industry's decline. A small but good sand beach spreads next to the disused industrial cranes.

Folklore Museum
📞 22850 61725 🕐 Jul-Aug: 10:30am-7:30pm; erratic hours rest of the year

> Approaching from Kóronos the road becomes a tortuous succession of hairpin bends before finally arriving in pretty Koronída (formerly known as Komiakí).

Geological Museum
♿ 🏫 Village school 📞 22850 61725 🕐 May-Sep: 10:30am-4pm daily 🚫 Main public hols

⑤

Koronída

📍 42 km (26 miles) E of Náxos town

Approaching from Kóronos, a small village dating from around 1200 AD, the road becomes a tortuous succession of hairpin bends before finally arriving in pretty Koronída (formerly known as Komiakí). This is the highest village on Náxos and a former home of the emery miners. It is covered with vines and is known for being the place where the local *kítro* liqueur originated more than two

←
Traditional stone and marble alleyway, characteristic of Apírathou village

centuries ago. *Kítro* is made from the leaves of citron trees (and the fruit is candied).

From the village there are lovely walks with wonderful views over the surrounding terraced vineyards.

⑥

Apóllonas

📍 49 km (30 miles) NE of Náxos town

Originally a fishing village that has become a resort, Apóllonas gets busy in the summer for the sake of its beach, fish tavernas and the huge *koúros* found here. There is also a lively festival in the village for St John the Baptist on 28–29 August.

Steps lead up the hillside above the village to ancient marble quarries where a vast unfinished statue has lain abandoned since 600 BC. The epic bearded marble figure, 10.5 m (35 ft) long and weighing 30 tonnes, is believed to

↑ Natural rock formation, ideal for bathing, on the island of Koufoníssi

represent the god Apollo. At Agiá, 10 km (6 miles) west of Apóllonas, stands the fortified monastery of Kímisis tis Theotókou, now uninhabited but still hosting a lively festival on 14–15 August. Further along the north coast road lies the idyllic sand-and-pebble beach at Abram with a good family-run taverna.

The abandoned Moní Faneroménis, dating from 1606, is 13 km (8 miles) south on the road winding down the west coast from Apollonas. Slightly further south towards Galíni, a road leads up to the looming fortification of Moní Ypsilotéra, built in 1660 by the same Orthodox Cocco (Kokkos) clan responsible for the similar monastery at Agiá. They feuded with the Catholic Barozzis for two decades until a marriage united the two families.

Minor Cyclades

Between Náxos and Amorgós lie the islands of Donoússa, Koufoníssi, Skhinoússa and Irakliá, the "Lesser Cyclades" or, informally "Back Islands". They are all developed, to varying degrees, for tourism.

Irakliá, the largest, has marked walking trails, one ending at the sacred cave of Aï Giánnis. Koufoníssi consists of two islands: Ano (upper), the most developed and busiest of the Back Islands, with excellent sandy beaches, and the uninhabited Káto (lower). Skhinoússa's bays are popular with yachties but land access to some of the coast is blocked by development.

Donoússa, the most northerly, is more isolated but is the second most popular destination after Koufoníssi. It has good walking on the remaining path network, superb sandy beaches at Kéndros and Livádi, and a few relaxed tavernas in the port.

Did You Know?

Although he was born in a cave on Crete, the king of the gods, Zeus, was brought up on Náxos.

STAY

Hotel Grotta
Rooms are nicely decorated, more in the style of a multi-starred hotel. Vast, delicious breakfasts are served in a spacious lounge.

⌂ Grótta district, Náxos town
🌐 hotelgrotta.gr

€€€

Chateau Zevgoli
Stay in an antique-fitted suite or a double with sea views at this inn, in restored Venetian-era buildings.

⌂ Boúrgos district, Kástro
🌐 naxostown hotels.com

€€€

Kavos Naxos
A lovely hillside oasis of stone bungalows comfortably kitted out, suitable for families. There is an excellent restaurant and assiduous service.

⌂ Stelída peninsula, Ágios Prokópios, Náxos
🌐 kavos-naxos.com

€€€

Naxian Collection
Offering a range of suites and villas, many with pools, the scenic Naxian Collection is incredibly luxurious, and has white decor throughout.

⌂ Stelída peninsula, Náxos
🌐 hotel.naxian collection.com/en/

€€€

16

TÍNOS
ΤΗΝΟΣ

🏛 Tínos town 🚢 Quay 🛈 Corner of Kionian, Tínos town

A craggy yet green island, Tínos was first settled by Ionians in Archaic times. It has a long history of religious significance: in the 4th century BC it was known for its Sanctuary of Poseidon and Amphitrite, and it now has over 800 Christian chapels scattered across the island. In the 1960s, the military junta ruling Greece declared it a holy island and Greek Orthodox pilgrims still flock to the large church complex of the Panagía Evangelístria in Tínos town. Under Venetian rule from medieval times, in 1715 Tínos was conquered by the Ottomans, the last island in the Cyclades to fall.

Did You Know?

People still go up the steps of the Panagía Evangelístria in the hope of being healed from illness.

① Tínos Town

A typical island capital, Tínos town has narrow streets, white-washed houses and a bustling port lined with restaurants and hotels. Situated at the top of Megalóharis, the main street that runs up from the ferry, **Panagía Evangelístria**, the church of the Annunciation, dominates Tínos town. The pedestrianized Evangelístrías, which runs parallel to the main street, is packed with stalls full of votive offerings and icons. Built in 1830, the church houses Tínos's miraculous icon. In 1822, during the Greek War of Independence, a nun at Moní Kechrovouníou, Sister Pelagia, had visions of the Panagía showing where an icon had been buried. In 1823, acting on the nun's directions, excavations revealed the icon of the Annunciation of the Archangel Gabriel, unscathed after 850 years underground. Known in Greece as the Megalóhari (the Great Joy), the icon was found to have healing powers, and the church built around it has became a pilgrimage for Orthodox Christians.

During the annual festivals of the Annunciation and the Assumption, the icon is paraded through the streets. The church is a treasury of offerings, such as the orange tree made of gold and silver, gifted by pilgrims whose prayers have been answered. The icon itself is so smothered in gold and jewels it is hard to see the painting. The crypt where it was found is known as the chapel of Évresis, or Discovery. Where the icon lay is now lined with silver, and the holy spring here is said to have healing powers.

On Megalóharis, halfway to Panagía Evangelístria, is the **Archaeological Museum**, which has displays of sculptures of nereids (sea-nymphs) and dolphins found at the Sanctuary of Poseidon and Amphitrite near Kiónia. There are also some enormous 8th-century-BC storage jars from ancient Tínos, sited on the rock of Exómbourgo.

East of town, the closest beach is shingly Agios Fokás. To the west is the popular beach at Stavrós, with a jetty

↑ The vast complex of Panagía Evangelístria in Tínos town

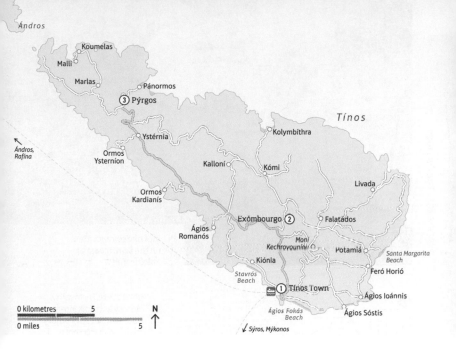

0 kilometres 5

0 miles 5

N ↑

that was built in Classical times. To the north near Kiónia are the foundations of the 4th-century-BC Sanctuary of Poseidon and Amphitrite, his sea-nymph bride.

North of Tínos town is the 12th-century walled Moní Kechrovouníou, one of the largest convents in Greece. You can visit the cell where Sister Pelagia had her visions and the chest where her embalmed head is kept.

Panagía Evangelístria
🕒 Daily 🌐 panagiatinou.gr

Archaeological Museum
◈ 🏛 Megalóharis 📞 22830 29063 🕒 8am–3pm Tue–Sun 🚫 Main public hols

---

Exómbourgo

🏛 15 km (9 miles) N of Tínos town

Dominating the central part of the island, at 640 m (2,100 ft) high, the rock of Exómbourgo was the site of the Archaic city of Tínos and later became

home to the Venetian fortress of St Elena. Built by the Ghisi family after the Doge, leader of the Republic of Venice, handed over the island to them in 1207, the fortress was the toughest stronghold in the Cyclades, and was not surrended to the Ottomans until 1715. You can see remains of ancient walls on the crag, medieval houses, a fountain and three churches.

---

③
Pýrgos

🏛 23 km (14 miles) NW of Tínos town

Overlooking the harbour of Pánormos in the northwest of the island, the pretty village of Pýrgos is famous for its marble, and has a notable tradition of creating marble-work, particularly sculptures. There are studios throughout town, and the old grammar school is now the School of Fine Arts, where students learn the craft. There are fantastic examples at the Museum of Marble Crafts in town.

↑ Kleftiko cove, located on the south coast of Mílos island

17

MÍLOS
ΜΗΛΟΣ

🛫 7 m (4 miles) SE of Adámas 🚤 Adámas
🚌 Adámas ℹ Harbourfront, Adámas

Volcanic Mílos is the most dramatic of the Cyclades with its extraordinary rock formations, hot springs and white villages perched on cliffs. Under the Minoans and Mycenaeans the island became rich from trading obsidian. Minerals remain the main source of the island's wealth, although tourism is growing.

① Pláka

On a clifftop 4 km (2 miles) above the port of Adámas, Pláka is a pretty mix of churches and white cubic houses. These blend into the suburb of Trypití, which is topped by windmills.

Pláka is believed to be sited on the acropolis of ancient Mílos, built by the Dorians between 1100 and 800 BC. The town was destroyed by the Athenians and later settled by the Romans.

The principal sight is the **Archaeological Museum**, its entrance hall dominated by a plaster copy of the *Venus de Milo*, found on Mílos. The collection includes Neolithic finds, particularly obsidian, Mycenaean pottery, painted ceramics and terracotta animals from 3500 BC, found at the ancient city of Phylakopi. The most famous of the ceramics is the *Lady of Phylakope*, an early Cycladic goddess decorated in Minoan style. The Hellenistic 4th-century-BC statue of Poseidon and the *koúros* of Mílos (560 BC) found here are now in the National Archaeological Museum in Athens (*p292*). There are also finds from the neighbouring island of Kímolos. The nearby History and Folk Museum is housed in a 19th-century mansion in the centre of Pláka. It has costumes, four-poster beds and handicrafts.

Steps lead to the ruined *kástro*, which was built by the Venetians on a volcanic plug 280 m (920 ft) above sea level. Only the houses that formed the outer walls of the fortress remain. Above the *kástro*, the church of Mésa Panagía was bombed during World War II. It was rebuilt and renamed Panagía Skhiniótissa (Our Lady of the Bushes) after an icon of the Virgin Mary appeared in a bush where the old church used to stand. Just below, the church of Panagía Thalassítra (Our Lady of the Sea), built in 1728, has icons of Christ, the Virgin Mary and Ágios Elefthérios. The massive stone blocks of the Cyclopean walls that formed the city's East Gate in

←

Copy of *Venus de Milo*, Pláka Archaeological Museum

450 BC remain, while 15 m (50 ft) west there are marble relics and a Christian baptismal font from a Byzantine basilica.

Archaeological Museum

 ⚑ Main square ☏ 22870 28026 🕒 9am–4pm Tue–Sun (also closed Thu Apr–Oct) 🗓 1 May

---

② Trypití

⚑ 2 km (1 mile) SE of Pláka

In the nearby town of Trypití are well-preserved 2nd-to-4th-century-AD **Christian Catacombs**. Carved into the hillside, the massive complex of galleries has tombs in arched niches (arcosolia), each one containing up to seven bodies. The catacomb network is 184 m (605 ft) long, with 291 tombs. Archaeologists believe that as many as 2,000 bodies were interred here.

From the catacombs, a track leads to the place where the Venus de Milo was discovered, marked by a plaque. It was found on 8 April 1820 by a farmer, Georgios Kentrotas. He uncovered a cave in his field with half of the marble statue inside. The other half was found by a visiting French officer. The statue is now on show in the Louvre, Paris. The missing arms are thought to have been lost in the struggle for possession.

Christian Catacombs

⚑ Trypití, 2 km (1 mile) SE of Pláka 🕒 8:30am–6:30pm Tue–Sun (to 3pm Sun) 🌐 catacombs.gr

---

③ Bay of Mílos

⚑ 12 km (7 miles) SE of Pláka

This rugged island is scattered with volcanic relics and long stretches of beach. The vast Bay of Mílos, the site of the

volcano's central vent, is one of the finest natural harbours in the Mediterranean.

South of Adámas, the Bay of Mílos has a succession of attractive beaches, including Hivadolímni, backed by a turquoise saltwater lake.

---

④ Agía Kyriakí

⚑ 13 km (8 miles) SE of Pláka

On the south coast are a succession of beaches; one of the best is the lovely Agía Kyriakí, beyond Zefyría village. Neighbouring Paleohóri is unique as some of the sand is volcanically heated – enough to cook an egg.

---

⑤ Pollónia

⚑ 12 km (7 miles) NE of Pláka

Situated on the northeast tip of the island is Pollónia, a popular resort with a tree-fringed beach. Small ferries leave here for the island of Kímolos, named after the chalk (kimolía) mined there.

Once an important centre of civilization, little remains of Ancient Phylakope, southwest of Pollónia. You can make out the old Mycenaean city walls, houses and grave sites, but a large part of the city has been submerged under the sea.

CRETE

For nearly 3,000 years the ruins of an ancient Minoan civilization lay buried and forgotten beneath the coastal plains of Crete. It was not until the early 20th century that the remains of great Minoan palaces at Knosós, Phaestos, Mália and Zákros were unearthed. Their magnificence demonstrates the level of sophistication and artistic imagination of the Minoan civilization, now considered the wellspring of European culture. The Romans brought their administrative expertise to the island, and the ancient city-state of Górtys became capital of the Roman province of Crete in 65 BC. Byzantine rule was followed by the Venetians, who built formidable fortresses, such as Frangokástello, and elegant buildings in cities, such as those found in Réthymno and Haniá. The Venetians were defeated by the Ottomans, who ruled Crete until 1913, when, led by revered statesman Elefthérios Venizélos (1864–1936), Crete became a part of unified Greece. The island was again occupied in World War II by German forces, but these invaders were fiercely resisted by the local populace until they were eventually defeated by the Allied army. Through all these long occupations, Cretan identity and pride remained strong, and today many cultural traditions, including costume, continue across the island.

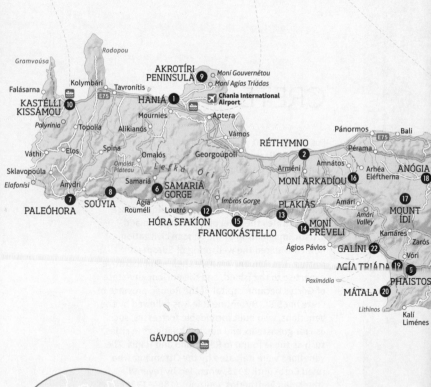

Kýthira ↑

Sea of Crete

Gramvoúsa

Rodopoú

Falásarna

Kolymbári

Tavronítis

AKROTÍRI PENINSULA 9

Moní Gouvernétou
Moní Agías Triádas

KASTÉLLI KISSÁMOU 10

E75

HANIÁ 1

✈ **Chania International Airport**

Polyrínia

Topoliá

Mourniés

Aptera

PALEÓHORA 7

SOÚYIA

Alikianós

Vámos

Váthi

Elos

Spína

Omalós

Georgoúpoli

RÉTHYMNO 2

Pánormos

E75 Bali

Sklavopoúla

Elafonísi

Anýdri

Omalós Plateau

Lefká Óri

Samariá

SAMARIÁ GORGE 6

8

Arméni

Amnátos

Péríma

MONÍ ARKADÍOU 16

Arhéa Eléftherna

ANÓGIA 18

Ágia Rouméli

Loutró

Ímbros Gorge

PLAKIÁS 13

Amári

MOUNT ÍDI 17

HÓRA SFAKÍON 12

15

FRANGOKÁSTELLO 14

MONÍ PRÉVELI

Amári Valley

Kamáres

Zarós

Vóri

Ágios Pávlos

GALÍNI 22

AGÍA TRIÁDA 19

PHAISTOS 5

Paximádia

MÁTALA 20

Lithínos

Kalí Liménes

GÁVDOS 11

CRETE

CRETE

Must Sees
1. Haniá
2. Réthymno
3. Iráklio
4. Palace of Knosos
5. Phaistos
6. Samariá Gorge

Experience More
7. Paleóhora
8. Soúyia
9. Akrotíri Peninsula
10. Kastélli Kissámou
11. Gávdos
12. Hóra Sfakíon
13. Plakías
14. Moní Préveli
15. Frangokástello
16. Moní Arkadíou
17. Mount Ída
18. Anógia
19. Agía Triáda
20. Mátala
21. Gortys
22. Galíni
23. Arhánes
24. Hersónisos
25. Mália
26. Lasíthi Plateau
27. Eloúnda
28. Ágios Nikólaos
29. Kritsá
30. Ierápetra
31. Gournia
32. Moní Toploú
33. Sitía
34. Váï Beach
35. Zákros

→

1 The fortress at Spinalónga.

2 Inside the fortifications of Moní Toploú.

3 The famous palms at Vaï.

4 A lovely sunset at a beach resort, Mýrtos.

5 DAYS
in Eastern Crete

Day 1

Your east coast exploration starts at Malia *(p275)*, a short drive east of Crete's capital, Iráklío. This bustling resort is home to the little-visited Minoan palace of Malia, one of the most important ancient sites on the island. After an hour or so of exploration, drive east to scenic Lasíthi plateau *(p275)*. You'll know you've arrived when you see the windmills and smell thyme in the air. Stop for lunch at family-run Dionyssos in Magoulás hamlet *(Main road, Magoulás)*. The main attraction in this part of Crete is the eerie Diktean Cave *(p275)*, the legendary birthplace of Zeus; the path to the cave starts from the small village of Psychró. After you've marvelled at the eerie rock formations, head to lively Ágios Nikólaos *(p276)* for dinner under the vines at friendly, traditional Avli taverna *(Prigkipos Georgiou 12)*.

Day 2

By daylight, Ágios Nikólaos is delightful, situated as it is around Mirabéllo Bay and the supposedly bottomless Voulismémni Lake. Wander around town, ending up at one of the lakefront cafés for breakfast. After, hop back in the car for the short trip to Kritsá *(p266)*, a mountain village known for Panagía Kéra, a Byzantine church with magnificent, if dilapidated, frescoes, and for its local crafts – explore the market and pick up some ceramics or lace to take home. Drive on to Pláka village, where you can catch the ferry to Spinalónga *(p277)*, a fascinating islet with a Venetian-fortress-turned-leper colony, made famous by Victoria Hislop's novel *The Island* (2005). Back at Ágios Nikólaos, have dinner at colourful Chrisofyllis *(Akti Pagalou, Kitroplateia)* on the waterfront.

Day 3

You could spend a whole day lazing in the gentle, turquoise water at Voúlisma beach, but limit yourself to the morning. Have lunch at venerable Ta Kohylia in the little resort of Móhlos *(p278)*, now a culinary destination, then take in the nearby Moní Toploú *(p278)*, a dramatic fortress-church with spectacular frescoes and museum-treasury. It's freshly caught fish on the menu at Agistri taverna, under the olive trees in little Angathiás village, a short drive further around the coast.

Day 4

Váï beach *(p279)* is a slice of Jamaica in Crete, and a morning lounging on the palm-fringed bay is a dream. It does get crowded, so escape to the Minoan palace at Káto Zákros *(p279)*, where you can also explore the several excellent seaside tavernas. Suitably fortified, spend the afternoon hiking in the Gorge of the Dead *(p279)*, a misnomer as this landscape thrives with life. You've earned dinner at water-front Votsalakia in Koutsourás village, one of the best spots around.

Day 5

After a night on the coast, get an early start to arrive in time for the 10:30am excursion boat from Ierápetra out to Chrysí islet *(p277)* with its two beautiful white-sand beaches, Caribbean-hued sea and exceedingly rare juniper forests. After a day spent exploring the island, head back to the mainland and west towards the laid-back beach resort of Mýrtos. Park yourself at a restaurant on the waterfront for the night, and toast to your trip.

1

2

3

7 DAYS
in Western Crete

Day 1

Big and bustling Iráklio *(p256)*, Crete's main port and capital, can feel a bit manic. Spend an hour wandering the pedestrianized Platía Venizélou, before escaping into the past at the Iráklio Archaeological Museum *(p258)*, which has the best collection of Minoan treasures in the world. After spending a few hours exploring the 27 galleries, head to Efta Baltades *(p257)*, a friendly taverna in the middle of town, for lunch in its sunny courtyard. Many of the artifacts in the Archaeological Museum were discovered in the Palace of Knosos *(p260)*, which rewards an afternoon's exploration. In the evening, come back to the present with a movie at summer-only open-air cinema, Bethlehem, in Iraklio's old walls.

Day 2

Crete is imbued with the ruins of numerous civilizations and the remains at Gortys *(p273)* are particularly impressive. After so much food for thought, replenish at Alekos *(Odos Stefanidi; 28920 91094)* in nearby Vóri, which serves traditional dishes in a courtyard-meets-garden

paradise. Continue to the Minoan palace of Phaistos *(p265)*, which, unlike recon-structed Knosós, was left as a ruin. After-wards, cool down in the water at craggy Damnóni beach, before finally arriving in Réthymno *(p254)*. Tonight, enjoy dinner at the special Ta Dyo Rou *(Pánou Koronéou 28)*.

Day 3

Drive southeast out of Réthymno to historic Moní Arkadíou *(p279)*, with its glorious Baroque façade and a shrine to the failed 1866 revolt against the Ottoman occupiers. After a few hours at the monas-tery, head to nearby Margarítes for lunch and to pop into some of the village's renowned potteries. Return to Réthymno in time for dinner. To Pigadi *(Xanthoudídou 31)* is a fantastic option.

Day 4

Bid farewell to Réthymno with breakfast at one of the charming eateries on Dimitrakaki, and then make your way to Lake Kourná – Crete's only natural lake – for a morning swim. Have lunch at a lakeshore taverna, then carry on to Hánia

1 Sculptures in the Iráklio
Archaeological Museum. ↑

2 The cloister of Arkádi monastery.

3 Canoeing on Lake Kourná.

4 The path to the top of Samariá Gorge.

5 Boats in Loutró's beautiful bay.

(p252). The many years of Venetian occupation are clear in this port town's grand Italianate buildings. After a wander around, dine at busy Tamam (p253), perhaps tasting a few local beers. If you want to extend your evening, have a nightcap at Ta Chalkina (www.chalkina.com) while listening to live Cretan music.

Day 5

Spend part of your morning browsing the collection at the small but exquisite Byzantine Museum in the Venetian San Salvatore church, before pilgrimaging to the nearby Etz Hayyim Synagogue (p253). This restored building is the sole legacy of Hánia's Jewish community, many of whom were victims of the Holocaust in World War II. Pop into the market hall to shop for souvenirs – and pick up a few snacks for a picnic on the beach at Ágii Apostóli (p253). Spend the afternoon swimming at the two sandy coves found here. Back in Haniá, have dinner in the colourful Splántzia Quarter at Well of the Turk (p253). Afterwards, catch jazz – recorded or live – at Fagotto Bar (Angélou 16, 28210 71877).

Day 6

Pack a small overnight bag and take a morning bus from Haniá up to Ómalos and the top of the Samariá Gorge (p266). This national park is one of Europe's longest gorges, and the 7-hour hike through the valley drops steeply through the mountains on the way to the coast. You will arrive at Agía Rouméli in time for a late-afternoon swim and a well-deserved dinner. Crete is blessed with clear skies, so spend some time admiring the stars before spending the night in this sleepy port.

Day 7

Take the morning ferry further along the wild Sfaria coast, hopping off at the tiny village of Loutró for a swim and an explore. Hike further along the coast to Hóra Sfakíon (p269) for lunch and another swim, before boarding a bus back to Haniá and retrieving your car. Your flight out may be from Haniá, in which case the airport is close by – though clarify one-way-car-rental charges beforehand. Otherwise, it's a challenging drive back to Iráklio.

The mosque of Giáli Tzamí on the water's edge in the outer harbour, Haniá

HANIÁ
XANIA

✈ 16 km (10 miles) E of Haniá ⛴ Soúda bay 🚌 Kydonías (long distance), Platía Agorás (local) ℹ Kriári 40; www.chania.eu

Set against a spectacular backdrop of majestic mountains and aquamarine seas, Haniá is one of the island's most appealing cities and a good base from which to explore western Crete. The city's stately Neo-Classical mansions and Venetian fortifications testify to its turbulent and diverse past: once a Minoan settlement, Haniá has been fought over and controlled by groups from the Romans to the Germans.

The Harbour

Most of the city's interesting sights are in the old Venetian quarter, around the harbour and surrounding alleyways. At the northwest point of the outer harbour, the **Naval Museum**'s collection of model ships and maritime artifacts is displayed in the well-restored Venetian Fort Firkás. On the other side of the harbour, the áli Tzamí (Shore Mosque) es back to the arrival of Turks in 1645 and is the 's oldest Ottoman g. It was damaged in War II and rebuilt soon

after. Its famous dome is particularly atmospheric at dusk. Behind the mosque rises the hilltop quarter of Kastélli, the oldest part of the city, where the Minoan settlement of Kydonia is being excavated. The site, closed to the public but visible from the road, is approached along Líthinon. Many of the finds are on display in the city's Archaeological Museum.

By the inner harbour stand the now derelict 16th-century Venetian dockyards, where ships were repaired. The Venetian lighthouse, at the end of the seawall, offers superb views over Haniá.

Naval Museum

 📍 Fort Firkás, Aktí Koundourióti 🕐 16 Apr–31 Oct: 9am–5pm Mon–Sat, 10am–6pm Sun 🚫 Main public hols 🌐 mar-mus-crete.gr

② 🛍

The Market and the Stivanádika

Connected to the harbour by Hálidon road, this covered market sells local fruit and vegetables and Cretan souvenirs. Alongside the market, the bustling Skrýdlof, or Stivanádika, has shops selling leather goods, including Cretan boots (*stivánia*) and made-to-measure sandals.

③

Archaeological Museum

📍 Hálidon 21 📞 28210 90334 🕐 Apr–Oct: 8am–8pm daily; Nov–Mar: 8:30am–3pm Tue–Sun 🚫 Main public hols

Near Stivanádika in the former church of San Francesco is the Archaeological Museum. It displays artifacts from western Crete; most notably, a collection of Minoan clay tablets inscribed with Linear A script.

④ Etz Hayyim Synagogue

⌂ Párados Kondyláki ⌚ May–Oct: 10am–6pm Mon–Thu; Nov–Apr: 10am–5pm Sat–Thu, 10am–3pm Fri ⓦ etz-hayyim-hania.org

Near the Archaeological Museum is the restored 15th-century Etz Hayyim Synagogue, which was used by Haniá's Jewish population until the German occupiers deported them to Auschwitz in June 1944. The only Jewish structure remaining in the city, Etz Hayyim is now a memorial with displays about the 2,000 years of Jewish life in Haniá.

⑤ The Splántzia Quarter

Picturesque houses with wooden balconies overhang the cobbled backstreets of Splántzia. The tree-lined square of Platía 1821 commemorates a rebellion against the Ottomans, during which an Orthodox bishop was hanged. Overlooking the square is the Venetian church of Ágios

Nikólaos, the 16th-century church of Ágii Anárgyri, with its beautiful icons and paintings, and the church of Ágios Rókkos, built in 1630.

⑥ Historical Museum

⌂ Ioánnou Sfakianáki 20 ☏ 28210 52606 ⌚ 8:30am–2:30pm Mon–Fri ⌖ Main public hols

The Historical Museum and Archives is housed in a Neo-Classical building. Devoted to the Cretan preoccupation with rebellions and invasions, the exhibits include photographs and letters of the statesman Elefthérios Venizélos (1864–1936), as well as many other historical records.

⑦ Ágii Apostóli Beaches

Sandy beaches stretch west from Haniá to the town of Tavronítis, 21 km (13 miles) away. The closest good beaches are 3 km (2 miles) west, at the sandy coves of Ágii Apostóli. There are four beaches here, popular with locals and tourists.

EAT

Tamam
Located in a medieval bathhouse, Tamam offers Cretan platters plus Med-fusion recipes.

⌂ Spyridónos Zambelíou 49, Old Port ⓦ tamamrestaurant.com

€€€

Well of the Turk
Middle Eastern fare and superior Armenian pizza outnumber the Cretan platters here.

⌂ Kaliníkou Sarpáki 1–3, Splántzia ⓦ welloftheturk.gr

€€€

To Magazaki
This reliable, jolly local hangout on the seafront serves local dishes.

⌂ Aktí Papanikolí 14, Neahóra ☏ 28210 99177

€€€

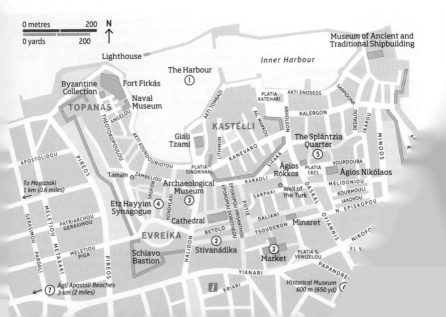

↑ Réthymno's harbour, buzzing with tavernas and bars

② RÉTHYMNO
PEΘYMNO

🏠 55 km (35 miles) SE of Haniá 🚌 Kefalogiánnidon
ℹ️ Kountourioti 80; 28210 92000

Despite modern development and tourism, the city of Réthymno has kept much of its charm and remains the intellectual capital of Crete. The old quarter is rich in elegant, well-preserved Venetian and Ottoman architecture. The huge Venetian Fortétsa overlooks the picturesque harbour, which is skirted by a sandy beach.

①
Fortétsa

🏠 Kateháki 📞 2831028101
🕐 8:30am-8pm; winter: to 3pm daily 🚫 Main public hols

Located at the western end of Réthymno's bustling water-ront is a small inner harbour, re a restored 16th-century ouse stands on its ater. Above this spot, étsa, or citadel, s the city. Designed allavicini in the built to defend st pirate attacks ing threat of he ramparts

are still largely intact. Within them, a superb mosque, a small church with the largest dome in Greece and parts of the governor's quarters can still be seen, though most are in ruins. In the summer there are open-air concerts.

②
Archaeological Museum

🏠 Himáras 📞 2831027506
🕐 Apr-Oct: 10am-6pm Tue-Sun; Nov-Mar: 9am-3pm Tue-Sun 🚫 Main public hols

Directly opposite the main entrance to the Fortétsa, the

Archaeological Museum occupies the former town prison. Its collection is set out chronologically from Neolithic through Minoan to Roman times. The most compelling exhibits are Minoan clay *larnakes* (burial caskets), vividly painted with stylized animals.

③
Old Town

Clustered behind the Fortétsa, the Old Town is characterized by a maze of vine-canopied streets and Venetian and Ottoman houses with wrought-iron balconies. Off Platía Títou Petiháki is the best-preserved mosque in the city, Nerantzés Mosque. Built as the church of Santa Maria by the Venetians, it was converted in 1657 by local Muslims. It now serves as the local conservatory and occasional concert venue; just before or after rehearsal is the most likely time to catch a glimpse of the wonderful vaulted ceiling inside. In a little square on Paleológou, the still-running 17th-century stone Venetian Rimóndi Fountain gushes alongside busy cafés and shops.

The small **Historical and Folk Art Museum** is housed in a Venetian mansion. On display upstairs are collections of embroidery, weavings, pottery and rural tools.

Historical and Folk Art Museum

 🌐 📍 Vernárdou 30 📞 28310 23398 🕐 Apr–Oct: 9:30am–2:30pm & 6–9pm Mon–Sat 🚫 Main public hols

---

④
Minoan Cemetery

📍 7 km (4 miles) S of Réthymno 🕐 8:30am–6pm Tue–Sun (winter: to 3pm) 🚫 Main public hols

On the main road between Réthymno and Agía Galíni, there is an extensive late Minoan cemetery where a large number of graves have been excavated. Bronze weapons, vases and *larnakes* have been unearthed here and many of these finds are now on display in the archaeological museums of Haniá *(see p252)* and Réthymno. Even though they are empty, the ancient tombs – some with imposingly long entrances – still merit exploration.

⑤
Georgioúpoli

📍 22 km (14 miles) W of Réthymno

Despite tourist development, this small village still has a traditional feel. Eucalyptus trees line the streets and a turtle-inhabited river flows down to the sea. Located around 5 km (3 miles) inland, Lake Kournás is perfect for a swim, or you can hire a kayak. Tavernas line the north shore.

↑ Georgioúpoli's little white church standing in an isolated spot

STAY

Kapsalianá Village
Rooms occupy Venetian or more recent Cretan cottages with sea or olive-grove views.

📍 Kapsalianá 🌐 kapsalianavillage.gr

€€€

Palazzo Vecchio
Suites and maisonettes with beamed ceilings and kitchenettes.

📍 Melissinoú 🌐 palazzovecchio.gr

€€€

Veneto
Studios and suites, all unique, with a pretty arcaded courtyard.

📍 Epimenídou 2–4 🌐 veneto.gr

€€€

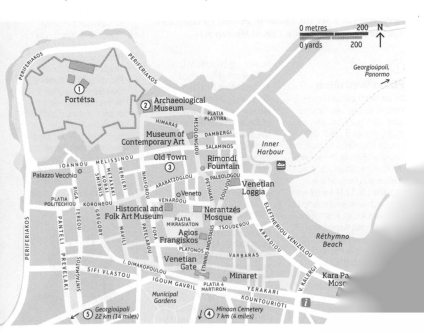

↑ The Venetian fortress, a major landmark at the end of the old harbour, Iráklio

❸

IRÁKLIO
ΗΡΑΚΛΕΙΟ

130 km (80 miles) E of Haniá ✈5 km (3 miles) E of town
🚌E of Venetian harbour 🚌Outside of ferry port (for
Réthymno, Haniá, Ágios Nikólaos and Ierápetra); outside
Haniá Gate (for points southwest) ℹXanthoudídou 1;
www.heraklion.gr

The sprawl of traffic-jammed streets does not make
the best first impression of Crete's capital. But look
again and you'll see the wealth of Venetian architecture
and the world's best collection of Minoan art.

①
Platía Venizélou

At the heart of Iráklio is Platía
Venizélou, a pedestrianized
zone with buzzing cafés and
shops grouped around the
ornate 17th-century Morosini
Fountain. Facing the square,
the restored church of Ágios
Márkos was built by the
Venetians in 1239 and is now
used as a venue for concerts
and exhibitions. From here,
Ikostipémptis Avgoústou (25
...reet) leads north to
...en harbour. Found
...t, the elegantly
...century Loggia
...place for the
...nd now
...ity hall.
...in a small

square set back from the
road, is the refurbished
16th-century church of Ágios
Títos, dedicated to the island's
patron saint. On the other side
of Ikostipémptis Avgoústou,
the tiny El Greco Park is
named after Crete's most
famous painter.

②
Fortress Arsenali

Venetian Harbour
📞28102 88484 🕐Apr-Oct:
8:30am-7pm Tue-Sun; Nov-
Mar: 8:30am-3pm Tue-Sun
🚫Main public hols

Located at the northern end of
Ikostipémptis Avgoústou, the
old harbour is dominated by

this Venetian fortress, whose
dauntingly massive structure
repulsed prolonged assaults
by the invading Turks in the
17th century. It was erected
between 1523 and 1540 and
named Rocca al Mare (Fort
on the Sea) by the Venetians.
Opposite the fortress are the
arcades of the 16th-century
Venetian Arsenali where ships
were built and repaired.

THE GREEK

El Greco (Domenikos
Theotokopoulos) was
born in Crete in 1541.
His art was rooted in
the Cretan School of
Painting, an influence
that permeates his
individualistic use of
dramatic colour and
elongated human
forms. In Italy, El Greco
became a disciple of
Titian before moving to
Spain. He died in 1614
and his works are now
on display in museums
around the world.

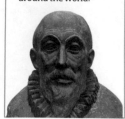

Historical Museum

Kysimáhou Kalokerinoú 7 **28102 83219** Apr-Oct: 9am-5pm Mon-Sat; Nov-Mar: 9am-3:30pm Mon-Sat **Main public hols**

West along the waterfront, the Historical Museum traces the history of Crete since early Christian times. Its displays include Byzantine icons and friezes, sculptures and archives of the Battle of Crete. Pride of place is given to the only El Greco painting in Crete, *View of Mt Sinai and the Monastery of St Catherine*.

Agía Ekateríni

Platía Agías Ekaterínis Apr-Sep: 9am-2pm & 5-8pm daily; Oct-Mar: 9am-1pm daily

Once a monastic centre famous for art and learning, the Venetian church of Agía Ekateríni, dating from the 16th century, now houses the **Museum of Religious Art**, with a magnificent collection of Byzantine icons, frescoes and manuscripts. Particularly notable are six icons by 16th-century Cretan artist Mihaíl Damaskinos, who learned his craft here.

Next door, the 19th-century cathedral of Ágios Minás towers over the square.

Museum of Religious Art

 Agía Ekateríni of Sinai, Platía Agías Ekaterínis **28103 36316** 9:30am-7:30pm Mon-Sat, 10:30-7:30pm Sun

Platía Kornárou

In this square, coffee is served from a charming converted Ottoman-era pump-house, next to which a headless Roman statue graces the historic Bembo Fountain.

EAT

Avli tou Devkaliona
Among the *mezédes* served here, the fluffy *keftedákia* (meatballs) are generous. The courtyard features an ornate fountain.

Lysimáhou Kalokerinoú 8 **2810 244215**

€€€

Efta Baltades
Besides grills and stews, starters like *askordouláki* (hyacinth bulbs) feature on the menu at this converted medieval house.

Idomenéos 10a **2810 226533**

€€€

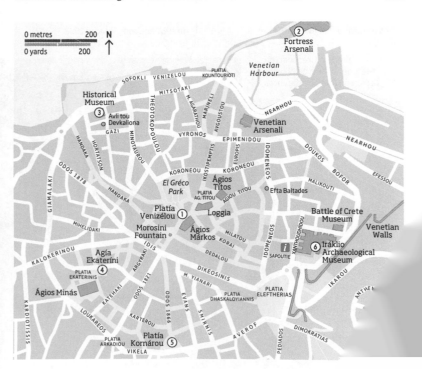

⑥ 🗺 🖵

IRÁKLIO ARCHAEOLOGICAL MUSEUM

ΑΡΧΑΙΟΛΟΓΙΚΟ ΜΟΥΣΕΙΟ ΗΡΑΚΛΕΙΟΥ

🏛 Corner of Xanthoudídi & Mpofór, Plateía Eleftherías, Iráklio 🕐 May-Oct: 8am-8pm daily; Nov-Apr: 10am-4pm Mon, 10am-5pm Tue-Sun 🌐 heraklionmuseum.gr

The Iráklio Archaeological Museum houses the world's most important collection of Minoan artifacts, giving a unique insight into a highly sophisticated civilization that existed on Crete over 3,000 years ago. The vast museum contains discoveries from all over the island, including the famous Phaistos Disc *(p265)*.

The museum was refurbished in 2014 and now has state-of-the-art interactive exhibits. Its 27 galleries house archaeological treasures including well-preserved Minoan frescoes from Knosos *(p260)*, finely carved stone vessels, jewellery, Minoan double axes and other artifacts The Minoan double axe was an extremely powerful sacred symbol thought to have been a cult object connected with the Mother Goddess. Evidence of the importance of the axe for the Minoans is clear from the many vases, larnakes (clay coffins), seals, frescoes and pillars on display that feature the axe.

↑ The exterior of the museum, designed in 1937 and completed in 1952

The sculpture rooms on the ground floor, displaying Greek and Roman influences ↓

↑ The spectacular display of frescoes
collected from around Crete

GALLERY GUIDE

The exhibits, arranged chronologically, showcase the history of the Cretan civilization from the prehistoric era to Roman times, with a focus on religious and ceremonial practices, mortuary habits, bureaucratic administration and daily life. The ground floor chronicles the seafaring dominance of the Minoans across the Aegean; the second floor focuses on the emergence of Minoan city-states. Labels are in Greek and English, and there are multimedia displays throughout. There are also thematic displays: the first floor is home to famous frescoes from Knosos.

Bull's Head Rhyton

▷ This vessel, made in the 16th-century BC, was used for the pouring of ritual wines. Found at Knosos, it is carved from steatite, a black stone, with inset rock crystal eyes and a mother-of-pearl snout.

The Hall of Frescoes

The famous Minoan frescoes and other fantastic examples of Minoan art can be found in this room. The display includes the elaborately frescoed Agía Triáda sarcophagus, dating from around 1400 BC, giving insight into Minoan funerary rites, as well as frescoes found at the Palace of Knosos (p260), with pieces like the "Lily Prince" displayed.

Gold Bee Pendant

Found in the Chrysólakkos cemetery at Mália (p287), this exquisite gold pendant shows two connected bees storing honey. The pendant dates from the Bronze Age, around the 17th century BC, and is one of the best examples of Minoan jewellery here.

Snake Goddesses

▷ This female holds a snake in either hand, and is the smaller of two faïence figurines thought to represent the snake goddess or a priestess performing religious rituals. Both date from around 1600 BC, and were found at Knosos.

The Minoan Double Axe

◁ The Minoan double axe was both a tool used by carpenters, masons and ship-builders, and a sacred symbol. The famous Labyrinth at Knosos (p260), home of the Min is believed to have be "dwelling place of double axe"; the *labrys* being th Greek name f The ceremor depicted be horns or wit

④ ⊛ ⓜ ▭ 🏛

PALACE OF KNOSOS
ΑΝΑΚΤΟΡΟ ΤΗΣ ΚΝΩΣΟΥ

📍5 km (3 miles) S of Iráklio 📞2810 231940 🚌2 from Iráklio 🕐Hours vary, check website 📅Main public holidays 🌐odysseus.culture.gr

In the Bronze Age, Crete was ruled by the Minoans, an advanced civilization that built cities and palaces across the island, and used a language that is yet to be deciphered. Knosos was this civilization's capital, and the largest and most impressive palace was built here in 1900 BC.

This palace is famous in legend as the domain of King Minos, half-human son of Zeus, who kept the ferocious Minotaur in a labyrinth underneath the building. In reality, the palace was the centre of a Bronze Age empire that ruled much of the Aegean, as evidenced by the sophistication of the complex.

The first palace of Knosos was destroyed by an earthquake in about 1700 BC and was soon completely rebuilt. The restored ruins visible today are almost entirely from this second palace. These two palaces have been used to mark distinct eras in Minoan civilization, referred to as the First Palace Period and Second Palace Period.

↑ An elaborate fresco at Knosos, restored imaginately by Evans

↑ rth entrance to ...ce, showing a ...ed walkway

Timeline

c 2000 BC
First palace period: construction of the palace.

c 1370 BC
Second palace destroyed by fire.

c 800 BC
City-state of Knosós emerges

7000 BC
Arrival of the first inhabitants of Knosós.

1750–1700 BC
First palace destroyed by earthquake; construction of the second palace.

c 1100 BC
Dorian invasion of Greece. End of Bronze Age and beginning of Dark Ages.

67 BC
Roman conquest of Crete.

Unlike other Minoan sites, the Palace of Knosós was imaginatively restored by Sir Arthur Evans, who excavated the site, between 1900 and 1929. While his intepretation is the subject of academic controversy, his reconstructions of the second palace gives visitors an impression of life in Minoan Crete that cannot be easily gained from the remains of other palaces on the island.

The focal point of the site is its vast north–south aligned Central Court, off which lie many of the palace's most important areas (p262). The original frescoes are in the Archaeological Museum of Irákleio (p280), although a replica of the major frescoes remain at the palace.

THE MINOTAUR

The half-bull, half-man Minotaur was born of a white bull and Queen Pasiphaë, wife of King Minos of Crete, part of a trick played by Poseidon. Rather than kill the monster, Minos imprisoned it in a labyrinth constructed by Daedalos. When Androgeos, son of Minos, was murdered during the Panathenaic Games, Minos demanded that 14 Athenian youths be sent to Crete as food for the Minotaur each year. Theseus, prince of Athens, volunteered. Aided by Daedalos and Princess Ariadne, he penetrated the labyrinth, slew the Minotaur and escaped with his life in tact.

Visitors at the South
Propylo, looking at the ↑
impressive frescoes

AROUND THE SOUTH PROPYLON

Entry to the palace complex is via the West Court, the original ceremonial entrance now marked by a bust of Sir Arthur Evans. To the left are three circular pits known as *kouloúres*, which probably served as granaries. Ahead, running along the length of the west façade, are the West Magazines. These contained numerous large storage jars *(pithoi)*, and, along with the granaries, the central position give an impression of how important the control of resources and storage was within the palace.

At the far right-hand corner of the West Court, the west ntrance leads to the Corridor the Procession. Now cut t by erosion of the hill- the corridor was painted series of elaborate depicting a number arers. This seems that state and ents at the palace were accompanied by much ceremony. There were also impressive frescoes in the South Propylon, off the corridor. From the South Propylon, steps lead up to the reconstructed Piano Nobile, the name given by Sir Arthur Evans to the probable location of the grand state apartments and reception halls. Stone vases found in this part of the palace were used for ritual purposes and indicate the centrality of religion to palace life. The close link between secular and sacred power is also reinforced by the Throne Room, where ritual bathing in a lustral basin (sunken bath) is thought to have taken place. Steps lead from the Throne Room to the once-paved Central Court. Now open to the elements, this would have been the heart of the palace, flanked by high buildings on all four sides.

THE HISTORY OF THE PALACE

The capital of Minoan Crete, Knosós was the largest and most sophisticated of the palaces on the island. It contained over 1,000 rooms across multiple storeys and enjoyed the comforts of an elaborate drainage system, flushing toilets and paved roads. The Minoans left behind numerous scripts that have not yet been deciphered, meaning that much of what is understood about the palace complex is conjecture. Luckily, the site was also written into numerous myths, including the Minotaur *(p261)* and Icarus, who flew too close to the sun.

THE ROYAL APARTMENTS

On the east side of the Central Court lie rooms of such size and elegance that they have been identified as the Royal Apartments. The apartments are built into the side of the hill and accessed by the Grand Staircase, one of the most impressive surviving architectural features of the palace. A drainage system was provided for the toilet beside the Queen's Megaron, or hall, which enjoyed the luxury of an en suite bathroom with clay bathtub. Corridors and rooms alike in this area were decorated with frescoes of floral and animal motifs. The walls of the Hall of the Royal Guard, a heavily guarded landing leading to the Royal Apartments, were decorated with a shield motif. The King's Megaron, also known as the Hall of the

↑ The extravagantly decorated and expansive Royal Apartments

Double Axes, takes its name from the Minoan double-axe symbols incised into its stone walls. Remains of what may have been a plaster throne were found here, suggesting that the room was also used for some state functions.

NORTH AND WEST OF THE CENTRAL COURT

The north entrance of the Central Court was adorned with remarkable figurative decoration, including the Charging Bull fresco, of which a replica is displayed on site. The north entrance leads to the North Pillar Hall, dating from the second palace period. This building was named as the Customs House by Sir Arthur Evans, who believed merchandise was inspected here. Immediately to the west is a room with restored steps leading into a pool, known as the North Lustral Basin. Traces of burning and the discovery of oil

jars seems to indicate that those coming to the palace were purified and annointed here before entering. Further west is the Theatre, a stepped court whose position at the end of the Royal Road suggests that the reception of visitors, and any ritual

welcoming ceremonies, may have occurred here. The Royal Road leading away from the palace to the Minoan town of Knosós was lined with houses. Just off the Royal Road lies the so-called Little Palace. This building has been excavated, but is not open to the public. It is architecturally very similar to the main palace and was destroyed at the same time.

→ The colourfully rebuilt north entrance to the Central Court

The ruined palace of Phaistos, with Mount Idi looming behind

5 PHAISTOS

ΤΟ ΑΝΑΚΤΟΡΟ ΤΗΣ ΦΑΙΣΤΟΥ

📍 65 km (40 miles) SW of Iráklio ☎ 28920 42315 🕐 Hours vary, check website 🚫 Main public hols 🌐 odysseus.culture.gr

One of four great Minoan palaces discovered on Crete, Phaistos was first excavated by Italian archaeologist Federico Halbherr between 1884 and 1904, who unearthed two palaces on site. Situated south of Iráklio on the Messara plain, Phaistos is backed by Mount Ida.

Remains of the first palace, constructed around 1900 BC and destroyed by an earthquake in 1700 BC, are still visible. However, most of the present ruins are of the second palace, which was severely damaged around 1450 BC, possibly by a tidal wave. Although a large number of inscriptions were found on site, they are all in Linear A script, which remains largely undeciphered. This, and the superimposed ruins of the two palaces, have made it more challenging to discover who lived on the site.

Phaistos was the second largest palace in Minoan Crete. Unlike at larger Knosós (p260), where the ruins were creatively interpreted and partially rebuilt by Sir Arthur Evans, Phaistos remains an archaeological site. Visitors, free to wander around the site, can imagine the structure of the complex, which is laid out similarly to the other Minoan palaces with a central courtyard and grand staircase, the star feature of the site.

↑ One of the ancient storerooms found in the palace

← A visitor wandering through the ruins of the palace

THE PHAISTOS DISC

This round clay disc *(right)*, 16 cm (6 in) in diameter, was discovered at Phaistos in 1908. It is inscribed on both sides with pictorial symbols, similar to hieroglyphs, that spiral from the circumference into the centre. While no one has yet been able to completely decipher its meaning or identify its origins, a number of the disc's symbols have been cracked after years of study. The disc is now thought to be a sacred hymn, referring to a pregnant goddess. The disc is one of the most important exhibits at the Irákleio Archaeologi Museum *(p258)* – although a small number of scholars have suggested the disc is a hoax.

EXPERIENCE Crete

SAMARIÁ GORGE
ΦΑΡΑΓΓΙ ΤΗΣ ΣΑΜΑΡΙΑΣ

📍 44 km (27 miles) S of Haniá 🚌 To Xylóskalo entrance ⛴ Agía Rouméli to Hóra Sfakíon (via Loutró); to Paleóhora (via Soúyia); time of last boat back varies, check before travel 🕐 May–Oct: 7am–4pm daily (if weather permits) 🌐 samaria.gr

A spectacular, deep-cut canyon, Samariá Gorge is one of Europe's longest ravines. Situated in the White Mountains, it hides a landscape of narrow paths cutting through towering cliffs. Declared a national park in 1962, Samariá Gorge protects a number of endemic species.

Samariá Gorge is home to the Greek Islands' most-famous hiking trail: the tortuous 18-km (11-mile) route from the 1,250-m- (4,000-ft-) high northern entrance to the sea at Agía Rouméli. The hike starts at Xylóskalo, a breathtaking zigzag path that drops a staggering 1,000 m (3,280 ft) in the first 2 km (1 mile) of the walk. At the bottom nestles the tiny chapel of Agios Nikólaos, a reminder of life in the gorge before it was declared a national park. Further down the path are the remains of Samariá village, abandoned in 1962. The most famous part of the hike comes 12 km (7 miles) along the gorge at the Gates, where the route squeaks between two 300-m- (1,000 ft) high rock walls, only 3 m (10 ft) apart. The walk continues down to the seaside village of Agía Rouméli, a whitewashed collection of houses facing the turquoise sea. It used to be the haunt of pirates, but now caters for the hiking crowd. The only transport from the village is a boat; the last one is usually at 5:30pm.

→

A *kri-kri*, or wild goat, often found leaping around the gorge

HIKE ALONG THE SFAKIÁ COAST

From Agía Rouméli, keen hikers can continue east along the coast, on the seven-hour-hike to Hóra Sfakíon. The main path, waymarked as route E4, passes medieval Ágios Pávlos chapel and nearby beach tavernas. At the fork, stay alongside the sea, which leads to Loutró resort, via Mármara beach and palm-tree-studded Fínikas cove. Beyond, the footpath ﹍reads along the shore ﹍til arriving at Hóra ﹍íon. The journey ﹍e broken with an ﹍ght at Mármara ﹍ó.

↑ Xylóskalo, the entrance to the gorge, dropping sharply into the national park

2,000

The number of endemic *kri-kri*, a type of wild goat, still found on Crete.

↑ Visitors cla▯
the rough▯
path thro▯

EXPERIENCE MORE

7

Paleóhora
Παλαιόχωρα

 70 km (44 miles) SW of Haniá 🚌🚐

This small port began life as a Venetian castle in 1279. Today the remains of the fort, destroyed by pirate attacks in 1539, stand guard on the little headland that divides the village's two beaches, both excellent: to the west, a wide sandy beach with gently shelving sea; to the east, a rocky but sheltered beach.

Discovered in the 1960s by the hippie community, the town became a haven for backpackers and is now popular with the package holiday-maker crowd.

Winding up through the Lefká Ori (White Mountains), a network of roads passes through a stunning landscape of terraced hills and mountain villages, noted for their Byzantine churches. The closest of these villages is Anýdri, 5 km (3 miles) east of Paleóhora, with the 14th-century double-naved church of Ágios Geórgios containing frescoes by Cretan Ioannis Pagomenos from 1323.

In summer, a daily boat service runs to Elafonísi, a lagoon-like beach of golden sand and brilliant blue water. Some 5 km (3 miles) north of Elafonísi (sometimes included in the same tour) stands Moní Chrysoskalítissas (Golden Step), named for the steps leading up to its church, one of which is said to appear golden in the eyes of the virtuous. From Paleóhora, ferries sail the 35 nautical miles to forested, beach-fringed Gávdos island twice weekly.

8

Soúyia
Σούγια

 60 km (37 miles) E of Haniá 🚌🚐

At the mouth of the Agía Iríni Gorge, the hamlet of Soúyia was once isolated from the rest of the world, but is now linked with Haniá and the north coast by a good road. Although the village has accommodation, several tavernas and two bars, it has never taken off as a resort, and retains something of a countercultural vibe. The beach is sand and pebbles, and the water is pristine. Inland, the village church is built on top of a Byzantine structure, whose mosaic floors have been largely removed.

9

Akrotíri Peninsula
Χερσόνησος Ακρωτηρίου

17 km (11 miles) E of Haniá 🚌 Soúda 🚐 Haniá & Soúda

Flat by Cretan standards, the Akrotíri Peninsula lies

between Réthymno (p254) and Haniá (p252). At its base, on top of Profítis Ilías hill, is a shrine to Crete's national hero, Elefthérios Venizélos. His tomb is a place of pilgrimage, for it was here that fiercely independent Cretan rebels raised the Greek flag in 1897 to fight against the Ottoman Empire occupying the island.

There are several wonderful monasteries in the north-eastern hills of the peninsula. Moní Agías Triádas, which has an impressive multidomed church, is 17th century, while Moní Gouvernétou dates back to the early Venetian occupation. Nearby, but accessible only on foot, the abandoned Moní Katholikoú is partly carved out of the rock.

At the neck of the peninsula is the Commonwealth War Cemetery, the burial ground of over 1,500 British, Australian and New Zealand

 Beach on the Gramvoúsa Peninsula with amazing turquoise waters

soldiers killed during the Battle of Crete in World War II, and a military base.

10

Kastélli Kissámou

Καστέλλι Κισσάμου

 37 km (23 miles) E of Haniá 🚌🚢

The small, unassuming town of Kastélli Kissámou, also known simply as Kastélli, sits at the eastern base of the virtually uninhabited Gramvoúsa Peninsula. While not a touristy town, it has a few hotels and restaurants along its pebbly shore. In the town square is an **Archaeological Museum** with spectacular Roman mosaics excavated in the area. Boat trips run to the tip of the Gramvoúsa Peninsula, where there are sandy beaches.

Some 7 km (4 miles) south of Kastélli, the ruins of the ancient city of Polyrínia are scattered above the village of Ano Paleókastro. Dating from the 6th century BC, the fortified city-state was developed by the Romans and later the Byzantines and Venetians. A further 16 km (10 miles) west

← Moní Chrysoskalítissa, perched on the southwest coast of Crete near Paleóhora

of Kastélli, on the coast of the Gramvoúsa Peninsula, a winding road descends to the excellent and isolated beach at Falásarna. Once the site of a Hellenistic city-state of that name, earthquakes have obliterated almost all trace of the once-thriving harbour and town. Today many small guesthouses and tavernas are scattered along the long and often windy beach.

About 20 km (12 miles) east of Kastélli lies the picturesque fishing village of Kolymbári. Head north of Kolymbári for the impressive 17th-century Moní Panagías Goniás, with a lovely seaside setting and a fine collection of 17th-century icons. Every year on 29 August (Feast of St John the Baptist), hundreds of pilgrims make the 3-hour walk up the peninsula to the church of Ágios Ioánnis to witness the mass baptism of boys named John (Ioánnis).

Archaeological Museum
 Platía Tzanakáki (near the bus station) 📞 28220 83308 🕐 8:30am–3pm Tue–Sun

---

11

Gávdos

Γαύδος

🚢 Platía Agías Ekaterínis

A triangular, juniper-flecked speck in the Libyan Sea 27 nautical miles from Hóra Sfakíon or Paleóhora, Gávdos is Europe's southernmost land mass. Not widely known, it has a cult-like popularity, with thousands of Greek and foreign devotees.

Many visitors camp behind excellent beaches, but the port hamlet of Karabé and the dune-backed beach resort of Sarakíniko just north have tavernas and accommodation. Naturists have colonized Ágios Ioánnis, 3 km (2 miles) west, while at the southeastern tip of Gávdos, Trypití sports a giant wood throne on which pilgrims sit to contemplate the view.

12

Hóra Sfakíon

Σφακιά

 71 km (44 miles) S of Haniá 🚌

Overlooking the Libyan Sea from near the mouth of the breathtaking Ímbros Gorge, Hóra Sfakíon (the main town of wild Sfakiá district) enjoys a commanding position as the last coastal community of any size until Paleóhora. Cut off from the outside world until recently, historically the local clansmen have a reputation for rugged self-sufficiency and individualism, albeit accompanied by feuds and vendettas until the 1990s. The village today is devoted to tourism and is a stepping-off point for the southwest coast.

EAT

Methexis
Methexis delights with unusual recipes such as goat with *askólymbri* (oyster thistle).

🍴 Easterly shore road, Paleóhora
📞 28230 41431

€€€

Anchorage
This vine-shaded courtyard inland serves creative local dishes.

🍴 Papandérou St, Soúyia
📞 28230 51487

€€€

Kali Kardia
For a great meal at this old-fashioned taverna, ask the owners for recommendations.

🍴 Frangokástello be
📞 28250 9212?

€€€

 13

Plakiás
Πλακιάς

🏠 **35 km (22 miles) S of Réthymno** 🚌

Once a simple fishing harbour serving the villages of Mýrthios and Selliá, Plakiás is now a full-scale resort with all the usual facilities and a grey sandy beach, 2-km (1-mile) long. Sited at the mouth of the Kotsyfoú Gorge, and with good road connections, Plakiás makes an excellent base for exploring the region.

A 5-minute drive, or a scenic walk around the headland, leads east to the beach of Damnóni, now a fully fledged resort. Tiny, pretty coves beyond it are good spots for swimming. Just west of Plakiás, Soúda is an excellent beach.

 14

Moní Préveli
Μονή Πρέβελη

🏠 **14 km (9 miles) E of ...iás** 🚌 ☎ **28320 31246**
...n-1 hour before sunset
...h monasteries; call
... in winter

...by road through
...ótiko Gorge, the
...astery of Préveli
...lated but

beautiful spot overlooking the sea. It played a prominent role in the evacuation of Allied forces from nearby beaches during World War II.

Some 17th-century buildings cluster around a large central courtyard, where the fountain bears the inscription "wash your sins, not just your face". A small museum displays ecclesiastical artifacts, including silver candlesticks and highly decorative robes. En route to the courtyard, you pass the original 10th-century monastery of Káto Préveli, now restored as a museum. A short walk east of Píso Préveli, a steep path leads to Préveli beach. This charming beach is also known as Kourtaliótiko, or Palm Beach, after the grove of Cretan palms along the river. Excursion boats call here in large numbers.

15

Frangokástello
Φραγκοκάστελλο

🏠 **14 km (9 miles) E of Hóra Sfakíon** 🚌 ⏰ **Daily**

This fortress was built by the Venetians as a bulwark against pirates and unruly Sfakiots in 1371. Its interior was recently restored, with an event stage and the ability to climb one of the towers. The curtain walls

have been well preserved and, above the south entrance, the Venetian Lion of St Mark looks out to sea.

In May 1828, Frangokástello was the scene of an ultimately futile battle in the Greek War of Independence, when Hatzimihalis Daliannis, an Epirot adventurer, seized the fortress. A superior force of Cretan Muslims charged Frangokastello and slaughtered the entire garrison. On the anniversary of the battle, the soldiers' ghosts are said to appear at dawn, march towards the fortress and vanish.

Below the fortress is a sandy beach where the waters are shallow and warm. A scattering of rented rooms and tavernas cater for holiday-makers.

16

Moní Arkadíou
Μονή Αρκαδίου

🏠 **20 km (12 miles) SE of Réthymno**
🚌 **To Réthymno**
⏰ **From 9am daily**

The monastery of Arkadíou stands at the top of a winding

→
 The Greek Orthodox two-nave church at Moní Arkadíou

A man hiking the winding mountain paths near Plakiás

gorge. The most impressive of its buildings is the double-naved church with an ornate Venetian façade that figured on the retired 100-drachma Greek banknote.

The monastery provided a safe haven for its followers in times of religious persecution. It came under attack from the Ottoman army in 1866, when its buildings were crowded with hundreds of refugees. The outer wall was breached, and the defenders torched their gunpowder store, killing Christian and Muslim alike. This created instant martyrs who are remembered in a small museum, which also displays sacramental vessels, icons and vestments. A sculpture outside the monastery is a memorial to the only survivor, a girl, and the abbot who lit the gunpowder.

 Mount Ídi
Ψηλορείτης

📍 **58 km (36 miles) SE of Réthymno**
🚌 **To Anógia & Kamáres**

At 2,456 m (8,080 ft) the soaring peaks of Mount Ídi (or Psilorítis) are the crowning glory of the massive Psilorítis range. The highest mountain

in Crete, it is home to many sanctuaries including the famous Idean Cave. To reach the cave from Anógia, follow the paved road towards the Nída plateau, a walk of 23 km (14 miles) through rocky terrain, punctuated by the occasional stone shepherd's hut. Here a lone taverna caters to visitors en route to the cave, a further 20-minute hike up hill. This huge cavern is where Zeus was said to be reared, and has yielded artifacts including remarkable bronze shields dating from around 700 BC. From the plateau, marked trails lead up to the peak of Mount Ídi. The trek to the summit and chapel of Timios Stavros is an 8-hour round trip from the Nída plateau taverna.

On the mountain's southern face, a 3.5-hour scramble from Kamáres village leads to the Kamáres Cave, where Minoan pottery known as Kamáres ware was discovered.

 Anógia
Ανώγεια

📍 **46 km (29 miles) SE of Iráklio** 🚌

The village of Anógia was established in the 12th century, high up the Psilorítis mountains. It has had a turbulent past; destroyed by the Muslims in 1822, and then by the Germans in 1944, the town has since been rebuilt.

CRETAN CAVES AND THE MYTH OF ZEUS

The island of Crete is home to 4,700 caves, of which some 2,000 have been explored. Since Neolithic times, caves have been used as cult centres by successive religions. Bound up with ancient Cretan mythology, the Diktian and Idean caves are two of the island's most visited. According to legend, Rhea gave birth to the infant god Zeus in the Diktian Cave. He was protected by *kourítes* (warriors) and nurtured by a goat, before being concealed and raised in the Idean Cave. This was to protect him from his father, Kronos, who had swallowed his other offspring after a warning that he would be dethroned by one of his sons.

Modern Anógia runs along a rocky ridge. Its square has a war memorial – a bronze statue of a Cretan hero in traditional dress – inscribed with significant dates in Crete's recent past. Shops and tavernas are also in the new village.

The old village tumbles down the steep slopes into a warren of narrow stepped alleys, ultimately converging on a little square of stalls and tavernas. Here, a marble bust of local politician Vasilios Skoulas stands next to a woodcarving of his friend Eleftherios Venizelos, by local artist Manolis Skoulas.

The stalls in the old part of the village abound in lace, rugs and embroidery, and form one of Crete's main centres for embroidered woven goods. Fans of 1970s singer Nikos can pay homage to washed house the main squa

19

Agía Triáda

Αγία Τριάδα

🅰 3 km (2 miles) W of Phaistos 🚌 To Phaistos 📞 28920 91564 🕒 9am–4pm daily 🔒 Main public hols

The Minoan villa of Agía Triáda was excavated from 1902 to 1914. An L-shaped structure, it was built around 1700 BC, the time of the Second Palace Period (*p260*), over earlier houses. Magnificent frescoes used to adorn the walls of private apartments and public reception rooms. Minoan treasures, like the carved stone Harvester vase, Boxer rhyton and Chieftain cup, were all found in this area and are on display at the great Irákleio Archaeological Museum (*p258*). Evidence of the villa's importance is provided by the discovery of clay seals and tablets bearing the undeciphered Minoan Linear A script.

After the villa's destruction by fire in around 1400 BC, a Mycenaean *megaron* (hall) was built on the site. The ruined settlement to the north, with its porticoed row of shops, dates mostly from this period, as does the magnificent sarcophagus that was found in the cemetery to the north. The paintwork on the sarcophagus depicts a burial procession; it can be seen in the Irákleio Archaeological Museum.

At the village of Vóri, 6 km (4 miles) northeast of Agía Triáda, is the **Museum of Cretan Ethnology**. On display are tools and materials used in the everyday life of rural Crete up to the mid-1900s.

Museum of Cretan Ethnology

 🕒 Apr–Oct: 10am–6pm daily 🔒 Main public hols 🌐 cretanethnology museum.gr

---

20

Mátala

Μάταλα

🅰 70km (44 miles) W of Iráklio 🚌

Clustered around an idyllic bay, Mátala was a small fishing hamlet until the hippies discovered it in the 1960s. The tourist boom of the mid-1970s transformed it into a pulsating resort with hotels, bars and restaurants.

Despite what its modern appearance suggests, Mátala has not been untouched by history. Homer described Menelaos, husband of Helen of Troy, being shipwrecked here on his way home from Troy. During Hellenistic times, in around 220 BC, Mátala

Did You Know?

The singer-songwriter Joni Mitchell lived in the Mátala caves with other hippies in the late 1960s.

served as the port for the ancient city-state of Gortys. The resort's sandstone cliffs were carved out for use as tombs in the Roman era. Later they were extended as cave dwellings for early Christians, then hippies, who lived here in the 1960s.

The area around Mátala has some beautiful beaches, like the bay of Kalí Liménes to the southeast, said to have been the landing place of St Paul the Apostle on his way to Rome. To the north, a track leads to Kommós, one of the best sandy beaches on the south coast. A Minoan settlement just inland is thought to have been a port serving Phaistos (*p264*) and is under excavation.

Boat excursions run daily from Mátala to the Paximádia islands in the bay and to pebbly Ágio beach, at the mouth of the Ágio Farago gorge. There are also several bus tours to the archaeological sites of Agía Triáda, Phaistos and Gortys.

arved out of the cliffs ↑ beach, used first as later as dwellings

→
Ruins at Gortys, in ancient times the most important city on Crete

Gortys
Γόρτυς

🏛 52 km (32 miles) S of Iráklio 📞 28920 31144
🚌 ⏰ Apr–Oct: 8am–8pm daily; Nov–Mar: 8am–3pm daily 🚫 Main public hols

The ancient city-state of Gortys began to flourish under Dorian rule during the 6th century BC. Following its defeat of Phaistos in the 2nd century BC, Gortys became the main city on Crete. Its pre-eminence was sealed after the Roman invasion of 65 BC, when Gortys was appointed capital of the newly created Roman province of Crete and Cyrene (modern-day Libya). The city continued to flourish under Byzantine rule, but in the late 7th century AD it was destroyed by Arab invaders.

The remains of the 6th-century basilica of Ágios Títos, whose floor plan is still clearly visible, are immediately beyond the entrance to the site. In its heyday it was the premier Christian church of Crete, traditionally held to be the burial place of St Titus, first bishop and patron saint

of the island. Behind the basilica is thought to be a Greek agora, or marketplace. Beyond this stand the semi-circular tiered benches of the Roman odeion (theatre), now home to the famous stone slabs inscribed with the Law Code of Gortys.

A path leads up to the acropolis hill, where a post-Minoan settlement was built around 1000 BC. On the east slope of the hill are the foundations of the 7th-century-BC Temple of Athena.

To the south of the main road, an extensive area of Roman Gortys remains only partially excavated. Standing in a grove of olive trees is the 7th-century-BC Temple of Pythian Apollo. Converted

into a Christian basilica in the 2nd century AD, it was super-seded by the basilica of Ágios Títos in AD 600.

In the village of Ágii Déka, east of Gortys, a 13th-century Byzantine church stands on the spot where ten early Christian Cretans were martyred for their opposition to the Roman Emperor Decius in AD 250. An icon in the nave portrays the ten martyrs.

In the mountains north of Górtys, the village of Zarós is famous for its spring water. From here, a trail leads north through Rouvás Gorge.

THE LAW CODE OF GORTYS

The most extensive set of early written laws in the Greek world was found at ancient Gortys and dates from around 500 BC. Each stone slab of the law code contains 12 columns of inscriptions in a Doric Cretan dialect. There is a total of 600 lines. The laws were on display to the public and related to domestic matters such as marriage, divorce, adoption, the obligations and rights of slaves and the sale and division of property

Clear waters at the small, sheltered beach of Galíni, a former fishermen's village ↑

22

Galíni
Γαλήνη

 70 km (43 miles) E of Réthymno

Formerly a fishing village, Galíni is today a full-blown tourist resort. The original village, now only a handful of old houses and narrow streets, is dwarfed by the mass of holiday apartments. The harbourfront is alive with busy tavernas; just beyond it is a small sandy beach popular with sunbathers.

Taxi boat trips sail daily from Galíni's harbour to the neighbouring beaches of Agios Geórgios and Agios Pávlos and, further still, to Palm Beach at Moní Préveli. There are less frequent excursions to the Paximádia islands, where there are good sandy beaches.

23

Arhánes
ρχάνες

km (10 miles) S
klio

m Crete's coastal
sorts, Arhánes is
earth farming
e olive groves and
ds chequer the
e. Lying at the
unt Gioúhtas,

in local tradition the burial place of Zeus, Arhánes was a thriving and important settlement in Minoan times.

In 1964, the remains of a Minoan palace were found in the centre of the village. A short walk out of town, on Foúrni Hill to the west, lies a vast **Minoan Cemetery**. Among the treasures uncovered here was the tomb of a princess with mirror and gold diadem in place, as well as exquisitely engraved signet rings. Some of these are on display in Arhánes at the Archaeological Museum.

On the north slope of Mount Gioúhtas at Anemospiliá is the site of a Minoan sanctuary. Though little remains to be seen today, the views of Mount Ídi are sensational.

The **Kazantzákis Museum** at Myrtiá has memorabilia of the Cretan author of *Zorba the Greek*. The museum is located next to his ancestral home.

The surrounding area is an important winemaking region. Among the wineries offering tours is **Nikos Gavalas**, which produces superb organic wine.

Minoan Cemetery
Foúrni Hill ⏱ Daily Main public hols

Kazantzákis Museum
⊕ Myrtiá Apr–Oct: 9am–5pm daily; Nov–Mar: 10am–3pm Sun Main public hols kazantzakis.gr

Nikos Gavalas
Voriás Monofatsíou 8am–4pm Mon–Fri; weekends by arrangement gavalascretewines.gr

24

Hersónisos
Χερσόνησος

26 km (16 miles) E of Iráklio

A busy port from Classical to early Byzantine times, Hersónisos (more correctly Liménas Hersonísou) is today the centre of the package-holiday business. Amid the plethora of tavernas, souvenir shops and bars, the harbour still retains faint intimations of the old Hersónisos. Along the waterfront a pyramid-shaped Roman fountain with fish mosaics dates from the 2nd–3rd century AD. Some remains of the Roman harbour, now mostly submerged, can also be seen here.

On the coast, at the eastern edge of town, traditional Cretan life is recreated at the **Cretan Open-Air Museum**, where exhibits cover a range of subjects, including a windmill, a stone house and native herbs. The **Crete Golf Club**, just inland, is one of only two golf courses on the island. To cool off in, the **Acqua Plus Water Park** is a playground of pools and waterslides.

Cretan Open-Air Museum

⊗ 🖈 Lychnostátis ⏱ Apr-Oct: 9am–2pm Sun-Fri 🚫 Main public hols 🌐 lychnostatis.gr

Crete Golf Club

🖈 7 km (4 miles) S of Hersónisos ⏱ Daily 🌐 cretegolfclub.com

Acqua Plus Water Park

⊗ 🖈 5 km (3 miles) S of National Highway ⏱ Mid-May–early Oct: 10am–6pm daily (to 7pm Jul & Aug); 🌐 acquaplus.gr

---

25

Mália

Μάλια

🖈 36 km (22 miles) E of Iráklio 🚌

Mália, a popular resort with the package-holiday crowd, bustles noisily with sunseekers bent on enjoying the crowded beaches by day and the cacophony of competing clubs by night.

In marked contrast, the Minoan **Palace of Mália** lies in ruins along the coastal plain to the east. The first palace was built in 1900 BC, but it

→

A reconstructed urn found at the Minoan Palace of Mália

was destroyed in 1700 BC; it was later rebuilt and destroyed again in 1450 BC. The site incorporates many features characteristic of other Minoan palaces – the great central court with its sacrificial altar, royal apartments, lustral basins (water pools) and lightwells. In a small sanctuary in the west wing of the palace, the Minoan religious symbol of the double axe *(labrys)*, as seen on vases at the Iráklio Archaeological Museum *(p258)* are inscribed on twin pillars.

Beyond the palace, the remains of what is thought to be a town are under excavation, while further north is the burial site of Chrysólakkos. Treasures uncovered here include a famous gold bee pendant, also displayed in the Iráklio Archaeological Museum.

The fast-developing fishing village of Sísi, 7 km (4 miles) east of Mália, has a charming port and a sheltered beach for swimming. There are a few good tavernas. Continuing eastwards, there are stunning views down to Mílatos.

From here a trail leads to the Mílatos Cave, where a shrine and glass-fronted casket of bones are a memorial to those massacred by Ottomans in 1823 during the Greek War of Independence.

Palace of Mália

⊗ 🖈 3 km (2 miles) E of Mália 📞 2897 031597 ⏱ Apr–Oct: 8am–8pm Tue–Sun; Nov–Mar: 8am–3pm daily 🚫 Main public hols

26

Lasíthi Plateau

Ωροπέδιο Λασιθίου

🖈 56 km (35 miles) SE of Iráklio 🚌 To Tzermiádo

A row of stone windmills at the Séli Ambélou Pass marks the entry to the plain of Lasíthi, a flat agricultural area 800 m (2,625 ft) above sea level.

Along the perimeter of the plain are several villages, the largest of which is Tzermiádo, with good tourist facilities. On the southern edge of the plain, the village of Ágios Geórgios has a small **Folk and Historical Museum** displaying embroidery, paintings and Venizelos memorabilia.

The highlight of a visit to Lasíthi is the climb to the **Diktian Cave**, birthplace of Zeus. Artifacts unearthed here include votive offerings, double axes and statuettes, now in the collection at the Iráklio Archaeological Museum *(p258*

Folk and Historical Museum

⊗ 🖈 Ágios Geórgios 📞 Oct: 10am–6pm Mon–

Diktian Cave

⊗ 🖈 Psychró 📞 22462 ⏱ Apr– 6:30pm daily 8:30am–2:3 🚫 Main pu

Eloúnda

Ελούντα

⌂ 11 km (7 miles) N of Ágios Nikólaos 🚌

Once the site of the ancient city-state of Olous, the town of Eloúnda was developed by the Venetians in 1579 as a fortified port situated on the Mirabéllo Bay. Today, it is an idyllic, well-established resort.

East of the town a narrow strip joins the mainland to the long piece of land forming the Spinalónga peninsula. Just below the water's surface here can be seen remains of the Greco-Roman city-state of Olous, with its temples of Zeus and Artemis. To the north of the peninsula is the small island of **Spinalónga**, fortified by a 16th-century Venetian fortress. Surrendered to the Ottomans in 1715, it later contained a Muslim village before serving as a leper colony (from 1903 to 1957). Boats regularly ferry tourists to the island from Eloúnda and Pláka, a nearby hamlet that offers a pleasant retreat from the town's bustle.

Spinalónga
◈ ⌚ Apr–Oct: 9am–7pm daily

Did You Know?

Legend has it that Athena bathed in Ágios Nikólaos' Lake of Voulisméni.

Ágios Nikólaos

Αγιος Νικόλαος

⌂ 65 km (40 miles) W of Iráklio 🚌🚌 ℹ 28413 40100

One of the most delightful holiday centres in Crete, Ágios Nikólaos boasts a superb setting on the Mirabéllo Bay. In Hellenistic times, according to inscriptions dating back to 193 BC, this was one of two flourishing cities called Lato: Lato pros Kamara (towards the arch) and Lato Etera (Other Lato). Having declined in importance under Venetian rule, it was not until the 19th century that modern Ágios Nikólaos began to develop; it is now the busy capital of Lasíthi province.

A thriving resort, the pretty harbour is the centre of Ágios Nikólaos. Nearby, with a depth of 64 m (210 ft), is the Lake of Voulisméni. Overlooking the lake, the **Folk Museum** houses a colourful display of traditional Cretan crafts and domestic items. Just north of town, in the grounds of the Mínos Palace Hotel, is the tiny 10th- to 11th-century church of Ágios Nikólaos, after which the town is named.

Unfortunately, the town's **Archaeological Museum** has been closed for years and seems destined to remain so. The only part of the building open is a small photography exhibition on the development of the modern town.

Folk Museum
◈ ⌂ Kondyláki 2 ⌚ 10am–2pm & 5–8:30pm Tue–Sun ⌛ Main public hols

Archaeological Museum
⌂ Paleológou 74 📞 28410 24943 ⌚ 8am–3pm Tue–Sun

Kritsá

Κριτσά

⌂ 10 km (6 miles) W of Ágios Nikólaos 🚌

Set at the foot of the Lasíthi mountains, Kritsá is a small village known for its Byzantine church. Also a popular centre for Cretan crafts, during the summer month its main street is awash with lace, elaborately woven rugs and embroidered tablecloths. From the cafés and tavernas along the main street, you can enjoy fine views of the valley leading down to the coast.

East of Kritsá, just off the road among olive groves, the 13th-century church of **Panagia Kerá** contains some of the finest frescoes in Crete, dating from the 13th to mid-14th century. The building is triple-aisled, with the central aisle being the oldest.

North of Kritsá lie the ruins of a fortified city founded by the Dorians in the 7th century BC. **Lato Etera** flourished until Classical times, when its fortunes declined under Roman rule: it was superseded by the

← Well-preserved frescoes in the Byzantine church of Panagía Kerá, Kritsá

more easily reached port of Lato pros Kamara (today's Ágios Nikólaos). Perched on a saddle between two mountain peaks, the site offers fine views of Mirabéllo Bay. A paved road, with workshops and houses clustered on the right, climbs up to a central agora, or marketplace, where there is a cistern to collect rainwater and a shrine. On the north side of the agora is a staircase flanked by two towers; to the south are a temple and a theatre.

Panagía Kerá

⊗ 🏠 Approach road to Kritsá
🕐 8:30am–3pm Tue–Sun

Lato Etera

🏠 4 km (2 miles) N of Kritsá
🕐 Unrestricted access

 30

Ierápetra

Ιεράπετρα

🏠 33 km (20 miles) S of Ágios Nikólaos 🚌

On the southeast coast of Crete, Ierápetra is Europe's most southerly city. A settlement since pre-Minoan times, trade and cultural connections with the Middle East and with North Africa were a key reason for the city's existence. Sir Arthur Evans declared it the "crossroads of Minoan and Achaian civilizations". Once a flourishing city with villas, temples, amphitheatres and imposing buildings, the town today has an air of decline.

The entrance to the old harbour is guarded by the 13th-century Venetian **Fort Kalés**. West of the fortress is the former Muslim quarter, where a restored 18th-century mosque and elegant Ottoman fountain can be seen. Also in this area, on Kougioumtzáki, is the 14th-century church of Aféntis Christós.

The small **Archaeological Museum** displays local artifacts that managed to survive marauders and archaeological predators. The exhibits date from Minoan to Roman times and include *larnakes* (burial caskets), *pithoi* (storage jars), statues, bronze axes and stone carvings.

An almost unbroken line of sandy beaches stretches eastwards from Ierápetra, overlooked by a plethora of hotels and restaurants. From Ierápetra's harbour, daily boat excursions (mid-May–late October) run to the idyllic white sands and juniper forests of the uninhabited Chrysí island, also known as Gaidouronísi. The island, a protected nature reserve, has only one bar and one taverna.

Fort Kalés

🏠 Old port 🕐 Daily 🕐 Main public hols

Archaeological Museum

🏠 Dimokratías 2 📞 28420 28721 🕐 8am–3pm Tue–Sun 🕐 Main public hols

← The charming, taverna-lined harbour of the resort of Ágios Nikólaos

STAY

White River Cottages

Fifteen stone cottages in an abandoned hamlet have been transformed into apartments with minimalist decor.

🏠 Aspropótamos district, Makrýgialos
🌐 whiterivercottages. com

€€€€

Stella's Traditional Apartments

These rustic yet comfortable units are set in lush terrace-gardens near the beach.

🏠 Káto Zákros
🌐 stelapts.com

€€€€

St Nicolas Bay Resort Hotel and Villas

Elegant luxury with spacious standard rooms, superior suites with private pools, and family villas. A spa completes the package.

🏠 Nisí peninsula, 1.5 km (1 mile) N of Ágios
🌐 stnicolasbay.gr

€€€€

Minos Beach Art Hotel

This seaside boutique hotel has whitewashed bungalows by the

🏠 Aktí Ilía Sot Ágios Ni
🌐 minos

Gourniá
Γουρνιά

🏛 **19 km (12 miles) E of Ágios Nikólaos** 🚌
🕐 **8:30am–3pm Tue–Sun**
🚫 **Main public hols**

The Minoan site of Gourniá stands on a low hill overlooking the tranquil Mirabéllo Bay. Excavated by the American archaeologist Harriet Boyd-Hawes between 1901 and 1904, Gourniá is the best-preserved Minoan town in Crete. A mini-palace (one-tenth the size of Knosos) marks its centre, surrounded by a labyrinth of narrow, stepped streets and single-room dwellings. The site was inhabited as early as the 3rd millennium BC, though what remains dates instead from the Second Palace Period, around 1700 BC. A fire, caused by seismic activity in 1450 BC, destroyed the settlement.

Along the National Highway, 2 km (1 mile) west of Gourniá, an old concrete road turns left up to Moní Faneroménis, a spectacular 6-km (4-mile) climb. Here, the 15th-century chapel of the Panagía was built into a deep cave and is the repository for sacred (and some say miraculous) icons.

East along the National Highway, a left turning from Sfáka leads to the delightful resort village of Móhlos. Just offshore is a small island, once joined to the mainland by a narrow strip of land, which is the site of a Minoan settlement and cemetery.

Moní Tóploú
Μονή Τοπλού

🏛 **10 km (6 miles) E of Sitía, Lasíthi** 📞 **28430 29630**
🚌 **Towards Vaï** 🕐 **Apr–Oct: 9am–6pm daily; Nov–Mar: 9am–6pm Fri only**

Founded in the 14th century, Moní Tóploú is now one of the wealthiest and most influential monasteries in Crete. The present buildings date from Venetian times, when the monastery was fortified against pirate attacks. The Turkish name "Tóploú" refers to the cannon installed here. During World War II, Resistance radio broadcasts were transmitted from the monastery, an act for which Abbot Siligknakis Gennadios and two of his monks were executed by the Germans at Agiá prison in western Crete.

There are three levels of cells overlooking the inner courtyard, where a small 14th-century church contains icons and frescoes. The most famous of these is the Lord, Thou Art Great icon, completed in 1770 by the Cretan artist Ioannis Kornaros, comprising 61 miniature but meticulously detailed scenes. On the façade of the church, an inscription records the Arbitration of Magnesia in 132 BC. This was a landmark decision that settled a dispute between the rival city-states of Ierapytna (which is today's Ierápetra) and Itanos over the control of the Temple of Zeus Diktaios at Palékastro. The inscription stone was used originally as a tombstone. The monastery's small but worthwhile museum houses etchings and 15th- to 18th-century icons.

← The vibrantly decorated refectory (*inset*) of the fortress-like 14th-century Moní Tóploú

Sitía
Σητεία

🚗 70 km (44 miles) E
of Ágios Nikólaos 🚌🚆

Snaking its way through the mountains between Gourniá and Sitía, the National Highway traverses some of the most magnificent scenery in Crete. Towards Sitía, the landscape gives way to barren ridges and vineyards.

Although there is evidence of a large Greco-Roman city in the region, modern Sitía dates from the 4th century AD. It flourished under Byzantine and early Venetian rule, but its fortunes took a downturn in the 16th century as a result of earthquakes and pirate attacks. When rebuilding took place in the 1870s Sitía began to prosper once again.

Today, the production of wine and olive oil is important to Sitía's economy, and the town has replaced Ágios Nikólaos as the ferry port for eastern Crete.

At the centre of Sitía's old quarter lies a picturesque harbour, with tavernas and cafés clustering around its edges. Above the north end of the harbour the restored Venetian fort (now used as an open-air theatre) is all that remains of the once extensive fortifications of the town. The Kornaria Festival is a cultural event held in the fort from mid-June until mid-August and is a great way for visitors to learn about the customs and traditions of Sitía. Festival events include music, theatre and dance performances, exhibitions and sports.

On the southern outskirts of town, the **Archaeological Museum** displays artifacts from the Sitía district. Exhibits range from Neolithic to Roman times and include an exquisite Minoan ivory statuette known as the Palékastro *kouros*, a large pottery collection and a sizeable haul of material from Zákros Palace.

HIKES AROUND ZÁKROS

Just inland from the port at Káto Zákros, the Gorge of the Dead (so called for the ancient tombs in its flanks) extends inland as far as modern Zákros village. It's actually a very alive canyon, with vegetation, birds and potable water from the aqueduct threading it. Hikers should allow two hours for a round trip. A 45-minute walk from Hohlakiés village takes hikers down the gorge to Karoumés beach. A coastal trail also links Karoumés with Káto Zákros – handy if you've left a car there.

Archaeological Museum
⚕ ♿ South edge of town, on corner of National Highway to Palékastro 📞 28430 23917 🕐 8am–3pm Tue–Sun 🚫 Main public hols

Vái Beach
Παραλία Βάι

🚗 93 km (58 miles) E
of Ágios Nikólaos 🚌

Exotic Vái Beach is a tropical paradise of palm trees known to have existed in ancient times. This inviting sandy cove is tremendously popular with holiday-makers. Although thoroughly commercialized, with overpriced tavernas and the constant arrival of tour buses, great care is taken to protect the palm trees.

In the desolate landscape 3 km (2 miles) north of Vái, the ruins of the ancient city-state of Itanos stand on a hill between two sandy coves. Minoan, Greco-Roman and Byzantine remains have been excavated (the scant traces of which can be seen today), including a Byzantine basilica and the ruins of some Classical temples.

The agricultural town of Palékastro, 10 km (6 miles) south of Vái, is the gateway to sandy Kouraménos beach, a major windsurfing centre.

Zákros
Ζάκρος

🚗 104 km (65 miles) SE
of Ágios Nikólaos 🚌
🚫 Main public hols

In 1961, Cretan archaeologist Nikolaos Platon discovered the unplundered Minoan palace of Zákros. The fourth largest of the Minoan palaces, it was built around 1700 BC and destroyed in the island-wide disaster of 1450 BC.

The two-storey palace was arranged around a central courtyard, the east side of which contained the royal apartments. Remains of colonnaded cistern ha' still be seen, as can a lined well in which preserved 3,000-' olives were four Finds from th an exquisite and nume the Irákli' Museu'

A DRIVING TOUR
THE AMÁRI VALLEY

Locator Map
For more detail see p246

Tour length 92 km (57 miles) **Stopping-off points** There are local tavernas in every village en route (Ano Méros offers spectacular views) **Terrain** Twisting but well-paved roads

Dominated by the peaks of Mount Ídi to its east, the Amári Valley offers staggering views over the region's rocky peaks, broad green valleys and dramatic gorges. Winding roads link the many small agricultural communities of the Amári where, even today, traditional life, including wearing folk dress, continues. An area of Cretan resistance in World War II, many of the villages were destroyed in the 1940s.

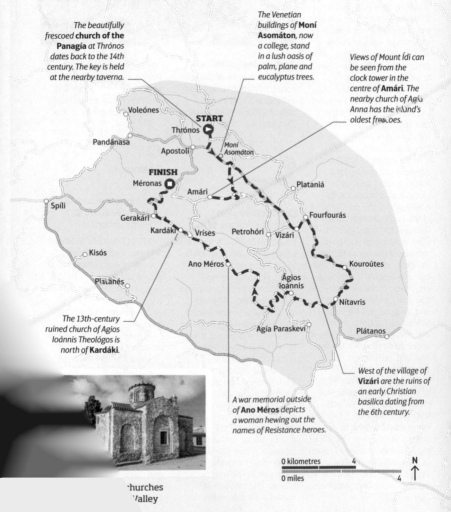

The beautifully frescoed **church of the Panagía** at Thrónos dates back to the 14th century. The key is held at the nearby taverna.

The Venetian buildings of **Moní Asomáton**, now a college, stand in a lush oasis of palm, plane and eucalyptus trees.

Views of Mount Ídi can be seen from the clock tower in the centre of **Amári**. The nearby church of Agía Anna has the island's oldest frescoes.

The 13th-century ruined church of Agios Ioánnis Theológos is north of **Kardáki**.

A war memorial outside of **Ano Méros** depicts a woman hewing out the names of Resistance heroes.

West of the village of **Vizári** are the ruins of an early Christian basilica dating from the 6th century.

0 kilometres   4
0 miles   4

N

churches
Valley

↑ The lush valley, wit[...]
hidden villages, sh[...]
and churches

ATHENS

The birthplace of European civilization, Athens
has been inhabited for millennia. The ancient city
experienced a golden age in the 5th century BC,
when Athenian leader Perikles commissioned
many new buildings, including most of the
structures on the Acropolis. This was the time
when great tragedies and comedies were written
and performed, and Aristotle and Socrates opened
schools of philosophy. Athens led the Delian
League, a union of Greek cities, but came into
conflict with the other leading city-state, Sparta,
resulting in a major 30-year-conflict known as
the Peloponnesian War. By its end, Athens lay
defeated, its golden age over. The city became a
part of the Roman Empire in 146 BC, starting
centuries of occupation by various powers from
the Byzantine to the Ottoman empires. In 1821,
Greek people across the islands and mainland rose
up in the War of Independence against the ruling
Ottomans and created the Greek State. Athens
was declared its capital in 1834. After World War II,
which Athens spent occupied by the German army,
the city sprawled out into suburbs housing the
multitudes of people migrating from rural areas.
A military coup overthrew the democratically
elected government in 1967, and mass protests
by students in 1973 resulted in a violent suppres-
sion by military forces. Now a large, buzzing and
democratic city, still with a significant student
population, Athens is a concrete metropolis, it
walls a noted canvas for world-class street a

ATHENS

Must See
1. Acropolis

Experience More
2. Ancient Agora
3. National Archaeological Museum
4. Anafiótika
5. Exárhia
6. Monastiráki
7. Pláka
8. Lykavittós Hill
9. Benaki Museum

10. Museum of Cycladic Art
11. National Gallery of Art
12. Byzantine and Christian Museum

Eat
1. Rififi
2. Ama Lahei
3. Diporto

Stay
4. Emporikon Athens
5. Marble House Pension

① The view from the Acropolis rock.

② A walkway over ruins at the Acropolis Museum.

③ A bustling market in central Monastiráki square.

④ Musicians playing *rembétika* music.

24 HOURS
in Athens

Morning

Say *kaliméra* ("good morning") with a coffee from Little Trees Books & Coffee *(Kavalloti 2, Athina 117 42)*, a bookshop-cum-café whose outdoor tables sit charmingly under striped awnings. It's handily close to the Acropolis, where your best chance of beating the crowds is getting there close to opening at 8am. Spend the morning among the most remarkable ancient structures in the world, from the Pantheon to the Temple of Athena Nike *(p288)*. Descend to pedestrianized Dionysíou Areopagítou, down the east hill past the late Classical Theatre of Dionysos, where many ancient tragedies and comedies had their premieres, on your way to the Acropolis Museum *(p288)*, where you could easily spend a few hours – but limit yourself to one or two. The most notable displays here include half of the surviving Parthenon Marbles, housed in a gallery with a view of the Acropolis.

Afternoon

Throw yourself headlong into vibrant and bustling Monastiráki *(p293)*, with its range of shops – if you're there on a Saturday, it will be buzzing with the odd and the amazing at the weekly flea market. Have lunch at the basement Diporto taverna near Athens Central Market *(p293)*. There's no sign, and no English menu, which is part of the reason it has remained authentic. From Monastiráki station, take Metro Line 1 north to Omónia, then change to a bus along Trítis Septemvríou, alighting near Márni for the National Archaeological Museum *(p292)*. Budget a couple of hours to absorb the collection which spans thousands of years, from the Neolithic to the Roman eras. Unmissable crowd-pleasers include the Cycladic Harp Player from the third millennium BC and the Youth of Antikythera salvaged from a shipwreck near that island, along with the so-called Antikythera mechanism of 100 BC, an advanced ancient computer used to calculate astronomical events.

Evening

Walk a few blocks southeast to buzzing and alternative Exárhia district, where tavernas and bars stay up all night. If it's a Tuesday, Thursday or Friday, bookstores and music shops purveying legacy vinyl will sell their wares long into the night. Head for the characterful stone taverna Efimeron *(Methonis 58, Athina 106 81)*, known for its live *rebétika* music, a local Greek blues variation that emerged from dive bars and tavernas. Feast traditional Greek dishes and loc here. Head back to the Acropo' the Odeon of Herodes Atticu an ancient amphitheatre th partially restored. Catchir or perfomance at this an magical, and not to be

ACROPOLIS

⊙ B5 ⌂ Dionysíou Areopagítou (main entrance), Pláka
⊜ Acropoli ⊞ 230, X80 ⊙ May–Oct: 8am–8pm daily;
Nov–Apr: 8am–3pm daily ⊠ 1 Jan, 25 Mar, Easter Sun, 1 May,
25 & 26 Dec ⊠ odysseus.culture.gr

One of the most famous archaeological sites in the world, the
Acropolis and its temples stands as a monument to the political
and cultural achievements of Greece. The Acropolis overlooks the
city from a plateau that has been in use for 5,000 years.

In the mid-5th century BC, after the Athenians had defeated
the invading Persian Empire, Athenian leader Perikles
persuaded Athens' citizens to begin a grand programme of
building work in the city, sparking a new golden age. This work,
constructed by Athens' leading architects, sculptors and
painters, transformed the Acropolis with three contrasting
temples, two dedicated to Athena and one shared between
Athena and Poseidon, and a monumental gateway called the
Propylaia. The most well-known temple is the Parthenon, a
massive temple to the city's patron goddess Athena, which is
being restored. The Theatre of Dionysos on the south slope
was developed further in the 4th century BC, and the Odeon
of Herodes Atticus was added in the 2nd century AD.

INSIDER TIP
Early Bird

Your best chance to
catch the Acropolis
before the large crowds
descend in summer is
at 8am, immediately
after the complex opens
to visitors.

THE ACROPOLIS MUSEUM

Located in the historic Makrigiánni
district at the foot of the Acropolis, this
€130 million showpiece was designed
by Bernard Tschumi and constructed
over excavations of an early Christian
settlement; a glass walkway hovers
over the ruins. The collection has been
installed in chronological order and
starts with finds from the slopes of the
Acropolis, including statues and reliefs
from the Shrine of Asklepios. The skylit
Parthenon Gallery on the top floor is the
highlight, showcasing the parts of the
Parthenon frieze that remain in Greece,
in their original order.

The awe-inspiring columns
of the Parthenon, with ↑
restoration underway

3000 BC

▽ First settlement on the Acropolis during the Neolithic period.

BC 447–438

▽ Construction of the Parthenon begins under noted Athenian leader Pericles.

510 BC

△ Delphic Oracle declares the Acropolis a holy place of the gods, banning habitation by mortals.

AD 1985

△ Restorations begin on the Acropolis site, starting with the Erechtheion.

Exploring the Acropolis

Once through the Propylaia, the grand gateway built between 437 and 432 BC as the entrance to the site, the Parthenon exerts an overwhelming fascination. The other fine temples on "the Rock" include the Erechtheion, the temple dedicated to both Athena and Poseidon, and the Temple of Athena Nike. The Erechtheion is particularly notable for the Porch of the Caryatids, statues of women used in place of columns on the south porch of the temple. Since 1975, visitors have not been allowed to enter the temples. It is a miracle that anything remains at all, as the ravages of war, the removal of temple treasures and pollution have all taken their toll on the Acropolis.

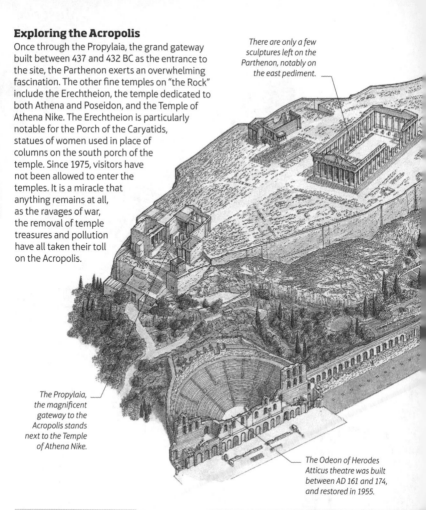

There are only a few sculptures left on the Parthenon, notably on the east pediment.

The Propylaia, the magnificent gateway to the Acropolis stands next to the Temple of Athena Nike.

The Odeon of Herodes Atticus theatre was built between AD 161 and 174, and restored in 1955.

THE PARTHENON MARBLES

The most famous ancient sculptures in the world, the Elgin (Parthenon) Marbles are also the most controversial. Half of the surviving sculptures were taken to Britain by Lord Elgin in 1803, allegedly with the permission of the Ottomans. Since 1832, independent Greece has petitioned Britain to return the marbles, which are on display in the British Museum, without success.

The partially restored Odeon of Herodes Atticus, now used for summer festivals

← Illustration of the Acropolis rock as it looks today

The Theatre of Dionysos visible today was built by Lykourgos between 333 and 330 BC.

The stoa of Eumenes is a long colonnaded walkway connecting the odeon and Theatre of Dionysos.

Must See

The Parthenon

▷ One of the world's most recognizable structures, work began on the Parthenon in 447 BC, when the sculptor Pheidias was entrusted with supervising the building of a magnificent new Doric temple to Athena, the patron goddess of the city. It was designed primarily to house the Parthenos, Pheidias's impressive 12-m- (39-ft-) high cult statue of Athena covered in ivory and gold. Taking nine years to complete, the temple was dedicated to the goddess during the Great Panathenaia festival of 438 BC. The famous Parthenon Marbles consist of the pediments, metopes and friezes that decorated the temple. These marbles show a range of scenes from both mythology and daily life. The magnificent frieze, which ran around the four walls of the structure, depicted the ancient Panathenaic procession, which happened every four years in the city on Athena's birthday.

Temple of Athena Nike

The second dedicated to Athena, this particular temple on the west side of the Propylaia worships Athena as goddess of victory. It was built between 427 and 424 BC.

Theatre of Dionysos

◁ Nestled on the southeastern flank of the Acropolis, the Theatre of Dionysos – dedicated to the local cult of Dionysos Eleutherios – was originally erected during the 5th century BC and upgraded in about 330 BC to seat 17,000. The first performances of many works by Sophokles, Aristophanes and Euripides were performed here. The most interesting architectural details are the ancient front-row thrones for VIPs, including one with lion-paw detail for the priest of Dionysos. The stage building shows scenes from the life of the god.

Odeon of Herodes Atticus

Herodes Atticus (101–177 AD) was a wealthy Athenian scholar and Roman consul, who endowe the giant odeon (building for musical peformanc that bears his name, completed in 161 AD, to t of Athens. The orchestra area would have be in cedar, though seating was apparently c sky, as no supports for an extended roof found. Extending to three storeys in p is immensely tall – particularly comp modest odeons found in other sit Restored during the 20th centu the main venues for the summ and is not normally open du

EXPERIENCE MORE

2

Ancient Agora

Αρχαία Αγορά

🏛 **Main entrance at Adrianoú 24, Monastiráki** 📞 **210 32 10 185** Ⓜ **Thiseío, Monastiráki** 🕐 **8am–8pm daily (to 3pm Nov–Apr)** 🚫 **Main public hols**

The Agora was the political and religious heart of ancient Athens. Also the centre of commercial and daily life, it abounded with schools and elegant stoas filled with shops. The state prison was here, as was the mint, which made the city's coins inscribed with the famous owl symbol.

The main building standing today is the impressive two-storey stoa of Attalos. This was rebuilt between 1953 and 1956 on the original foundations and using ancient building materials. Founded by King Attalos II of Pergamon (ruled 159–138 BC), it dominated the eastern quarter of the Agora until it was destroyed in AD 267. It is used today as a museum, exhibiting the finds from the site. These include legal artifacts, such as a *klepsydra* (a water clock that was used for timing plaintiffs'

speeches), bronze ballots and items from everyday life such as some terracotta toys and leather sandals. The best-preserved ruins on the site are the Odeion of Agrippa, a covered theatre, and the Hephaisteion, a temple to Hephaistos, which is also known as the Theseion.

---

3 🏛 Ⓜ 🖥

National Archaeological Museum

Εθνικό Αρχαιολογικό Μουσείο

🏛 **44 Patissíon, Exárhia** Ⓜ **Omónia or Viktória** 🕐 **Apr–Oct: 8am–8pm daily (from 1pm Mon); Nov–Mar: 9am–4pm Tues–Sun (1–8pm Mon)** 🌐 **namuseum.gr**

When it opened in 1891, this museum brought together pieces that had previously been stored all over the city. During World War II this priceless collection was dispersed and buried underground to protect it from any possible damage. The museum reopened in 1946, but it took another 50 years of renovation and reorganization to finally do justice to its

formidable collection. It is a good idea to plan ahead and be selective when visiting the museum and not attempt to cover everything in one visit.

The exhibits can be divided into five main collections: Neolithic and Cycladic; Mycenaean, Geometric and Archaic; Classical sculpture; Roman and Hellenistic sculpture; and the pottery collections. Smaller collections that are also worth seeing include the stunning Eleni Stathatou jewellery collection and the Egyptian rooms.

The many high points of the museum range from the unique finds of the grave circle at Mycenae, in particular the gold *Mask of Agamemnon*, to the Archaic *kouroí* statues and the unrivalled collection of Classical and Hellenistic statues. Two of the finest

Did You Know?

The Odeion of Agrippa was built by a Roman statesman as a gift to the people of Athens.

bronzes are the *Horse with the Little Jockey* and the *Poseidon*. Also housed here is one of the world's largest collections of ancient ceramics, comprising elegant figure vases from the 6th and 5th centuries BC and some Geometric funerary vases dating back to 1000 BC. The Library of Archaeology holds a large collection of rare books, including the diaries of Heinrich Schliemann, who uncovered the remains of Mycenae and Troy.

 4

Anafiótika
Αναφιώτικα

 Monastiráki or Akrópoli

Nestling beneath the northern slopes of the Acropolis, this area is one of the oldest settlements in Athens. Today, its whitewashed houses, cramped streets and pots of basil on windowsills still give it the atmosphere of a typical Cycladic village. Its first residents were refugees from the Peloponnesian War. By 1841, it had been colonized by workmen from Anáfi, in the Cyclades, who eventually gave the area its name. Part of the influx of island craftsmen who

 ←

The imposing stoa of Attalos, on the site of the Ancient Agora

 ←

The charming streets of Anafiótika, lined with whitewashed houses

helped to build the new city following independence, they ignored a decree declaring the area an archaeological zone, and completed their houses overnight, installing their families by morning. By Ottoman law, this meant the authorities were powerless to knock the new houses down.

The area is bounded by two 17th-century churches: Agios Geórgios tou Vráhou to the southeast, which has a tiny courtyard filled with flowers, and Agios Symeón to the west, which contains a copy of a miraculous icon, originally brought from Anáfi.

 5

Exárhia

 Omónia

An area of about a dozen blocks southeast of the National Archaeological Museum, around the *platía* at the junctions of Spyrídonos, Themistokléous, Trikoúpi and Stournára, Exárhia is the traditional student quarter, the long-time headquarters of the Greek publishing industry, and a major alternative culture hub.

It is a heavily graffitied area, and some of the murals are well worth seeking out. Tavernas, cafés, bars and quirky shops abound.

6

Monastiráki
Μοναστηράκι

Monastiráki Market
Daily

This area, named after the little monastery church in Platía Monastirakíou, is synonymous with Athens' famous flea market. Located

next to the Ancient Agora, it is bounded by Platía Agíon Asomáton in the west and Eólou in the east. The streets of Pandrósou, Iféstou and Áreos leading off Platía Monastirakíou are full of shops, selling a range of goods from antiques, leather and silver to tourist trinkets.

The heart of the flea market is Platía Avyssinías where every weekend dealers arrive with furniture and varic and ends. During nearby shops a offer antique: books, rugs taverna ch gear and

7

Pláka
Πλάκα

 Monastiráki 🚋 1, 2, 4, 5, 9, 10, 11, 12, 15, 18

Considered the historic heart of Athens, the Pláka district buzzes with tourists as well as Athenians who come to eat in old-fashioned tavernas or browse in the antique and icon shops. Despite the crowds, Pláka still retains the atmosphere of a traditional neighbourhood and while only a few of its buildings date back further than the Ottoman period, it remains the oldest continuously inhabited area in the city.

One explanation of its name comes from the Albanian soldiers in the service of the Turks who settled here in the 16th century – *pliaka* (old) was how they described the area.

Among the notable remains here is the only choregic monument intact in Athens, the Lysikrates Monument in Lysikrátous. Built to commemorate the victors at annual dramatic and festival at the Theatre the monuments from the *...os*) of the

...e Winds, in ..., is in the ... Agora.

It was built by the Syrian astronomer Andronikos Kyrrestes around 100 BC as a weather vane and waterclock. On each of its marble sides, the eight recognized winds are depicted in relief form.

Many churches here are worth a visit: 11th-century Agios Nikólaos Rangavás has ancient columns as its walls.

Tower of the Winds
 ⬛ Platía Aerídon ☎ 210 32 45 220 🕐 May–Oct: 8am–5pm daily; Nov–Apr: 8am–3pm daily ◻ Main public hols

R

Lykavittós Hill
Λυκαβηττός

 Megaro Moussikis

At 277 m (910 ft), this hill is the highest point in Athens and the apex offers the best view over town. A steep path climbs it from the top of Loukianoú Street, at the southwestern tip of the ridge; alternatively, the easy way up is the funicular a block away on Aristíppou, at the top of Ploutárhou. Near the summit, the little chapel of Ágios Geórgios is well attended on 23 April, when every George celebrates his name-day. Beyond, the outdoor Lykavittós Theatre is a popular venue for concerts in the summertime.

9

Benaki Museum
Μουσείο Μπενάκη

⬛ Corner of Koumbári and Vasilíssis Sofías, Sýntagma ⬛ Sýntagma 🚋 3, 7, 8, 13 🕐 10am–6pm Wed & Fri, 10am–12am Thu & Sat, 10am–4pm Sun ◻ Main public hols 🌐 benaki.gr

This outstanding museum, which opened in 1931, contains a diverse collection of Greek art and crafts, regional costumes, jewellery and political memorabilia spanning from the 3rd century BC to the 20th century. There are also fantastic artifacts from Egypt and the rest of the world. The museum was founded by Andonios Benakis (1873–1954), the son of Emmanouil Benakis, a wealthy Greek who made his fortune in Egypt. Andonios Benakis was, from an early age, interested in Greek, Persian, Egyptian and Ottoman art, and started collecting while living in Alexandria. When he moved to Athens in 1926, he donated his collection to the Greek State and used his family house as the museum. The elegant Neo-Classical mansion housing the museum was built towards the end of the 19th century by Anastasios Metaxas, who was also behind Athen's Kallimármaro stadium. Due to generous donations,

Aerial view across
Monastiraki Square
and Pláka in Athens

the collection is ever-
expanding and there have
been several extensions
added to the original building,
subsequent to its conversion
into a museum.

Museum of Cycladic Art

Μουσείο Κυκλαδικής Τέχνης

🏠 Neofýtou Doúka 4,
Kolonáki 🚍 3, 7 🕐 10am-
5pm Mon, Wed, Fri & Sat;
10am-8pm Thu; 11am-5pm
Sun ⌚ Main public hols
🌐 cycladic.gr

Opened in 1986, this modern
museum has the world's
finest collection of Cycladic
art. Assembled by Nikolaos
and Dolly Goulandris and
helped by the donations of
other Greek collectors, it
brings together a fantastic
selection of ancient Greek art
spanning 5,000 years of
history, spread over five
fantastic floors.

The displays start on the
first floor, home to the
Cycladic collection. Dating
back to the 3rd millennium
BC, the Cycladic figurines
were found mostly in graves,
although their exact usage
remains a mystery. One of the
finest examples is
the marble sculpture
of the Harp Player.

Ancient Greek art
is exhibited on the
second floor and the
Charles Politis
collection of Classical
and Prehistoric art is
on the fourth floor;
highlights include
some terracotta
figurines of
women from
Tanágra, central
Greece. The third

floor of the museum is used
for often compelling
temporary exhibitions. The
adjoining Neo-Classical
Stathátos Mansion is named
after its original inhabitants,
Otto and Athiná Stathátos,
and houses the Greek Art
Collection of the Athens
Academy. Temporary exhibitions are often on display on
the first floor of the mansion.

11

National Gallery of Art

Εθνική Πινακοθήκη

🏠 Vasiléos Konstandínou
50, Ilísia Ⓜ Evangelismós
🚍 3, 13 🕐 9am-3:30pm Mon
& Thu-Sun, 2-9pm Wed
🕐 Main public hols
🌐 nationalgallery.gr

This gallery holds a
permanent collection of
European and Greek art,
mainly paintings. In one
gallery, the marvellous
European collection includes
works by the great masters of
Van Dyck, Cézanne, Dürer and
Rembrandt, as well as
Picasso's *Woman in a White
Dress* (1939) and Caravaggio's
Singer (1620). Most of the
collection is made up of Greek
art from the 18th to 20th
centuries. The 1800s feature
evocative paintings of the
War of Independence. There
are also some excellent
portraits, including *The Loser
of the Bet* (1878) by Nikólaos
Gýzis (1842–1901), *Waiting*
(1900) by Nikifóros Lýtras
(1832–1904) and *The Straw
Hat* (1925) by Nikólaos
Lýtras (1883–1927).
The neighbouring
building, which houses
the excellent, sizeable
sculpture collection,
remains closed for
extensive renovation.

Marble idol on display
in the Museum of
Cycladic Art

12

Byzantine and Christian Museum

Βυζαντινό και χριστιανικό μουσείο

🏠 Vasilíssis Sofías 22
🕐 summer: 8am-8pm daily
(from noon Mon); winter:
much earlier closing time
🌐 byzantinemuseum.gr

One of Athens's best for both
quality of displays and clarity
of presentation. Exhibits, not
just ecclesiastical, are grouped
thematically and chronologically. A compelling aspect is
the visual transition from
Roman and pagan practices
and architecture in early
Christianity. Star exhibits
include the mosaic floor of
the Ilissós basilica; a carved
marble altar screen with a lion
attacking a stag; the Hoard of
Mytilene, hastily buried during
7th-century Arab raids; and
many 13th-century frescoes
from vulnerable churches.

NEED TO KNOW

Before You Go 298

Getting Around 300

Practical Information 304

BEFORE YOU GO

Forward planning is essential to any successful trip. Be prepared for all eventualities by considering the following points before you travel.

AT A GLANCE

CURRENCY
Euro (EUR)

AVERAGE DAILY SPEND

SAVER	SPEND	SPLURGE
€65	€110	€170

BOTTLED WATER	COFFEE	BEER	DINNER FOR TWO
€1.20	€3.50	€3.00	€35+

ESSENTIAL PHRASES

Hello	Geia sas
Goodbye	Adío
Please	Parakalo
Thank you	Efharisto
Do you speak English?	Miláte Angliká?
I don't understand	Den katálava

**ECTRICITY
PLY**

sockets are
nd F, fitting
ged plugs.
ltage is
s.

Passports and Visas

EU nationals and citizens of the UK, US, Canada, Australia and New Zealand do not need visas for stays of up to three months. Consult your nearest Greek embassy or the **Greek Ministry of Foreign Affairs** website if you are travelling from outside these areas.
Greek Ministry of Foreign Affairs
w mfa.gr/en/visas

Travel Safety Advice

Visitors can get up-to-date travel safety information from the **US Department of State**, the **UK Foreign and Commonwealth Office**, and the **Australian Department of Foreign Affairs and Trade**.
Australia
w smarttraveller.gov.au
UK
w gov.uk/foreign-travel-advice
US
w travel.state.gov

Customs Information

Limits vary if travelling from outside the EU, so check restrictions before travelling. An individual is permitted to carry the following within the EU for personal use:
Tobacco products 800 cigarettes, 400 cigarillos, 200 cigars or 1 kg of tobacco.
Alcohol 10 litres of alcoholic beverages above 22 per cent strength, 20 litres of alcoholic beverages below 22 per cent strength, 90 litres of wine (60 litres of which can be sparkling wine) and 110 litres of beer.
Cash If you plan to enter or leave the EU with €10,000 or more in cash (or equivalent in other currencies), you must declare it to the customs authorities prior to departure.

Insurance

It is wise to take out an insurance policy covering theft, loss of belongings, medical problems, cancellation and delays, as well as coverage for car hire and adventure activities. EU nationals with an **EHIC** (European Health Insurance Card), available online through national health services, are entitled to free care in state-run clinics or hospitals, provided you enter via the casualty ward. It is highly recommended travellers get comprehensive travel insurance covering private clinics, particularly if you don't have an EHIC .

EHIC

gov.uk/european-health-insurance-card

Vaccinations

No vaccinations are required for travel in the Greek Islands.

Money

Major credit and debit cards are accepted in most shops and restaurants, while pre-paid currency cards are accepted in some, as well as contactless credit cards. However, it is always worth carrying some cash, as many smaller businesses and markets still operate on a cash-only policy.

Booking Accommodation

Booking accommodation far in advance is recommended in high season and you should be aware that prices can double (at least) in major tourist centres. Santoríni, Mýkonos, Crete and Rhodes in particular have hotels where you can spend four-figure sums per night on luxury suites. Only smaller, off-the-radar places like Anáfi, Nísyros or Arkí will be significantly cheaper. These islands offer *enikiazómena domátia* (rented rooms) and small apartments, alongside fully fledged hotels.

It is also advisable to book during low season, as beachside accommodation is closed during this time, though there will be a few town hotels that should remain open.

Travellers with Specific Needs

Greece has made some progress in meeting the requirements of travellers with accessibility requirements. As of 2018, all hotels must by law provide at least one wheelchair-adapted en-suite room, but compliance will vary. Most museums built recently have disabled access. Many island towns have ramps to access

pedestrian crossings – when parked vehicles aren't blocking them – but announcements for the visually impaired to cross safely are rare.

Language

Greek is the official language. The level of English and other foreign languages spoken can be limited, particularly in rural areas, and locals appreciate visitors' efforts to speak Greek. Larger towns have tourist police who speak at least one foreign language well.

Closures

Opening hours tend to be vague in Greece, varying from day to day, season to season, and place to place. Although the opening times have been checked at the time of going to print, it is advisable to use the times given in this book as a rough guideline only and to check locally before visiting a remote or inconvenient sight.

Afternoon Many shops stay closed after 2:30pm but are open from 5:30–8:30pm on Tuesday, Thursday and Friday; monasteries and churches close for a few hours

Mondays Many archaeological museums and minor sites are closed for the day.

Sundays Most shops outside of major resorts stay closed, though there is usually at least one town supermarket with limited hours.

Public holidays Major sights, shops and restaurants are closed.

Low season Many hotels, restaurants and smaller attractions close during winter.

PUBLIC HOLIDAYS	
1 Jan	New Year's Day
6 Jan	Epiphany
25 Mar	Greek Independence Day
April/May	Orthodox Easter
1 May	May Day/Labour Day
Early June	Whit (Penecost) Monday
15 Aug	Dormition Day
28 Oct	Ohi Day
25 Dec	Christmas Day
26 Dec	Gathering of the Mother of God

GETTING AROUND

Whether you are visiting for a short one-stop escape or island-hopping for weeks, discover how best to reach your destination and travel like a pro.

PUBLIC TRANSPORT COSTS

VÓLOS TO SKÓPELOS

€30 seat

€80 for a car berth

ATHENS TO SANTORÍNI

€42 seat

€62 for a cabin

ATHENS TO RHODES

€64 seat

€111 for a cabin

SPEED LIMIT

BUILT-UP AREAS

30 km/h
(18 mph)

COUNTRY ROADS

80 km/h
(50 mph)

MOTORWAYS

120 km/h
('5 mph)

Arriving by Air

Most people travelling to the Greek Islands arrive into Athens or Thessaloníki, which have good onward connections to the islands on several domestic airlines. Both airports are well-connected and have regular flights from Europe, North America and Asia.

In Athens, Metro line 3 (blue line) links the airport to Syntagma and Monastiraki in the city centre every 30 minutes. The X95 bus runs from the airport to Synagma Square in the city centre every 10–15 minutes. Bus X96 runs from the airport to Piraeus port every 20–25 minutes, where you can catch ferries to the islands. You can look up timetables on **TrainOSE**.

Some airlines, like **Ryanair**, **Jet2** or **EasyJet**, offer direct flights from Europe – mainly from the United Kingdom and Ireland – to larger islands, including Corfu, Lefkáda (Préveza airport), Kefaloniá, Zákynthos, Crete, Mýkonos, Santoríni, Rhodes, Kos and the northern Sporádes (Vólos airport). Most, but not all, islands with airports have some sort of dedicated bus service to and from the airport, but they don't always dovetail well with flight arrivals and departures.

EasyJet
W easyjet.com
Jet2
W jet2.com
Ryanair
W ryanair.com
TrainOSE
W trainose.gr/en/

Arriving by Sea

There are high-speed ferry services from the Italian ports of Venice, Ancona, Brindisi and Bari to the mainland ports of Igoumenítsa and Pátra, as well as Corfu. You can check ferry schedules on **Greek Travel Pages** or **Open Seas**. Healthy competition means that you can expect to pay affordable fares except in high season. Winter sees limited service. Smaller ferries make various crossings from Turkey, although these are usually more expensive.

GETTING BETWEEN ATHENS AND THE GREEK ISLANDS

Airport	Distance to city	Journey time
Corfu	381 km (237 miles)	40 mins
Crete	318 km (198 miles)	45 mins
Kos	324 km (201 miles)	45 mins
Límnos	252 km (157 miles)	45 mins
Mýkonos	153 km (95 miles)	30 mins
Páros	157 km (98 miles)	35 mins
Rhodes	426 km (265 miles)	45 mins
Santoríni	228 km (142 mile)	40 mins
Skiáthos	135 km (84 miles)	30 mins
Skýros	128 km (80 miles)	40 mins

Greek Travel Pages
Ⓦ gtp.gr
Open Seas
Ⓦ openseas.gr

Domestic Air Travel

Olympic Air (OA), a subsidiary of **Aegean**, uses prop planes to handle most domestic routes, although Aegean occasionally steps in with small jets. Flights to the islands from the mainland are also operated by **Astra** and **Sky Express**, which both have major hubs in Athens and Thessaloníki, as well as Ryanair, which has a minor hub in Athens.

Corfu is served by Ioannis Kapodistrias International Airport, which is located less than 2 km (1 mile) from Corfu town. It is served by regular buses and taxis from the rank right outside the terminal. Corfu's fellow Ionian island Kefaloniá has its own international airport, which is situated 8 km (5 miles) from the centre of the principal town of Argostóli. The best way to reach central Argostóli is by taxi.

Zákynthos is served by Dionýsios Solomós International Airport, which is less than 5 km (3 miles) from Zákynthos town. Taxis are again the best way into town.

Lésvos is served by Odyseas Elitís Mytilíni International Airport, 7 km (4 miles) from the centre of the main town of Mytilíni. KTEL buses and taxis link the airport with the town. On the nearby island of Límnos, Ifestos International Airport is 18 km (11 miles) from the centre of

Mýrina, its main town. It is served by taxis and primarily tourist buses. Sámos is served by Aristarchós of Sámos International Airport, 14 km (9 miles) southwest of Vathý. Buses link the airport with many of the towns and villages on Sámos.

In the Dodecanese, Ippokratis International Airport serves the island of Kos. KTEL buses from outside the arrivals exit make the 40-minute journey into Kos town centre.

Rhodes is served by Rodos Diagoras International Airport. Located 15 km (9 miles) west of Rhodes town, KTEL airport buses link it to the city centre. The journey time is around 45 minutes.

Crete has two international airports – Nikos Kazantzakis at Iráklio, only 5 km (3 miles) away from the city centre, and Ioannis Daskalogiannis Airport in Haniá, which is situated around 15 km (9 miles) northwest of the city. KTEL buses and taxis run from outside the terminal to Haniá's main square, with the journey taking about 45 minutes. Siteía also has a domestic airport.

Mýkonos and Santoríni receive international flights from within Europe during the popular summer months.

Aegean
Ⓦ en.aegeanair.com
Astra
Ⓦ astra-airlines.gr
Olympic Air
Ⓦ olympicair.com
Sky Express
Ⓦ skyexpress.gr

Domestic Sea Travel

Islands are linked with each other, and the mainland, by an assortment of ferries, including fast ferries, catamarans, small caïques (taxi boats), modern speedboats, and Soviet-era hydrofoils which only ply the Argo-Saronic and Sporades islands.

Modern catamarans lack the romance of traditional ferries, which, with open-air deck seating, are perhaps the best way to enjoy a sunny Aegean summer day.

Fares on fast ferries, catamarans, speedboats and hydrofoils cost roughly twice as much as on conventional ferries, and they travel twice as quickly. Bigger conventional ferries always have cabins available on overnight trajectories, while most catamarans lack cabins. All large craft have space for cars – even the Dodecanese catamarans fit five vehicles. Hydrofoils do not take cars. Car ferries serve, with varying frequency, all islands except Ýdra and Spétses, where their use is forbidden or highly restricted.

Smaller ports have limited services, so check the timetable on arrival to see if you can depart for your next destination on a particular day. The larger ports, such as Piraeus in Athens and Thessaloníki, have many more services. Piraeus is Greece's busiest port and has many routes initiating from its harbour. The hub of activity is at Plateía Karaïskáki, where most ticket agents reside, as well as the *limenarcheío* (port police). A number of companies, including **Blue Star Ferries**, **Hellenic Seaways**, **Sea Jets**, **Anek Lines**, **Minoan Lines**, **Aegean Speedlines**, **Small Cyclades Lines** and **Skyros Shipping Co**, run the ferry services from here, each with its own agents. This makes the task of finding out when ferries sail, and from which dock, a more challenging one. The ferries are approximately grouped by destination, but when the port is busy ferries dock wherever space permits. Finding your ferry usually involves studying the agency's information board or asking the *limenarcheío*.

Aegean Speedlines
w www.aegeanspeedlines.gr
Anek Lines
w www.anek.gr
Blue Star Ferries .
w www.bluestarferries.com
Hellenic Seaways
w hellenicseaways.gr
Minoan Lines
w www.minoan.gr
Sea Jets
w www.seajets.gr
Small Cyclades Lines
w www.smallcycladeslines.gr
Skyros Shipping Co
w sne.gr

Ferry Tickets

Cars can cost as much as two or three times the passenger fare. Children under two travel free, those aged from two to nine pay half the stated fare, and once over the age of ten, children must pay the full adult fare. On major routes, ferries have essentially three classes, ranging from deck class to deluxe – the latter costing almost as much as flying. First class usually entitles you to a two-bunk exterior cabin with bathroom facilities. A second-class ticket costs around 25 per cent less and gives you a three- or four-bunk cabin with washing facilities, such as a basin. Second-class cabins are usually within the interior of the vessel. A deck-class ticket gives you access to most of the boat, including a lounge with reclining seats. During the summer, the deck is often the best place to be.

Local Inter-Island Ferries

In addition to the large ferries that cover the main routes, there are smaller ferries making inter-island crossings in the summer. These boats provide direct connections to the islands, which shortcut circuitous routes via mainland ports, saving you valuable time. Local ferries, regardless of size, are subject to government price controls, but boats chartered by tourist agencies can charge what they like, and often prove expensive. It is therefore worth doing some research locally on the various options before purchasing a ticket.

Taxi Boats

Taxi boats (or caïques) operate on an ad hoc basis, sailing along coastlines and making short trips between adjacent islands. They are usually only available during high season and, as the smallest vessels, are most prone to cancellation in adverse sea conditions. They tend to be more expensive than ferries, given the short distances involved, but often provide a route where few or no others are available. Routes and itineraries are at the discretion of the boat owners, and the only place to determine if a caïque is going your way is at the quayside.

Public Transport

Athens operates public transport services comprising buses, trams and metro. Islands are serviced by bus services, often limited, and taxis.

Metro

Athens has a three-line metro system, which shares tickets with the small tramway network and extensive bus routes. The plastic ATH.ENA cards are reusable and give discounts the more journeys you load onto them. Tickets are most reliably purchased from the machine, or staffed window, at metro station.

Buses

All islands, except tiny ones like Foúrni or Lipsí, have big Mercedes buses, usually coloured cream and sea-green, which are run by **KTEL** consortium. Routes and service frequencies vary, and are often based on the size of the island; buses are excellent on major island hubs like Crete, Mýkonos, Skiáthos and Corfu. During summer, main routes, especially on popular islands like Santoríni, are packed. Tickets are usually sold on board, though in some towns, including Rhodes and Mýkonos, you buy in advance from booths next to the bus stop. Évvia is connected to the mainland with a bridge at the capital Halkída, served from Athens by both buses (the station is well inland, beyond Halkída town centre) and trains, whose schedules are found on TrainOSE (p300).

KTEL

🌐 ktelbus.com

Taxis

Island taxis are metered, and there should be a list of per-kilometre rates and allowable surcharges affixed to the dashboard. Never engage a taxi without having small euro notes (5, 10, 20) and coins. Some short local runs have set rates (often overpriced), such as the drive from Páros airport to the ferry dock for Andíparos. Many taxis now issue receipts automatically. Taxis are usually coloured grey, but on some islands may be navy or burgundy, and take a maximum of four passengers.

Driving

Driving to the Greek Islands

Driving to the islands isn't recommended, given the cost of shipping cars on domestic ferries and the fact that most larger islands have car-rental agencies. Travelling overland to Greece makes more sense if you are driving to Lefkáda (bridge to the mainland) or to northern Greece to access nearby islands like Thásos, Samothráki or Límnos (the latter two have limited car hire options).

Car Rental

The minimum age for car rental is 21 years old, although some companies require drivers to be over 25. In low season rental cars can be arranged on the spot, but in summer it is advisable to reserve one in advance on a third-party website, such as **Auto Europe**, or directly with a local agency. All the major international chains have local affiliates. Take out a policy insuring you for the collision damage waiver excess beforehand.

Auto Europe

🌐 autoeurope.co.uk

Licences

Driving licences issued by any of the European Union member states are valid throughout the EU. If visiting from outside the EU, you will need to apply for an International Driving Permit. Check with your local automobile association before you travel.

Rules of the Road

The blood alcohol limit is 0.5 g per litre, and driving under the influence will result in heavy fines and possible loss of licence and prosecution. Seatbelts must be worn in front seats, with a €350 fine for non-compliance. Children aged under ten must sit in the back seat and under-threes must ride in approved child seats (rental agencies will supply these). Fines for minor infractions must be paid within ten days to avoid court proceedings. It's an offence to drive away from an accident involving another car – or to move the vehicles from the positions at which they came to rest – before the police arrive, who will breathalyze all drivers and write an accident report. This will be required by your car-hire company and your insurer, even if you are driving your own vehicle.

Parking

All island town centres are congested and, to avoid getting a parking ticket (which start at €80), it is suggested you park on the outskirts of the centre, in an unrestricted zone on the outskirts and walk in from there.

Scooter Rental

Island holidays used to be synonymous with hiring what the Greeks call a *papáki* ("little duck") or *mihanáki* ("little machine"). Agencies now enforce the Greek requirement for a basic motorcycle licence, even for 50cc scooters. Customers without one will have to take quad bikes instead. Helmets will be supplied and should be worn.

Cycling

Road cycling on touring bikes is now common in the Greek Islands, particularly in summer or the cooler months of autumn. You'll share the road with locals, as well as increasing numbers of fellow visitors.

Rental outlets are most easily found on Égina, Corfu, Zákynthos, Kos, Rhodes and Páros. Rental agencies tend to have stock of either fairly basic models – with fat tires and maybe three speeds – or mountain bikes. Daily rates but are generally around €5–15.

Cyclists should be aware that grades are often steep, and the only island with dedicated cycle lanes is Kos, which are more often found in the flatter areas around the main town.

PRACTICAL
INFORMATION

A little local know-how goes a long way in the Greek Islands. Here you will find all the essential advice and information you will need during your stay.

AT A GLANCE

EMERGENCY NUMBERS

TOURIST POLICE (ATHENS ONLY)	POLICE
1571	**100**

AMBULANCE	FIRE
166	**171**

TIME ZONE
EET/EEST: Eastern European Summer Time runs from the last Sunday in March to the last Sunday in October.

TAP WATER
Unless otherwise stated, tap water in the Greek Islands is safe to drink, though usually extremely hard. Spring water is avidly collected and the best fountains often have queues.

TIPPING

Waiter	10 per cent
Taxi Drivers	Round up the bill
Porters and Chambermaids	€2 each day of stay
Concierge	€1-2

Personal Security

Overall island crime rates are low, although car break-ins are an increasing problem on both Athens and in the island groups. If you suffer a theft or are assaulted, report the crime as soon as possible to your nearest police station or tourist police, if a branch exists on the island.

The tourist police – often just one person inside the main police station – should be consulted for issues with taxi drivers, hoteliers, shops and tavernas; they wear a uniform and speak at least one foreign language.

Pickpocketing is rife in the cities of Athens and Thessaloníki, particularly on crowded buses such as the X95 buses from the airport in Athens to Sýndagma. Monastiráki station on the Piraeus–Kifisiá metro line is notorious as a spot targeted by thieves. If you are coming from Piraeus (the port) towards the centre with luggage, it's recommended to alight at Néo Fáliro, walk the short distance to the SEF (Stathmós Irínis ke Filías) station, and continue into town on a tram.

Health

Pharmacies, indicated by a green cross, have both conventional and homeopathic remedies available at accessible prices without prescriptions. When they are shut, there will be a duty pharmacist elsewhere (the rota should be posted on the door).

Emergency medical care is free for EU nationals with an EHIC (*p299*) at state-run clinics or hospitals, provided you enter via the casualty ward. If you have an EHIC card, be sure to present this as soon as possible.

For visitors outside the EU, payment of medical expenses is the patient's responsibility. Organizing comprehensive medical insurance before your trip is essential, as private doctors or clinics are expensive.

Smoking, Alcohol and Drugs

In 2010, Greece introduced a law officially banning smoking in enclosed public spaces,

including in restaurants, bars and cafés; locals often ignore this law. Smoking in outdoor areas such as café terraces is permitted. Greek police will not tolerate rowdy or indecent behaviour, especially when fuelled by excessive alcohol consumption; Greek courts impose heavy fines or even prison sentences on people who behave indecently. Possession of narcotics is prohibited and could result in a prison sentence.

ID

Both locals and foreigners are required to have identification (either a national ID card or passport) on them at all times.

LGBT+ Safety

Homosexuality is legal and widely accepted in Greece. Skála Eresoú on Lésvos is a famous lesbian resort, while there are recognized gay scenes and beaches, most notably on Mýkonos, Ýdra, Rhodes and Sámos. However, smaller towns and rural areas are often more traditional in their views, and overt displays of affection may receive a negative response from locals.

Local Customs

Afternoon *mikró ýpno* ("little sleep") is sacrosanct and enforced by law: no noise is allowed between 3–5:30pm, and phone calls made during these hours are frowned upon. Topless sunbathing is tolerated except in front of "family" tavernas, but nudity is restricted.

Visiting Churches or Mosques

Modest attire (shoulders and above-the-knees covered for men and women) is required at churches, monasteries and (on Rhodes only) functioning mosques. Many monasteries have "modesty" wraps available for free at the door. Photography inside is often forbidden.

Mobile Phones and Wi-Fi

Visitors travelling to the Greek Islands with EU tariffs will be able to use their devices without being affected by data roaming charges; instead they will be charged the same rates for data, SMS and voice calls as they would pay at home.

There are three major local providers: Cosmote (with the widest coverage), Wind and Vodafone. If on Corfu (opposite Albania), or any Northeast Aegean or Dodecanese island (opposite Turkey), make sure that your phone does not use the non-EU network.

All hotels and most *domátia* (rooms) or apartments have Wi-Fi signal. Often it's free; otherwise, ascertain charges. Most tavernas, bars or cafés have password-protected Wi-Fi.

Post

Greece's postal service **ELTA** (Elliniká Tahydromía) has full-service branches (open 7:30am–2pm Monday–Friday) on almost every island. Post boxes are bright yellow (ordinary) or red (express), but collection frequencies are obscure.
ELTA
⬤ elta.gr

Taxes and Refunds

Usually included in the price, the top rate of FPA (Fóros Prostitheménis Axías) – the equivalent of VAT or sales tax – is 24 per cent in Greece, though taverna meals are assessed at 17 per cent. Visitors from outside the EU staying fewer than three months may claim this money back on purchases over €120. A Tax-Free form must be completed in the store, a copy of which is then given to the customs authorities on departure, along with proof of purchase.

WEBSITES AND APPS

Urban Rail Transport
Find travel times across metro, tramway and railway in Athens at www.stasy.gr.
Meteo
A great website for weather forecasts across Greece, found at www.meteo.gr.
Greece Is
For general information about the Greek Islands visit www.greece-is.com.
Odysseus
The official culture ministry site, covering archaeological sites, monuments and state-run museums with opening times and information, is found at odysseus.culture.gr.

INDEX

Page numbers in **bold** indicate main entries.

A

Accommodation
  booking 299
  see also Hotels
Achílleion Palace (Corfu) **76-7**
Achilles **77**
Acropolis (Athens) **288-91**
Agía Ánna (Évvia) **111**
Agía Ekateríni (Iráklio, Crete) 257
Agía Kyriakí (Mílos) **243**
Agía Marína (Léros) **191**
Agía Marína (Sými) 197
Agía Pelagía (Kýthira) **101**
Agía Rouméli (Crete) 266
Agía Sofía Cave (Kýthira) **100-101**
Agiásos (Lésvos) **134**
Agía Theokísti **233**
Agía Triáda (Crete) **272**
Agía Varvára (Corfu) **76**
Ágii Apostóli Beaches (Crete) 253
Ágii Iáson ke Sosípatros (Corfu Town) **68**
Ágios Efstrátios (Límnos) **149**
Ágios Kírykos (Ikaría) **142**
Ágios Nektários (Égina) **93**
Ágios Nikitas (Léfkáda) **80**
Ágios Nikólaos (Crete) **276**, 277
Ágios Nikólaos (Sými) 197
Ágios Nikólaos (Ýdra) **99**
Ágios Spyrídon (Corfu Town) **64**, 70
Agnóndas (Skópelos) **116-17**
Air travel 300, 301
Akrotíri Peninsula (Crete) **268-9**
Akrotíri (Santoríni) 201, 211, **214-15**
Alcohol 305
Alexander the Great 48
Álinda (Léros) **191**
All-inclusive resorts 35
Alónnisos 38, **112**
Alykí (Thásos) **146**
Amorgós 218, **220-21**
Anáfi 215
Anafiótika (Athens) **293**
Anávatos (Híos) 130
Ancient Agora (Athens) **292**
Ancient monuments 10, 22, 43
  Acropolis (Athens) **288-91**
    after dark 32-3
  Akrotíri (Santoríni) **214-15**
  Ancient Agora (Athens) **292**

Ancient monuments (cont.)
  Ancient Eretria (Évvia) **108**
  Ancient Ialysos (Rhodes) **178**
  Ancient Kameiros (Rhodes) **179**
  Ancient Paleópoli (Ándros) 227
  Ancient Thasos (Liménas, Thásos) **144-5**
  Ancient Thera (Santoríni) **214**
  Casa Romana (Kos Town) 187
  Christian Catacombs (Trypití, Mílos) 243
  Delos 10, **208-9**
  Dragon houses (Évvia) 108
  Efpalínio Órygma (Sámos) **138-9**
  Gortys (Crete) **273**
  Gourniá (Crete) **279**
  Hephaistia (Límnos) **149**
  Heraion (Sámos) **141**
  Kabeirio (Límnos) **149**
  Kastélli (Skála, Pátmos) 158
  Kéa 216
  Lato Etera (Kritsá, Crete) 276-7
  Lindos Acropolis (Rhodes) **174**
  Minoan Cemetery (Arhánes, Crete) 274
  Minoan Cemetery (near Réthymno, Crete) **255**
  Monte Smith (Rhodes New Town) **173**
  Odeon of Herodes Atticus (Athens) 288, 290, **291**
  Palace of Knosos (Crete) **260-63**
  Palace of Mália (Crete) 275
  Parthenon (Athens) **288-91**
  Phaistos **264-5**
  Poliohne (Límnos) **149**
  Sanctuary of the Great Gods (Samothráki) **151**
  Temple of Aphaia (Égina) 89, **94-5**
  Temple of Athena Nike (Athens) **291**
  Theatre of Dionysos (Athens) 288, **291**
  Tower of the Winds (Athens) 294
Andimáhia (Kos) **189**
Andíparos 233, **235**
Andípaxí **79**
Ándissa (Lésvos) **136**
Ándros 201, **224-7**
  restaurants 230
Ándros Town **224-5**

Angístri (Égina) **93**
Anógia (Crete) **271**
Ano Merá (Mýkonos) **223**
Apéri (Kárpathos) 199
Apírathou (Náxos) **238**
Apollo 208, 209
Apóllonas (Náxos) **238-9**
Archaeological museums *see* Museums and galleries
Archaic Period 47
Architecture **42-3**
  Streamline Moderne (Lakkí, Léros) 190
Arethousa Archaeological Museum (Halkída, Évvia) **107**
Argo-Saronic Islands 16, **88-101**
  Égina 92-5
  hotels 97, 98
  Kýthira 100-101
  map 90-91
  Póros 97
  restaurants 92, 101
  Salamína 96
  Spétses 96-7
  Ýdra 98-9
Argostóli (Kefaloniá) **84**
Arhánes (Crete) **274**
Arhángelos (Rhodes) **177**
Armenistís (Ikaría) **143**
Armólia (Híos) 128
Art
  art galleries *see* Museums and galleries
  Cycladic **227**, 294
  El Greco **256**
  religious **49**
Asfendioú Villages (Kos) **188**
Asklepion (Kos) **188**
Asklinió (Rhodes) **190**
Ássos (Kefaloniá) **85**
Astypálea **182**
Athens 19, **282-95**
  history 47
  hotels 295
  itinerary 286-7
  map 284-5
  restaurants 293
Atlantis **212**
Avgónyma (Híos) **130**
Avlémonas (Kýthira) **101**

B

Balkan Wars 50
Bars and clubs 33
Batsí (Ándros) **227**
Bay of Mílos **243**
Beaches **20-21**
  for children 34

Beer 26, 212-13
Benaki Museum (Athens) **294-5**
Bísti (Ýdra) **99**
Blue Caves (Zákynthos) **83**
British Ionian Protectorate 50
Brostá (Kálymnos) **193**
Bros Thermá (Kos) **187**
Burned Islands **215**
Bus travel 302
Byzantine Empire 49
Byzantine museums *see*
  Museums and galleries

C

Cape Zoúrva (Ýdra) **99**
Captain Corelli's Mandolin 41
Car rental 302
Castles and fortifications 23
  Angelókastro (Corfu) 74
  Castle of the Knights (Kos
    Town) 186, 187
  Fortétsa (Réthymno, Crete)
    254
  Fortress Arsenali (Iráklio) **256**
  Fortress (Ierápetra, Crete)
    277
  Frangokástello (Crete) 245,
    270
  Gardíki Castle (Corfu) 75
  Hálki castle 100
  Karababa Castle (Halkída,
    Évvia) 106
  Kástro Kritinías (Rhodes) **179**
  Kástro Mytilínis (Lésvos) 132
  Kástro (Híos Town) **124**
  Kástro (Kéa) 216
  Kástro (Mólyvos, Lésvos) 135
  Kástro (Plátanos, Léros)
    190-1
  Kástro (Thásos) **147**
  Káto Hóra (Kýthira) **100**
  Mastic Villages (Híos) 11,
    128-9
  Medieval City Walls (Rhodes
    Old Town) **162-3**, 171
  Monólithos castle (Rhodes)
    181
  New Fortress (Corfu Town)
    66
  Old Fortress (Corfu Town) **66**,
    70
  Pýrgoi (fortified
    watchtowers) 239
  see also Palaces
Caves
  Agía Sofía Cave (Kýthira)
    100-101
  Blue Caves (Zákynthos) **83**

Caves (cont.)
  Cave of Andíparos 235
  Cretan caves **271**
  Diktian Cave (Crete) 275
  Holy Cave of the Apocalypse
    (Pátmos) 158-9
Children **34-5**
Christianity 48, 49
Chrysoheriás (Kálymnos) **192**
Churches and cathedrals 23,
  305
  Agía Ekateríni (Iráklio, Crete)
    257
  Ágii láson ke Sosípatros
    (Corfu Town) **68**
  Ágios Nektários (Égina) **93**
  Ágios Spyrídon (Corfu Town)
    64, 70
  Ekatondapylianí (Parikiá,
    Páros) 232-3
  Kímisi Theotókou (Asklipió,
    Rhodes) 180
  Ómorfo Ekklissiá (Égina) **93**
  Panagía Evangelístria (Tínos
    Town) 240, 242
  Panagía Katholikí (Rhodes)
    177
  Panagía Kerá (Kritsá, Crete)
    276, 277
  Panagía Spiliótissa (Corfu
    Town) **68**, 70
  Panagía tou Kástrou (Rhodes
    Old Town) **163**
  see also Monasteries and
    convents
Cinema 33, **40-41**
Classical period 47
Closures 299
Colossus of Rhodes **173**
Corfu 55, **64-77**
  boat trips 73
  hotels 69
  itinerary 58-9
  restaurants 66
  writers on 68
Corfu Town **64-71**
  map 65
  shopping 68
  walk 70-71
Corporon, Yvette Manessis 68
Crete 19, **244-79**
  hotels 255, 277
  itineraries 248-51
  map 246-7
  restaurants 253, 257, 269
  spring flowers 39
Crusades 49
Culture **22-3**
Currency 298

Cyclades 18, 30, **200-43**
  Amorgós 220-21
  Ándros 224-7
  art 227, 294
  Delos 208-9
  Folégandros 219
  hotels 214, 221, 225, 239, 243
  Íos 221
  itineraries 204-7
  Kéa (Tziá) 216
  Kýthnos (Thermiá) 216-17
  map 202-3
  Mílos 242-3
  Minor Cyclades **239**
  Mýkonos 222-3
  Náxos 236-9
  Páros 232-5
  restaurants 213, 223, 230
  Santoríni 210-15
  Sérifos 217
  Sífnos 218
  Síkinos 220
  Sýros 228-31
  Tínos 240-41
Cycladic culture 46
Cycling 24, 303

D

Dance, Skýros Goat Dance **116**
Dark Ages 47
Delos 10, 201, **208-9**
De Villaret, Foulkes **167**
Diafáni (Kárpathos) **194**
Disabled travellers 299
Diving 25, 33
Dodecanese 18, 31, **152-99**
  Astypálea 182
  Hálki 184-5
  hotels 165, 183, 197
  itinerary 156-7
  Kálymnos 192-3
  Kárpathos 194-5
  Kastellórizo 185
  Kos 186-9
  Léros 190-1
  Lipsí 182
  map 154-5
  Nísyros 194-95
  Pátmos 158-61
  restaurants 159, 163, 181,
    187, 193, 199
  Rhodes 162-81
  Tílos 182-3
Donoússa 239
Dorians 201, 210, 214, 276
Dovecotes (Tínos) **241**
Driving 302
Durrell, Laurence & Gerald 68, **72**

E

Efpalínio Órygma (Sámos) **138–9**
Égina 89, **92–5**
Égina Town **92**
Electricity supply 298
El Greco 49, **256**
Elisabeth of Austria, Empress (Sisi) 76
Eloúnda (Crete) **276**
Émbona (Rhodes) **180**
Emboriós (Nísyros) **195**
Emergency numbers 304
Entertainment **32–3**
Eptá Pigés (Rhodes) **176–7**
Eretria (Évvia) **108**
Ermoúpoli (Sýros) **228–9**
Esplanade (Corfu Town) **66–7**, 70
Etz Hayyim Synagogue (Haniá, Crete) **253**
European Union 51
Evangelistrías Monastery (Skiáthos) **115**
Evans, Sir Arthur 261, 262, 263, 265
Évdilos (Ikaría) **142–3**
Évvia 103, **106–11**
 see also Sporádes and Évvia
Exárhia (Athens) **293**
Exómbourgo (Tínos) **241**

F

Faliráki (Rhodes) **176**
Ferries 31, 144, 300–301, 303
Festivals and events 11, 22
 A Year in the Greek Islands **44–3**
 Niptír ceremony (Hóra, Pátmos) **160**
 panegýria **142**
Filippos Argentis Folklore Museum (Híos Town) **125**
Firá (Santoríni) **210–11**
Fiskárdo (Kefaloniá) **85**
Folégandros **219**
Folk museums see Museums and galleries
Food and drink
 Alexandris Winery (Émbona, Rhodes) 180
 Greek Islands for Foodies **28–9**
 Nikos Gavalas (Arhánes, Crete) 274
 olives 13, **133**
 oúzo 27, **134**

Food and drink (cont.)
 Raise a Glass **26–7**
 Santoríni Brewing Company **212–13**
 seafood 11
Fortresses see Castles and fortifications
Foúrni (Ikaría) **143**
Fowles, John 97
Frangokástello (Crete) 245, **270**
Fríkes (Itháki) **86**

G

Gáïos (Paxí) **78**
Galíni (Crete) **274**
Galissás (Sýros) **231**
Gávdos (Crete) **269**
Gávrio (Ándros) **226**
Gennádi (Rhodes) 180
Genoese 49
George I 50
Georgioúpoli (Crete) **255**
Giustiniani Palace (Híos Town) **124**
Glóssa (Skópelos) **117**
Glýstra Cove (Rhodes) 180
Gods and goddesses
 Poseidon **79**
 Samothráki **151**
Golf, Crete Golf Club 274, 275
Gortys (Crete) 245, **273**
Gourniá (Crete) **278**
Grand Masters, Knights of St John 166–7
Greco-Turkish War 51
Greek Civil War 51
Greek War of Independence 50, 127
Gríkou (Pátmos) **159**

H

Hálki **198–9**
Halkída (Évvia) **106–7**
Haniá (Crete) 245, **252–3**
 hotels 277
Harbour (Haniá, Crete) **252**
Health 299, 304
Hellenistic culture 48
Hephaistia (Límnos) **149**
Hera **141**
Heraion (Sámos) **141**
Hersónisos (Crete) **274–5**
Hiking 24
 Crete 266, 279
 North Kárpathos **198**
Híos 121, **124–31**
 massacre 127

Híos Town **124–5**
Hippocrates 184, **185**
Historical museums see Museums and galleries
Historic buildings
 Etz Hayyim Synagogue (Haniá, Crete) **253**
 Inns of the Tongues (Rhodes Old Town) 168–9, 171
 Mon Repos Villa (Corfu) **69**
 Simantíris House (Hóra, Pátmos) 158, 169
 see also Ancient monuments; Castles and fortifications; Churches and cathedrals; Monasteries and convents; Palaces
History **46–51**
Hoklákia mosaics **199**
Homer 41, 55, 86, 97, 221, 272
Homosexuality 137, 305
Hóra (Kýthira) **100**
Hóra (Pátmos) **158–9**, 160
Hóra (Samothráki) **150**
Hóra Sfakíon (Crete) 266, **269**
Horió (Sými) 196
Hotels
 Argo-Saronic Islands 97, 98
 Athens 295
 Corfu 69
 Crete 255, 277
 Cyclades 214, 221, 225, 239, 243
 Dodecanese 165, 183, 197
 Ionian Islands 69, 83
 Northeast Aegean Islands 124, 145
 Sporádes and Évvia 110

I

Ialysos (Rhodes) **178**
Ía (Santoríni) **212**
ID 305
Ierápetra (Crete) **277**
Ikaría **142–3**
Inoússes (Híos) **131**
Insurance 298–9
Internet access 305
Ionian Islands 16, 30, **54–87**
 Corfu 64–77
 history 50
 hotels 69, 83
 Itháki 86–7
 itineraries 58–63
 Kefaloniá 84–5
 Léfkáda 80–81
 map 56–7
 Paxí 78–9

Ionian Islands (cont.)
  restaurants 66, 74, 78, 81, 84
  shopping 68
  Zákynthos 82-3
Íos **221**
Iráklio Archaeological Museum
  (Iráklio, Crete) 23, **258-9**
Irakliá **239**
Iráklio (Crete) **256-9**
  map 257
  restaurants 257
Island hopping **30-31**, 301
Itháki 55, **86-7**
Itineraries
  2 Weeks in the Southern
    Ionians 60-63
  5 Days around Corfu 58-9
  5 Days in Eastern Crete
    248-9
  8 Days in the Northern
    Cyclades 204-5
  8 Days in the Northern
    Dodecanese 156-7
  8 Days in the Southern
    Cyclades 206-7
  8 Days in Western Crete
    250-51
  24 Hours in Athens 286-7

K

Kabeirio (Límnos) **149**
Kaiser's Throne (Corfu) 12, 75
Kalámi (Corfu) **72**
Kallóni (Lésvos) **136**
Kálymnos **192-3**
Kalývia (farmhouses) **114**
Kamarí (Kos) **189**
Kámbos (Híos) **125**
Kameiros (Rhodes) **179**
Kamíni (Ýdra) **99**
Kanóni (Corfu) **69**
Kantádes **80**
Kapodistrias, Ioannis 50
Kapsáli (Kýthira) **100**
Karlóvasi (Sámos) **140**
Kárpathos **198-9**
Kárpathos Town **198**
Karyá (Léfkáda) **81**
Kárystos (Évvia) **108-9**
Kassiópi (Corfu) **72-3**
Kastélli Kissámou (Crete) **269**
Kástro Quarter (Halkída, Évvia)
  106-7
Kástro, *see also* Castles and
  fortifications
Kástro (Kefaloniá) **85**
Kástro (Skiáthos) **115**

Kástro (Thásos) **147**
Káto Hóra (Kýthira) **100**
Kávos **77**
Kazantzákis, Níkos 274, **275**
Kéa (Tziá) **216**
  hotels 243
Kefaloniá 55, **84-5**
  hotels 83
Kéfalos (Kos) **189**
Kíni (Sýros) **230**
Kióni (Itháki) **86**
Kiotári (Rhodes) 180
Kiteboarding 25
Knights of St John
  Hálki 198
  Kos 186
  Rhodes 153, 162-71, 187, 192,
    Tílos 196
Knosos, Palace of (Crete) 245,
  258-9, **260-63**
Kokkári (Sámos) **140**
Kondiás (Límnos) **148**
Kórakas (Rhodes) 181
Korissíon Lagoon (Corfu) **75**
Koronída (Náxos) **238**
Kos 125, 153, **186-9**
Koskinoú (Rhodes) **176**
Kos Town **186**
Koufoníssi **239**
Koukounariés (Skiáthos) **115**
Krithóni (Léros) **191**
Kritsá (Crete) **276-7**
Kými (Évvia) **109**
Kynops 158
Kyrá Panagiá (Kárpathos) 199
Kýthira **100-101**
Kýthnos (Thermiá) **216-17**
  hotels 243

L

Lace 174
Laganás (Zákynthos) **82**
Lákka (Paxí) **78-9**
Lakkí (Léros) 153, **190**
Lámpi (Pátmos) **159**
Language 299
  essential phrases 298
  phrasebook 314-18
Lasíthiu Plateau (Crete) **275**
Lato Etera (Kritsá, Crete) 276-7
Léfkáda **80-81**
Léfkáda Town **80**
Léfkes (Páros) **234**
Lefkós (Kárpathos) 199
Léros 153, **190-1**
Lésvos 121, 125, **132-7**
LGBT 305
Licences, driving 302

Liménas (Thásos) **144-5**
Límni (Évvia) **111**
Límnos 121, **148-9**
  hotels 145
  restaurants 147
Linariá (Skýros) **118**
Lindos (Rhodes) **174-5**
Lipsí **182**
Listón (Corfu Town) 66, 70, 71
Literature
  Níkos Kazantzákis 274, **275**
  writers on Corfu **68**
Local customs 305
Longós (Paxí) **79**
Loutrá Edipsoú (Évvia) **110**
Loutrá (Kýthnos) 216, 217
Lykavittós Hill (Athens) **294**

M

Magaziá (Skýros) **117**
Mália (Crete) **275**
Mamma Mia! 40
Mandamádos (Lésvos) **143-4**
Mandráki Harbour (Rhodes New
  Town) **172-3**
Mandráki (Nísyros) **194-95**
Maps
  Ándros 225
  Argo-Saronic Islands 90-91
  Athens 284-5
  Corfu Town 65
  Crete 246-7
  Cyclades 202-3
  Dodecanese 154-5
  Égina 93
  Greek Islands 14-15
  Halkída (Évvia) 107
  Haniá (Crete) 253
  Híos Town 125
  Ikaría 142
  Ionian Islands 56-7
  Iráklio (Crete) 257
  Kálymnos 193
  Kárpathos 198
  Kefaloniá 85
  Kos 187
  Kýthira 100
  Léfkáda 80
  Léros 191
  Límnos 149
  Mílos 243
  Mýkonos 223
  Náxos 237
  Nísyros 194
  Northeast Aegean Islands
    122-3
  Páros 233
  Pátmos 159

Maps (cont.)
  Paxí 78
  Réthymno (Crete) 255
  Rhodes New Town 173
  Rhodes Old Town 163
  Sámos 139
  Samothráki 151
  Santoríni 211
  Skiáthos 115
  Skópelos 117
  Skýros 119
  Sporádes and Évvia 104-5
  Sými 196
  Sýros 229
  Thásos 145
  Tínos 241
  Ýdra 99
  Zákynthos 83
Marathiás (Corfu) 76
Marathoúnda (Sými) 187
Market (Haniá, Crete) 252
Mastic Villages (Híos) 11, 128-9
Mátala 272
Medieval Rhodes and Ancient
  Rhodes Exhibitions (Rhodes
  Old Town) 162
Megális Panagías Monastery
  (Sámos) 139
Megálo Horió (Tílos) 197
Megálo Kazavíti (Thásos) 147
Mélanes Valley (Náxos) 237
Merikiá (Léros) 190
Merói (Skýros) 119
Mesariá (Ándros) 225
Mestá (Híos) 128
Metro (Athens) 302
Mikró Horió (Tílos) 197
Military junta 51
Mílos 242-3
Minoans 46, 201, 210, 214-15
  Crete 245, 258-65, 273, 274,
  275, 278
Minor Cyclades 239
Minotaur 260, 261, 262
Mobile phones 305
Modern Greek Art Museum
  (Rhodes New Town) 173
Mólyvos (Míthymna) (Lésvos)
  135
Monasteries and convents 13,
  43
  Agíou Nikoláou Galatáki
    (Évvia) 111
  Evangelistrías Monastery
    (Skiáthos) 115
  Megális Panagías Monastery
    (Sámos) 139
  Monastery of St John
    (Pátmos) 13, 160-61

Monasteries and convents (cont.)
  Moní Agíou Pandelímonos
    (Tílos) 197
  Moní Arhangélou Mihaïl
    (Thásos) 146-7
  Moní Arkadíou (Crete)
    270-71
  Moní Filerímou (Rhodes)
    178-9
  Moní Limónos (Kalloní,
    Lésvos) 136
  Moní Moundón (Híos) 131
  Moní Panachrándou (Ándros)
    226
  Moní Panagías Hozoviótissas
    (Síkinos) 220
  Moní Préveli (Crete) 270
  Moní Taxiárhi Mihaïl
    Panormítis (Sými) 197
  Moní Taxiárhi Mihaïl
    Roukounióti (Sými) 196
  Moní Thárri (Rhodes) 177
  Moní Theotókou (Corfu) 74
  Moní Toploú (Crete) 278
  Moní Ýpsiloú (Lésvos) 137
  Mount Paloúki Monasteries
    (Skópelos) 116
  Néa Moní (Híos) 121, 126-7
  Pamagía Kehreás Monastery
    (Skiáthos) 115
  Pamagías Kounístras
    Monastery (Skiáthos) 115
Monastiráki (Athens) 293
Money 299
Moní (Égina) 93
Monólithos (Rhodes) 191
Mon Repos Villa (Corfu) 69
Monte Smith (Rhodes New
  Town) 173
Moúdros (Límnos) 148-9
Mountain bikes 24
Mount Énos (Kefaloniá) 85
Mount Fengári (Samothráki)
  151
Mount Ídi (Crete) 271
Mount Kerketéfs (Sámos) 141
Mount Óhi (Évvia) 108, 109
Mount Paloúki Monasteries
  (Skópelos) 116
Mount Pandokrátor (Corfu) 72
Museums and galleries 23
  Acropolis Museum (Athens)
    288
  Archaeological Collection of
    Stavrós (Itháki) 86
  Archaeological Museum
    (Ándros Town) 224, 225
  Archaeological Museum
    (Argostóli, Kefaloniá) 84

Museums and galleries (cont.)
  Archaeological Museum
    (Corfu Town) 68
  Archaeological Museum
    (Égina Town) 92
  Archaeological Museum
    (Eretria, Évvia) 108
  Archaeological Museum
    (Ermoúpoli, Sýros) 228,
    229
  Archaeological Museum (Firá,
    Santoríni) 210
  Archaeological Museum
    (Haniá, Crete) 252
  Archaeological Museum
    (Hóra, Kýthira) 100
  Archaeological Museum
    (Ierápetra, Crete) 277
  Archaeological Museum
    (Kastélli Kissámou, Crete)
    269
  Archaeological Museum (Kéa)
    216
  Archaeological Museum (Kos
    Town) 186, 187
  Archaeological Museum
    (Mýkonos Town) 222, 223
  Archaeological Museum
    (Mytilíni, Lésvos) 132
  Archaeological Museum
    (Náxos Town) 237
  Archaeological Museum
    (Parikiá, Páros) 233
  Archaeological Museum
    (Pláka, Mílos) 242, 243
  Archaeological Museum
    (Póros Town) 97
  Archaeological Museum
    (Pythagório, Sámos) 139
  Archaeological Museum
    (Réthymno, Crete) 254
  Archaeological Museum
    (Rhodes Old Town) 162
  Archaeological Museum
    (Sífnos) 218
  Archaeological Museum
    (Sitía, Crete) 279
  Archaeological Museum
    (Tínos Town) 240, 241
  Archaeological Museum
    (Vathý, Sámos) 138
  Arethousa Archaeological
    Museum (Halkída, Évvia)
    107
  Benaki Museum (Athens) 295
  Bouboulina Museum (Spétses
    town) 96, 97
  Byzantine and Christian
    Museum (Athens) 295

Museums and galleries (cont.)
Byzantine Museum (Corfu Town) **65**
Byzantine Museum (Híos Town) **125**
Byzantine Museum (Mytilíni, Lésvos) 132
Byzantine Museum (Zákynthos Town) 82
for children 35
Christos Kapralos Museum (Égina Town) 92
Cretan Open-Air Museum (Hersónisos, Crete) 274, 275
Ecclesiastical and Folklore Museum (Lipsí) 196
Ecomuseum (Folégandros) 219
Faltaïts Museum (Skýros Town) 118, 119
Filippos Argentis Folklore Museum (Híos Town) **125**
Focas-Cosmetatos Foundation (Argostóli, Kefaloniá) 84
Folk and Historical Museum (Ágios Geórgios, Crete) 275
Folklore Museum (Apírathou, Náxos) 238
Folklore Museum (Halkída, Évvia) 107
Folklore Museum (Mandráki, Nísyros) 194-95
Folk Museum (Mýkonos Town) 222, 223
Folk Museum (Othos, Kárpathos) 199
Folk Museum (Síkinos) 220
Geological Museum (Apírathou, Náxos) 238
Hatzigiannis Mexis Museum (Spétses town) 96, 97
Historical and Folk Art Museum (Réthymno, Crete) 254-5
Historical Museum (Haniá, Crete) 253
Historical Museum (Iráklio, Crete) **257**
History and Folklore Museum of Corfu (Sinarádes) 74-5
History and Folk Museum (Pláka, Mílos) 242, 243
Iráklio Archaeological Museum (Iráklio, Crete) 23, **258-9**
Kazantzákis Museum (Arhánes) 274

Museums and galleries (cont.)
Lignos Folklore Museum (Firá, Santoríni) 210
Maritime Museum (Ándros Town) 224-5
Medieval Rhodes and Ancient Rhodes Exhibitions (Rhodes Old Town) **162**
Megaro Gyzi Cultural Centre (Firá, Santoríni) 210
Modern Greek Art Museum (Rhodes New Town) **173**
Museum of Asiatic Art 64, 71
Museum of Contemporary Art (Ándros Town) 224, 225
Museum of Cretan Ethnology (Agía Triáda, Crete) 272
Museum of Cycladic Art (Athens) **295**
Museum of Popular Arts and Folklore (Sífnos) 218
Museum of Religious Art (Iráklio, Crete) 257
National Archaeological Museum (Athens) **292-3**
National Gallery of Art (Athens) **295**
Natural History Museum of the Lésvos Petrified Forest (Sígri, Lésvos) 137
Naval Museum (Haniá, Crete) 252
New Archaeological Museum (Mytilíni, Lésvos) 132
Papadiamantis Museum (Skiáthos Town) 114
Paper Money Museum (Corfu Town) **67**, 70, 71
Polygnotos Vagis Museum (Potamiá, Thásos) 146
Prehistoric Museum (Firá, Santoríni) 23, 210
Solomos Museum (Corfu Town) **67**
Tériade Museum (Mytilíni, Lésvos) 23, 132
Theophilos Museum (Mytilíni, Lésvos) 132
Vamvakaris Museum (Ermoúpoli, Sýros) 229
War Museum (Merikiá, Léros) 186
Music
at ancient sites 32
Kantádes 80
rembétika 228
traditional 12
Mussolini, Benito 153
Mycenaeans 46, 47, 201

Mýkonos **222-3**
Mýkonos Town **222-3**
Mylonas, George 218
Mýrina (Límnos) **148**
Mytilíni (Lésvos) **132**

N

Nanoú (Sými) 197
Náousa (Páros) **235**
Napoleon 50
National Archaeological Museum (Athens) **292-3**
Náxos 201, **236-9**
Náxos Town **236-7**
Néa Agora (Rhodes New Town) **173**
Néa Kaméni **215**
Néa Moní (Híos) 121, **126-7**
Nightlife **32-3**
Nikiá (Nísyros) **195**
Nísyros **194-95**
geology 195
Northeast Aegean Islands 17, **120-51**
Híos 124-31
hotels 124, 145
Ikaría 142-3
Lésvos 132-7
Límnos 148-9
map 122-3
restaurants 131, 135, 139, 143, 147
Sámos 138-41
Samothráki 150-51
Thásos 144-7
Nydrí (Léfkáda) **81**

O

Odeon of Herodes Atticus (Athens) 288, 290, **291**
Odysseus 41, 55, 96, **97**
Okthoniá (Évvia) **109**
Olive growing **133**
Ólymbos (Kárpathos) **198-9**
Olýmpi (Híos) 128
Ómorfo Ekklissiá (Égina) **93**
Othos (Kárpathos) 199
Otto I 50
Ottoman Empire 50
Outdoor activities **24-5**
Oúzo 27, **134**

P

Palaces
Achílleion Palace (Corfu) **76-7**
Giustiniani Palace (Híos) **124**

Palaces (cont.)
Palace of the Grand Masters (Rhodes Old Town) **166-7**, 171
Palace of Knosos (Crete) 258-9, **260-63**
Palace of Mália (Crete) 275
Palace of St Michael and St George (Corfu Town) **64-5**, 71
Phaistos (Crete) **264-5**
see also Castles and fortifications
Paleá Kaméni **215**
Paleóhora (Crete) **268**
Paleohóra (Égina) **93**
Paleohóra (Kýthira) **100**
Paleokastritsa (Corfu) **74**
Paleókastro (Ándros) **226**
Pálli (Nísyros) **193**
Panagía Spiliótissa (Corfu Town) **68**, 70
Panagía tou Kástrou (Rhodes Old Town) **163**
Pandéli (Léros) **191**
Panormitis (Sými) 197
Pánormos (Skópelos) **117**
Papadiamantis, Alexandros **112**
Paper Money Museum (Corfu Town) **67**, 70, 71
Parikiá (Páros) **232-3**
Parking 302
Parks and gardens
Rodíni Park (Rhodes New Town) **173**
see also Water parks
Páros **232-5**
hotels 239
Parthenon (Athens) **288-91**
Parthenon Marbles **290**
Passports 298
Pátmos **158-61**
Paxí 55, **78-9**
Pédi bay (Sými) 197
Péfkos (Skýros) **117**
Pélekas (Corfu) **75**
Peloponnesian War 47, 283
Pérdika (Égina) **93**
Pericles 47, 283, 288
Persian Empire 47
Personal security 304
Petaloúdes (Páros) **234**
Petaloúdes (Rhodes) **178**
Pétra (Lésvos) **136**
Phaistos 245, **264-5**
Phaistos Disc **265**
Philip II of Macedonia 47, 48
Philip, Prince, Duke of Edinburgh 69

Photography **36-7**
Phrasebook **314-18**
Pigés Kallithéas (Rhodes) **176**
Píso Livádi (Páros) **234-5**
Pláka (Athens) **294**
Pláka (Mílos) **242-3**
Plakiás (Crete) **270**
Plakás (Léros) **190-1**
Plátanos (Léros) **190-1**
Platía Dimarhíou (Corfu Town) **68**
Platía Kornárou (Iráklio, Crete) **257**
Platía Venizélou (Iráklio, Crete) **256**
Platýs Gialós (Mýkonos) **223**
Plimýri Bay (Rhodes) 180-81
Plomári (Lésvos) **134**
Poliohne (Límnos) **149**
Political exiles **218**
Pollónia (Mílos) **243**
Polykrates 121, 209
Póros **97**
Poseidon 78, **79**
Posidonía (Sýros) **231**
Postal services 305
Potamiá (Thásos) **146**
Potámi (Sámos) **140**
Póthia (Kálymnos) **192**
Prassonísi **180**, 181
Prehistory 46
Prices
average daily spend 298
public transport 300
Prokópi (Évvia) **110-11**
Psará **131**
Psérimos (Kálymnos) **193**
Public holidays 299
Public transport 302
prices 300
Pyli (Kos) **184-5**
Pyrgí (Híos) 11, 128
Pýrgos (Tínos) **241**
Pythagoras 139
Pythagório (Sámos) **139**

R

Ráhes Villages (Ikaría) **143**
Reasons to Love the Greek Islands **10-13**
Refugee crisis 51, **125**
Restaurants
Ándros 230
Athens 293
Corfu 66, 74
Crete 253, 257, 269
Égina 92
Évvia 107
Folégandros 219

Restaurants (cont.)
Híos 131
Ikaría 143
Kálymnos 193
Kárpathos 199
Kefaloniá 84
Kos 183
Kýthira 101
Léfkáda 81
Léros 191
Lésvos 135
Límnos 147
Mýkonos 223
Pátmos 159
Paxí 78
Rhodes 163, 181
Sámos 139
Samothráki 147
Santoríni 213
seafood 11
Sífnos 218
Skiáthos 115
Skýros 119
Sýros 230
Thásos 147
Réthymno (Crete) 245, **254-5**
Rhodes 49, 153, **162-81**
restaurants 163, 181
Rhodes New Town **172-3**
Rhodes Old Town **162-71**
map 163
walk 170-71
Rhodes, Siege of **169**
Rock climbing 25
Rodíni Park (Rhodes New Town) **173**
Romans 48
Rules of the road 300, 302

S

Safety
personal security 304
travel safety advice 298
Salamína 89, **96**
Salamis, Battle of 47, 89, 96
Samariá Gorge (Crete) 13, **266-7**
Sámi (Kefaloniá) **85**
Sámos 121, 125, **138-41**
Samothráki **150-51**
restaurants 147
Sanctuary of the Great Gods (Samothráki) **151**
Santoríni 201, **210-15**
geological history 215
Santoríni Brewing Company **212-13**
Sappho 121, **137**
Scooter rental 302

Sea Peoples 46, 47
Sea travel 31, 300–301, 303
Seïtáni (Sámos) **140**
Septinsular Republic 50
Sérifos **217**
   hotels 243
Shipwreck Bay (Zákynthos) 10,
   82-3
Shopping, Corfu 65
Siánna (Rhodes) 181
Sidári (Corfu) **73**
Sífnos **218**, 219
Sígri (Lésvos) **137**
Síkinos **220**, 221
Sinarádes (Corfu) **74-5**
Sísi 275
Sitía (Crete) **279**
Skála Eresoú (Lésvos) **137**
Skála (Pátmos) **158**
Skhinoússa 239
Skiáthos **114-15**
Skiáthos Town **114**
Skópelos **116-17**
Skópelos Town **16**
Skýros **118-19**
Skýros Town **118-19**
Smoking 304–5
Solomos, Dionysis 67, 68
Solomos Museum (Corfu Town)
   67
Sotíra (Thásos) **147**
Soúyia (Crete) **268**
Specific needs, travellers with
   299
Speed limit 300
Spétses 89, **96-7**
Spinalónga (Crete) 276
Splántzia Quarter (Haniá, Crete)
   253
Sponge fishing (Kálymnos) **192**
Sporádes and Évvia 17, **102-19**
   Alónnisos **112**
   Évvia 106–11
   hotels 110
   map 104–5
   restaurants 107, 115, 119
   Skiáthos 114-15
   Skópelos **116-17**
   Skýros 118-19
Sporádes Marine Park 12, **113**
St John 158-9
St Paul 48
Stáfylos (Skópelos) **116**
Stavrós (Itháki) **86**
Stení (Évvia) **108**
Stivanádikia (Hanlá, Crete) **252**
Street of the Knights (Rhodes
   Old Town) **168-9**, 171
Stýra (Évvia) **110**

Süleyman the Magnificent 50,
   153, 169, 171
Sun-bathing **20-21**
   topless and nude 305
Swimming 24
Sykaminiá (Lésvos) **134**
Sými **196-7**
Sými Town **196**
Sýros 201, **228-31**

T

Tap water 304
Taxis 302
Télendos (Kálymnos) **193**
Telephone services 305
Temples *see* Ancient
   monuments
Thásos **144-7**
Theatre of Dionysos (Athens)
   288, **291**
Themistokles 96
Theológos (Thásos) **147**
Theophilos Hatzimihail 132
Thera, Ancient (Santoríni) **214**
Thérma (Samopthráki) **150**
Tílos **182-3**
Time zone 304
Tinqkáki (Kos) **188**
Tínos 201, **240-41**
Tínos Town **240-41**
Tipping 304
Trageá Valley (Náxos) **237**
Travel
   getting around **300-303**
   safety advice 298
Trypití (Mílos) **243**
Turkey, day trips to 199
Tzermiádo 275

V

Vaccinations 299
Vagis, Polygnotos 146
Váï Beach (Crete) **279**
Vamvakaris, Markos **228**, 229
Vári (Sýros) **231**
Vasilikí (Léfkáda) 10, **81**
Vasilikós Peninsula (Zákynthos)
   82
Vathý (Itháki) **86**
Vathý (Sámos) **138**
Vathýs Valley (Kálymnos) **193**
Vátos (Corfu) **75**
Vávili (Híos) 128
Velanió (Skópelos) **116**
Venetians 49, 50
Visas 298
Volcanic activity 191, 215

Vollissós (Híos) **130**
Votsalákia (Sámos) **141**
Vourliótes (Sámos) **140**
Vromólithos (Léros) **191**

W

Walks
   A Short Walk: Corfu Old Town
      70-71
   A Short Walk: Rhodes Old
      Town 170-71
Water parks
   Acqua Plus Water Park
      (Hersónisos, Crete) 274,
      275
   Faliráki Water Park (Rhodes)
      176
Websites 305
Wi-Fi 305
Wildlife **38-9**
   Aquarium (Rhodes New
      Town) 34, 173
   for children 34
   Jersey tiger moths
      (Petaloúdes, Rhodes) 178,
      179
   loggerhead turtles 33, 39, **82**,
      85
   monk seals 12, 38, 119
   photography 37
   Sporádes Marine Park 12,
      112
Wilhelm II, Kaiser 75, 76
Windmills 43
Windsurfing 10, 25
   Rhodes **180**
Wine **27**, 180, 274
World War I 50, 51, 148-9
World War II 51, 153, 186, 245
   Battle of Crete **268**

X

Xerxes 96
Xirókambos (Léros) **191**

Y

Ýdra 89, **98-9**
Ýdra Town **98**

Z

Zákros (Crete) **279**
Zákynthos **82-3**
Zákynthos Town **82**
Zeus **271**
Zorba the Greek 40

PHRASE BOOK

There is no universally accepted system for representing the modern Greek language in the Roman alphabet and not all Greek phonemes have exact English equivalents. The system of transliteration adopted in this guide is adapted from the one used by the Greek government.

For Classical names this guide uses the most commonly accepted Greek spelling without accents, with a preference for –os endings on names, as opposed to the more old-fashioned -us. In a few cases, such as Socrates, the more familiar Latin form has been used. Likewise, where a well-known English form of a name exists, such as Athens or Corfu, this has been used.

Guidelines for Pronunciation

The accent over Greek and transliterated words indicates the stressed syllable. In this guide the accent is not written over capital letters nor over monosyllables, except for question words and the conjunction ή (meaning "or"). In the right-hand "Pronunciation" column below, the syllable to stress is given in bold type.

On the following pages, the English is given in the left-hand column with the Greek and its transliteration in the middle column. The right-hand column provides a literal system of pronunciation and indicates the stressed syllable in bold.

THE GREEK ALPHABET

Α α	A a	c*a*t
Β β	V v	*v*ote
Γ γ	G g	*y*ear (when followed by e and i sounds) but *g* as in *g*as (when followed by a, o or ou sounds)
Δ ᴅ	D d	*th*at
Ε ε	E e	*e*gg
Ζ ζ	Z z	*z*oo
Η η	I i	sk*i*
Θ θ	Th th	*th*ink
Ι ι	I i	sk*i*
Κ κ	K k	*k*id
Λ λ	L l	*l*ap
Μ μ	M m	*m*an
Ν ν	N n	*n*ot
Ξ ξ	X x	ta*xi*
Ο ο	O o	f*o*x
Π π	P p	*p*ot
Ρ ρ	R r	*r*ed, but more rolled as in Scottish
Σ σ	S s	*s*it (zero when followed by μ)
ς	s	(used at end of word)
Τ τ	T t	*t*ea
Υ υ	Y y	sk*i*
Φ φ	F f	*f*ish
Χ χ	Ch ch	lo*ch* in most cases, but *h*e when followed by a, e or i sounds
Ψ ψ	Ps ps	ma*ps*
Ω ω	O o	f*o*x

COMBINATIONS OF LETTERS

In Greek there are two-letter vowels that are pronounced as one sound:

Αι αι	Ai ai	*e*gg
Ει ει	Ei ei	sk*i*
Οι οι	Oi oi	sk*i*
Ου ου	Ou ou	l*u*te

There are also some two-letter consonants that are pronounced as one sound:

Μπ μπ	Mp mp	*b*ut, sometimes *numb*er in the middle of a word
Ντ ντ	Nt nt	*d*og, sometimes un*d*er in the middle of a word
Γκ γκ	Gk gk	*g*o, sometimes bi*ng*o in the middle of a word
Γξ γξ	nx	tha*nks*
Γγ γγ	Gg gg	bi*ng*o, only in the middle of a word

IN AN EMERGENCY

Help!	Βοήθεια! Voïtheia!	vo-ee-thee*a*
Stop!	Σταματήστε! Stamatíste!	sta-ma-tee-steh
Call a doctor!	Φωνάξτε ένα γιατρό! Fonáxte éna giatró!	fo-n*a*k-steh *e*-na ya-tro
Call an ambulance/ the police/the fire brigade!	Καλέστε το ασθενοφόρο/την αστυνομία/την πυροσβεστική! Kaléste to asthenofóro/tin astynomía/tin pyrosvestikí!	ka-le-steh to as-the-no-fo-ro/ teen a-sti-no-mia/ teen pee-ro-zve-stee-kee

COMMUNICATION ESSENTIALS

Yes	Ναι Nai	neh
No	Οχι Ochi	*o*-chee
Please	Παρακαλώ Parakaló	pa-ra-ka-l*o*
Thank you	Ευχαριστώ Efcharistó	ef-cha-ree-st*o*
You are welcome	Παρακαλώ Parakaló	pa-ra-ka-l*o*
OK/alright	Εντάξει Entáxei	en-d*a*k-zee
Excuse me	Με συγχωρείτε Me synchoreíte	me seen-cho-ree-teh
Hello	Γειά σας Geiá sas	yeea sas
Goodbye	Αντίο Antío	an-dee-o
Good morning	Καλημέρα Kaliméra	ka-lee-m*e*-ra
Good night	Καληνύχτα Kalinýchta	ka-lee-neech-ta
Morning	Πρωί Proí	pro-ee
Afternoon	Απόγευμα Apógevma	a-po-yev-ma
Evening	Βράδυ Vrádi	vr*a*th-i
This morning	Σήμερα το πρωί Símera to proí	see-me-ra to pro-ee
Yesterday	Χθές Chthés	chthes
Today	Σήμερα Símera	see-me-ra
Tomorrow	Αύριο Avrio	*a*v-ree-o
Here	Εδώ Edó	ed-*o*
There	Εκεί Ekeí	e-kee
What?	Τί? Tí?	tee?
Why?	Γιατί? Giatí?	ya-tee?
Where?	Πού? Poú?	pou?
How?	Πώς? Pós?	pos?
Wait!	Περίμενε! Perímene!	pe-ree-me-neh

USEFUL PHRASES

How are you?	Τί κάνεις? Tí káneis?	tee ka-nees
Very well, thank you	Πολύ καλά, ευχαριστώ Poly kalá, efcharistó	po-lee ka-l*a*, ef-cha-ree-st*o*
How do you do?	Πώς είστε? Pós eíste?	pos ees-te?
Pleased to meet you	Χαίρω πολύ Chaíro polý	che-ro po-lee

What is your name?	Πώς λέγεστε? Pós légeste?	pos le-ye-ste?
Where is/are...?	Πού είναι? Poú eínai?	poo ee-ne?
How far is it to...?	Πόσο απέχει...? Póso apéchei...?	po-so a-pe-chee?
How do I get to?	Πώς μπορώ να πάω...? Pós mporó na páo...?	pos bo-ro-na pa-o?
Do you speak English?	Μιλάτε Αγγλικά; Miláte Angliká?	mee-la-te an-glee-ka?
I understand	Καταλαβαίνω Katalavaíno	ka-ta-la-ve-no
I don't understand	Δεν καταλαβαίνω Den katalavaíno	then ka-ta-la-ve-no
Could you speak slowly?	Μιλάτε λίγο πιο αργά παρακαλώ? Miláte lígo pio argá parakaló?	mee-la-te lee-go pyo ar-ga pa-ra-ka-lo?
I'm sorry	Με συγχωρείτε Me synchoreíte	me seen-cho-ree te
Does anyone have a key?	Έχει κανένα κλειδί? Echei kanénas kleidí?	e-chee ka-ne-nas klee-dee?

USEFUL WORDS

big	Μεγάλο Megálo	me-ga-lo
small	Μικρό Mikró	mi-kro
hot	Ζεστό Zestó	zes-to
cold	Κρύο Krýo	kree-o
good	Καλό Kaló	ka-lo
bad	Κακό Kakó	ka-ko
enough	Αρκετά Arketá	ar-ke-ta
well	Καλά Kalá	ka-la
open	Ανοιχτά Anoichtá	a-neech-ta
closed	Κλειστά Kleistá	klee-sta
left	Αριστερά Aristerá	a-ree-ste-ra
right	Δεξιά Dexiá	dek-see-a
straight on	Ευθεία Eftheía	ef-thee-u
between	Ανάμεσα / Μεταξύ Anámesa / Metaxý	a-na-me-sa/ me-tuk-see
on the corner of...	Στη γωνία του... Sti gonía tou...	stee go-nee-a tou
near	Κοντά Kontá	kon-da
far	Μακριά Makriá	ma-kree-a
up	Επάνω Epáno	e-pa-no
down	Κάτω Káto	ka-to
early	Νωρίς Norís	no-rees
late	Αργά Argá	ar-ga
entrance	Η είσοδος I eísodos	ee ee-so-thos
exit	Η έξοδος I éxodos	eee-kso-dos
toilet	Οι τουαλέτες /WC Oi toualétes / WC	ee-tou-a-le-tes
occupied/engaged	Κατειλημμένη Kateiliméni	ka-tee-lee-me-nee
unoccupied/vacant	Ελεύθερη Eléftheri	e-lef-the-ree
free/no charge	Δωρεάν Doreán	tho-re-an
in/out	Μέσα/Έξω Mésa/ Exo	me-sa/ek-so

MAKING A TELEPHONE CALL

Where is the nearest public telephone?	Πού βρίσκεται ο πλησιέστερος τηλεφωνικός θάλαμος? Poú vrísketai o plisiésteros tilefonikós thálamos?	pou vrees-ke-te o plee-see-e-ste-ros tee-le-fo-ni-kos tha-la-mos?
I would like to place a long-distance call	Θα ήθελα να κάνω ένα υπεραστικό τηλεφώνημα Tha íthela na káno éna yperastikó tilefónima	tha ee-the-la na ka-no e-na ee-pe-ra-sti-ko tee-le-fo-nee-ma
I would like to reverse the charges	Θα ήθελα να χρεώσω το τηλεφώνημα στον παραλήπτη Tha íthela na chreóso to tilefónima ston paralípti	tha ee-the-la na chre-o-so to tee-le-fo-nee-ma ston pa-ra-lep-tee
I will try again later	Θα ξανατηλε φωνήσω αργότερα Tha xanatilefoníso argótera	tha ksa-na-tee-le-fo-ni-so ar-go-te-ra
Can I leave a message?	Μπορείτε να του αφήσετε ένα μήνυμα? Mporeíte na tou afísete éna mínyma?	bo-ree-te na tou a-fee-se-teh e-na mee-nee-ma?
Could you speak up please?	Μιλάτε δυνατότερα, παρακαλώ? Miláte dynatótera, parakaló?	mee-la-teh dee-na-to-a little te-ra, pa-ra-ka-lo
Local call	Τοπικό τηλεφώνημα Topikó tilefónima	to-pi-ko tee-le-fo-nee-ma
Hold on	Περιμένετε Periménete	pe-ri-me-ne-te
OTE telephone office	Ο ΟΤΕ / Το τηλεφωνείο O OTE / To tilefoneío	o O-TE / To tee-le-fo-nee-o
Phone box/kiosk	Ο τηλεφωνικός θάλαμος O tilefonikós thálamos	o tee-le-fo-ni kos tha-la-mos
Phone card	Η τηλεκάρτα I tilekárta	ee tee-le-kar-ta

SHOPPING

How much does this cost?	Πόσο κάνει? Póso kánei?	po-so ka-nee?
I would like...	Θα ήθελα... Tha íthela...	tha ee-the-la...
Do you have...?	Έχετε...? Echete...?	e-che-te
I am just looking	Απλώς κοιτάω Aplós koitáo	u-plos kee-ta-o
Do you take credit cards?	Δέχεστε πιστωτικές κάρτες? Décheste pistotikés kártes?	the-ches-te pee-sto tee-kes kar-tes
What time do you open/close?	Ποτέ ανοίγετε/ κλείνετε? Póte anoígete/ kleinete?	po-teh a-nee-ye-te/ kloe-ne-te?
Can you ship this overseas?	Μπορείτε να το στείλετε στο εξωτερικό? Mporeíte na to steilete sto exoterikó?	bo-ree-te na to stee-le-te sto e-xo-te-ree ko?
This one	Αυτό εδώ Aftó edó	af-to e-do
That one	Εκείνο Ekeíno	e-kee-no
expensive	Ακριβό Akrivó	a-kree-vo
cheap	Φθηνό Fthinó	fthee-no
size	Το μέγεθος To mégethos	to me-ge-thos
white	Λευκό Lefkó	lef-ko
black	Μαύρο Mávro	mav-ro
red	Κόκκινο Kókkino	ko-kee-no
yellow	Κίτρινο Kítrino	kee-tree-no
green	Πράσινο Prásino	pra-see-no
blue	Μπλε Mple	bleh

TYPES OF SHOP

| antique shop | Μαγαζί με αντίκες
Magazí me antíkes | ma-ga-zee me an-dee-kes |
| bakery | Ο φούρνος
O foúrnos | o four-nos |

bank	Η τράπεζα I trápeza	ee tra-pe-za
bazaar	Το παζάρι To pazári	to pa-za-ree
bookshop	Το βιβλιοπωλείο To vivliopoleío	to vee-vlee-o-po-lee-o
butcher	Το κρεοπωλείο To kreopoleío	to kre-o-po-lee-o
cake shop	Το ζαχαροπλαστείο To zacharoplasteío	to za-cha-ro-plastee-o
cheese shop	Μαγαζί με αλλαντικά Magazí me allantiká	ma-ga-zee me a-lan-dee-ka
department store	Πολυκάταστημα Polykátastima	Po-lee-ka-ta-stee-ma
fish market	Το ιχθυοπωλείο/ ψαράδικο To ichthyopoleío/ psarádiko	to eech-thee-o-po-lee-o/psa-ró-dee-ko
greengrocer	Το μανάβικο To manáviko	to ma-na-vee-ko
hairdresser	Το κομμωτήριο To kommotírio	to ko-mo-tee-ree-o
kiosk	Το περίπτερο To períptero	to pe-reep-te-ro
leather shop	Μαγαζί με δερμάτινα είδη Magazí me dermátina eídi	ma-ga-zee me ther-ma-tee-na ee-thee eídi
street market	Η λαϊκή αγορά I laïkí agorá	ee la-ee-kee a-go-ra
newsagent	Ο εφημεριδοπώλης O efimeridopólis	O e-fee-me-ree-tho-po-lees
pharmacy	Το φαρμακείο To farmakeío	to far-ma-kee-o
post office	Το ταχυδρομείο To tachydromeío	to ta-chee-thro-ee-o
shoe shop	Κατάστημα υποδημάτων Katástima ypodimáton	ka-ta-stee-ma ee-po-dee-ma-ton
souvenir shop	Μαγαζί με "souvenir" Magazí me "souvenir"	ma-ga-zee me "souvenir"
supermarket	Σουπερμάρκετ/ Υπεραγορά "Supermarket"/ Yperagorá	"Supermarket"/ee-per-a-go-ra
tobacconist	Είδη καπνιστού Eídi kapnistoú	Ee-thee kap-nee-stou
travel agent	Το ταξειδιωτικό γραφείο To taxeidiotikó grafeío	to tak-see-thy-o-tee-ko gra-fee-o

SIGHTSEEING

tourist information	Ο ΕΟΤ O ΕΟΤ	o E-OT
tourist police	Η τουριστική αστυνομία I touristikí astynomía	ee too-rees-tee-kee a-stee-no-mee-a
archaeological	αρχαιολογικός archaiologikós	ar-che-o-lo-yee-kos
art gallery	Η γκαλερί I gkalerí	ee ga-le-ree
beach	Η παραλία I paralía	ee pa-ra-lee-a
Byzantine	βυζαντινός vyzantinós	vee-zan-dee-nos
castle	Το κάστρο To kástro	to ka-stro
cathedral	Η μητρόπολη I mitrópoli	ee mee-tro-po-lee
cave	Το σπήλαιο To spílaio	to spee-le-o
church	Η εκκλησία I ekklisía	ee e-klee-see-a
folk art	λαϊκή τέχνη laïkí téchni	la-ee-kee tech-nee
fountain	Το συντριβάνι To syntriváni	to seen-dree-va-nee
hill	Ο λόφος O lófos	o lo-fos
historical	ιστορικός istorikós	ee-sto-ree-kos
island	Το νησί To nisí	to nee-see
lake	Η λίμνη I límni	ee leem-nee
library	Η βιβλιοθήκη I vivliothíki	ee veev-lee-o-thee-kee

mansion	Η έπαυλις I épavlis	ee-pav-lees
monastery	Μονή moní	mo-nee
mountain	Το βουνό To vounó	to voo-no
municipal	δημοτικός dimotikós	thee-mo-tee-kos
museum	Το μουσείο To mouseío	to mou-see-o
national	εθνικός ethnikós	eth-nee-kos
park	Το πάρκο To párko	to par-ko
garden	Ο κήπος O kípos	o kee-pos
gorge	Το φαράγγι To farángi	to fa-ran-gee
grave of...	Ο τάφος του… O táfos tou…	o ta-fos tou
river	Το ποτάμι To potámi	to po-ta-mee
road	Ο δρόμος O drómos	o thro-mos
saint	άγιος/ άγιοι/ αγία/αγίες ágios/ágioi/agía/agíes	a-yee-os/ a-yee-ee/ a-yee-a/a-yee-es
spring	Η πηγή I pigí	ee pee-yee
square	Η πλατεία I plateía	ee pla-tee-a
stadium	Το στάδιο To stádio	to sta-thee-o
statue	Το άγαλμα To ágalma	toa-gal-ma
theatre	Το θέατρο To théatro	to the-a-tro
town hall	Το δημαρχείο To dimarcheío	To thee-mar-chee-o
closed on public holidays	κλειστό τις αργίες kleistó tis argíes	klee-sto tees aryee-es

TRANSPORT

When does the... leave?	Πότε φεύγει το …? Póte févgei to…?	po-teh fev-yee to...?
Where is the bus stop?	Πού είναι η στάση του λεωφορείου? Poú eínai i stási tou leoforeíou?	poo ee-neh ee sta-see tou le-o-fo-ree-ou?
Is there a bus to...?	Υπάρχει λεωφορείο για…? Ypárchei leoforeío gia...?	ee-par-chee le-o-fo-ree-o yia...?
ticket office	Εκδοτήρια εισιτηρίων Ekdotíria eisitiríon	Ek-tho-tee-reea ee-see-tee-ree-on
return ticket	Εισιτήριο με επιστροφή Eisitírio me epistrofí	ee-see-tee-ree-o meh e-pee-stro-fee
single journey	Απλό εισιτήριο Apló eisitírio	a-plo ee-see-tee-reeo
bus station	Ο σταθμός λεωφορείων O stathmós leoforeíon	o stath-mos leo-fo-ree-on
bus ticket	Εισιτήριο λεωφορείου Eisitírio leoforeíou	ee-see-tee-ree-o leo-fo-ree-ou
trolley bus	Το τρόλλεϋ To trólley	to tro-le-ee
port	Το λιμάνι To limáni	to lee-ma-nee
train/metro	Το τρένο To tréno	to tre-no
railway station	σιδηροδρομικός σταθμός sidirodromikós stathmós	see-thee-ro-thro-mee-kos stath-mos
moped	Το μοτοποδήλατο / το μηχανάκι To motopodílato / To michanáki	to mo-to-po-thee-la-to/to mee-cha-na-kee
bicycle	Το ποδήλατο To podílato	to po-thee-la-to
taxi	Το ταξί To taxí	to tak-see
airport	Το αεροδρόμιο To aerodrómio	to a-e-ro-thro-mee-o
ferry	Το φερυμπότ To "ferry-boat"	to fe-ree-bot

hydrofoil	Το δελφίνι / Το υδροπτέρυγο	to del-fee-nee / To ee-throp-te-ree-go
	To delfíni / To ydroptérygo	
catamaran	Το καταμαράν	to catamaran
	To katamarán	
for hire	Ενοικιάζονται	e-nee-kya-zon-de
	Enoikiázontai	

STAYING IN A HOTEL

Do you have a vacant room?	Έχετε δωμάτια;	ee-che-teh tho-ma-tee-a?
	Echete domátia?	
double room with double bed	Δίκλινο με διπλό κρεβάτι	thee-klee-no me thee-plo kre-va-tee
	Díklino me diplò krevàti	
twin room	Δίκλινο με μονά κρεβάτια	thee-klee-no me mo-na kre-vat-ya
	Díklino me monà krevàtia	
single room	Μονόκλινο	mo-no-klee-no
	Monóklino	
room with a bath	Δωμάτιο με μπάνιο	tho-ma-tee-o me ban-yo
	Domátio me mpánio	
shower	Το ντους	To dooz
	To douz	
porter	Ο πορτιέρης	o por-tye-rees
	O portiéris	
key	Το κλειδί	to klee-dee
	To kleidí	
I have a reservation	Έχω κάνει κράτηση	e-cho ka-nee kra-tee-see
	Echo kánei krátisi	
room with a sea view/balcony	Δωμάτιο με θέα στη θάλασσα/μπαλκόνι	tho-ma-tee-o me the-a stee tha-la-sa/bal-ko-nee
	Domátio me théa sti thálassa/mpalkóni	
Does the price include breakfast?	Το πρωινό συμπεριλαμβάνεται στην τιμή;	to pro-ee-no seem-be-ree-lam-va-ne-teh steen tee-mee?
	To proïnó symperilamvánetai stin timí?	

EATING OUT

Have you got a table?	Έχετε τραπέζι;	e-che-te tra-pe-zee?
	Echete trapézi?	
I want to reserve a table	Θέλω να κρατήσω ένα τραπέζι	the-lo na kra-tee-so e-na tra-pe-zee
	Thélo na kratíso éna trapézi	
The bill, please	Τον λογαριασμό, παρακαλώ	ton lo-gar-yas-mo pa-ra-ka-lo
	Ton logariazmó parakaló	
I am a vegetarian	Είμαι χορτοφάγος	ee-meh chor-to-fa-gos
	Eímai chortofágos	
What is fresh today?	Τί φρέσκο έχετε σήμερα;	tee fres-ko e-che-teh see-me-ra?
	Tí frésko échete símera?	
waiter/waitress	Κύριε / Γκαρσόν / Κυρία (female)	Kee-ree-e/Gar-son/Kee-re-a
	Kýrie/Garson"/Kyría	
menu	Ο κατάλογος	o ka-ta-lo-gos
	O katálogos	
cover charge	Το κουβέρ	to koo-ver
	To "couvert"	
wine list	Ο κατάλογος με τα οινοπνευματώδη	o ka-ta-lo-gos meh ta ee-no-pnev-ma-to-thee
	O katálogos me ta oinopnevmatódi	
glass	Το ποτήρι	to po-tee-ree
	To potíri	
bottle	Το μπουκάλι	to bou-ka-lee
	To mpoukáli	
knife	Το μαχαίρι	to ma-che-ree
	To machaíri	
fork	Το πηρούνι	to pee-roo-nee
	To piroúni	
spoon	Το κουτάλι	to koo-ta-lee
	To koutáli	
breakfast	Το πρωινό	to pro-ee-no
	To proïnó	
lunch	Το μεσημεριανό	to me-see-mer-ya-no
	To mesimerianó	
dinner	Το δείπνο	to theep-no
	To deípno	
main course	Το κυρίως γεύμα	to kee-ree-os yev-ma
	To kyríos gévma	
starter/first course	Τα ορεκτικά	ta o-rek-tee-ka
	Ta orektiká	

dessert	Το γλυκό	to ylee-ko
	To glykó	
dish of the day	Το πιάτο της ημέρας	to pya-to tees ee-me-ras
	To piáto tis iméras	
bar	Το μπαρ	To mpar
	To "bar"	
taverna	Η ταβέρνα	ee ta-ver-na
	I tavérna	
café	Το καφενείο	to ka-fe-nee-o
	To kafeneío	
fish taverna	Η ψαροταβέρνα	ee psa-ro-ta-ver-na
	I psarotavérna	
grill house	Η ψησταριά	ee psee-sta-rya
	I psistariá	
wine shop	Το οινοπωλείο	to ee-no-po-lee-o
	To oinopoleío	
dairy shop	Το γαλακτοπωλείο	to ga-lak-to-po-lee-o
	To galaktopoleío	
restaurant	Το εστιατόριο	to e-stee-a-to-ree-o
	To estiatório	
ouzeri	Το ουζερί	to ou-ze-ree
	To ouzerí	
meze shop	Το μεζεδοπωλείο	To me-ze-do-po-lee-o
	To mezedopoleío	
take away kebabs	Το σουβλατζίδικο	To sou-vlat-zee-dee-ko
	To souvlatzídiko	
rare	Ελάχιστα ψημένο	e-lach-ees-ta psee-me-no
	Eláchista psiméno	
medium	Μέτρια ψημένο	met-ree-a psee-me-no
	Métria psiméno	
well done	Καλοψημένο	ka-lo-psee-me-no
	Kalopsiméno	

BASIC FOOD AND DRINK

coffee	Ο καφές	o ka-fes
	O Kafés	
with milk	με γάλα	me ga-la
	me gála	
black coffee	σκέτος	ske-tos
	skétos	
without sugar	χωρίς ζάχαρη	cho-rees za-cha-ree
	chorís záchari	
medium sweet	μέτριος	me-tree-os
	métrios	
very sweet	γλυκύς	glee-kees
	glykýs	
tea	τσάι	tsa-ee
	tsái	
hot chocolate	ζεστή σοκολάτα	ze-stee so-ko-la-ta
	zestí sokoláta	
wine	κρασί	kra-see
	krasí	
red	κόκκινο	ko-kee-no
	kókkino	
white	λευκό	lef-ko
	lefkó	
rosé	ροζέ	ro-ze
	rozé	
raki	Το ρακί	to ra-kee
	To rakí	
ouzo	Το ούζο	to oo-zo
	To oúzo	
retsina	Η ρετσίνα	ee ret-see-na
	I retsína	
water	Το νερό	to ne-ro
	To neró	
octopus	Το χταπόδι	to chta-po-dee
	To chtapódi	
fish	Το ψάρι	to psa-ree
	To psári	
cheese	Το τυρί	to tee-ree
	To tyrí	
halloumi	Το χαλούμι	to cha-loo-mee
	To chaloúmi	
feta	Η φέτα	ee fe-ta
	I féta	
bread	Το ψωμί	to pso-mee
	To psomí	
bean soup	Η φασολάδα	ee fa-so-la-da
	I fasoláda	
houmous	Το χούμους	to chou-mous
	To houmous	
halva	Ο χαλβάς	o chal-vas
	O chalvás	
meat kebabs	Ο γύρος	o yee-ros
	O gýros	
Turkish delight	Το λουκούμι	to loo-koo-mee
	To loukoúmi	
baklava	Ο μπακλαβάς	o bak-la-vas
	O mpaklavás	
klephtiko	Το κλέφτικο	to klef-tee-ko
	To kléftiko	

NUMBERS

1	ένα éna	e-na
2	δύο dýo	thee-o
3	τρία tría	tree-a
4	τέσσερα téssera	te-se-ra
5	πέντε pénte	pen-deh
6	έξι éxi	ek-si
7	επτά eptá	ep-ta
8	οχτώ ochtó	och-to
9	εννέα ennéa	e-ne-a
10	δέκα déka	the-ka
11	έντεκα énteka	en-de-ka
12	δώδεκα dódeka	tho-the-ka
13	δεκατρία dekatría	de-ka-tree-a
14	δεκατέσσερα dekatéssera	the-ka-tes-se-ra
15	δεκαπέντε dekapénte	the-ka-pen-de
16	δεκαέξι dekaéxi	the-ka-ek-si
17	δεκαεπτά dekaeptá	the-ka-ep-ta
18	δεκαοχτώ dekaochtó	the-ka-och-to
19	δεκαεννέα dekaennéa	the-ka-e-ne-a
20	είκοσι eíkosi	ee-ko-see
21	εικοσιένα eikosiéna	ee-ko-see-e-na
30	τριάντα triánta	tree-an-da
40	σαράντα saránta	sa-ran-da
50	πενήντα penínta	pe-neen-da
60	εξήντα exínta	ek-seen-da
70	εβδομήντα evdomínta	ev-tho-meen-da
80	ογδόντα ogdónta	og-thon-da
90	ενενήντα enenínta	e-ne-neen-da
100	εκατό ekató	e-ka-to
200	διακόσια diakósia	thya-kos-ya
1,000	χίλια chília	cheel-ya
2,000	δύο χιλιάδες dýo chiliádes	thee-o cheel-ya-thes
1,000,000	ένα εκατομμύριο	e-na e-ka-to-mee-ree-o

TIME, DAYS AND DATES

one minute	ένα λεπτό éna leptó	e-na lep-to
one hour	μία ώρα mía óra	mee-a o-ra
half an hour	μισή ώρα misí óra	mee-see o-ra
quarter of an hour	ένα τέταρτο éna tétarto	e-na te-tar-to
half past one	μία και μισή mía kai misí	mee-a ke mee-see
quarter past one	μία και τέταρτο mía kai tétarto	mee-a ke te-tar-to
ten past one	μία και δέκα mía kai déka	mee-a ke the-ka
quarter to two	δύο παρά τέταρτο dýo pará tétarto	thee-o pa-ra te-tar-to
ten to two	δύο παρά δέκα dýo pará déka	thee-o pa-ra the-ka
a day	μία μέρα mía méra	mee-a me-ra

a week	μία εβδομάδα mía evdomáda	mee-a ev-tho-ma-tha
a month	ένας μήνας énas mínas	e-nas mee-nas
a year	ένας χρόνος énas chrónos	e-nas chro-nos
Monday	Δευτέρα Deftéra	thef-te-ra
Tuesday	Τρίτη Tríti	tree-tee
Wednesday	Τετάρτη Tetárti	te-tar-tee
Thursday	Πέμπτη Pémpti	pemp-tee
Friday	Παρασκευή Paraskeví	pa-ras-ke-vee
Saturday	Σάββατο Sávvato	sa-va-to
Sunday	Κυριακή Kyriakí	keer-ee-a-kee
January	Ιανουάριος Ianouários	ee-a-nou-a-ree-os
February	Φεβρουάριος Fevrouários	fev-rou-a-ree-os
March	Μάρτιος Mártios	mar-tee-os
April	Απρίλιος Aprílios	a-pree-lee-os
May	Μάιος Máios	ma-ee-os
June	Ιούνιος Ioúnios	ee-ou-nee-os
July	Ιούλιος Ioúlios	ee-ou-lee-os
August	Αύγουστος Avgoustos	av-gou-stos
September	Σεπτέμβριος Septémvrios	sep-tem-vree-os
October	Οκτώβριος Októvrios	ok-to-vree-os
November	Νοέμβριος Noémvrios	no-em-vree-os
December	Δεκέμβριος Dekémvrios	the-kem-vree-os

ACKNOWLEDGMENTS

The publisher would like to thank the following for their kind permission to reproduce their photographs:

Key: a-above; b-below/bottom; c-centre; f-far; l-left; r-right; t-top

4Corners: Johanna Huber 112-3b; Mel Manser 286bl.

akg-images: Sotheby's 46t.

Alamy Stock Photo: AJ Adelmari 209crb; AegeanPhoto 95cb, 210cr, 219br; AF archive 41cr; AGE Fotostock 23tr, 24cla; AGF Srl 209bc; Germaine Alexakis 28br, 110clb, 241br; Alexandria 44bl; Ancient Art and Architecture 49bl; ART Collection 79br; Penny Atkinson 82bl; George Atsametakis 10-1bc; Erin Babnik 94cl; Peter Barritt 60crb, 87cr; Steve Bentley 62cla; Iosif Luclan Bulca 16cl, 54-5; George Brice 67br; Josse Christophel 49cra; Chronicle 46br; Classic Image 48tl, 137br; Roy Conchie 162t, 166-7b, 168bl; Chris Craggs 22bl; David Crossland 44cr; Cultura Creative (RF) 17bl, 120-1; Ian Dagnall 134bc, 286t; Debu55y 179br; Kathy deWitt 44cl; Mike Drosos 164b; Robert Dziewulski 266-7; Adam Eastland 185tr; Peter Eastland 292b; Entertainment Pictures 40br; Greg Balfour Evans 35cla, 180tl, 184b; Everett Collection Inc 50-1t; Peter van Evert 189br; eye35.pix 8-9b; F1online digitale Bildagentur GmbH 27cl, 256br; Falkensteinfoto 48bc; Kirk Fisher 288clb; FLHC 1A 50bc; Florilegius 289ca; Peter Erik Forsberg 263br; Peter Forsberg 68tl, 258cr; Werli Francois 25cr; freeartist 78-9t, 81b, 194b, 220-1b, 228-9b, 237br; funkyfood London - Paul Williams 46clb, 95br, 99cr, 127tr; Martin Garnham 234tl; Elly Godfroy / © Succession Picasso / DACS, London 2018 227cr; Milan Gonda 129, 143t, 186t, 217t, 293tl; Grant Rooney Premium 71tr; Hackenberg-Photo-Cologne 11br, 259tl; Terry Harris 146-7t; Andrew Hasson 206tl; Hemis 136b, 157tr, 190-1b, 277tl, 279cra, 280clb, 281, 295bl; Heritage Image Partnership Ltd 48crb, 48br; Brian Hoffman 48-9t; Peter Horree 67bc, 87b, 262bl; Eduardo Huelin 77br; Stephen Hughes 171br; Ian west 117tr; idp greek collection 109bl; Constantinos Iliopoulos 58br, 76b, 96tr, 168-9t, 176bl, 238-9t; imageBROKER 24b, 58clb, 63tr, 167cra, 236b; imageimage 256t; Images & Stories 128cl; Interfoto/ Austrian National Library 50tl; Ivy Close Images 47tr, 47cla; JHeiniman 214bl; Inge Johnsson 138b; Panagiotis Karapanagiotis 150; Brenda Kean 211tr; Jason Knott 232-3b; Kokixx 130b; Panagiotis Kotsovolos 235t; Art Kowalsky 208br; Katho Menden 134tr; Hercules Milas 13br, 60bl, 106-7t, 108bc, 108-9t, 110-1b, 148bl, 165tl, 188b, 207cla, 228tr, 230-1t, 238bl, 248cl, 250cra, 264, 265cb, 268b, 278b; Sergio Monti 289cla; muART 178cr; Remy Musser 2-3; Adrian Muttitt 113tr; Melinda Nagy 147bl; National Geographic Image Collection 12-3b; Odyssey-Images 137tl, 160clb; George Papapostolou 36-7b; Sanga Park 288-9b; Pictures Colour Library 33cl; Peter Ptschelinzew 232crb; Realy Easy Star 126bc; ReligiousStock 23cl; Rolf Richardson 226bl; robertharding 20bl, 71br, 112tl, 172t, 180-1b, 205cla; Jeff Rotman 33br; Samothraki / Roger Cracknell 02 151cr; Sagaphoto.com / Forray Didier 75b; Seewhatmitchsee 199bc; Iain Sharp 60cr; David Shield 209clb; TCD / Prod. DB 41cla; The Picture Art Collection 169br; David Tomlinson 86tr; Konstantinos Tsakalidis 291tr; Nevena Tsvetanova 45cl; Grethe Ulgjell 139bc; Lucas Vallecillos 286crb; Haris Vithoulkas 182-3t; Washington Imaging 275bc; Jan Wlodarczyk 6-7, 19t, 20-1t, 97b, 174-5, 214-5t, 244-5, 254t, 269tl; Ian Woolcock 178-9t; World History Archive 50br, 51bc; Rawdon Wyatt 26br.

AWL Images: Robert Birkby 86br; Danita Delimont Stock 12cl; Neil Farrin 74tr, 161t.

Bridgeman Images: De Agostini Picture Library / St. Martin, by an anonymous artist of the Venetian-Cretan School, Icon, 1500, Greece 49cr.

Depositphotos Inc: Wujekspeed 278clb.

Dorling Kindersley: Stuart West 29br.

Dreamstime.com: Adisa 84-5b; Arsty 273tr; Ivan Bastien 43b; Yuriy Brykaylo 248br; Carafoto 17t, 102-3; Costas1962 45bl; Maciej Czekajewski 156cra; Ionut David 210-1t; Debu55y 167tl; Dimaberkut 45tr; Elenimac28 230br; Elifranssens 255c; Serban Enache 205tr; Eugenz 37tr, 76clb; F8grapher 98-9b, 206-7t; Alexandre Fagundes De Fagundes 169clb; Evgeniy Fesenko 286cr; Freesurf69 40-1t; Frizzantine 58cl; Gelia 262-1t; Milan Gonda 11tl, 16bl, 18tl, 19bl, 42bl, 88-9, 118b, 140-1t, 152-3, 157clb, 192t, 204tl, 248t, 259crb, 259bc, 282-3; Gorelovs 251tr; Sven Hansche 93tr; Fritz Hiersche 133cl; Patricia Hofmeester 265cr; Irakite 266cr; Jordeangjelovik 62tl; Thomas Jurkowski 250-1t, 260cra; Tzogia Kappatou 27br; Karaevgen 44tr; Panagiotis Karapanagiotis 156tl; Mikhail Laptev 72-3b; Lev Levin 167tr; Lucianbolca 271bl, 274-5t, 276b; Mangojuicy 141b; Vitaliy Mateha 8bc; Martin Molcan 42-3t; Olgacov 212-3b; Anna Pakutina 258-9b, 259tr; Photobac 25t; Photostella 96bl, 111tr, 218t; Marek Rapicki 37clb; Pavlos Rekas 45tl; Rndmst 234br; Saiko3p 23crb; Santorines 26t; Valery Shanin 47tl; Josef Skacel 34-5t; Slasta20 58t; Calin Andrei Stan 60t; Stockbksts 195tr; Julia Sudnitskaya 13cr, 133tr; Tolgaildun 126clb, 128bl; Georgios Tsichlis 133b, 248clb, 260-1b, 263tr, 272-3b, 290-1b; Ultraone 47br; Ivan Ushakovskiy 174cb; Vasilis Ververidis 44br; Alvaro German Vilela 291cb; Natalia Volkova 250tl, 265bl; Dennis Van De Water 62-3t; Maren Winter 8cb.

Getty Images: 51tr; B&M Noskowski 206cra; Bettmann 72c; Paul Biris 38-9t; Matteo Colombo 8cl, 21crb; Creative Touch Imaging Ltd. / NurPhoto 213tl; Ian Cumming 34bl; James Davis 289tr; DEA / De Agostini / G. Dagli Orti 95bc; Dreamer Company 28-9t; John Elk III 296-7t; Louisa Gouliamaki 32tl; Dzianis Kadyrko 10c; Izzet Keribar 45cr, 128cra; Glenn van der Knijff 294t; Christian Marquardt 204-5t; ME Studio 39cl; Sakis Mitrolidis 44tl; George Pachantouris 33tr; Bastian Parschau 29cl; Nicholas Pitt 21c; Print Collector 289tc; David C Tomlinson 39b; Tuul & Bruno Morandi 43cl; ZU_09 87cl.

iStockphoto.com: Adisa 4; al_ter 270t; Amriphoto 45br; AndrijTer 73t; Charalambos Andronos 101t; ankarb 77t; Borchee 31cra; BrettCharlton 66b; ChrisHepburn 18cb, 200-1; cunfek 117tl, 135b; czekma13 189tl; DanilluAndjus 36tl; Engineervoshkin 196b; FevreDream 114b; FRAARTIST 13t, 31crb, 158-9t; Freemixer 24tr; Louisa Gouliamaki 32b; Imgorthand 35br; Joakimbkk 207tr; JustinBlackStock 208-9t; kelvinjay 252t; Konstantinos_K 131tl; kwasny221 82-3t; Lefteris 242t; LeszekCzerwonka 52-3; majaiva 64-5t; MichaelUtech 51cra; milangonda 30-1t, 92t, 204cra, 216b, 221tl, 240b; nejdetduzen 124-5t, 132bl; newsfocus1 194cr; Kate OMalley 224b; Onepony 10clb; Oleg_P 177t; Pldjoe 156-7t; Poike 67t; Rusm 62-3c; sam74100 30-1b; Santorines 11cr; Saro17 266bc; Seewhatmitchsee 198b; sjhaytov 144-5b; spooh 222b; THEPALMER 69b; Uchar 49tr; ultramarinfoto 25b; Vasiliki 22-3t; Wabeno 12t; yrabota 251cla; Zackwool 38br.

The Metropolitan Museum of Art: 227bl, 227bc, 227fbl, 227br.

Rijksmuseum, Amsterdam: 87tr.

Robert Harding Picture Library: ProCip 116bl.

Front flap:
Alamy Stock Photo: Milan Gonda cla; Jan Wlodarczyk cb; **Dreamstime.com:** Byvalet bl; Mikhail Laptev tc; Carafoto br; **iStockphoto.com:** Adisa cra.

Cover images:
Front and spine: **Getty Images:** usabin.
Back: **Alamy Stock Photo:** Iosif Lucian Bolca c, Jan Wlodarczyk cla; **Dreamstime.com:** Photobac tr; **Getty Images:** usabin bc.

For further information see: www.dkimages.com

Main Contributors Marc Dubin,
Nick Edwards, Stephanie Ferguson,
Mike Gerrard, Andy Harris, Tanya Tsikas

Senior Editor Ankita Awasthi Tröger

Senior Designer Owen Bennett

Project Editor Lauren Whybrow

Project Art Editors Tania Gomes, Stuti Tiwari
Bhatia, Hansa Babra, Priyanka Thakur

Designer William Robinson

Factchecker Marc Dubin

Editors Elspeth Beidas, Rebecca Flynn,
Jackie Staddon, David Tombesi-Walton,
Sylvia Tombesi-Walton

First edition 1997

Published in Great Britain by Dorling Kindersley Limited,
80 Strand, London, WC2R 0RL

Published in the United States by DK Publishing,
1450 Broadway, 8th Floor, New York, NY 10018

Copyright © 1997, 2019 Dorling Kindersley Limited
A Penguin Random House Company
19 20 21 22 10 9 8 7 6 5 4 3 2 1

A CIP catalog record for this book
is available from the British Library.

A catalog record for this book is available
from the Library of Congress.

ISSN: 1542-1554
ISBN: 978-0-2413-5836-8

Printed and bound in China.

www.dk.com

MIX
Paper from
responsible sources
FSC FSC™ C018179
www.fsc.org

**The information in this
DK Eyewitness Travel Guide is checked regularly.**

Every effort has been made to ensure that this book
is as up-to-date as possible at the time of going to
press. Some details, however, such as telephone
numbers, opening hours, prices, gallery hanging
arrangements and travel information, are liable to
change. The publishers cannot accept responsibility
for any consequences arising from the use of this
book, nor for any material on third party websites,
and cannot guarantee that any website address
in this book will be a suitable source of travel
information. We value the views and suggestions
of our readers very highly. Please write to: Publisher,
DK Eyewitness Travel Guides, Dorling Kindersley,
80 Strand, London, WC2R 0RL, UK, or email:
travelguides@dk.com